D1028294

THE DELIBERATIVE DEMOCRACY HANDBOOK

Strategies for Effective Civic Engagement in the Twenty-First Century

EDITORS

John Gastil
Peter Levine

This edited volume is a project
of the Deliberative Democracy Consortium.
Learn more about the programs described in this
book at www.deliberative-democracy.net/handbook

JOSSEY-BASS
A Wiley Imprint
www.josseybass.com

Published by Jossey-Bass
A Wiley Imprint
989 Market Street, San Francisco, CA 94103-1741   www.josseybass.com

Jossey-Bass books and products are available through most bookstores. To contact Jossey-Bass directly call our Customer Care Department within the U.S. at 800-956-7739, outside the U.S. at 317-572-3986, or fax 317-572-4002.

Jossey-Bass also publishes its books in a variety of electronic formats. Some content that appears in print may not be available in electronic books.

Used as the title for Chapter Five, Deliberative Polling® is a registered trademark of James S. Fishkin. 21st Century Town Meeting® is a registered trademark of America*Speaks*. Citizens Jury® is a trademark of the Jefferson Center, registered in the U.S. All rights reserved. For purposes of readability, the trademark symbol is used only at the first appearance of the term in the book.

Library of Congress Cataloging-in-Publication Data

The deliberative democracy handbook : strategies for effective civic engagement in the twenty-first century / John Gastil, Peter Levine, editors.—1st ed.

 p. cm.

Includes bibliographical references and index.

ISBN: 978-1-118-10510-8

1. Political participation—United States. 2. Political culture—United States. 3. Democracy—United States. I. Gastil, John. II. Levine, Peter, date.

JK1764.D445 2005

323'.042'097309051—dc22

2005010920

FIRST EDITION

HB Printing 10 9 8 7 6 5 4 3 2 1

CONTENTS

John Gastil, William M. Keith

The idea of public deliberation has come in and out of vogue over the past century, and its recent arrival is no guarantee that it is here to stay. A deliberative movement appeared in the early twentieth century in the United States, only to dissipate by World War II. The reemergence of deliberation in the 1990s could also come to an end, and this chapter explains what cultural, technological, and geopolitical forces bring about deliberation and cause its collapse. Understanding the interplay of these forces might help us sustain the present deliberative movement.

Mark Button, David Michael Ryfe

This chapter provides a general survey of a wide range of practical efforts to
foster more citizen deliberation in American politics. Deliberative programs differ
in terms of who is included in the forums, how deliberation is conducted, and how
success is determined. A useful theory of deliberative democracy must engage the
realities and constraints of deliberative practice, and public deliberation programs
need to recognize the theoretical and cultural consequences of the practical
choices they make. Deliberation may have a number of positive outcomes, but
it is more important to understand deliberation as a powerful socialization
experience that reminds participants what it means to be a true citizen in a
democratic society.

Keith Melville, Taylor L. Willingham, John R. Dedrick

The National Issues Forums is a grassroots movement of diverse organizations
and individuals committed to framing, moderating, and convening inclusive
public discussions. Organizations across the country use nationally developed
discussion guides, often adapting them to reflect the circumstances of their
local community. A growing number of communities are applying the theoretical
principles of the forums to name and frame their own local issues for public
deliberation. The result is a growing network of communities that are using
deliberation to make thoughtful decisions based on a common understanding
of an issue and the costs, consequences, and benefits of their shared
decision.

Michelle Charles, Harris Sokoloff, Chris Satullo

How can a local newspaper work with the public to inform its judgment about
which candidate to endorse in an election? How can mutual trust be built among
the public and the press to arrive at such a conclusion? This chapter documents
a major metropolitan newspaper's endeavor to engage citizens in a citywide
civic journalism project. How did it happen? What were the outcomes? Charles,
Sokoloff, and Satullo discuss their best practices and principles for weaving civic
mapping, public deliberation, and the business of running a newspaper into a
positive electoral experience for citizens.

*Deliberative Polling® is a registered trademark of James S. Fishkin. Any fees from the trademark are used to support research at the Center for Deliberative Democracy.

**Citizens Jury® is a registered trademark of the Jefferson Center.

PART THREE: DELIBERATIVE GOVERNANCE 139

*21st Century Town Meeting® is a registered trademark of America*Speaks*.

11 Collaborative Learning and the Public's Stewardship of Its Forests 164

Antony S. Cheng, Janet D. Fiero

In the western United States, federal agencies often find themselves entangled in drawn-out conflicts with local communities and interest groups over the stewardship of local public lands. In many cases, these conflicts are artifacts of agency planning processes that favor highly technical analyses over meaningful civic engagement. In a break from traditional planning approaches, the Forest Service in western Colorado has adapted the Collaborative Learning approach to enable local citizens to deliberate about the future of public lands. This chapter focuses on how the Forest Service used place-based working groups to develop a forest plan for the three-million-acre Grand Mesa, Uncompahgre, and Gunnison Forest. The landscape working groups used Collaborative Learning principles to make progress in improving stakeholder relationships, clarifying substantive issues, and enhancing capacity for multiparty deliberation.

12 Participation and Public Policies in Brazil 174

Vera Schattan P. Coelho, Barbara Pozzoni, Mariana Cifuentes Montoya

Brazil leads the world in establishing local councils through legislation to enable ordinary citizens to participate in the formulation and monitoring of public policies on health, education, and social assistance. In this context, the notion of citizen participation raises two critical challenges: building institutions that allow poor and marginalized citizens to influence policies and ensuring that these institutions are accountable to their needs. Our analysis of the experiences and achievements of the Municipal Health Council of São Paulo brings attention to the need to improve the process of council member selection and devise appropriate procedures to ensure the inclusion of all participants in discussions and decision-making processes.

13 Deliberative City Planning on the Philadelphia Waterfront 185

Harris Sokoloff, Harris M. Steinberg, Steven N. Pyser

Beginning in January 2003, more than eight hundred residents of Philadelphia participated in three months of robust public dialogue about the future of the city's waterfront at Penn's Landing. They participated in a series of facilitated public meetings, including expert presentations and deliberative forums, to discuss and share their thoughts about the redevelopment of the waterfront and the city's future. This chapter presents a model process for engaging the public on issues of urban design and empowering residents to inform their elected officials on issues that affect the quality of their built environment. This powerful civic engagement model meshes public values and professional expertise.

PART FOUR: COMMUNITIES AND DELIBERATIVE CULTURE   197

14 Study Circles: Local Deliberation as the Cornerstone
    of Deliberative Democracy   199

Patrick L. Scully, Martha L. McCoy

Since its establishment in 1989, the Study Circles Resource Center has helped
make face-to-face deliberation a regular part of public life. In the United States,
study circles have played a leading role in connecting deliberation to individual,
community, institutional, and policy change. This chapter details the process by
which study circles are conducted and provides illustrations of their many varieties.

15 e-thePeople.org: Large-Scale, Ongoing Deliberation   213

G. Michael Weiksner

The mission of e-thePeople is to improve civic participation through the use of the
Internet. The e-thePeople Web site provides a free on-line forum for public discussion
and political action. A distinctive characteristic of the forum is the degree to which the
participants themselves govern the forum, creating and enforcing the rules, deciding on
the topics of discussion, and framing those discussions; it's an attempt at a citizen-driven
town hall. This chapter describes the methods and successes of e-thePeople, and it
examines the special challenges and opportunities of on-line deliberation.

16 Learning Democracy Centers: Where the Public Works   228

Carole J. Schwinn, John T. Kesler, David R. Schwinn

While academics, politicians, and pundits wrangle over the relative power of
federal, state, and local governments, a growing number of civic organizations are
putting power back into the hands of ordinary citizens. The authors of this chapter
refer to these organizations as *learning democracy centers*. These associations and
initiatives are trusted, neutral, institutionalized conveners that have the capacity to
engage diverse members of their community in solving their most pressing social,
economic, and environmental problems. The chapter examines the methods by
which these associations organize, deliberate, and promote citizen action.

17 Disagreement and Consensus: The Importance
    of Dynamic Updating in Public Deliberation   237

Christopher F. Karpowitz, Jane Mansbridge

This chapter examines some specific methods of public deliberation that were
deployed to facilitate town planning in Princeton, New Jersey, using this case to
discuss the dynamics of deliberation more broadly. Karpowitz and Mansbridge
raise a point that pertains to all methods of deliberation—the importance of an
open-minded, ongoing discovery of each party's values and interests—and discuss
what can be done to ensure that this *dynamic updating* takes place.

TABLES AND FIGURES

Tables

Figures

PREFACE

Were democracy a simple matter, it would not require a handbook. *The Deliberative Democracy Handbook* helps the reader learn new methods of citizen engagement that emphasize face-to-face and on-line deliberation among publics large and small. This book is possible because public-minded citizens have accumulated years of experience with many innovative approaches to public participation. We now know how these programs run and what makes them work; the purpose of this book is to share that knowledge.

The first two chapters provide a context for understanding deliberation in the United States. In Chapter One, John Gastil and William Keith explain that a deliberative movement appeared in the early twentieth century in the United States, only to dissipate by World War II. The reemergence of deliberation in the 1990s could also falter, and Chapter One explains what cultural, technological, and geopolitical forces bring about deliberation and cause its collapse. Chapter Two, by Mark Button and David Ryfe, provides an overview of a wide range of programs designed to promote citizen deliberation. The authors present a typology that highlights the shared and distinct features of these deliberation programs so that the reader can understand the full diversity of deliberative practices. Button and Ryfe argue that there are significant trade-offs among the different approaches and that anyone hoping to promote public deliberation should take these into account. The authors also argue that deliberation may have a number of positive outcomes, but it is most important to understand deliberation as a powerful socialization experience that reminds participants what it means to be true citizens in a democratic society.

Chapters Three through Eighteen describe in detail the methods and outcomes of over fifteen different models of public deliberation. The authors of these chapters include the practitioners and scholars who have the best firsthand knowledge of these deliberative practices. To make it easier for the reader to jump from one part of the book to another, each chapter uses a similar organization. There is a quick illustration of the model, an overview of the model's origins and purposes, a detailed description of the model's design, a history of its use, and reflections on its potential uses in the future. In addition, we have created a companion Web site at http://www.deliberative-democracy.net/handbook. The Web site provides additional detail and periodic updates on each of the models described in this volume.

We have grouped the deliberative models into three categories, although the models overlap more than this simple division might suggest. Chapters Three through Eight focus on programs designed to improve the public's judgment through carefully designed deliberative forums and meetings. In Chapter Three, Keith Melville, Taylor Willingham, and John Dedrick describe the many successes of the National Issues Forums, one of the earliest contemporary processes for public deliberation. Michelle Charles, Harris Sokoloff, and Chris Satullo review the design and impact of Philadelphia's Citizen Voices project in Chapter Four. *The Philadelphia Inquirer* brought together the principles of public journalism and the methods of deliberative innovations, such as the deliberative polling method that James Fishkin and Cynthia Farrar describe in Chapter Five. Deliberative polling has now been employed in several countries, and that is also true for the consensus conferences and planning cells that Carolyn Hendriks describes in Chapter Six and the Citizens Juries that Ned Crosby and Doug Nethercut discuss in Chapter Seven. The final chapter of Part Two, coauthored by Lyn Carson and Janette Hartz-Karp, discusses deliberation programs in Australia that have integrated the features of many of these approaches to public meetings.

Chapters Nine through Thirteen bring together a set of deliberation models that typically involve governmental agencies and other public entities. In Chapter Nine, Patricia Bonner, Robert Carlitz, Laurie Maak, Rosemary Gunn, and Charles Ratliff describe the on-line dialogues they have conceived as an improvement on more conventional public hearings. Carolyn Lukensmeyer, Joe Goldman, and Steve Brigham have also explored the applications of new technologies in public meetings, although their 21st Century Town Meetings (described in Chapter Ten) use high-tech communication tools in large-scale face-to-face public gatherings. In the next chapter, Antony Cheng and Janet Fiero focus on Collaborative Learning, a process that was successfully used to help bring public input into the forest management process in the United States. In Chapter Twelve, Vera Coelho, Barbara

Pozzoni, and Mariana Cifuentes Montoya describe the remarkable Brazilian experiment in municipal councils, which give real power to members of civil society organizations. They sound a more cautious note about public deliberation than do most of the authors in this volume, but they believe that the cure for what ails the municipal councils is readily available in the form of more transparent council elections and better deliberation. Part Three ends with Harris Sokoloff, Harris Steinberg, and Steven Pyser's description of the Penn's Landing Forums in Philadelphia, which brought together city planners, urban designers, the general public, and the city's main newspaper to establish a set of principles for developing their blighted waterfront.

Part Four looks at our third category of deliberation programs, those that seek to build community and foster a more deliberative civic culture. In Chapter Fourteen, Patrick Scully and Martha McCoy explain how the Study Circles Resource Center has taken the idea of small, face-to-face study circles and developed it into a model for learning and practicing deliberation throughout neighborhoods, cities and towns, states, school districts, college campuses, and other communities. G. Michael Weiksner, in Chapter Fifteen, shows how a different kind of deliberative community has been created on the Internet through the on-line discussion Web site e-thePeople.org. In Chapter Sixteen, Carole Schwinn, John Kesler, and David Schwinn step back from the specifics of particular approaches to deliberation and look at an array of what they call *learning democracy centers*, initiatives that combine a variety of deliberative methods with other tools to improve local communities.

Not all efforts to promote civic engagement and deliberation come to fruition quickly and seamlessly. In Chapter Seventeen, Christopher Karpowitz and Jane Mansbridge show that in one case in Princeton, New Jersey, a flawed deliberative process yielded a premature consensus, and many citizens found their voice only in more traditional public hearings. In the final chapter of Part Four, William Potapchuk, Cindy Carlson, and Joan Kennedy describe the case of Hampton, Virginia, which has creatively and painstakingly built its capacity for dialogue and deliberation but still has a long way to go before meeting its goals for civic reform.

In the final chapter of this volume, Peter Levine, Archon Fung, and John Gastil consider the challenges that those who wish to improve deliberation face in the coming decades. Persistent challenges include balancing unity and disagreement, ensuring effective organization and facilitation, conducting deliberation on larger scales, and influencing decision makers. As deliberation becomes more influential, practitioners should also take care to preserve the integrity of the deliberative process. In addition, we suggest that some controversial issues may require what we call *cultural accommodation*. If deliberation can successfully reach across cultural divides, it may even become an appropriate mode for addressing international issues, such as trade and terrorism.

The future of democratic governance depends on the articulation of a clear theory of deliberation and the development of effective methods for public engagement. The authors of this volume have done much to advance both purposes. We hope that this handbook will be a useful guide for all who seek to better their communities and their world through common talk and action with their fellow citizens.

April 2005

John Gastil
Seattle, Washington

Peter Levine
College Park, Maryland

ABOUT THE EDITORS

John Gastil (faculty.washington.edu/jgastil) is associate professor in the Department of Communication at the University of Washington. He has conducted survey research for the University of New Mexico Institute for Public Policy, convened citizens' conferences, and managed political campaigns. Gastil is the author of *Democracy in Small Groups* and *By Popular Demand: Revitalizing Representative Democracy Through Deliberative Elections*. His current research examines the civic impact of jury service, the interplay of political culture and deliberation, and the social and psychological aspects of group decision making. He is also the principal author of the Election Day computer simulation game (www.election-day.info).

Peter Levine (www.peterlevine.ws) is research scholar at the Institute for Philosophy and Public Policy and deputy director of the Center for Information and Research on Civic Learning and Engagement (CIRCLE) at the University of Maryland. He is author of four books, most recently *The New Progressive Era: Toward a Fair and Deliberative Democracy*. He serves on the steering committee of the Deliberative Democracy Consortium and is an associate of the Charles F. Kettering Foundation. He also chairs the steering committee of the Campaign for the Civic Mission of Schools. His current work concerns young people's civic engagement and civic uses of the Internet.

ABOUT THE CONTRIBUTORS

Patricia A. Bonner (bonner.patricia@epa.gov) is director of the customer service program at the U.S. Environmental Protection Agency and led the development and implementation of the agency's Public Involvement Policy. In addition to program and policy development, she provides training, feedback, measurement coordination, and support to eleven cross-agency committees. Bonner worked previously in private industry as well as in county and federal government in the United States and in Canada, often with a focus on education and communications related to water policy. She is a graduate of Carnegie Mellon University and earned an M.S. degree from Rensselaer Polytechnic Institute.

Steven Brigham is chief operating officer of America*Speaks*. In addition to managing the organization's operating and financial functions, he serves as project manager on multiple projects. Most recently, he managed a visioning and planning project for the Hamilton County Regional Planning Commission that led to a thousand-person countywide town meeting in January 2002.

Mark Button (mark.button@poli-sci.utah.edu) is assistant professor in the Department of Political Science at the University of Utah. His previous work on deliberative democracy has appeared in *Polity* and the *PEGS Journal*, and he has recently published on the role of religion in American politics. His current research is concerned with the moral virtues necessary to sustain democratic citizenship in diverse societies.

Robert Carlitz (rdc@info-ren.org) developed an interest in public use of the Internet following a career in theoretical physics. Building on this interest, he has organized a number of local, regional, and national networking projects. In 1996, he founded Information Renaissance (www.info-ren.org), where he has guided the development of large-scale on-line dialogues with over one thousand participants; the Smart Building project; and the Wireless Neighborhoods project, in which community groups played an essential part. Information Renaissance is currently working toward participatory electronic rule making at the national level, which has the potential to increase meaningful dialogue between citizens and government on regulatory issues.

Cindy Carlson (www.hampton.gov/foryouth) is director of the Hampton Coalition for Youth. As a department head within city government, she is responsible for long-range and strategic planning for youth and families and for implementing the city's youth development agenda through a partnership of professionals, citizens, and youths. She also oversees the Hampton Youth Commission. Carlson is a presenter and trainer on youth civic engagement, youth and adult partnerships, and Search Institute's 40 Developmental Assets. She has authored articles, training curricula, and a manual on how to create and sustain a successful youth commission.

Lyn Carson (www.activedemocracy.net) is a senior lecturer in applied politics at the University of Sydney. She has written many handbooks, journal articles, and book chapters on public participation. She is coauthor, with Brian Martin, of *Random Selection in Politics*. A former elected representative in local government, she now teaches and undertakes research in the field of public participation and deliberation. She has been involved in many examples of active democracy, including Australia's first consensus conference, Australia's first two deliberative polls, citizens' juries, Australia's first youth jury, and a combined citizens' panel and televote.

Michelle Charles is a consultant in civic engagement and group dialogue facilitation. She has designed and implemented grassroots civic engagement initiatives with the Harwood Institute for Innovation, the Charles F. Kettering Foundation, the University of Pennsylvania, and the *Philadelphia Inquirer*. Michelle is author of the race relations discussion guide "Race Relations: Where Are We Now?" Her main area of expertise is the civic engagement practices of marginalized African American and Latino American citizens of the inner cities as distinct from the civic engagement practices of mainstream America. She lives in Philadelphia.

Antony S. (Tony) Cheng (http://www.cnr.colostate.edu/frws/people/faculty/cheng.html) is assistant professor of forestry and natural resource policy in the Department of Forest, Rangeland, and Watershed Stewardship at Colorado State University in Fort Collins. He teaches undergraduate and graduate courses in natural resource policy and specializes in research on community-based, collaborative natural resource management. His current work, sponsored by the Ford Foundation, is on advancing understanding and practice of community-based forestry in the United States. He is coauthor of *Forest Conservation Policy: A Reference Handbook* and is a senior research fellow with the Pinchot Institute for Conservation.

Mariana Cifuentes Montoya is a research associate at the Institute of Policy Analysis and Research in Kenya. She worked with the Brazilian Center for Analysis and Planning during her postgraduate work, analyzing the municipal health councils in São Paulo. She is interested in processes that strengthen citizens' participation in decentralized decision making. Her current research examines Kenyan local reform that is developing participatory mechanisms to improve service delivery in poor urban areas. She is also researching the use of art and participatory processes in creating and disseminating HIV/AIDS prevention campaigns in East Africa.

Vera Schattan P. Coelho is a researcher and project coordinator at the Brazilian Center of Analysis and Planning in São Paulo and convenes the Brazilian team of the Development Research Centre on Citizenship, Participation and Accountability, which is linked to the Institute of Development Studies at the University of Sussex. She does research on new forms of citizen participation and deliberation and conducts capacity-building programs to improve social policies and participatory democracy. She is author of numerous articles on health policy, pension reform, and the citizen-government relationship. She recently edited *Pension Reform in Latin America* (2003), co-edited "New Democratic Spaces" for the *Institute of Development Studies Bulletin* (2004) and *Participation and Deliberation in Brazil* (2004).

Ned Crosby has pursued a career in public affairs, concentrating on democratic reforms (www.healthydemocracy.org). In 1971, he invented the Citizens Jury process while getting a Ph.d. degree in political science from the University of Minnesota. In 1974, he founded the Jefferson Center to do research and development on new democratic processes. He has worked extensively to coordinate and support lobbying efforts in Washington, D.C. (African affairs in the 1970s, human rights in Central America in the 1980s) and in Minnesota (children's issues in the 1990s).

John R. Dedrick (jrdedrick@kettering.org) is director of programs at the Charles F. Kettering Foundation, Inc. (www.kettering.org). He has been an observer of deliberative forums for more than fifteen years.

Cynthia Farrar (www.yale.edu/isps/programs) is director of urban academic initiatives and lecturer in political science at Yale University. She runs a project on deliberation and local governance at Yale's Institution for Social and Policy Studies. She coordinates the citizen deliberations for MacNeil/Lehrer Productions' By the People project and organizes the annual Greater New Haven Citizens Forum on behalf of the Community Foundation for Greater New Haven and the League of Women Voters of Connecticut. Farrar is author of *The Origins of Democratic Thinking: The Invention of Politics in Classical Athens* and articles and essays on deliberation and on the implications of ancient democracy for modern challenges.

Janet D. Fiero is a consultant who specializes in organizational and community development. She has over thirty years' experience in management and consulting. Her passion is improving the ways in which citizens are engaged in public policy—particularly environmental policy. She started her own consulting company, Bricolage, in 1985 and is an associate of America*Speaks*, a Washington nonprofit that is known for designing and facilitating large public meetings that use intimate deliberation and the power of numbers through technology. She is a roster member of the U.S. Institute of Environmental Conflict Resolution in facilitation and mediation services.

James Fishkin is the Janet M. Peck Chair in International Communication and director of the Center for Deliberative Democracy at Stanford University (http://cdd. stanford.edu), where he is also professor of communication and professor of political science. He is author of a number of books, including *Democracy and Deliberation: New Directions for Democratic Reform* (1991), *The Dialogue of Justice* (1992), *The Voice of the People: Public Opinion and Democracy* (1995), and, with Bruce Ackerman, *Deliberation Day* (2004).

Archon Fung (http://www.archonfung.net/) is associate professor of public policy at the John F. Kennedy School of Government, Harvard University. His research examines the impacts of civic participation, public deliberation, and transparency on public and private governance. His book *Empowered Participation: Reinventing Urban Democracy* (2004) examines two participatory democratic reform efforts in low-income Chicago neighborhoods. His recent books and edited collections include *Deepening Democracy: Institutional Innovations in Empowered Participatory Governance* (2003), *Can We Eliminate Sweatshops?* (2001), *Working Capital: The Power of Labor's Pensions* (2001), and *Beyond Backyard Environmentalism* (2000). His articles on regulation, rights, and participation have appeared in *Politics and Society, Governance, Environmental Management, American Behavioral Scientist,* and *Boston Review.*

Joe Goldman is a senior associate at America*Speaks* (www.americaspeaks.org), where he plays a leadership role in the organization's 21st Century Town Meetings. He has managed and consulted on a wide array of citizen engagement initiatives around the world, including the redevelopment of the World Trade Center site after the attacks of September 11, the creation of Washington, D.C.'s municipal budget, and the development of the Chicago metropolitan area's comprehensive land-use plan. Goldman also conducts research at the John F. Kennedy School of Government at

Harvard University. His current research, funded by the Charles F. Kettering Foundation, investigates the long-term impacts of public deliberation on communities. Goldman is coauthor of the book *A National Town Hall: Bringing Citizens Together Through Interactive Video Teleconferencing*, published by The Pew Charitable Trusts in 1999.

Rosemary Gunn (rgunn@info-ren.org) works with Information Renaissance toward use of the Internet to increase citizen involvement in government. She assisted with two dialogues described in Chapter Nine; for the dialogue on the Master Plan for California Education, she constructed the library, negotiated discussion questions, and wrote the evaluation. Her longtime interest in public participation began in community organizations; later, she was a consultant to agencies and city government and a university program coordinator. More recently, she served as a commissioning editor for publications on development cooperation in health and agriculture, emphasizing participation, stakeholder involvement, training, organization development, and gender, at the Royal Tropical Institute in the Netherlands.

Janette Hartz-Karp is a community engagement consultant to Western Australia's minister for planning and infrastructure. Her role is to implement innovative ways of engaging community and industry in joint decision making with government. Her methods have included citizens' juries, consensus conferences, consensus forums, multicriteria analysis conferences, deliberative surveys, and a 21st Century Town Meeting (Dialogue with the City). Hartz-Karp has lectured in sociology and management at universities in the United States, Israel, and Australia. She has held policy, change agent, and executive positions in Western Australian public service and is currently director of JHK Quality Consultants.

Carolyn M. Hendriks is a research fellow in political science at the University of Amsterdam. She recently completed her doctoral thesis at the Australian National University on the tensions between inclusive forms of public deliberation and interest-based politics. Hendriks has published and conducted workshops on the principles of deliberative forms of public participation. She has also conducted participatory processes for state and local government organizations, including the world's first combined televote and citizens' jury process. She has a background in environmental engineering.

Christopher F. Karpowitz is a Quin Morton Writing Fellow, an affiliate graduate student at the Center for the Study of Democratic Politics, and a doctoral candidate at Princeton University. He is coauthor of *Democracy at Risk*, a report of the American Political Science Association's Standing Committee on Civic Education and Engagement. His research explores how citizens experience democratic institutions and processes, with special attention to deliberation and democratic theory. His dissertation seeks to understand the relationship between deliberative reforms and existing decision-making institutions, such as public hearings.

William M. Keith is associate professor of communication at the University of Wisconsin–Milwaukee. He is currently writing about the history of speech pedagogy in the twentieth century and its relationship to democratic communication forms, especially the forum movement. He has published in numerous journals, including *Rhetoric and Public Affairs, Communication Theory,* and *Rhetorical Society Quarterly.* He also co-edited *Rhetorical Hermeneutics* with Alan Gross.

Joan Kennedy (www.hampton.gov/neighborhoods) is director of the Hampton Neighborhood Office. She served as Hampton planning director prior to accepting the challenge of starting the Neighborhood Initiative for Hampton, which has been nationally recognized for redefining the relationship between city government and neighborhood leaders, shifting it from adversarial to a valued resource partnership. She has presented extensively to national organizations on Hampton's work in neighborhoods and community building and has authored articles and participated in forums on how to deepen the field of community collaboration.

John T. Kesler is an attorney, consultant, and lecturer. His consulting and speaking activities concentrate on civic and democratic capacity building, as well as integrative approaches to personal and societal transformation. In 2003, he ended three years of part-time service as executive director of the Coalition for Healthier Cities and Communities (the American healthy communities organization), and he is currently national chair of the healthy communities section of the successor organization, the Association for Community Health Improvement. Kesler is chairman of the consulting group Learning Democracy Associates and chairman of the Integrative Health Network. He has consulting affiliations with the Integral Institute and the Berkana Institute.

Carolyn J. Lukensmeyer is president and founder of America*Speaks*. From 1997 to 1999, she was executive director of Americans Discuss Social Security, a $12 million project of The Pew Charitable Trusts. Prior to founding America*Speaks,* Lukensmeyer worked as a consultant to the White House Office of the Chief of Staff and served as deputy project director of management of the National Performance Review, Vice President Al Gore's reinventing government task force. From 1986 to 1991, Lukensmeyer served as chief of staff to Governor Richard F. Celeste of Ohio; she was the first woman to serve as Ohio's chief of staff. She holds a doctorate in organizational behavior from Case Western Reserve University.

Laurie E. Maak develops and manages Web dialogues (www.webdialogues.net) for WestEd, a research, development, and service agency based in San Francisco. Her current focus is on using the Web to increase communication between citizens and legislative committees; to facilitate large issue-based discussions; and to enable organizations and government entities to independently produce Web dialogues. Prior to her work at WestEd, she developed and produced large-scale on-line dialogues with Information Renaissance. Her work integrates previous experience in cultivating educational networking, creating public information campaigns, developing extracurricular classes for gifted students, and serving as a school psychologist.

Jane Mansbridge is the Adams Professor at the John F. Kennedy School of Government, Harvard University. She is author of *Beyond Adversary Democracy* and *Why We Lost the ERA,* editor of *Beyond Self-Interest,* co-editor (with Susan Moller Okin) of *Feminism,* and co-editor (with Aldon Morris) of *Oppositional Consciousness.* Her recent publications include "Should Women Represent Women and Blacks Represent Blacks? A Contingent 'Yes'" (*Journal of Politics*), "Rethinking Representation" (*American Political Science Review*), and "Consensus in Context: A Guide for Social Movements (*Consensus Decision Making,* edited by P. G. Coy). Her work in progress, *Everyday Feminism,* argues that "everyday activists" play an important and relatively unnoticed role in social movements.

Martha L. McCoy is president of The Paul J. Aicher Foundation and began working with the foundation's Study Circles Resource Center at its inception in 1989. She has been the center's executive director since 1995. McCoy's academic background is in political science, with a master's degree and doctoral work in political theory and methods, international relations, and comparative politics. She writes and speaks extensively on the need for inclusive, democratic, diverse "public spaces" in which citizens can address public issues and work together for lasting community change.

Keith Melville (KEMelville@aol.com) has been working in the field of public deliberation for more than twenty years. He was senior vice president at Public Agenda Foundation, where he worked with Daniel Yankelovich, helping policymakers move beyond public opinion to understand the public's concerns and perspectives. He was one of the founders of the National Issues Forums and for fifteen years was its editorial director as well as senior writer of more than fifty issue books. He worked with James Fishkin and MacNeil/Lehrer Productions on the 2003 National Issues Convention and wrote the issue book on America's role in the world. Melville has been a faculty mentor in the Fielding Graduate Institute's program in human organization and development since 1982.

Doug Nethercut (dougneth@usinternet.com) is an independent consultant based in Minneapolis. He served as executive director of the Jefferson Center, where he directed several Citizens Jury projects on local, regional, and national issues. Nethercut has directed nonprofit organizations and projects in Minnesota, New

York, and Ghana. He continues to collaborate with Ned Crosby on research and development concerning deliberative processes. Nethercut holds a master's degree from Columbia University's School of International and Public Affairs.

William R. Potapchuk (www.communitytools.net) is president and founder of the Community Building Institute (CBI), based in Annandale, Virginia. CBI works to strengthen the capacity of communities to conduct public business inclusively and collaboratively in order to build healthy, sustainable futures. Potapchuk is the former executive director of the Program for Community Problem Solving and has worked as a consultant, trainer, facilitator, and mediator with states and local governments across the country—in particular, on a variety of projects over a sixteen-year period in Hampton, Virginia. He also has authored numerous publications, including chapters in *The Consensus Building Handbook* and *The Collaborative Leadership Fieldbook*.

Barbara Pozzoni is a consultant to the Operations Evaluation Department of the World Bank and a member of the core team that is evaluating community-driven development interventions promoted by the World Bank. Her interest in deliberative processes at the local level is grounded in her experience as a development practitioner in Central America, where she worked extensively to promote the inclusion of women in participatory local governance spaces.

Steven N. Pyser (http://thedialogue.blogspot.com/) is a principal in a consulting firm that provides dialogue, strategic planning, conflict management, and synergy services to educational institutions, corporations, and nonprofit organizations. He is a faculty member at University of Phoenix, Greater Philadelphia Campuses, where he teaches undergraduate and graduate business and management courses. He facilitates public conversations and dialogues and conducts workshops on diversity, issues of public importance, group facilitation skills, and conflict management. Pyser serves on the editorial boards of *Conflict Resolution Quarterly* and the *Journal of Cognitive Affective Learning* and as a staff editor for the *Journal of Legal Studies Education*.

Charles A. Ratliff (charles@putstudents1st.org) is director of the Office of the Education Master Plan in California. He served as a senior consultant and primary writer of the Master Plan, a comprehensive plan to improve the quality of education for all students, from preschool through university levels. Previously, he served as chief deputy director of the California Postsecondary Education Commission. His expertise spans strategic and long-range planning, public policy, organizational change and leadership, issues of educational equity, and academic support services to students.

David Michael Ryfe is assistant professor of journalism at Middle Tennessee State University. He has published one book, *Presidents in Culture: The Meaning of Presidential Communication*, and many articles, including a series of essays on the practice of deliberative democracy. His current work focuses on ethnographic studies of news media and civic learning in small to midsize American communities.

Chris Satullo has been editorial page editor of the *Philadelphia Inquirer* since March 2000. He is founder and director of the paper's Citizen Voices program, an effort to engage readers in deeper political dialogue. He won the 2000 James F. Batten Award for Excellence in Civic Journalism for his work on Citizen Voices.

Carole J. and David R. Schwinn share a twenty-year history of working with organizations and geographical communities and currently share a consulting practice, Learning Democracy Associates, with John Kesler. The Schwinns' work has taken them throughout the United States, as well as to Canada, Puerto Rico, Japan, New Zealand, India, Aruba, South Africa, and Thailand. After a twenty-five-year career in the community college system, Carole now serves as steward of Berkana Partnering, the outreach and service arm of the Berkana Institute, a nonprofit educational organization founded by Margaret Wheatley. Prior to his consulting practice, David spent twenty years at Ford and General Motors in various engineering and management positions. He is currently a professor in the management department of Lansing Community College.

Patrick L. Scully is executive vice president of the Paul J. Aicher Foundation, where he also serves as deputy director of the Study Circles Resource Center. Before joining the Aicher Foundation, Scully served for nine years as a program officer and director of research at the Charles F. Kettering Foundation. Following his time with Kettering, Scully was a project manager at the Harwood Group, a nonpartisan public issues research firm. He holds an interdisciplinary doctorate in social science (with emphasis on American studies, U.S. political history, and political science) from the Maxwell School of Citizenship and Public Affairs at Syracuse University.

Harris Sokoloff (http://www.gse.upenn.edu/faculty/sokoloff.html) is adjunct associate professor and director of the Center for School Study Councils at the University of Pennsylvania Graduate School of Education, where he also teaches in the School of Design. His applied research focuses on issues of student civic engagement and community development, particularly rebuilding the "public" support for public education through the use of deliberative public forums on school and community issues. Articles on that work have appeared in the *American School Board Journal* and *School Administrator.* He has worked with the editorial board of the *Philadelphia Inquirer* in designing and implementing the public engagement aspects of their Citizen Voices projects and is an associate of the Charles F. Kettering Foundation.

Harris M. Steinberg, AIA, is executive director of Penn Praxis (www.design.upenn. edu/pennpraxis) and a faculty member in the Department of Architecture in the School of Design at the University of Pennsylvania. Penn Praxis is the clinical consulting arm of the School of Design, whose mission is to foster faculty and student collaboration on real-world projects across the five disciplines of the school: architecture, landscape architecture, city and regional planning, historic preservation, and fine arts. Steinberg's work in civic engagement focuses on the relationship between civic design and civic discourse. The Penn's Landing Forums, designed and produced in a partnership with the *Philadelphia Inquirer* and the Center for School Study Councils at the University of Pennsylvania, received a 2003 Citation for Architectural Excellence from the Pennsylvania chapter of the American Institute of Architects and the 2004 Clearwater Award from the Waterfront Center.

G. Michael Weiksner (mike@e-thePeople.org) has been chairman of e-thePeople (www.e-thePeople.org) since October 1999. Prior to cofounding e-thePeople, Weiksner was a manager at Fulcrum Analytics and a consultant at Mercer Oliver Wyman. Michael graduated cum laude from Princeton University with dual degrees from the Woodrow Wilson School of Public and International Affairs and the computer science department. He is a member of the steering committee of the Deliberative Democracy Consortium and founding chairman of its on-line committee. He lives in New York City.

Taylor L. Willingham (taylor@austin-pacific.com) is the founder of Texas Forums (www.texasforums.org), a member of the LBJ Family of Organizations funded by the Lyndon B. Johnson Presidential Library. She is a research associate for the Charles F. Kettering Foundation's New Dartmouth project that is exploring United States–Russia relations and was a National Issues Forums Institute board member. She helped frame issue books on health care, terrorism, America's role in the world, reinventing Iowa's high schools, and issues affecting the Kansas City region. She has been on the faculty of over thirty public policy institutes across the country and in Russia and is adjunct faculty for graduate library schools at the University of Illinois and San Jose State University.

PART ONE

BACKGROUND

CHAPTER ONE

A NATION THAT (SOMETIMES) LIKES TO TALK

A Brief History of Public Deliberation in the United States

John Gastil, William M. Keith

The creation of this book is a testament to the strength of a new deliberative democracy movement. Chapters Two through Eighteen document the many ways in which people in the United States and other countries have developed the idea of deliberation into real methods for public discussion and self-government. Some of the programs detailed in this volume have refined their techniques over decades, whereas others represent a new wave of deliberative experimentation.

Although the following chapters reveal important differences in approach and method, all of the deliberation programs that are described share a set of premises. Advocates of deliberation presume that it is worthwhile for diverse groups of citizens—not just experts and professional politicians—to discuss public issues. Civic discussions, moreover, should have an impact on something important— usually law or public policy but sometimes mass behavior, public knowledge and attitudes, or cultural practices. Even in a representative democracy, direct, participatory democracy plays an important role in emphasizing and furthering public discussion, dialogue, or deliberation and thereby addressing public problems in ways that respect diverse interests and values.

After reading the chapters that follow, one might conclude that American democracy has taken a bold new step forward by adding civic deliberation to its repertoire of institutions and practices. This conclusion would fit comfortably with the conventional view that democracy has consistently improved in the United States as the electorate has expanded and citizens have won new political rights.

Many modern nations share a mythology emphasizing their linear, inexorable progress toward civic perfection.

The reality is more sobering. There is nothing inevitable or irreversible about the deliberative democracy movement, and irrational exuberance about deliberation could lead unwary readers to overlook countertrends that could undermine recent advances. In this chapter, we hope to demonstrate that the deliberative mode of democracy can ebb and flow under changing circumstances. As broadly as we can, we discuss the rise and fall of deliberation in the United States from 1910 to 1940, then consider what recent events have caused it to rise (and might cause it to fall) once again.

History and Democracy

To plan for democracy's future, we need to know its past. Some might fear that such ruminations could trigger paralytic self-doubt and undermine the United States' campaign to win the world's allegiance to democracy; they believe that the romantic version of the story is more palatable. Yet a historical perspective could help Americans recognize that our own historical journey remains unfinished, and this modest self-appraisal could prevent the reckless export of unpolished democratic ideology.

According to its authorized biography, the United States has progressed through a succession of cultural and institutional improvements. Just as the rise and fall of the stock market has occurred within a steady long-term ascent, so has this nation moved, in fits and starts for over two hundred years, toward an increasingly democratic polity. The adoption of the Constitution, followed quickly by the Bill of Rights, set the process in motion by bringing together a nascent nation and equipping it with a set of rights now taken to be fundamental to any democracy. The power of the electorate has grown through the popular election of senators (ratified in 1913), which removed a barrier between the expression of popular will and the creation of national policy. In the same period, many states began to implement direct democratic devices, such as the initiative and recall, which are practiced with greater fervor (and controversy) today than ever before.

Some changes have gradually increased the number and kind of people who can and do vote. The eligible voting public was enlarged by the passage of women's suffrage in 1919, the admission of African Americans (officially, anyway) to citizenship after the Civil War, and the increasing attention to enfranchising minorities as a consequence of the civil rights movement. Lowering the voting age to eighteen in 1972 expanded the franchise further. Since then, there have been reforms designed to enlarge the electorate even more by making voter registration easier; expanding absentee voting, early voting, and voting by mail; and making participation more accessible to people with disabilities.

Beyond expanded voting rights, many other recent changes have enhanced the scope and quality of citizenship. These advances include the explicit rejection, in the last half century, of government intrusions on the right to assembly, such as those perpetrated by the House Committee on Un-American Activities or COINTELPRO, the counterintelligence programs of the Federal Bureau of Investigation. The amount and variety of information available to voters has increased through expanded freedom of the press (by means of the Freedom of Information Act and the precedent set by the publication of the Watergate papers), in addition to voter information guides, many of which are now available on-line.

These changes and many others caused democratic theorist Robert Dahl to suggest that the history of the United States is a roughly linear movement through stages toward ever-higher levels of "polyarchy" on the road to democracy. More and more groups of people (or their representatives) have a seat at the table, and nearly every issue is (or could be) on the public's agenda.[1]

Yet some changes in the political landscape suggest a nonlinear history. These anomalous historical sequences suggest that the process of democratization can have a cyclic character or even fall into steady decline. Some modern trends and events appear to be weakening democratic institutions. The news media, from newspapers to television, have undergone massive technological changes since the early nineteenth century that have coincided with their changing business structure. Many Americans worry today, just as they did in 1900 (but not in 1850 or 1950) about increased concentration of media ownership and how it could affect the democratic functions of the fourth estate.

Every time the United States goes to war, restrictions on civil liberties spring up; 2001's Patriot Act is only the most recent example. Jay Martin has recently argued that John Dewey's objections to World War I stemmed mostly from his fear that democratic reforms would not survive the inevitable authoritarian fervor that surrounds a war. Dewey was worried not only about institutional changes, such as restrictions on the press, but also about changes in the public's civic attitudes and habits during a military campaign. Dewey was concerned about the vitality of the nation's civic culture—its tolerance, sense of duty, public spiritedness, and political efficacy.[2]

These cultural threads of democratic life are difficult to trace across time. It is possible that as we craft ever more democratic public *institutions*, we may be losing or weakening important cultural habits and traditions. In *Democracy in America*, Alexis de Tocqueville described in detail the cultural aspects of American life in the 1830s that he thought provided the substructure that held up America's prized democratic institutions.[3] One of the most popular academic books in recent years is Robert Putnam's *Bowling Alone,* which documents a precipitous decline in "social capital"—the social networks and mutual trust that sustain democratic institutions. Although others have disputed his findings, his book resonated with many readers who sensed a steady decline in social trust and civic engagement.[4]

Rather than see the history of democracy in America as a linear story of either progress or decline, it might be more helpful to view it as a succession of experiments in different places on a continuum ranging from populist democracy to modest republicanism to elitist republicanism. Populist democracy, or radical democracy, emphasizes the inclusion of as many citizens as possible in voting on decisions; referenda are a characteristic tool of populist democracy. Representative forms of democracy emphasize deliberative institutions placed at a remove from the ebb and flow of public opinion, institutions where elected representatives can deliberate carefully. In our view, the United States has oscillated between populist and representative democratic traditions, periodically renegotiating the balance originally struck between the federalists and the democrats in the Constitution. Sometimes the United States has been more populist, such as in the 1820s or in the Progressive era. At other times, the nation has been more elitist, such as during the founding era or the Gilded Age.

Institutional safeguards both in the federal government and in the relation of the states to federal power have been set up to prevent succumbing to either the sins of mobocracy or the vices of oligarchy or plutocracy, but even these safeguards have been amended, dismantled, shored up, and rebuilt at various times. Cultural trends have tended sometimes toward populist and sometimes toward elitist conceptions of citizenship and politics, shaping our social practices as much as our public institutions.

These changes represent more than the changing democratic fashions and tastes. Sometimes unambiguously democratic habits fade or disappear altogether, representing a genuine move away from the ideal. When this happens, it is essential that we study such fragile democratic practices so that we might reintroduce them to the political system. Accordingly, in this essay, we will trace the emergence, decline, and reemergence of one particular democratic art, public deliberation, which has begun to reemerge after fifty years of dormancy.

Late Twentieth-Century Deliberation in the United States

Deliberation is a commonplace word, used most often to describe the process used by juries, councils, legislatures, and other bodies that make decisions after a period of reasoned discussion. Slowly, over the past twenty years, this humble term has taken on a more precise and demanding meaning when used to designate a particular form of democracy. In *Beyond Adversary Democracy* (1983), Jane Mansbridge explains that there are two contrasting models of American democracy—one adversarial and one unitary. The former has dominated our political culture, but there is also an oft-forgotten unitary tradition represented by town meetings and the pursuit of consensus. In the unitary mode, a public engages in respectful deliberation, weighs conflicting evidence and sentiments, and arrives at an enlightened understanding of the general will.[5] In the aftermath of the 1960s, it was common to indict the unitary model as a covert sort of conformism that inevitably stifles dissent and difference. More recent scholarship, such as Francesca Polletta's *Freedom Is an Endless Meeting*, has begun to rehabilitate the democratic experiments of that era.[6] At the time of Mansbridge's book, however, it was revelatory to discover anything of value in tedious discussions that sought to reach consensus.

The next year, in 1984, Benjamin Barber published *Strong Democracy*, one of the best-selling scholarly books on democratic theory.[7] For Barber, a democracy built on representative institutions, adversarial competition among conflicting interests, and the protection of private rights was weak compared to one that gave equal or greater emphasis to community action, public talk, and civic responsibility. Barber recommended a complex array of reforms, many of which have since reappeared in the hundreds of subsequent academic articles on deliberative democracy in political science, communication, and philosophy journals.

Of all the ideas advanced by deliberative theorists, one has received the most attention—the deliberative poll, first suggested in a 1988 *Atlantic Monthly* essay by political science professor James Fishkin.[8] In 1996, Fishkin and a team of nonprofit foundations brought a random sample of over four hundred American citizens to Austin, Texas, to deliberate on pressing national issues, interview prospective presidential candidates, and record their opinions. Fishkin dubbed the event the National Issues Convention, and it was his hope that the postconvention opinions expressed by the attendees would have a "recommending force" and that for the first time, the nation would hear the voice of a *deliberative* public. (See Chapter Five for more on deliberative polling.)

The National Issues Convention received considerable press, and many of its sessions aired on PBS's public television stations. It may even have had an impact on the formats of that year's presidential debates and other media events, which incorporated quasi-random samples of the public as questioners and discussants. The outcomes of the deliberative poll, however, had no clear impact on the election. When another national deliberative poll was held in January 2003, it received little notice. Despite its relevance at the time, policymakers and the media did not notice the surprising shift in participants' opinions; as they deliberated, more of them came to support a United Nations–sponsored solution to the Iraq crisis.[9]

The renewed impulse for deliberation has had other dramatic manifestations, such as President Clinton calling for a national dialogue on race. Delivering the commencement address at the University of California, San Diego, on June 14, 1997, Clinton announced a plan to "promote a dialogue in every community of the land to confront and work through these issues, to recruit and encourage leadership at all levels to help breach racial divides."[10]

Clinton's reference to *dialogue* rather than deliberation emphasized that in addition to encompassing reasoned policy analysis, talk about race must confront differences in experiences and perspectives, requiring as much emotional as intellectual labor. "Honest dialogue," he acknowledged, "will not be easy at first. We'll all have to get past defensiveness and fear and political correctness and other barriers to honesty. Emotions may be rubbed raw, but we must begin." The ultimate impact of the dialogue on race eludes measurement, but the point here is that a sitting president thought it appropriate to launch an initiative promoting public deliberation and dialogue. Such an action indicates that something— whether political or cultural—was needed beyond the thirty years of civil rights legislation.

Beyond dramatic events such as the racial dialogue and deliberative polls, innumerable programs, organizations, and local initiatives have been undertaken in the name (or spirit) of deliberative democracy over the past fifteen years. Many public officials, lay citizens, activists, and academics are interested in increasing the quality of deliberation that takes place in public settings and creating more venues in which citizens and policymakers can meet and talk intelligently and honestly about values and policies.

A sampling of the different deliberative activities initiated in recent years might include the National Issues Forums, a program organized by the Kettering Foundation but convened across the country by a decentralized network of community organizers, local leaders, public officials, educators, and public-spirited citizens (see Chapter Three). These forums bring together communities, church groups, prisoners, adult literacy students, and others to talk about current issues in a distinctive format that breaks issues down into three or four choices and emphasizes the trade-offs of each approach.

Another program that has gained in popularity over the past decade consists of a variety of study circles and community dialogues assisted by the Study Circles Resource Center (see Chapter Fourteen). The study circles approach seeks to improve the quality of public talk by combining open dialogue with focused deliberation and, using community organizing techniques, attracting a large and diverse body of participants. Local organizers adapt study circle processes to achieve a variety of outcomes ranging from shifting individual attitudes and behaviors to sparking collective action to engendering institutional or public policy changes.

The Internet has made possible a new generation of deliberative discussions, such as those convened by meetup.org, MoveOn.org, and e-thePeople.org (see Chapter Fifteen). Thousands of chat rooms, listservs, moderated discussions, and other on-line processes bring together people from across the country (and, in some cases, across the globe) to discuss public issues with one another in a way that was not possible before the widespread adoption of the Internet. Some innovators have created software, such as UnChat, that is specifically designed to facilitate careful deliberation rather than the ranting cross fire that takes place during the less sober on-line exchanges.

The U.S. government has recognized the potential benefits of harnessing public deliberation in its rule-making processes and has created an infrastructure for this purpose. Although public hearings have existed for many decades, on-line versions of these hearings have made it possible for a broader public to participate. They have also made it easier for agencies to give participants direct feedback, including explicit references to on-line input in amended policy documents.

Bodies as diverse as the U.S. Environmental Protection Agency, public utilities, state transportation departments, and school districts have experimented with face-to-face deliberative methods to improve the quality of public input. For example, in 1998, the Orono Board of Education, located just outside Minneapolis, Minnesota, convened a Citizens Jury to learn why citizens kept rejecting school bonds. The jury, composed of a representative sample of the electorate, drafted a novel bond proposal, which the board then placed on the ballot. The bond passed, but only after its proponents campaigned with the Citizens Jury as a key justification.[11] (See Chapters Seven and Eight for more on citizens' juries.)

Though diffuse in their methods, locations, and goals, the theorists and practitioners of deliberative democracy are sufficiently connected that one might say there is a nascent movement to make deliberation a central feature of our political culture and, perhaps, our institutions. A greater quantity and quality of public dialogue and deliberation would likely make the United States more democratic, but it would be a mistake to assume that the deliberative turn represents yet another sure step in the steady march toward the democratic ideal. After all, this is not the first time this country has celebrated the virtues of deliberation.

Early Twentieth-Century Deliberation in the United States

Deliberation emerged as an important cultural force in the early part of the twentieth century. This earlier appearance of deliberation was not just another peak in a cycle that repeats every fifty years, and this historical emergence was different from the more recent reemergence in important ways. It is necessary to revisit this earlier period to understand what characteristics were shared with today's emergence of deliberation, what was different and, ultimately, what causes the deliberation movement to appear and disappear periodically. We can learn by revisiting the past with our contemporary concerns and constraints in mind.

By the second and third decades of the twentieth century, both the public and academics were aware that the New England town meeting, the model of democracy that was sentimentally favored in the public imagination, was no longer viable. (And never mind that those meetings never were the ideal sites of populist democracy that legend had made them out to be.) Not only had the industrial transformation of the U.S. economy moved the majority of the population from farms into rapidly expanding cities, but this population was increasingly diverse. No longer secluded in isolated rural communities, Americans in cities were confronted with just how many of their fellow citizens spoke a different language, ate different food, or worshipped at a different church. The nation lacked the small size and homogeneity that both Pericles and Jefferson had assumed to be necessary for democracy. The connectedness provided by newspapers and radio only served to demonstrate the vastness of the geographical distances that separated different communities, because reliance on them meant surrendering the face-to-face traditions of civic communication. People knew that others, all over the country, were listening to the same broadcast, but couldn't know or speak to one another. The Populist mentality of the late nineteenth century seemed to have foundered on the sheer scale of the populace, in terms of geography, numbers, and diversity.

Progressive reformers at the turn of the century had responded to the crisis of the Gilded Age by increasing some means of direct representation (the direct election of Senators and the ballot initiative are artifacts of this period); at the same time, they increased the size and complexity of public bureaucracies, thereby distancing citizens from government. But as Kevin Mattson showed in *Creating a Democratic Public,* urban governments across the country developed techniques for opening up government to popular participation. In addition, many of the characteristic Progressive civic and nongovernmental institutions sponsored deliberative practices, as Peter Levine has documented. Settlement houses and community centers sponsored debate clubs and forum series, and granges provided places where farmers could discuss the issues of the day.[12]

One of the new methods of citizen involvement was the "open forum." In spurts from about 1900 onward, the open forum movement (later called *the forum movement*) gained ground, especially in urban areas. The word *open* designated the (then) novel idea that such discussion would not be limited to private clubs but would be open to the general public. The open forum reproduced a Chautauqua practice in which a speaker on a current topic would take questions from the audience and a *discussion* would ensue. For many people, this sort of discussion seemed to exemplify the democratic spirit of the town meeting. Such discussions didn't directly lead to laws or policies, but they embodied the spirit of deliberation in a public setting.[13]

One of the most memorable examples of these deliberative institutions was Ford Hall. In 1908, George Coleman opened the Ford Hall Forum in Boston, based on a bequest from recently deceased local philanthropist Daniel Sharp Ford. Coleman met Ford's wishes by providing a diverse and often working-class audience with a place to hear speakers and respond to them. The original handbills "were printed in English, Italian and Yiddish." No one imagined that this was in fact *direct* democracy; a 1930 account of the Ford Hall Forum was subtitled "A Demonstration in Adult Education." Yet it seemed to fit with an emerging sense of expanded political participation. In a 1915 article in the new *Quarterly Journal of Public Speaking*, "The Forum as an Educative Agency," Rollo Lyman of the University of Chicago claimed that the most valuable part of the Chautauqua was not the entertainments but the educational part, the forum. He recommended that forums be detached from the singing, theater, poetry, and oratory and that they be sponsored by colleges in their local communities.[14]

Lyman voiced a widely felt sentiment, and forums spread across the country. In 1920, the League for Political Education opened the Town Hall in New York City; in the wake of the Nineteenth Amendment, the pro-suffrage forces sought a place where newly enfranchised women could obtain a political education that would equip them to cast enlightened votes. Town Hall specialized in forums open to the general public as well as educated women, and they also ran short courses on topics of current interest.[15]

Many people in the early part of the century blamed the problems of democratic communication on the evils of debate as practiced both by legislatures and competitive college teams. In a 1915 *Outlook* magazine essay, Teddy Roosevelt explicitly attacked the model of debate taught in the colleges. By the 1930s, speech departments at universities across the United States began to teach "discussion" courses. An outgrowth of (and in some cases, an alternative to) courses in debate, discussion courses focused on cooperative small group problem solving. Explicitly grounded in the writings of John Dewey, they aimed at equipping students to participate in forums, and they emphasized techniques of reasoned exchange, mutual respect, and equal participation.[16]

The highlight of the forum movement was the Federal Forum Project. In 1932, the Carnegie Corporation of New York gave a grant to John Studebaker, superintendent of schools in Des Moines, Iowa, to run a two-year series of forums as an experiment in continuing adult civic education. Studebaker's innovations included using public school buildings (since they were empty at night anyway), as well as having weekly forums at the neighborhood elementary school (where people would meet with their immediate neighbors), monthly forums at the high school to bring together several elementary school groups, and twice-yearly city-wide forums. Studebaker recruited high-quality speakers, and the forums were very successful. When Franklin Roosevelt tapped him to be U.S. commissioner of education in 1934, Studebaker set about replicating his success on a national scale. Beginning with eight (and eventually eleven) well-funded *demonstration forums* in big cities, the U.S. Office of Education sponsored dozens of forums all over the country. For some forums, the office contributed relief workers; to others, the office gave no more than *The Forum Planning Handbook* and speaker lists. The groundswell of interest in the forums during the Depression still astonishes: by 1938, more than a million people per year were participating in these forums, which were all free of charge and held at least once a week during the school year.[17]

Whereas some of the forums consisted of little more than polite middle-class audiences listening to a speaker and going home, many had diverse audiences, and interesting discussion might follow the speaker's presentation. In contrast to the orchestrated public relations events that often pass for forums today, the forums of the early twentieth century involved speakers (usually academics) who were deliberately neutral and audiences that were encouraged not to be. The goal of these forums was sometimes cast as voter instruction, but Studebaker and others often envisioned a loftier goal—adult civic education.

The point was not merely to educate the public about the issues of the day but, rather, to develop a cultural habit of democratic talk. As Studebaker (1935) makes clear in *The American Way*, deliberation is not important only when done by legislators; all citizens should form and test their views in collaborative interaction with other citizens: "If we are to have that trained civic intelligence, that critical open-mindedness upon which the practical operation of a democracy must rest, we must soon take steps to establish throughout the nation a . . . system of public forums. . . . We should be as thorough in our provision of educational machinery for the development of civic intelligence among adults as we are in our plans for teaching the three R's to children."

Part of what the forums taught was a method of democratic discussion whereby diverse and divided communities might nonetheless engage one another. (Today, this goal typically is cast as "the need for dialogue.")

In 1932, educational philosopher and forum advocate Harry Overstreet invented the *panel discussion*, a now-familiar form in which panelists discuss issues with one another on the stage before the audience joins the discussion. Overstreet realized that not everybody would automatically understand and practice appropriate forms of democratic communication, and he wanted a format that would allow educators to model best practices. Little of this mentality remains; today's Sunday morning talk shows have reduced Overstreet's idea to a parody, and the viciousness of talk radio reveals the popularity of a decidedly nondeliberative form of citizen participation.

The Federal Forum Project disappeared as the priorities of the federal budget shifted to preparations for World War II, and despite the fervent beliefs of forum advocates, nothing on a national scale took its place. Given so much continuity in the language, ideas, and practices of deliberation between the early and late twentieth century, what happened in the interim? We can easily endorse the goals and the methods of the forum movement, but why are we just now rediscovering them? Why did the forum movement mostly disappear, except for the versions that migrated to television and radio? This is important to know because it is a key to understanding the demise of deliberative practices, their resurgence, and the potential for sustaining them in the twenty-first century.

The Mid-Twentieth-Century Decline of Deliberation in the United States

Broadly, we think that a variety of forces in the period from the 1940s to the early 1960s eroded deliberative norms and institutions. The intensity of anticommunism did not provide fertile ground for open debate. Combined with a suspicion (which was partly justified) that there was something potentially subversive about the status quo in all this open debating (some forum activists of the 1930s, though not Studebaker, had been leftists), the Cold War strategy generally favored state-run censorship and propaganda over the marketplace of ideas. The House Un-American Activities Committee, for example, did little to encourage a diversity of voices. At the same time, the rise of new and complex technologies, especially mass communication technologies, drew attention away from the face-to-face context of democracy. Localism was also waning due to a renewed emphasis on urbanization and connecting the nation through a federally designed infrastructure of highways, agencies, and laws. In this growing nation, hurtling into a tomorrow made better through technology, could the quiet tradition of the school board meeting really exemplify efficient and rational governance?

In addition, as a host of B movies made clear, scientists became the exemplars of rational leadership. Science was allied, of course, with democracy and capitalism, and the persistence of a mythology of expertise was not likely to encourage ordinary Joe and Jane Citizen to believe that they had a fundamental role in the larger democratic picture. The emergence of think tanks, especially the RAND Corporation, embodied Walter Lippmann's view that the work was too complex to be run by democracy. Leaders needed experts more than citizens, a policy elite more than an active public.

After World War II revealed our capacity for succumbing to fascism, even the public itself doubted its capacity for reason. Works such as *The Authoritarian Personality* (1950) and Stanley Milgram's experiments on obedience to authority in the 1960s held a mirror up to a public that some regarded as too malleable and impulsive to self-govern.[18] Open-ended public discussion might just as soon percolate madness and sweep tyrants into power as produce anything resembling a reasoned public voice. In the shadow of the communist threat, the old Jacobin arguments were brought out in new garb: "We cannot trust and must control those who question our way of life. This may mean that we cannot trust ourselves."

Finally, the political scene was populated with new actors. Interest groups, representing coalitions of people with common cause, exerted influence, increasingly through the use of professional lobbyists; those with access to the halls of power broadened from the traditional insiders but only to a new elite class—the professionals. If Mr. Smith went to Washington now, he had better know whom to hire as his lobbyist. By the end of this period, people were thinking and talking about democracy as a pluralistic system in which professional planners and politicians adjudicated competing private wants and needs. The only deliberation that might take place would be among the elite, who depended on the public for legitimation and labor rather than leadership. The most democratic movements of the 1960s and 1970s raised new and important voices, but for the most part, they aimed to change the balance of power more than the means by which power was exercised.

Explaining the Deliberative Renaissance

What led to the reemergence of deliberative democracy was a confluence of many of the same factors that had led to its decline—technology, culture, and politics. Over the past thirty years, the worlds of computing, networking, and telecommunications have changed dramatically. In *Emergence*, Steven Johnson explains that in the modern world, people connect and coordinate through loosely coupled networks and local signals rather than a centralized system of command and control.[19] The widespread adoption of the Internet in the United States has lowered the cost of deliberating across geographic borders and even within communities. City hall is now in the kitchen, the office, or wherever you have a computer. E-mail, cell phones, and instant messaging not only facilitate quick one-to-one exchanges, but they also make it much easier to convene virtual and face-to-face meetings. The old problems of distance and communication have radically changed.

No significant discourse would fill these virtual public spaces, however, if the larger society eschewed deliberation. The cultural force behind renewed deliberation is a confluence of multiculturalism and a renewed civic impulse. Rapid globalization and the growing ethnic diversity within the political borders of the United States have pressured companies, government agencies, communities, and other social systems to improve their understanding of cultural differences. The metaphor of the melting pot has given way to that of the complex multicultural stew, and Americans are now expected to leverage difference rather than ignore it, deny it, or melt it away. Dialogue and deliberation can be tools for eliciting, appreciating, and utilizing differences to arrive at collective decisions. In this spirit, Clinton's dialogue on race was not simply a means to resolve an ongoing problem but a process by which people can grow and a society can become stronger. Certainly, there are countertendencies, but there remains a powerful impulse to steer between what Benjamin Barber describes as the stark cultural battles of "Jihad" and the totalizing nonpolitics of "McWorld."[20]

Coupled with this move toward diversity is a renewed civic spirit. At least as interesting as the decline in social capital documented by Robert Putnam's *Bowling Alone* is the acclaim that Putnam's writings have received from both the left and the right of the political spectrum. Referring to Putnam's original article in the 1995 issue of the *Journal of Democracy*, William Galston observed, "Seldom has a thesis moved so quickly from scholarly obscurity to conventional wisdom. By January 1996 the *Washington Post* was featuring a six-part series of front-page articles on the decline of trust, and Beltway pundits had learned the vocabulary of social capital."[21] Social capital may or may not have been waning, but the timing was certainly right for Putnam's thesis.

In the years since, critics have found other wellsprings of public spirit beyond the more traditional civic activities that Putnam traced over time. Charitable giving, volunteerism, and more diffuse civic networking may be supplanting lodges, PTA meetings, and bowling leagues. After September 11, even Putnam acknowledged that the national tragedy may have provided the very spark needed to reignite the public's passion for civic life.

The modern political context also includes new civic actors, such as the Kettering Foundation and The Pew Charitable Trusts, that are committed to promoting public deliberation and dialogue. Whereas most think tanks continue to advance particular political agendas, these new civic foundations and organizations promote a vigorous civil society and deliberative politics rather than a particular partisan outcome. This civic mission sometimes sounds more revolutionary than reformist. The Kettering Foundation describes itself as not looking "for ways to improve on politics as usual." Rather, according to its mission statement, "We are seeking ways to make fundamental changes in how democratic politics are practiced."[22] If the authors of the chapters in this book realize their vision of a deliberative democracy, then deliberation will become the answer to Robert Dahl's 1970 book title, *After the Revolution?*[23]

When deliberation goes wrong, it can degenerate into clumsy compromise or meaningless dialogue that masks the uninterrupted workings of political and economic elites. But deliberation—or mediation or alternative dispute resolution or any number of common forms of dialogue through difficulty—can be so much more than this. When Athenian critics of rhetoric pointed to its potential for misuse, Aristotle replied that the same could be said of strength, health, wealth, and generalship; these powers are not good or bad in themselves, only in the uses to which they are put. Successes from the 1920s and the 1990s alike have demonstrated that deliberation can be a robust process for finding solutions across differences of faith, value, culture, or life experience. Sometimes this means the discovery of an overlooked consensus position, but more often it means arriving at an informed, reflective accommodation of conflicting cultures, or it means parties finding provisional solutions that work within continuing disagreements. It is true that power differences make deliberation more difficult. But they don't make it impossible, and they don't make it useless.

Looking Forward

The conditions may be right for deliberation today, but one point of this essay is to help us recognize the fragility of this particular democratic practice. Changing conditions might sweep it away just as surely as they brought it back to us. But the ebb and flow of history is partly of our choosing, and a quick glance at the present helps us understand what forces could sustain or undermine the present movement toward a more deliberative democratic process.

The shifting international context has proven a factor in the emergence and disappearance of deliberation; no current account of democratic deliberation can ignore globalism the way Federal programs did in the 1930s. The present context is complex in this regard. President George W. Bush has set course for a unilateral, preemptory approach to foreign policy, but even within his administration, there are many who favor a more multilateral approach—one that is more auspicious for the give-and-take of deliberation. In the economic realm, entities such as the World Trade Organization might be taken as signs of ever greater concentration of power in the hands of elites who are accountable only through multiple layers of delegations and trade representatives appointed by executives. At the same time, global activism from Seattle to Prague to Cancún suggests that as the economy globalizes, pressure is likely to increase for more deliberative international bodies that take into account the concerns of a diverse global population.

The physical infrastructure of the modern era might seem more unambiguously felicitous for deliberation. The Internet's reach is only going to grow, and the cost of entering the global village drops every year. The creation of open-source software, such as the Linux operating system, not only has provided cheap, high-powered software to the world but also models the deliberative process in its rigorous exchange of code among equals in public venues. Yet equality of access, either in the United States or other parts of the world, remains a distant goal. Those with Internet access are still disproportionately white and well-off.

In addition, innovations in interactive software provide new opportunities for talking and working together through electronic media. On-line games, in particular, may carve out a virtual space in which the avatars that human players control clamor to become citizens. In a medieval fantasy gaming environment, it does not take one long to discover the need for rules, and players may ultimately want to wrest social control away from the game designers, drafting their own on-line Magna Carta. From the bloody fields of battle may arise public arenas designed for deliberation rather than combat. Players may become accustomed to negotiating the rules of the game, and those lessons cannot help but transfer to the larger public realm, where disputes simply concern different sorts of public goods.[24]

A countervailing trend, however, is the move toward media concentration and market differentiation. Congressional action in 2004 stopped, for the moment, the further relaxation of rules that limit how many media outlets can be owned by one company, but the issue is far from settled. Beyond ownership, the danger remains that the public will be dissipated into little more than segmented audiences who passively consume media content as isolated individuals. Although they may have a varied menu available to them, viewers and readers may become increasingly selective, seeking only political content, for instance, that suits their tastes. The creation of the new radio network Air America, with host Al Franken, is, in this sense, an attempt to create a space for liberals to hear liberals on the air, just as conservatives can cuddle up to Rush Limbaugh. The market for more balanced, thorough reportage may shrink as these ideologically delimited spaces grow, as Cass Sunstein has argued in his book *Republic.com*.[25] Nestled among ideological siblings, we may use interactive technology to cheer one another rather than take part in a more diverse deliberative experience.

In cultural terms, the struggle continues between fundamentalism and cultural relativism and between a withdrawal from public life and an eagerness to join a community. Modern forms of religious extremism remain intolerant of many of the diversities native to public life in a secular democracy. Gated communities remain skeptical of the value of the commons, supplanting public schools with private academies, public parks with members-only fishing holes, public safety with private security. Concerns about terrorism and safety push people further within their homes and their smaller kinship networks.

Against all of these and similar trends, however, are stubborn trends toward tolerance, which seem just as much a part of American culture as *Leave It to Beaver*'s patriotic conformity once did. One can take heart in the ever-increasing (albeit gradual) representation of minorities and women in professions, as well as the widening range of social roles available to people of varied backgrounds and interests.

More directly encouraging is the continuing proliferation of individuals, organizations, and associations committed to promoting public deliberation. Two large civic networks have formed, the Deliberative Democracy Consortium and the National Coalition for Dialogue and Deliberation. These networks bring together thousands of efforts, such as the Public Conversations Project, America*Speaks*, Information Renaissance, and other names that evoke the public-spirited associations of the 1920s.

These observations are of interest to more than the historian and futurist. The cycle of demise and rebirth need not be repeated, and it is possible at this moment in history to intervene in meaningful ways to sustain the momentum toward deliberative democracy. By promoting the most positive trends and monitoring and countering the negative ones, deliberative democratic practices may be sustained and continually developed well into our future.

Notes

1. Dahl, R. A. (1989). *Democracy and Its Critics*. New Haven, Conn.: Yale University Press.
2. Martin, J. (2002). *The Education of John Dewey*. New York: Columbia University Press, 269ff.
3. Tocqueville, A. de. (1961). *Democracy in America*. New York: Schocken Books. (Originally published 1835.)
4. Putnam, R. D. (2000). *Bowling Alone: The Collapse and Revival of American Community*. New York: Simon & Schuster. A critique of Putnam's general thesis of declining social capital is provided by Bennett, W. L. (1998). "The Uncivic Culture: Communication, Identity, and the Rise of Lifestyle Politics." *PS: Political Science & Politics, 31*, 741–761. A critique of Putnam's core explanation for the decline in social capital is provided by Moy, P., Scheufele, D. A., and Holbert, R. L. (1999). "Television Use and Social Capital: Testing Putnam's Time Displacement Hypothesis." *Mass Communication & Society, 21*, 27–45.
5. Mansbridge, J. J. (1983). *Beyond Adversary Democracy*. Chicago: University of Chicago Press.
6. Polletta, F. (2002). *Freedom Is an Endless Meeting: Democracy in American Social Movements*. Chicago: University of Chicago Press.
7. Barber, B. R. (1984). *Strong Democracy: Participatory Politics for a New Age*. Berkeley: University of California Press.
8. Fishkin, J. (1988, Aug.). "The Case for a National Caucus." *Atlantic Monthly*, pp. 16–18.
9. More on this and related projects is available in "By the People: A National Conversation About America in the World." (n.d.). [http://www.pbs.org/newshour/btp].
10. The full text of the speech is available at the following Web site: Clinton, W. J. (1997, June 14). "Remarks by the President at University of California at San Diego Commencement." [http://usinfo.org/USIA/usinfo.state.gov/usa/race/pres616.htm].
11. This case is discussed in relation to deliberative electoral reform in Gastil, J. (2000). *By Popular Demand: Revitalizing Representative Democracy Through Deliberative Elections*. Berkeley: University of California Press.

12. Mattson, K. (2001). *Creating a Democratic Public.* State College: Pennsylvania State University Press; Levine, P. (2000). *The New Progressive Era.* Lanham, Md.: Rowman & Littlefield; Carson, M. (1990). *Settlement Folk: Social Thought and the American Settlement Movement, 1885–1930.* Chicago: University of Chicago Press; Simkhovitch, M. K. (1926). *The Settlement Primer.* New York: n.p.

13. Orchard, H. A. (1923). *Fifty Years of Chautauqua.* Cedar Rapids, Iowa: Torch Press.

14. Lurie, R. L. (1930). *The Challenge of the Forum—The Story of Ford Hall and the Open Forum Movement: A Demonstration in Adult Education.* Boston: Richard R. Badger; Lyman, R. L. (1915). "The Forum as an Educative Agency." *Quarterly Journal of Public Speaking, 1,* 1–8.

15. Overstreet, H. A., and Overstreet, B. W. (1938). *Town Meeting Comes to Town.* New York: Harper & Brothers; Young, L. (1989). *In the Public Interest: The League of Women Voters, 1920–1970.* New York: Greenwood.

16. Roosevelt, T. R. (1913, Feb. 22). "Chapters in an Autobiography." *Outlook,* 393–408. Some examples of popular texts at the time are Pellegrini, A., and Stirling, B. (1936). *Argumentation and Public Discussion.* New York: Heath; McBurney, J., and Hance, K. (1939). *Principles and Methods of Discussion.* New York: Harper & Brothers; Ewbank, H. L., and Auer, J. J. (1941). *Discussion and Debate: Tools of Democracy.* New York: F. S. Crofts.

17. Studebaker, J. W. (1935). *The American Way.* New York: McGraw-Hill; Studebaker, J. W. (1936). *Plain Talk.* Washington, D.C.: National Home Library Foundation; Studebaker, J. W., and Williams, C. S. (1937). *Choosing Our Way.* Office of Education Bulletin 1937, Misc. No. 1. Washington, D.C.: Office of Education, U.S. Department of the Interior.

18. Adorno, T. W., Frenkel-Brunswik, E., Levinson, D. J., and Sanford, R. N. (1950). *The Authoritarian Personality.* New York: Norton.

19. Johnson, S. (2001). *Emergence: The Connected Lives of Ants, Brains, Cities, and Software.* New York: Scribner.

20. Barber, B. R. (1995). *Jihad Vs. McWorld: How Globalism and Tribalism Are Reshaping the World.* New York: Ballantine Books.

21. Galston, W. (1996, May–June). "Unsolved Mysteries: The Tocqueville Files II." *American Prospect, 26,* 20–25.

22. Kettering mission statement is from http://www.kettering.org.

23. Dahl, R. A. (1970). *After the Revolution?* New Haven, Conn.: Yale University Press.

24. Lively discussions of these issues are already occurring on-line. See, for example, Dan Hunter, "Avatar Rights" (October 12, 2003), http://terranova.blogs.com/terra_nova/2003/10/avatar_rights.html.

25. Sunstein, C. (2002). *Republic.com.* Princeton, N.J.: Princeton University Press.

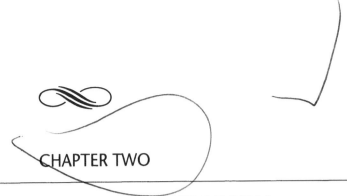

CHAPTER TWO

WHAT CAN WE LEARN FROM THE PRACTICE OF DELIBERATIVE DEMOCRACY?

Mark Button, David Michael Ryfe

If, as one recent author has wryly noted, "Democracy is hard to love," then it is difficult to know what to make of deliberative democracy.[1] The ideal of deliberative democracy not only suggests that decisions must derive from the collective will of its members but also insists that the decision-making process foreground the public reasoning of its members.[2] The attempt, let alone its accomplishment, can be a hard slog. Even the most committed advocates of deliberation can sometimes find the process tedious. For instance, we witnessed much eye rolling and many a shoulder shrug during sessions of the first National Conference on Dialogue and Deliberation held in Washington, D.C., in October 2002. Despite their enthusiasm, participants sometimes could barely suffer through yet another soliloquy on this or that deliberative process. And these were the putative experts! No wonder deliberation is difficult to imagine in large, complex, heterogeneous societies. Nevertheless, theorists of deliberative democracy remain hard at work to make good on its intuitive appeal, and a growing chorus of practitioners seeks to institutionalize deliberation in actually existing society.

In this chapter, our goal is to address what these theorists and practitioners can learn from one another and why it matters. Of course, theory and practice are always linked at some level. But there is still surprisingly little cross-communication going on between these camps. We think that remedying this deficiency could benefit normative accounts of deliberative democracy, which can tend toward ethereal accounts of political practice. But it could also benefit the institutional design and practice of deliberation, which at times can become acutely pragmatic.

To connect theorists and practitioners, we begin with a critical discussion and typology of a diverse group of practical initiatives that seek to foster more citizen deliberation in American politics. In our survey, we show that practical choices related to the institutional design of deliberative initiatives often have conceptual consequences that practitioners would do well to consider. Next, we evaluate some of the normative, democratic goals of deliberative models and consider some of their practical consequences and constraints in light of the empirical cases discussed in this chapter and throughout the book. In this context, we address some of the practical implications for conceptual choices as they bear on the idea of deliberative democracy. By demonstrating these connections, we hope to encourage a better-informed and more critically self-reflective dialogue between theorists and practitioners. We will conclude with a broad defense of deliberative democracy as a means of civic education. We hope that this defense will solidify the connections between the theory and practice of deliberation.

The Conceptual Implications of Practical Choices

It is fair to say that the deliberative movement around the globe is spearheaded by a relatively small cadre of experts. This is especially true in the United States, where experts in facilitation, conflict resolution, talk therapy, dialogue, and a host of other models dominate the field. The chapters in this volume bear the point out. National Issues Forums, deliberative polling, planning cells, Citizens Juries, America*Speaks*, Collaborative Learning, and study circles are all expert-created models circulating among state and local community leaders. We do not mean to disparage the populist sentiment that lies at the heart of many of these models, nor do we wish to denigrate the real work that local civic leaders do to make these models fit their particular community's circumstances. We only mean to highlight the fact that these models are crafted and modeled by individuals who make their living by thinking about how to deliberate. Such individuals are, by definition, experts in at least their own deliberative processes. We do not claim that every deliberative initiative is driven by experts, but we do suggest that, on balance, deliberative initiatives are expert-driven. This profile lends the movement an entrepreneurial cast. Experts of the kind represented in these pages (both as subjects and authors) are in the business of promoting deliberation—both as an abstract ideal and in the specific form of the models they employ.

This entrepreneurial profile has a further consequence that is worthy of some critical self-reflection. In their otherwise admirable spirit of pragmatism, deliberative experts may overlook the conceptual implications of their practical choices. As pragmatists, deliberative leaders are perfectly willing to mold their models to the needs of local communities. Such customization, however, may obscure the fact that the local ways in which they model deliberation offer more general, culture-wide lessons.

Two pragmatic questions of great conceptual significance are the following: Who initiates deliberation? And who will participate in the deliberation? As we will show in this chapter, specific models answer these questions in different ways at different times. The answers they provide go a long way toward defining the nature and substance of the public exchanges that will occur in a deliberative encounter, and these answers clarify the meaning of deliberative democracy itself.

In societies that are often impatient with or hostile to deliberative modes of collective decision making, it can seem that the key decision confronting various constituencies is whether to engage in deliberation at all. This decision is important, but it masks the fact that deliberation is not a uniform activity. As these chapters attest, it can take different forms, be oriented to different purposes, and have different outcomes. Moreover, as our fellow authors are acutely aware, deliberation is also fragile, open to both internal and external constraints, and highly unpredictable. The best of intentions can sometimes produce less than desirable outcomes.

Researchers have found, for instance, that ostensibly deliberative forums can be dominated by nondeliberative talk, strategic behavior, and elite opinions. Paradoxically, deliberation can be organized in such a way as to produce nondeliberative outcomes and more rather than less political cynicism.[3] Thus, although a decision to initiate deliberation is necessary, it is not sufficient to actually achieve the desired outcome. In our view, two subsequent questions play a particularly important role in determining the relative success of deliberative encounters: Who ought to initiate a deliberative encounter? And, once initiated, who ought to participate? The answers to these questions can determine the extent to which a public event or discussion program can overcome the aforementioned obstacles to deliberation.

Although practitioners put great thought into the question of whether or not to deliberate, these latter two questions often are not seen as choices at all. Some local entity—a planning agency, a chapter of the League of Women Voters, a high school, the YMCA—identifies a problem, decides that deliberation is necessary, and contacts deliberative experts for assistance in organizing the process. Similarly, the question of who participates is often made by default. Sometimes this choice is folded into the deliberative model that organizers select. The use of deliberative polls, planning cells, or citizens' juries, for instance, requires that participants be chosen by random selection. Participants in Brazil's public budgeting processes are elected by the organizations for which they work. In other cases, the choice is determined by the context of deliberation. For example, a school clearly has its own students and families in mind when it organizes a deliberative forum. Whether made consciously or not, however, these choices have significant normative and conceptual consequences. Decisions about who initiates and who participates in forums shape the talk that will ensue, the outcomes one might expect, and the challenges likely to arise in a deliberative encounter.

A Typology of Deliberative Processes

To see the conceptual consequences of practical decisions more clearly, we offer the following typology. Suppose for the moment that each of our two questions has three possible answers. For example, in our survey of the deliberative field, we find that three kinds of entities typically initiate a deliberative encounter: grassroots civic groups, such as neighborhood associations; nongovernmental organizations (NGOs), such as the League of Women Voters or the YMCA; or government organizations, such as planning agencies or health commissions. Similarly, there are three basic kinds of participant selection schemes: self-selection, random selection, and what we call *stakeholder selection*. Random selection is self-explanatory. Stakeholder selection involves organizers in a process of identifying groups likely to be affected by a decision and issuing a formal invitation to representatives of these groups. Self-selection involves a more personal invitation, from friend to friend, neighbor to neighbor, or community organizer to citizen.[4] Taken together, the kinds of entities and methods of participation selection produce a tidy three-by-three table, as shown in Table 2.1.

TABLE 2.1. CONFIGURATIONS OF DELIBERATIVE FORUMS

Who Initiates?	Who Participates?		
	Self-Selection	**Random Selection**	**Stakeholder Selection**
Civic association	School-based deliberations; neighborhood associations; on-line dialogues; National Issues Forums; study circles	N/A	National Issues Forums; study circles; on-line dialogues
Nongovernmental association	National Issues Forums; study circles; America*Speaks*; on-line dialogues	Deliberative polls; planning cells; Citizens Juries	National Issues Forums; study circles; participatory budgeting and management councils
Governmental organization	Town meetings; community forums; local councils; deliberative stewardship	Deliberative polls; planning cells; Citizens Juries	Deliberative city planning; deliberative meetings; deliberative stewardship; participatory budgeting and management councils

As Table 2.1 shows, many of the models discussed in this volume may fit two or more of the possible configurations. Yet each configuration constitutes deliberation in different ways and raises a different set of issues for both organizers and participants.

For example, consider forums initiated by voluntary civic groups that rely on a self-selection scheme. Such groups may put up flyers at a local library, announce initiatives to church groups, or go door to door in their community. The resulting forums are strongly shaped by this underlying structure. For example, precisely because participants self-select, they may exit with relatively little cost.[5] One way to keep them involved is to promise them a real input into decision-making processes. However, a voluntary association—unlike a government agency—can offer participants few assurances that their discussions will lead to specific outcomes. Indeed, moderators of such meetings often state explicitly that the purpose of the encounters is educational, not political.[6] Combined, these structural conditions often lead groups to emphasize politeness, familiarity, and even intimacy in group discussions. The idea seems to be to foster an environment in which participants will stay because they enjoy one another's company.[7] This is a perfectly legitimate outcome, but it can lead such groups to stress what Robert Putnam calls "bonding" over "bridging" experiences.[8] Over time, as participants shuffle in and out of self-selected groups initiated by voluntary associations, the groups risk becoming more exclusive and homogeneous. The bonding that takes place among the participants who return is bought at the price of cognitive diversity.[9] One consequence may be that deliberation in such forums actually exacerbates group polarization, leaving participants with more extreme versions of the opinions with which they started.[10]

Other cells in our typology produce deliberation in slightly different permutations. Limited space prevents us from a thorough discussion of each type of deliberation. The aforementioned example, however, illustrates how different organizational forms produce different kinds of deliberative possibilities.[11] In making this observation, our intention is not to show that organizing a deliberative forum is difficult; practitioners know this all too well. Rather, it is that the nature of any given initiative can be made clearer when organizers recognize the conceptual implications of their pragmatic choices. Mundane, practical decisions, such as allowing participants to self-select or allowing a civic association to initiate a deliberative encounter, constitute deliberation in particular ways. Knowing more about how this happens may not lead organizers to make different choices. After all, if an NGO is the only organization in a community willing to initiate deliberation, then merely wishing for the involvement of a government organization will not make it so. Similarly, if an organization has limited resources with which to reach out into a given community, knowing the pitfalls of self-selection will be of little solace. It may, however, help practitioners to anticipate the shape of the talk that is likely to ensue and the challenges that are likely to arise, given the configuration of the forums they have organized. It may make them more reflective and nimble as they confront issues on the ground and in the moment.

It is also worth stressing that conceptual choices have important, if often unacknowledged, pragmatic consequences as well. To this point, we have described practitioners as pragmatists wholly driven by facts on the ground. In reality, like deliberative theorists, practitioners have ideas about the normative value of deliberation and about how it ought to be practiced. Indeed, deliberative theory has inspired many practical initiatives. The connection between theorists and practitioners is deeper still. Both groups work within liberal democratic societies that tend to be at best indifferent and at worst hostile to widespread public deliberation.[12] As such, they confront deep skepticism about the value and purpose of deliberation—from theorists who question the feasibility of deliberative schemes, to policymakers who question the value of public input, to ordinary citizens who discount their potential impact on policymaking or who have grown (quite understandably) averse to politics.[13]

In this context, we detect a growing preference among practitioners and theorists alike for instrumental justifications of deliberation.[14] In their zeal to show its benefits, theorists and practitioners increasingly justify the value of deliberation as a means for addressing specific issues or public controversies. Often this impulse manifests itself in the claim that communities ought to embrace democratic deliberation because it produces better, wiser, and more legitimate public policies. This conception of deliberation, though useful in certain respects and for certain issue domains, has two problems. First, it remains to be shown that deliberative models provide forms of decision making that are superior to traditional voting procedures.[15] Second, it is often quite difficult to empirically establish that deliberation sustains this promise in practice.[16] Instrumental conceptions of deliberation are also questionable as a normative democratic matter. Suppose we could show that deliberation does in fact produce good outcomes. Is this the only reason we might prefer it as a method of public decision making? Our sense is that instrumentalism may blind us to other equally significant ways of conceiving and justifying deliberation and thus constrain our ability to fashion or embrace different configurations of the practice. Just as practical choices have conceptual implications, so do the ways that we conceive of deliberation have pragmatic consequences.

The Practical Implications of Conceptual Choices

Democratic theory remains a significant resource for the advocates and practitioners of public deliberation. In this section, we detail some of the most significant reasons that theorists advance in support of the work of democratic deliberation, and we address some of the practical challenges that confront this branch of democratic theory today. Some of the same problems that we have identified within the institutional design of deliberative forums are mirrored at the level of theoretical reflection as well. By critically attending to these interconnections, the theory and practice of deliberation can ultimately stand on firmer ground. In the conclusion to this chapter, we offer more specific ideas on how deliberative democracy might be best conceived, evaluated, and defended.

It is important to recognize, as suggested in Chapter One, that the contemporary revival of deliberative democracy is taking place within a unique historical-political context. Whereas one frequently hears, at least within academic circles, that deliberative democracy is offered as an alternative to liberal, pluralist, and interest-group models of democracy, it is also the case that a renewed interest in the specific value of public deliberation for democratic self-governance has taken place against a sociopolitical backdrop that includes increasing political and economic inequalities, the ongoing marginalization of already disadvantaged groups, steady declines in various forms of political participation, the institutional demobilization of the public, a widespread distrust of government, and a general disaffection with politics. Deliberative democracy has taken on renewed significance in recent years not only because of a certain measure of theoretical dissatisfaction with traditional aggregative models of bargaining and decision making but also because of more fundamental concerns about the health and future of democracy as a distinct political and cultural mode of life. These dual phenomena—theoretical reflection on democracy and the proliferation of institutional and political alternatives—are often separated within the academic division of labor but remain intimately connected by the shared commitment to creatively re-imagine the conditions necessary to bolster and sustain a democratic political culture. Can deliberative democracy make good on this promise? We believe it can, and in this section, we provide a general framework that strengthens the link between the theory and the practice of deliberative democracy today.

As we have seen—and as the rest of this book bears out in even greater detail—a variety of deliberative practices exist, and the diversity of these programs range along a number of important variables (such as who initiates deliberative forums and methods of participant selection) that shape both the nature of deliberative processes and their overall inclusiveness and representativeness. But what are the implications of this variability when we are thinking more broadly about the status and prospects of deliberative democracy today? What can we realistically expect from deliberative democracy? For what reasons should we give deliberative procedures moral or political priority over more traditional forms of strategic or aggregative decision making? Given the scale, complexity, and pluralism of contemporary political societies that depend in crucial ways on representative insti-

tutions and nondeliberative mechanisms like voting, what is the value of deliberation in our political lives?

There are a variety of answers to these questions on offer today. Indeed, deliberative democracy is not a unified theory but a diverse and growing field that is defined by a host of disagreements about how we might best address these and other questions. Although it is often difficult to discern the level of analysis at which theorists of deliberation pitch their accounts (and thus whether any serious attention has been given to the practical problems of establishing and sustaining more deliberative practices), the following are some of the most common reasons given in support of deliberative democracy. These theoretical accounts will continue to inform and inspire the practical design of deliberative forums.

Legitimacy

The specific procedures and preconditions of deliberative democracy are designed to generate legitimate outcomes. By stipulating fair procedures of public reasoning that are, in principle, open to everyone, the outcomes of a deliberative procedure will be seen as legitimate because they are the result of a process that is inclusive, voluntary, reasoned, and equal.[17] There are significant differences of opinion in regard to whether fair procedures are enough to legitimize a deliberative process. For instance, some observers have complained that formal equality means little if individual participants remain substantively unequal. However, there is general agreement that "the source of legitimacy is not the predetermined will of individuals, but rather the process of its formation, that is, deliberation itself."[18] Deliberative democracy takes seriously the idea that the exercise of collective political authority must be capable of being justified to all those who will be bound by it. To fail to accept this idea is to fail to take the freedom and equality of persons seriously.

Better Outcomes

Deliberative democrats not only want to generate outcomes that everyone can view as fair and legitimate but also hope to create more just and rational decisions. Under conditions of limited and costly information, value pluralism, and human fallibility (or "bounded rationality"), a deliberative process that is broadly inclusive and focused on the role of free and reciprocal reason giving among equals is intended to allow "no force except that of the better argument" to be exercised.[19] The specification of conditions of inclusion and norms of reciprocity in many accounts of deliberative democracy helps to ensure not only that a variety of voices will be heard on any public controversy but that individuals will also be motivated to give reasons that will be mutually acceptable to others. In this way, the decisions that issue from a process of deliberation, even when they fall short of consensus, can be considered just because they are the result of a process that has sought fair terms of cooperation and mutual justification for their own sake.[20]

Preference Formation or Transformation

One of the significant ways in which deliberative democracy is said to differ from other social choice mechanisms (such as voting or traditional polling) is that it does not treat individual preferences as fixed, rank-ordered, or exogenous to given institutional or political processes. From the vantage point of deliberative democracy, it is erroneous to suppose that individuals already possess a clear, enlightened, and coherent understanding of their preferences or opinions on complex social and political issues. Such reflective judgments, it is argued, can result only from a process of open and fair public deliberation.

Not only do deliberative democrats view individual preferences (and preference rankings) as an endogenous feature of political arrangements, but they also argue that an essential virtue of deliberation is that it deemphasizes the aggregation of (or bargaining among) pre-established preferences and individual interests. Instead, deliberation seeks the formation of a consensus view of shared interests and common goods. Such an understanding cannot come about if individuals are unwilling to set aside narrow self-interests or if political practices do not offer the necessary institutional settings and motivations to make this possible. A deliberative process cannot guarantee that individual preferences will change or that they will change in a uniquely more civic-minded direction; rather, defenders of deliberative democracy argue that they are more likely to do so in an inclusive, information-rich setting in which citizens are encouraged to reason with one another about broader issues of mutual concern in ways that are morally acceptable to everyone.[21]

Responding to Deliberation's Critics

As with the various configurations of deliberative forums that we discussed in the first part of this chapter, each one of the aforementioned goals of deliberative democracy raises a host of conceptual and practical difficulties. We cannot discuss these challenges in depth here, but it is important to recognize that the theory of deliberative democracy has been subjected to a number of thoughtful critiques that raise important questions about its basic feasibility for a large and heterogeneous society, its self-proclaimed superiority over aggregative decision-making procedures, and its normative desirability as a mode for addressing moral conflicts or as a way of understanding the proper relationship between individual or cultural differences and the wider polity.[22]

What the critics of deliberative democracy help us to appreciate is that as both a normative and an empirical matter, deliberative democracy remains an open question. Will deliberative forums produce policy consensus and help minimize moral disagreements, or will they heighten and reify moral and political divisions? Will deliberative encounters offer equal opportunities for a more inclusive understanding of the common good, or will the normative thrust toward consensus and mutual agreement run roughshod over those that may not enter the public domain with the skills and predispositions to enable their differences to be recognized in an arena of justificatory public reasoning? As our brief survey of both the practice and the theory of deliberation attests, deliberative democracy (as a largely procedural vision of politics) is full of uncertainty and is prone to a variety of internal and external constraints, pathologies, and abuses. Of course, it would be strange for any theory or practice of governance to be immune to challenges (for example, issues of pluralism, inequality, and power) that are endemic to political life as such. Although we should be modest and self-critical about what we claim for a more deliberative version of democracy, especially under the less-than-ideal circumstances of present social and economic realities, we should not succumb to a premature skepticism about deliberative democracy's value. What we want to suggest is that where we look for that value goes a long way in shaping the theoretical models and institutional designs that we pursue and defend.

One of the significant, if also surprising tendencies that we have observed in both the theoretical articulation and the practical design of deliberative democracy has been the overriding focus on the expected or hypothesized outcomes of deliberative procedures. In the case of deliberative practitioners, this tends to take the form of a preoccupation with policy input and policy effects. In the case of normative theory, it takes the shape of a defense of deliberation that is focused on the hypothetical benefits of deliberative procedures (political justification, legitimacy, rationality, preference transformation, and so on). In strictly logical terms, any account of deliberation will need to concern itself with the kinds of decisions and the types of results that can be realistically anticipated to result from such a process. Yet if a deliberative procedure is judged strictly in terms of its outcomes, then deliberative democracy would only seem to have instrumental value for us. To that extent, we may miss some of the intrinsic values that deliberative democracy holds for us, both individually and culturally.

Public Deliberation and a Civic Culture

What are the intrinsic values of democratic deliberation, and why do they matter? What sorts of evaluative standards or benchmarks would we propose in accordance with which we could judge the relative success of deliberative practices? From our point of view, deliberative democracy gives individuals the chance to live (however briefly) and to experience (however artificially) the essential meaning of democracy: free and equal citizens with an equal opportunity to participate in a shared public life and to shape decisions that affect their lives. A more fully deliberative form of politics is a more fully democratic kind of life because it enlists the skills and virtues that make it possible for individuals to see themselves as interdependent, equal, and sovereign members of a political association.

In this respect, then, deliberative democratic forums are a powerful political and cultural resource for combating the dual forces of privatism and demobilization, individual withdrawal, and institutional marginalization or exclusion that are taking place in our social and political lives today. As a variety of political thinkers from Jefferson to Tocqueville, Mill, and Arendt have helped us to appreciate, part of the intrinsic value of democracy is that it allows citizens to see things from different points of view and that it enables individuals to come to see themselves as equal, capable, and responsible members in a shared political life. The call for more deliberative forums within the dispersed, plural, and overlapping domains of civil society is at once a call for restoration of the conditions that make a civic culture and civic actors possible.

Hence, the kind of benchmarks that we might employ to assess relative degrees of success, in accordance with this civic cultural standard, would include feelings of personal and political efficacy; reports of changes in attitudes concerning social or political responsibility; changes in degrees of social trust and empathy; and rates of long-term social and political involvement. If we have in mind a theory of deliberative democracy that connects it to a larger concern about the formation and sustainability of a civic culture, then the empirical assessment side of this account must be calibrated so as to judge how well deliberation cultivates people who see themselves as democratic citizens—persons with the skills, qualities, dispositions, and virtues necessary to undertake the rights and obligations of citizenship effectively.

Any complete or adequate account of deliberation will have to resist the tendency to choose between its instrumental purposes and its value as an end in itself. If the focus on outcomes threatens to reduce deliberation to an instrumental process reminiscent of the aggregative procedures it was designed to supplement, an exclusive focus on deliberation as an end in itself will hardly bring people back

into politics. What is at stake in the deliberative movement is not series of contending models of democratic discourse but the renewal of a more fully democratic, civic culture, as well as the institutional spaces necessary to make democratic citizenship a meaningful and enduring reality.

There are ominous signs that the culture and values of democratic citizenship are under severe threat today—signs that American citizens have come to embrace a "stealth democracy."[23] Of course democracy doesn't work by stealth; plutocracy does. Hence, one of the most appropriate and most practical defenses of deliberative democracy is one that views it as part of a wider and longer-term effort to enliven active democratic citizenship and to bolster a democratic culture that will sustain such citizenship.

Ultimately, then, deliberative democracy is best viewed, in theory and in practice, as one part of an overall civic endeavor that aims to reproduce the necessary spaces, skills, and virtues to foster sovereign, self-governing members of a pluralistic society. If the public is to meet, as John Dewey might put it, the public must first be formed. To a significant degree, that is the most important purpose of the deliberative projects recounted in this book.

Notes

1. Young, I. M. (2000). *Inclusion and Democracy.* New York: Oxford University Press.
2. Barber, B. (1984). *Strong Democracy: Participatory Politics for a New Age.* Berkeley: University of California Press; Chambers, S. (2003). "Deliberative Democratic Theory." *Annual Review of Political Science, 6,* 307–326; Cohen, J. (1989). "Deliberation and Democratic Legitimacy." In A. Hamlin and P. Pettit (eds.), *The Good Polity: Normative Analysis of the State.* Oxford, U.K.: Blackwell, 17–34; Cohen, J. (1996). "Procedure and Substance in Deliberative Democracy." In S. Benhabib (ed.), *Democracy and Difference.* Princeton, N.J.: Princeton University Press, 95–119; Dryzek, J. (2000). *Deliberative Democracy and Beyond: Liberals, Critics, and Contestations.* New York: Oxford University Press; Gutmann, A., and Thompson, D. (1996). *Democracy and Disagreement.* Cambridge, Mass.: Belknap Press.
3. On this point, see Button, M., and Mattson, K. (1999). "Deliberative Democracy in Practice: Challenges and Prospects for Civic Deliberation." *Polity 31,* 609–637; and Ryfe, D. (in press). "Does Deliberative Democracy Work?" *Annual Review of Political Science, 8*(1).
4. Distinctions between these selection schemes can get fuzzy at the edges. For instance, when the League of Women Voters canvasses a community to promote a study circles initiative, is that self-selection or stakeholder selection? To our minds, self-selection has two key characteristics: self-representation and ease of exit. In self-selection schemes, participants represent no one but themselves. Moreover, precisely because they represent no one but themselves, participants in self-selection schemes may exit an initiative with relatively little cost. Thus, despite its similarities to stakeholder selection, by our definition the League of Women Voters initiative just described would be a self-selection scheme.
5. On this point, see Warren, M. (2001). *Democracy and Associations.* Princeton, N.J.: Princeton University Press.

6. See, for instance, Ryfe, D. (2003). "The Practice of Public Discourse: A Study of Sixteen Discourse Organizations." In J. Rodin and S. Steinberg (eds.), *Public Discourse in America.* Philadelphia: University of Pennsylvania Press, 184–200.

7. On the role of politeness in interpersonal conversations, see Brown, P., and Levinson, S. (1987). *Politeness: Some Universals in Language.* Cambridge, U.K.: Cambridge University Press; Mulkay, M. (1985). "Agreement and Disagreement in Conversations and Letters." *Text, 5,* 201–227; Pomerantz, A. (1984). "Agreeing and Disagreeing with Assessments: Some Features of Preferred/Dispreferred Turn Shapes." In J. M. Atkinson and J. Heritage (eds.), *Structures of Social Action.* Cambridge, U.K.: Cambridge University Press, 57–101; and Schiffrin, D. (1990). "The Management of a Cooperative Self During Argument: The Role of Opinions and Stories." In A. Grimshaw (ed.), *Conflict Talk: Sociolinguistic Investigations of Arguments in Conversations.* Cambridge, U.K.: Cambridge University Press, 241–259. For examples of this process in action, see Eliasoph, N. (1998). *Avoiding Politics: How Americans Produce Apathy in Everyday Life.* New York: Cambridge University Press; and Walsh, K. C. (2003). *Talking About Politics: Informal Groups and Social Identity in American Life.* Chicago: University of Chicago Press.

8. On the distinction between "bonding" and "bridging" forms of social capital, see Putnam, R. (2000). *Bowling Alone: The Collapse and Revival of American Community.* New York: Simon & Schuster, 22–23.

9. For research in psychology that explores the importance of cognitive and other forms of diversity in small-group communication, see Moscovici, S. (1976). *Social Influence and Social Change.* New York: Academic Press; Moscovici, S. (1980). "Toward a Theory of Conversion Behavior." *Advances in Experimental Social Psychology, 13,* 209–239; Nemeth, C. J. (1986). "Differential Contributions of Majority and Minority Influence." *Psychological Review, 93,* 23–32; Nemeth, C. J., and Kwan, J. (1985). "Originality of Word Associations as a Function of Majority and Minority Influence." *Social Psychology Quarterly, 48,* 277–282; Turner, J. C. (1991). *Social Influence.* Pacific Grove, Calif.: Brooks/Cole. Work in political science on these themes includes Huckfeldt, R. (1986). *Politics in Context: Assimilation and Conflict in Urban Neighborhoods.* New York: Agathon Press; and Huckfeldt, R., and Sprague, J. (1995). *Citizens, Politics, and Social Communication: Information and Influence in an Election Campaign.* New York: Cambridge University Press. On the relation of social networks to civic participation, see Knoke, D. (1990). *Political Networks: A Structural Perspective.* New York: Cambridge University Press; Krassa, M. (1990). "Political Information, Social Environment, and Deviants." *Political Behavior, 12,* 315–330; Leighley, J. (1990). "Social Interaction and Contextual Influences on Political Participation." *American Politics Quarterly, 18,* 459–475; and Walsh (2003), *Talking About Politics.*

10. On the process of group polarization, see Sunstein, C. (2002). "The Law of Group Polarization." *Journal of Political Philosophy, 10,* 175–195. This result is, of course, not preordained. But research on small-group communication indicates that it is a common one for groups organized along these lines. For a review of this literature, see Ryfe (in press). "Does Deliberative Democracy Work?" Responding to a prior draft, one reviewer offered the counterexamples of voluntary associations that hold deliberative sessions on race. His point is that even if they employ self-selection schemes as we have defined them, such groups often take extreme care to ensure diversity within the group. The point is well taken. But the key here is cognitive rather than racial diversity. If a group discussion on race has true cognitive diversity, then it may avoid the pitfalls we have described. However, as anyone who has attempted to conduct such meetings will agree, ensuring cognitive diversity is difficult. Race is such a painful subject that any hint of antagonism can easily lead groups to disband.

Those who stay behind may compose a mixed racial group, but one which nonetheless has little cognitive diversity, and this group will be prone to the same kinds of quirks as any other homogeneous group. For a good discussion of race and deliberation, see Mendelberg, T., and Oleske, J. (2000). "Race and Public Deliberation." *Political Communication, 17,* 169–171.

11. For another effort to think through the consequences of organizational formats on deliberation, see Fung, A. (2004). *Empowered Participation: Reinventing Urban Democracy.* Princeton, N.J.: Princeton University Press.

12. For wider discussions of this point, see Barber (1984), *Strong Democracy*; Bobbio, N. (1987). *The Future of Democracy: A Defense of the Rules of the Game* (R. Bellamy, ed.; R. Griffin, trans.). Cambridge, U.K.: Polity Press; and Macpherson, C. B. (1977). *The Life and Times of Liberal Democracy.* Oxford, U.K.: Oxford University Press.

13. On this point, see Hibbing, J., and Theiss-Morse, E. (2002). *Stealth Democracy: Americans' Beliefs About How Government Should Work.* Cambridge, U.K.: Cambridge University Press.

14. Notice that, as Gastil and Keith observe in Chapter One, the progressives of the early twentieth century had no such inclination. Their open forum movement was directed at education, not policymaking.

15. Robert Goodin (2004) provides an excellent comparison of aggregative and deliberative decision-making mechanisms. See his *Reflective Democracy.* New York: Oxford University Press. On this point, also see Knight, J., and Johnson, J. (1994). "Aggregation and Deliberation: On the Possibility of Democratic Legitimacy." *Political Theory, 22,* 277–298.

16. See, for instance, Hendriks, C. (2002). "Institutions of Deliberative Democratic Processes and Interest Groups: Roles, Tensions and Incentives." *Australian Journal of Public Administration, 61,* 64–75; Mansbridge, J. (1983). *Beyond Adversary Democracy.* Chicago: University of Chicago Press; and Mendelberg and Oleske (2000), "Race and Public Deliberation."

17. See Rawls, J. (1996). *Political Liberalism.* New York: Columbia University Press; Habermas, J. (1996). *Between Facts and Norms: Contributions to a Discourse Theory of Law and Democracy* (W. Rehg, trans.). Cambridge, Mass.: MIT Press; Cohen (1996), "Procedure and Substance in Deliberative Democracy"; Gutmann and Thompson (1996), *Democracy and Disagreement.*

18. Manin, B. (1987). "On Legitimacy and Political Deliberation." *Political Theory, 15,* 338–368.

19. See Habermas, J. (1975). *Legitimation Crisis* (T. McCarthy, trans.). Boston: Beacon Press, 108; see also Cohen (1996), "Procedure and Substance in Deliberative Democracy."

20. See Gutmann and Thompson (1996), *Democracy and Disagreement,* 52–55.

21. See Ackerman, B., and Fishkin, J. (2004). *Deliberation Day.* New Haven, Conn.: Yale University Press; Barber (1984), *Strong Democracy*; Chambers, S. (1996). *Reasonable Democracy.* Ithaca, N.Y.: Cornell University Press; Sunstein, C. (1991). "Preferences and Politics." *Philosophy and Public Affairs, 20;* Warren, M. (1992). "Democratic Theory and Self-Transformation." *American Political Science Review, 86;* and Warren, M. (1996). "Deliberative Democracy and Authority." *American Political Science Review, 90.*

22. See Knight and Johnson (1994), "Aggregation and Deliberation"; Stokes, S. (1998). "Pathologies of Deliberation." In J. Elster (ed.), *Deliberative Democracy.* Cambridge, U.K.: Cambridge University Press; Przeworski, A. (1998). "Deliberation and Ideological Domination." In J. Elster (ed.), *Deliberative Democracy.* Cambridge, U.K.: Cambridge University Press; Young, I. M. (1996). "Communication and the Other." In S. Benhabib (ed.), *Democracy and Difference.* Princeton, N.J.: Princeton University Press; Shapiro, I. (1999). "Enough of Deliberation: Politics Is About Interests and Power." In S. Macedo (ed.), *Deliberative Politics.* Oxford, U.K.: Oxford University Press; and Shapiro, I. (2003). *The State of Democratic Theory.* Princeton, N.J.: Princeton University Press.

23. Hibbing and Theiss-Morse (2002), *Stealth Democracy.*

PART TWO

DELIBERATION AND PUBLIC JUDGMENT

CHAPTER THREE

NATIONAL ISSUES FORUMS

A Network of Communities Promoting Public Deliberation

Keith Melville, Taylor L. Willingham, John R. Dedrick

If you crisscrossed the country and talked to people in hundreds of communities where citizens deliberate about local and national issues using the National Issues Forums (NIF) approach, you might hear accounts such as this one:

In El Paso, Texas—a city that is divided economically, geographically, and politically, where most people would expect low levels of civic participation and public involvement—National Issues Forums have been an integral part of public life for more than two decades. Local forums are publicized in the *El Paso Times* and held throughout the city in schools, churches, and libraries. Over the years, forums in this community have addressed dozens of issues, including abortion, education, and health care.

Participants in El Paso's forums are invited by the local public television station to take part in ninety-minute conversations that are notable for their lively exchanges and the absence of experts and elected officials. "We avoid the experts," says organizer Julie Zimet. "What's important here is grassroots participation, the value of talking to each other. When people deliberate together, everybody in the room comes out changed." Especially in a divided community, says Zimet, "the NIF is a critically important program because it enables us to learn about shared values and interests. The future of our city relies on our ability to talk to people who have different experiences and different philosophies about what we need to do for all of us."[1]

You might hear much the same thing from people who have taken part in NIF activities in other communities, such as Charleston, West Virginia, and

Panama City, Florida, where state legislators rely on reports and advisories from citizens who take part in a well-developed network of forums. Or you might hear about how the *San Jose Mercury News* and the California State Library, concerned that a ballot measure on affirmative action would further polarize a state that had been divided by a contentious ballot measure in the previous election, turned to NIF to convene forums throughout the state in 1995.[2]

Perhaps you would hear the story of how, in 2002, Cincinnati made front-page news nationwide when racial tensions were sparked by police shootings. Guided by Civic Life Institute, an initiative of Ohio State University Extension, and their experience with NIF, a series of some 150 deliberative forums on race took place, involving several thousand people in neighborhoods throughout Cincinnati. Those community discussions did not solve the city's race problem, but they did help defuse a dangerously tense situation by creating new bonds, including a grassroots organization called Neighbor to Neighbor, and identifying steps for community action. As illustrated by a series of forums on race described in *The Cincinnati Enquirer*, the city emerged from the experience with a stronger sense of its civic capacity.[3]

From one community to the next, you would hear about groups and institutions such as schools, libraries, churches, adult literacy programs, and even prisons coming together in creative ways to hold community forums. In Austin, Texas, over one hundred college students, young professionals, concerned citizens, and retirees participated in simultaneous forums on Medicare that were moderated by Texas Forums volunteers as part of a symposium hosted by the Lyndon B. Johnson Presidential Library and the Center for Health and Social Policy at the Lyndon B. Johnson School of Public Affairs.[4]

In most states, you would hear people describe overlapping networks of conveners based in a variety of civic institutions and organizations. In Alabama, for example, you would hear about forums and moderator training sessions at Shelton Community College in Tuscaloosa and at the Cooperative Extension Service, both part of a series coordinated by the Alabama Community Leadership Institute. You would encounter NIF in Alabama's schools and universities—at Hillcrest High School in Tuscaloosa, at the Honors College at Auburn University, and at the Blackburn Institute at the University of Alabama. And you would hear about statewide forums on health issues coordinated by the Department of Community and Rural Medicine at the University of Alabama's School of Medicine.[5]

In each of these communities, you would hear enthusiastic testimonials from moderators, participants, and public officials. "It is clear to me," one NIF convener said, "that traditional instruments for getting public input into public issues—such as public hearings—are largely a failure in helping citizens find common ground.

The National Issues Forums are one of the few frameworks that provide an opportunity for dialogue among people who hold divergent views on issues."[6]

Or consider this comment from a man who has moderated a series of forums: "I know that deliberative democracy works. I believe in it! There have been many instances in our community where public deliberation has made a difference. It diverted a potential riot at our high school. It has given citizens a chance to have their voices heard by our congressman. And it has made our community politically aware and active in the process."[7]

Enthusiastic endorsements also come from public officials and political leaders. Following the recent Medicare forums offered as part of Big Choices: The Future of Health Insurance for Older Americans Symposium in Austin, Texas, one of the organizers, Ken Apfel, director of the Center for Health and Social Policy and a former commissioner of the Social Security Administration, enthusiastically commented, "public engagement is critically important as we address these issues." He then committed to convene public deliberation on Social Security as part of Big Choices: The Future of Social Security Symposium in 2005.

Former president Jimmy Carter, who along with former president Gerald Ford was co-host of one of the National Issues Forums' early national meetings, put it in these words: "I think that part of the responsibility of this exciting new association ought to be how can we magnify what has been learned this year, not doubled but a thousand times over or ten thousand times over, by encouraging the responsible people who own and control the television, the radio, the newspapers to let this kind of effort be spread nationwide."[8]

A Nationwide Network

The National Issues Forums is a nonpartisan, nationwide network of organizations and individuals who sponsor public forums and training institutes for public deliberation. Although the NIF network does not compile specific records of forums that take place in a given year, several thousand forums were held in 2003, convened by service clubs, universities, libraries, membership groups, and other kinds of groups. Referred to as the flagship of contemporary groups that sponsor or encourage community forums, NIF is the largest such network.[9]

Each year, diverse organizations such as community colleges, leadership institutes, neighborhood associations, state humanities councils, presidential libraries, and even a prison society conduct public policy institutes. These institutes offer workshops and networking activities in which citizens learn to frame issues for public deliberation and to moderate and convene forums. Thirty-three organizations currently conduct such institutes in thirty states. NIF-style training is also offered at professional association conferences, including the American Library Association and the National Society for Experiential Education.

Some of the materials used in the network are developed by the National Issues Forums Institute, a 501(c)(3) organization of people who are in a position to promote public deliberation either through their own organization or through collaborative efforts. NIFI develops and promotes materials to support public deliberation, including issue books that provide background information about an issue and describe three broad approaches for deliberation; tools for moderators and conveners; and *NIF in the Classroom,* a curriculum for public deliberation in the schools. NIFI also works with members of the National Issues Forums network to frame issues and produce discussion guides.

NIF has influenced the design of various efforts to promote public deliberation. Political scientist Michael Briand adapted the NIF model when he designed a community convention process to help Trinidad, Colorado, plan for future economic development.[10] The NIF model and NIF-trained moderators were an important part of two prominent national events organized by James Fishkin: the first National Issues Convention, which took place as part of the 1996 presidential primary season, and a second National Issues Convention, which took place early in 2003 on the topic of America's global role, organized by MacNeil/Lehrer Productions (see Chapter Five).[11]

NIF has also influenced international efforts. Over the past decade, citizens and nongovernmental organizations in countries including Colombia, Russia, Croatia, and New Zealand have adopted deliberative forums and launched their own versions of the National Issues Forums.[12]

To those who champion strong democracy, NIF and the deliberative forums it has fostered represent an alternative to politics as usual—a draft version, at the very least, of the kind of public deliberation that should be a routine feature of public life in every community.

How the National Issues Forums Started

In the late 1970s, David Mathews, former Secretary of Health, Education, and Welfare and president of the University of Alabama, convened a group of scholars, community activists, public officials, and foundation leaders to explore ways to overcome public disengagement. When Mathews became president of the Charles F. Kettering Foundation in 1981, the foundation's trustees made the role of the public in democratic life the central theme of the foundation's mission. Mathews worked closely with Dan Yankelovich, a veteran public opinion analyst and founding president of Public Agenda.

National Issues Forums was launched in the summer of 1981 at the Wingspread Conference, when representatives of seventeen organizations agreed to pool their energies to create the Domestic Policy Association, a nonpartisan, nationwide network that would focus each year on three pressing issues. Public Agenda helped to select the issues and to prepare balanced, accessible, magazine-length books that laid out different approaches to key issues. The issue books were a vehicle for framing public discussion and a catalyst for the kinds of conversations that would move people beyond superficial and uninformed opinions toward *public judgment,* a term Yankelovich defines as "highly developed public opinion that exists once people have engaged an issue, considered it from all sides, understood the choices it leads to, and accepted the full consequences of the choices they make."[13]

Although its early organizers envisioned that universities would be the base for recruiting moderators and conveners, the network took on a life of its own, becoming a grassroots movement. Through word of mouth and the encouragement and training provided at public policy institutes, the network flourished and expanded across the country. Over the years, participants have become more diverse in terms of age, class, race, education, and region, and an ever wider range of collaborating institutions have initiated forums.

What's Distinctive About the National Issues Forums

NIF shares with other approaches to public deliberation a vision of how life in a democratic community ought to work. At local and national levels, we need to talk about common problems and agree on certain decisions about public actions. But *how* do we talk together in order to reach such agreement and decide on a course of action?

The NIF approach to public deliberation is an answer to one of the most basic problems facing any group that seeks to function democratically. It is an approach based on a specific understanding of *deliberation,* a term that is often used quite loosely. "To deliberate is not just to 'talk about' problems," according to David Mathews, an astute and energetic advocate of public deliberation. "To deliberate means to weigh carefully both the consequences of various options for action and the views of others."[14] Deliberations are the way we make sound decisions that allow us to act together. Through deliberation, people are challenged to face the unpleasant costs and consequences of various options and to work through the often volatile emotions that are a part of making public decisions.

In a sense, the NIF approach is most easily described by saying what it is *not.* Public hearings, a familiar means of soliciting comment on public decisions and a formal part of the public policy process, allow certain voices to be heard. Hearings, however, are often adversarial, and they rarely lead to anything resembling public deliberation.

Formal debates are appropriate in certain contexts, such as elections, as a way for the public to compare and contrast different views. But the debate format hardly serves the public's need to explore common concerns and think through the costs and consequences of various alternatives. Also, it provides no way of moving from entrenched opposition to complementary action.

For their part, the news media do little to provide a model of public discourse. Media commentary, attuned to the standards of spectacle and diversion, is typically confrontational and ideological, consisting of exchanges among people who have already made up their minds. Media accounts tend to focus on personalities rather than issues.

When, several years ago, the Harwood Group asked what kind of public conversations citizens wanted to be part of, people described the opposite of the "Crossfire" model: they wanted exploratory conversations in which they could test ideas and compare approaches, not score points or win arguments. What most people want is an alternative to partisan posturing and professional pundits.[15]

NIF is a radical alternative to the conviction that the public amounts to no more than an aggregation of stakeholders, a market waiting to be swayed by public officials. Through deliberation, a collection of individuals develop relationships and connections to one another. They become a public, a necessity for sustaining democracy and providing legitimacy and direction to governments.[16]

Whereas public deliberation needs to be anchored in facts, sound judgment—whether on the part of individuals or groups—is not based mainly on a command of pertinent facts, as policy experts often assume. Deliberation consists chiefly of exchanges about what individuals and groups value, their priorities and personal stories and their relevance to public concerns. People need to see issues named in a way that reflects their concerns and their way of thinking, which is often different from how policy experts or elected officials characterize issues. People are more likely to engage in forum discussions if what is most important to them is clearly reflected in the way the issue is named and if the framing leads to actions that can be taken at the local as well as the national level. Through such conversation, which bears little resemblance to expert analysis or exchanges among pundits that are featured in the media, groups arrive at common ground for public action. The most important collective decisions are about what *should* be, and in this respect, there are no experts.

Thus, NIF seeks to provide public spaces in which a different kind of conversation can take place. The commitment to democratic principles is hollow unless it is accompanied by a commitment to democratic practice. By approaching the task of naming and framing issues for public discussion in a particular way and facilitating community forums in a particular style, the NIF model lays out key features of deliberation as a core democratic practice.

How Issues are Chosen, Named, and Framed

When conveners begin to plan forums, they often use one of the existing issue books that have been prepared nationally for the NIF network on topics such as education, illegal drugs, youth at risk, immigration, or race. Over the past twenty-two years, issue books on more than seventy topics have been prepared by the NIF network, covering a wide range of concerns. Recent issues include juvenile violence, money and politics, governing America, gambling, alcohol abuse, racial and ethnic tensions, and responding to terrorism. Topics selected nationally for NIF issue books have a direct bearing on the lives of most Americans, and most of these issues remain timely for at least a few years.[17]

In its early years, the NIF network relied on the issue-framing capabilities of the Public Agenda Foundation, where Keith Melville was the senior writer on a team that prepared books on more than thirty issues. In recent years, various groups and individuals have developed the capacity to frame their own issues, working collaboratively in many cases. For example, an issue book on welfare reform was framed jointly by the Urban League of Portland, the National Association for Community Leadership, and staff at the Kettering Foundation. The Southern Growth Policies Board took the lead in framing a book called *Pathways to Prosperity.* The Farm Foundation took a leading role in preparing an issue book on biotechnology and the new science of food. And the American Bar Association developed and promoted an issue book entitled *And Justice for All.*[18]

Often, issue books are framed to reflect the unique circumstances and culture of particular communities. For example, the issue book *Breast Cancer: We Can Overcome,* framed by West Alabama Health Services, reflects approaches that can be taken in a rural, impoverished community where breast cancer rates tend to vary according to ethnicity. An issue book about community development on the Rosebud Reservation in South Dakota, framed by the Sicangu Policy Institute at Sinte Gleska University, incorporates Native American language, symbols, and values.

However they are framed, NIF issue books structure the work of deliberation. They focus on issues, not personalities or partisan divisions. They lay out three or four approaches to the issues, showing the values, arguments, and key facts on which each is based. Approaches to an issue are not mutually exclusive. Each embodies certain elements that are appealing to some participants and elements or costs that are problematic. The issue books provide, in an accessible form, a baseline of facts and background information that people need to understand complex issues. In these ways, issue books anchor the process and help structure discussion, serving as a reminder of the range of views that need to be considered.

Convening and Moderating Forums

Many NIF forums are organized jointly by several community groups and institutions. After all, the point of forums is to bring together diverse groups of people from different circumstances and different views. In most cases, no single organization or institution can mobilize the entire community, so associations of several groups work together to convene a forum.

The number of participants in NIF forums varies, as does the setting. The size of individual forums may be as few as a dozen people meeting in a church basement or as many as several hundred convening in a university auditorium. Some forums meet only once, addressing particular community concerns. More typically, however, NIF groups agree to meet with some regularity, addressing several issues over time. What has become clear in communities such as Panama City, Florida; Grand Rapids, Michigan; and Fairfield, California, where NIF forums are ongoing, is that after deliberating regularly and on a variety of issues, this practice becomes a part of people's civic habits and a familiar means of dealing with new issues and concerns as they arise.

Forums are moderated by individuals from diverse backgrounds, many of whom have participated in a training session hosted by organizations or individuals in the NIF network.[19] Moderators are not expected to be experts on the issue. In fact, a moderator known to be an expert on an issue can have a chilling effect on the free exchange of views and lead the participants to rely on the moderator for "answers." While not an expert on the issue, the moderator should be familiar with the issue book and the guidelines and practices that have served deliberative groups well in working through rather than just talking about issues. Above all, the moderator must be committed to remaining neutral.

What Do NIF Moderators Do?

Essentially, NIF moderators do five things. First, they lay out ground rules, charging the participants to listen with respect; to consider all perspectives, including those different from their own; and to seek common ground. As in most group settings, NIF moderators encourage everyone to participate, stressing the fact that listening is as important as talking. This applies especially to points of view with which individuals may disagree. Participants are encouraged to speak to one another and to listen for understanding.

Second, moderators introduce the issue and various approaches to it. The moderator may play a brief videotape containing a summary of the issue. The point is to provide enough information so that participants do not spend most of their time seeking pertinent facts. This step is intended to equalize participation, regardless of the education level or expertise of the participants.

Third, moderators draw people into the discussion by asking about their personal experience or concerns about the issue. Especially when issues seem abstract or distant, talking about personal experiences related to the issue helps create a sense of involvement in the discussion. Personal stories also help participants see the issue through one another's eyes and see how the things they value influence their perspective on the issue.

Fourth, moderators lead deliberation about the approaches. Moderators encourage participants to consider each approach fully and fairly, to illustrate each approach with personal stories and experiences, and to consider the related costs and consequences of each approach. Moderators often probe participants in order to encourage consideration of positions that are not fully expressed by members of the group. Moderators ask, for example, "Even if you do not agree with this approach, what is the strongest argument you could make in favor of it?"

Finally, after a discussion that may last from one to several hours, moderators lead a final segment of the discussion, often referred to as *reflections*. At this stage, moderators charge the group to identify common themes and common ground. They ask them to assess what is really at issue, what consequences are unacceptable, and what points remain unresolved. As participants strive to articulate a common understanding of the issue, they speak from the perspective of what they said as a group, not what they as individuals brought to the discussion. By doing so, they begin to see how they might move forward together. Often, the group identifies common ground for action. When little common ground is apparent, participants are at least able to articulate unresolved issues that need further deliberation.

The moderator is frequently joined by a recorder, who captures what is said, often summarizing by listing in two columns whether comments support an approach or indicate resistance to it. In this way, participants are able to weigh what takes place during deliberation.

NIF Forums and Their Outcomes

The Kettering Foundation, in collaboration with the NIF network, has supported the preparation of a series of summary reports.[20] Based in part on narrative reports or summaries from moderators, these reports enable local forum groups to lend their voices to national conversations. Summary reports are also used in national events that take place at the end of the forum season.[21] For several years, these took the form of Congressional briefings, as well as meetings at the Ford, Johnson, Kennedy, and Carter presidential libraries.

More recently, "A Public Voice," a one-hour program that is broadcast nationally on public television, has been the vehicle for reporting the results of forums on a specific topic.[22] Members of Congress, national news commentators, and subject experts gather at the National Press Club in Washington, D.C., to view videotaped segments of National Issues Forums that were conducted by the NIF network across the country. They then reflect on what this "public voice" means for those who report on current events and those who, as elected officials, are specifically entrusted with governing America. Mathews describes this public voice as "the voice of many citizens thinking aloud." "A Public Voice" captures the discernible and informed public voice that emerges as public knowledge grows, as opinion matures into judgment, and as common ground for action increases.[23]

What do these reports show? On some issues, deliberation produces the kind of eye-opening, horizon-widening impact that advocates of deliberative democracy have predicted. As a result of forum discussions on AIDS, for example, many reported becoming less judgmental and more sympathetic. In forums on health care for the elderly, many gained a new awareness of the nature and scope of the problem.

The main outcome of NIF forums in most cases is not that deliberation dramatically changes people's views but that it *alters* them. The process typically starts with the exchange of stories about how people experience certain problems and what they worry about. As David Ryfe notes, these stories play an important role in allowing the NIF conversation to continue when "complexity and ignorance threaten to grind the conversations to a halt at their beginning."[24]

In the course of deliberation, many participants move from a narrow sense of self-interest—an initial focus on "how this affects me"—to a broader sense of how a particular course of action is likely to affect others in their own community, in different circumstances, or even in other generations. Rather than abandoning their self-interest in favor of some perceived public interest, what typically happens is a more subtle change. Participants in forums build on one another's stories and create a shared narrative, or what Ryfe calls a *commonsense*. They integrate or accommodate different perspectives as they seek to identify areas of agreement about a course of common action. Positions do not necessarily change; rather, they expand in the course of deliberation.

After observing participants in a forum on family values, Scott London wrote, "They were neither as ideologically polarized nor as fixed in their political views as news coverage and opinion polls had led me to expect." He further stated, "I made a significant discovery: people's disagreements on given issues were usually the starting point, not the final outcome, of their deliberations. As people voiced their ideas, their experience, and their opinions, as they took in the perspectives of others and clarified points of tension and disagreement, the emphasis would gradually shift away from ideological differences toward common values."[25]

This is not to say that deliberation leads to consensus or significant changes in an individual's views. What *does* change is people's perceptions of those with whom they disagree. Even though forum participants may not agree with someone else's position, they often come to appreciate it and understand it better. The process of deliberation can serve to link people's private ideas and interests to something more closely resembling public values. This modification of their perception of others and of the problem itself creates an opening for identifying common ground and defining a broadly acceptable direction for public action.

While the aim of deliberation is to move toward decisions about purpose and direction, it doesn't necessarily end in agreement. As summary reports on various issues show, it is rarely the case—in individual forums or when results are aggregated at the national level—that forums lead to a consensus about what should be done. Instead, deliberation helps locate the area between agreement and disagreement, which might be called "common ground for public acting."[26] Common ground is neither consensus nor agreement that everyone wants the same thing. It is also different from compromise, when people disagree but are willing to split the difference. Common ground is defined as actions or policies that are acceptable to a group whose individual members may still cherish differing values and hold different opinions but have a shared frame of reference or sense of direction. As a practical matter, it is necessary to identify enough common ground to move ahead.

It is not clear that NIF deliberation typically increases participants' personal willingness to make hard choices, but there are indications of a wider recognition that hard choices need to be made for some of these problems to be resolved. At the end of the forum, participants often reflect that they have a newfound appreciation for the complexity of the issue and recognize the need not only to continue working toward a choice but to do so with a wider and more diverse circle of participants. Through deliberation, forum participants begin to identify which actions and consequences most people are prepared to live with over the long haul.

There is another aspect of the NIF forums that deserves to be noted as well. People are more likely to agree with decisions that they participate in making, as opposed to decisions that others make for them. When important community decisions are made openly, in deliberative forums, people are more likely to support those decisions and to accept their costs and consequences. This may explain the eagerness of public officials in many communities to support NIF forums on contentious issues.[27]

What happens as a result of NIF forums is more subtle than the shifts that are commonly reported in opinion polls, but it is far more than "just talk." The outcome of deliberative forums has the potential to open new avenues for public action by moving beyond political polarization to new avenues for public action, both in local communities and in the nation as a whole.

Impacts of the NIF Experience

As explained in Chapter Two, the advocates of deliberative democracy have made a variety of claims about its impact and salutary effects on individuals and communities as a whole. These claims are asserted repeatedly in the literature on deliberative democracy, often illustrated with testimonials or descriptions of what has happened in particular instances, but they are rarely tested with any rigor. As a result, scholarly conversation about deliberative democracy typically proceeds as a series of volleys between advocates (who generally speak on the basis of political theory or from personal conviction) and skeptics (who dismiss this model as unrealistic or at least unproven).

Twenty-two years of National Issues Forums have provided, among other things, a testing ground for assertions about the merits of deliberation. Its activities have been examined by more researchers than any of the other approaches to public deliberation. The Kettering Foundation, whose primary mission is to carry out research about public life, has initiated or supported many of these studies. Studies of different levels of rigor have addressed various aspects of the impact of the NIF experience on individuals and communities.

Impacts on Individuals

One overall claim made by those who advocate deliberative democracy—ranging from Alexis de Tocqueville to political scientist Jane Mansbridge—is that deliberative forums provide a school for citizenship. The experience of deliberation, these advocates have asserted, changes people in important and perhaps enduring ways. Observations of the NIF experience, interviews with participants, and a series of studies have shed light on six ways in which the experience of public deliberation seems to affect individuals:

Participation in NIF forums heightens interest in specific issues and in public affairs and leads to higher levels of public engagement. On one level, participation in NIF forums responds to the problem of public disengagement by increasing the motivation of many participants to seek out information about public issues and to take part in other similar group activities.[28] Other studies show that a majority of participants say their interest in issues is heightened as a result.[29]

Participants in literacy programs report that "this was the first time information [about public issues] was given to us in a form we could understand. It opened our eyes."[30] As a result, literacy students report increased political activity, including voting, writing to public officials, and attending forums.[31]

A civic initiative called Key to Community, which used National Issues Forums as a tool for addressing the concerns of adult literacy students who felt that their voice did not matter, found that the forums had clear and dramatic impacts. Many participants reported a better sense of their connection to others and became more confident that things could be changed for the better. As a group, the students who participated in the project voted at twice the rate of their demographic counterparts across the state.[32] High school students who participated in National Issues Forums in the classroom connected with their communities. They convened or attended community forums, became more involved with community projects, organizations, and groups, and began to read newspapers and talk about issues.[33]

Participation in NIF forums broadens the outlook of participants. By emphasizing forum activities that bring together diverse groups, joining parts of the community that do not normally meet together, NIF broadens participants' experiences. There is considerable evidence, some of it anecdotal, that participation opens a wider circle of contacts and establishes broader networks in many communities. When a group of twenty black and white churches decided to use National Issues Forums to address uneasy race relations in Dayton, Ohio, participants who ordinarily would have had little or no contact with one another not only worked together on issues but developed social relationships.[34]

As a result of participating in forums, individuals come to experience themselves in different ways, and they learn new ways of taking part in groups. Several studies have demonstrated behavioral or attitudinal change as a result of taking part in forums.[35] These include growing confidence on the part of participants that what they say matters, as well as enhanced listening skills, especially the willingness to listen to people who disagree with them.[36] Participation in NIF forums, as another study found, tends to change people's conversation habits, making them more egalitarian and reducing the habit of what one researcher calls "conversational dominance."[37]

Participation in NIF forums enhances people's sense of themselves as political actors who can make a difference in their communities. One of the more important effects of participation in NIF forums is that it increases what political scientists refer to rather dryly as "self-efficacy." That is, in the course of deliberative encounters, people begin to imagine an effective role for themselves as citizens. It increases not only their sense of involvement but also their sense of potential effectiveness.[38]

People construe their self-interest more broadly as a result of taking part in deliberative conversations. A fundamental and still largely unanswered question in political theory is whether most people are capable of transcending their narrow self-interest and moving toward a broader conception of the public good. Skeptics such as political scientist John Mueller dismiss the idea of a common good. (He refers to it as "that vaporous commodity, which so many supple philosophers have mused about at great and eloquent length.")[39] But judging from various observations of the impact of NIF forums, self-interest is neither inviolable nor all-pervasive. As noted in the previous section, there is considerable evidence that participation in deliberative forums helps to broaden participants' sense of their self-interest and seriously take into account others' experiences and situations.[40]

Deliberation helps people move beyond superficial preferences to considered public judgment. Both anecdotal accounts and several studies suggest that the experience of NIF-style deliberation does indeed help people move from superficial and largely unconsidered personal preferences to something like what Dan Yankelovich characterizes as public judgment. One study that compared the pre-forum and postforum questionnaires from NIF participants found that after attending forums, participants' views were more clearly considered, more logically consistent, and less volatile.[41]

Some commentators on public deliberation have minimized the usefulness of what comes out of NIF forums, characterizing it as atypical and a less accurate portrait of public thinking and preferences than what opinion polls provide. Most proponents of public deliberation would characterize the impact in quite a different way. One of NIF's strong claims is that the outcome of deliberative conversations is not mere talk but that the process of public deliberation does indeed enhance the ability to make well-considered public judgments. For example, forums on affirmative action in California didn't seem to change many minds, but they engendered the enlightenment that people could govern themselves in an informed and intelligent way, a sentiment expressed by Rob Elder, editor of the *San Jose Mercury News,* a leading convener of these deliberative forums.[42]

In summary, studies of the impact of NIF forums on individuals show various kinds of effects that, taken together, are impressive and significant. Many people are drawn to NIF forums because they provide a palpable and vivid experience of something normally an abstraction—the experience of being part of a public. Among those who have taken part in NIF forums and those who have observed and studied their impact, most come away convinced, as advocates of deliberation have asserted, that they make participants better citizens.

Impacts on Communities

With regard to the impact of NIF forums on communities as a whole, there is evidence of several effects, particularly in communities that hold forums repeatedly over several years. In such communities, deliberating about problems becomes a civic habit, an important aspect of public culture. Thomas Jefferson once commented, "The qualifications for self-government are not innate. They are the result of habit and long training."[43] What is apparent in many communities is that the habit of public deliberation builds skills and bolsters confidence that communities can respond effectively when problems arise.

The most important impact in many communities is the realization that it is possible to convene groups consisting of people who do not share the same views—and who come from very different circumstances—and create a civil atmosphere for talking about common concerns, even highly charged issues. In Owensboro, Kentucky, for example, forums on race succeeded in raising awareness among whites of the lack of trust felt by many African American citizens. Despite initial misgivings, the forums provided a civil setting in which people could talk across the racial divide, discuss their concerns, and reach agreement about a list of one hundred actionable ideas.[44]

Many communities have had similar experiences. In Grand Rapids, Michigan, the experience of almost two decades of forums has changed the way the community responds to its problems. Coming together as a community becomes a collective habit that changes the nature of political conversations. The authors of a study that compared various processes for bringing citizens and officeholders together concluded, "Collaborative forms of deliberation may be the most fruitful over the long run." The reason for the success of this approach, they said, is that it "transforms the way citizens and officeholders practice politics."[45] Another team of researchers concluded that when elected officials take part in forums or at least consult with moderators about the outcome of forums on specific topics, it tends to result in better outcomes than when decisions are made in more typical top-down, unilateral fashion.[46]

Although the most powerful impacts are apparent when people deliberate repeatedly on different issues, there are vivid examples of how even a single forum or a series of forums on a single issue can change a community. In Corona, California, a single forum on violent youth led by a first-time moderator—an adult literacy student—inspired the participants to form UNITY, an organization of students, parents, teachers, and public agencies, including the juvenile justice system.[47]

Deliberation is not a cure-all for civic disengagement or a one-size-fits-all technique for public problem solving. Some key claims made by advocates of deliberation have not yet been substantiated by anything more than personal testimony. However, the history of NIF provides ample evidence that when citizens grapple with common problems and deliberations continue over time, relationships change. In cities like Tupelo, Mississippi—where there is a strong sense of community, a high level of public participation, and ongoing networks that provide opportunities for people to talk together about common problems—deliberative practices are an integral part of the community's civic practices.[48]

Three Challenges

Today, twenty-two years after the first National Issues Forums were convened, NIF is no longer a start-up enterprise. It is a familiar and well-established feature in hundreds of communities and holds a prominent place in the public deliberation movement. New forms of public deliberation, in turn, play an important role within a larger movement to strengthen the role of citizens by building grassroots organizations; rethinking the professional practices of journalists, public officials, and experts; enhancing civic education; and improving the quality of public participation in development. As a whole, Sirianni and Friedland write, "the civic renewal movement has established its identity as a movement among a critical core of national, state, and local activists and professional practitioners, and it has achieved an important threshold of recognition in the media." Thousands of people and dozens of organizations have engaged in the work of "renovating the democratic foundations of American society," and they have made remarkable progress. "They have created forms of civic practice that are far more sophisticated in grappling with complex public problems and collaborating with highly diversified social actors than have ever existed in American history."[49]

"Nevertheless," Sirianni and Friedland point out, "these important foundational accomplishments should not be exaggerated, nor the obstacles to further development of a broad movement underestimated."[50] That is an accurate assessment of what has been accomplished as well as the challenges that lie ahead for the National Issues Forums and for the movement as a whole.

Three challenges are worth mentioning. The first is a challenge for individuals and organizations who take on the task of preparing issue books and other guides for public deliberation. The second is a challenge for convening organizations and moderators who take responsibility for creating a series of forums involving a cross section of the community. A third challenge is posed by the way deliberation is regarded by the media and by public officials.

The first challenge is to maintain the nonpartisan nature of deliberative forums.[51] Since its inception, NIF has been committed to a nonpartisan approach. It has made various efforts, especially in the preparation of issue books, to name and frame issues so as not to predispose readers to follow the principles or courses of public action advocated by any single political perspective.

After more than two decades of preparing guides on a wide range of issues, we are struck by the challenge of designing forums that are rigorously and consistently nonpartisan and by the importance of honoring that commitment. It is essential that NIF remain a nonpartisan enterprise—an inclusive, communitywide process in which people of different perspectives and persuasions meet to talk about common concerns. Carefully reviewing issue books to ensure that they are not unintentionally biased is especially important because of the perception in certain quarters that NIF, along with the deliberative democracy movement as a whole, is a Trojan horse harboring the left wing.[52] If, for whatever reason, such as the way issue books are framed or the personal bias of moderators, forums are inadvertently biased—or worse, if they are consistently biased in the same direction—the only people who are likely to attend forums will be those who share those biases. If forums consist of conversations among like-minded people, they lose most of their value.

A second challenge is attracting a diverse cross section of the community and sustaining a series of forums. By and large, people attend forums for either of two reasons. They attend because of their interest in a particular issue or community concern or because friends and acquaintances recruit or encourage them. Forum participants are likely to be well-educated people who are civically active. Thus, NIF forums often do not represent a true cross section of the community, limiting the claims that can be made for the outcomes of the forums.

It is an ongoing challenge for conveners to invite into forums as broad a group as possible and to create a series of forums rather than one-time events. As we have noted at several points in this chapter, deliberation is most likely to be a catalyst for deep changes in community life when forums are held repeatedly and when individuals attend forums regularly over the years. NIF is more likely to attract diverse participants and achieve sustainability when several community organizations, each able to recruit from a different part of the community's social network, collaborate on an ongoing basis. Developing and supporting a broad community collaborative is itself a looming challenge requiring resources that are often beyond the reach of many members of the NIF network.

A third challenge to the further growth and development of deliberative democracy hinges on the way such forums are regarded by elected officials and the media. The name of the game in electoral politics is numbers: how many turn out to vote, what percentage in a certain poll favor certain measures, how many participate in a political demonstration, and how representative they are of the public as a whole. Because NIF forums are typically fairly small and because participants are not normally representative of the community as a whole, many elected officials at local and national levels have tended not to take NIF forums or their outcomes seriously.[53]

Still, one of the key challenges for the NIF enterprise and for the deliberative democracy movement as a whole is cultivating close connections between forums and elected officials. It is one thing to receive endorsements of NIF from a few members of Congress and from former presidents such as Jimmy Carter and Gerald Ford. It is something else entirely to establish public deliberation as a routine and essential part of public life, something that officials ignore at their peril. It will, in all likelihood, require a series of initiatives and the creation of new reporting formats to convince elected officials on a broad scale of the significance of deliberative forums.[54]

Much the same thing can be said of the media and their response to public deliberation. In many cases, neither individual forums nor the outcome of a series of forums are considered newsworthy, in part because reporters don't know what to make of these events and the results are not easily summarized or readily characterized. As a result, when forum conveners seek media attention for local deliberations on a particular topic, they are obliged, in marketing parlance, not only to sell the brand but also to sell the product. NIF and the other programs described in this volume must make the case for public deliberation repeatedly and persuasively. This will require inventing new reporting formats for public judgment that are familiar, accessible, and persuasive in the same way that public opinion poll results have been for decades, becoming an indispensable part of the political process and a familiar ingredient in media reports.

The most important contribution of the National Issues Forums is not the light that these forums have shed on individual issues but the way this enterprise illustrates how democratic communities can function. NIF provides a rejoinder to those who have seriously underestimated the American public and a clear response to those who have dismissed anything like deliberative democracy as a utopian fantasy that is both unrealistic and unrealizable. What is happening throughout the country in thousands of community forums bears out the hope of those who have made the case for deliberative democracy.

Throughout the American experience, many have shared a vision of democratic communities in which people fully participate as citizens and take an active role in shaping their common destiny. NIF is an expression of that theme. Several years ago, the Harwood Group summarized the results of one of their studies in these words: "No interpretation of the public is less accurate than the often-repeated contention that people are apathetic and too consumed with private matters to care about politics. In fact, this study suggests just the opposite: these Americans feel that they have been pushed out of the political system."[55] The National Issues Forums, the most extensive and one of the oldest networks for public deliberation, shows what happens when a sustained effort is made to open the door and invite people back in.

Notes

1. London, S. (1999). "El Paso Forges Shared Outlook in Forums." In E. Arnone (ed.), *What Citizens Can Do: A Public Way to Act.* Dayton, Ohio: Charles F. Kettering Foundation, 1–3.

2. Heyser, H. A. (1999). "Newspaper Gives More Emphasis to Citizens' Views." In E. Arnone (ed.), *What Citizens Can Do: A Public Way to Act.* Dayton, Ohio: Charles F. Kettering Foundation, 9–14.

3. E-mail correspondence with Dave Patton, project coordinator, Civic Life Institute, an initiative of Ohio State University Extension, Aug. 20, 2004.

4. The Medicare forums occurred in the second year of a five-year joint project of the Lyndon B. Johnson Presidential Library and the Center for Health and Social Policy at the Lyndon B. Johnson School of Public Affairs. In the first year, the organizers convened a two-day panel presentation of experts on health care. Sensing that something was missing—namely, public interaction on the issue—the organizers turned to Texas Forums to assist in framing the Medicare issue and providing trained moderators to conduct seven simultaneous intergenerational forums. Participants listened to and questioned panel presenters on the first day, but the second day was devoted to NIF-style forums. This model was enthusiastically embraced by the participants and the organizers and will be replicated in 2005, when the issue will be Social Security.

5. Robert McKenzie, senior associate, Kettering Foundation, e-mail correspondence with Taylor Willingham, Feb. 5, 2005.

6. Heierbacher, S. (2003). "Final Report Submitted to the Kettering Foundation on the Online Survey of Practitioners of Public Deliberation, Conducted by the National Coalition for Dialogue and Deliberation." Unpublished manuscript.

7. Heierbacher (2003), "Final Report . . . "

8. Jimmy Carter, summary session of the First Presidential Library Conference at the Gerald R. Ford Library in Ann Arbor, Michigan, February 9–10, 1983.

9. Gastil, J. (2004). "Adult Civic Education Through the National Issues Forums: A Study of How Adults Develop Civic Skills and Dispositions Through Public Deliberation." *Adult Education Quarterly, 54,* 308–328.

10. Briand, M. (1999). *Practical Politics: Five Principles for a Community That Works.* Urbana: University of Illinois Press, 171–172. See also Gastil, J. (2000). *By Popular Demand: Revitalizing Representative Democracy Through Deliberative Elections.* Berkeley: University of California Press, 122–123.

11. See Chapter Five of this volume for more on Fishkin's deliberative polling method of deliberation.

12. Case studies of international programs can be found in London, S. (2004). *Creating Citizens Through Public Deliberation.* Dayton, Ohio: Charles F. Kettering Foundation.

13. Yankelovich (1991), *Coming to Public Judgment.* Syracuse, N.Y.: Syracuse University Press.

14. Mathews, D. (1994). *Politics for People: Finding a Responsible Public Voice.* Urbana: University of Illinois Press, 111. See also Mathews, D., and McAfee, N. (2002). *Making Choices Together: The Power of Public Deliberation.* Dayton, Ohio: Charles F. Kettering Foundation.

15. Harwood, R. (1991). *Citizens and Politics: A View from Main Street America.* Bethesda, Md.: Harwood Institute.

16. For a more thorough analysis of public expression in American politics, see Gastil (2000), *By Popular Demand,* chap. 5. See also Mathews (1994), *Politics for People,* chap. 6, for a more thorough description of the concept of the public and the public's role in politics.

17. Each year, the National Issues Forums Institute surveys the NIF network to determine two or three critical issues to be framed for deliberation. The focus of many of the 2004 forums is on four issues: immigration, Americans' role in the world, health care, and the news media and public trust.

18. For more information about National Issues Forums materials, visit www.nifi.org.

19. Visit http://www.nifi.org/network/index.aspx for a list of training sessions and locations.

20. Summary reports on the outcomes of forums have been prepared by Public Agenda; by Robert J. Kingston, senior associate at the Charles F. Kettering Foundation; by John Doble Research Associates; and by others.

21. Some communities, such as Grand Rapids, Michigan, hold capstone events that are attended by policymakers, at which the outcomes of forums are summarized and examined. Other communities, such as Panama City, Florida, and Charleston, West Virginia, hold regular briefings for local and state legislators on the implications of forum discussions. In many communities, local moderators help to prepare summaries of forum discussions.

22. "A Public Voice" is a Milton Hoffman production; Robert Kingston is its executive producer. It is the longest-running privately produced public television program. "Public Voice 2003: Terrorism" was aired by 210 public television stations. Over the years, this production has been moderated by Robert Kingston, David Gergen, and, most recently, Frank Sesno. See http://www.nifi.org/PrelimaryListingTelevisionStations.pdf for a list of public television stations broadcasting the latest program of "A Public Voice," called "Examining Health Care: The Publics' Prescription, 2004."

23. Mathews, D. (2002). *For Communities to Work*. Dayton, Ohio: Charles F. Kettering Foundation.

24. Ryfe, D. (Feb. 2003). "An Interim Report on Kinds of Talk in National Issues Forums." Unpublished memo, Charles F. Kettering Foundation, Dayton, Ohio.

25. London, S. (in press). "The Power of Deliberative Dialogue." In *Public Thought and Foreign Policy* (working title). Dayton: Charles F. Kettering Foundation.

26. Mathews, D. (2002). *For Communities to Work*. Dayton, Ohio: Charles F. Kettering Foundation, 27.

27. Mathews (1994), *Politics for People*, chap. 5, discusses the circumstances under which officials need the public: "when the public's attention is needed to keep an issue on the political front burner, when it is clear that a dispute turns on human values rather than technicalities, when public support is not forthcoming even after citizens have been 'educated,' or when the governing machinery is hopelessly deadlocked by a political stalemate." He writes, "Creating a sense of ownership among citizens and setting a long-term direction for the community require more public involvement."

28. John Doble Research Associates. (1996). *The Story of NIF: The Effects of Deliberation*. Dayton, Ohio: Charles F. Kettering Foundation, sections 1 and 2.

29. Farkas, S., Friedman, W., and Bers, A. (1996). *The Public's Capacity for Deliberation*. New York: Public Agenda, for the Charles F. Kettering Foundation.

30. Paget, G. (1989, Dec.). "Literacy Programs Open Doors for New Readers." *Connections* (Charles F. Kettering Foundation), *3*(1), 10–11.

31. Loyacano, M. (1991). "Attendant Effects of the National Issues Forums." Unpublished manuscript, Charles F. Kettering Foundation, Dayton, Ohio.

32. Clark, S., Wold, M., and Mayeri, H. (1996). "The Key to Community Voter Involvement Project: Fall 1996 Election Study." [http://literacynet.org/slrc/vip/whole.html].

33. Doble, J., Peng, I., with Frank, T., and Salim, D. (1999). *The Enduring Effects of National Issues Forums (NIF) on High School Students: A Report to the Kettering Foundation*. Dayton, Ohio: Charles F. Kettering Foundation, 37, 58.

34. Willey, S. (1999). "Public Deliberation Within Communities of Faith." In E. Arnone (ed.), *What Citizens Can Do: A Public Way to Act*. Dayton, Ohio: Charles F. Kettering Foundation, 35–38.

35. Gastil (2004), "Adult Civic Education Through the National Issues Forums"; Gastil, J., and Dillard, J. P. (1999). "The Aims, Methods, and Effects of Deliberative Civic Education Through the National Issues Forums." *Communication Education, 48*, 179–192.

36. For examples, see Doble, Peng, Frank, and Salim (1999), *The Enduring Effects of National Issues Forums;* John Doble Research Associates (1996), *The Story of NIF.*

37. Gastil (2004), "Adult Civic Education Through the National Issues Forums"; Burgoon, J. K., and Hale, J. L. (1984). "The Fundamental Topoi of Relational Communication." *Communication Monographs, 51,* 193–214.

38. Alamprese, J. A. (1995). "National Issues Forums Literacy Program: Linking Literacy and Citizenship." Unpublished report by COSMOS Corporation. Bethesda, Md.: For the Charles F. Kettering Foundation. See also Loyacano (1991), "Attendant Effects of the National Issues Forums"; Gastil (2004), "Adult Civic Education Through the National Issues Forums."

39. Mueller, J. (1999). *Capitalism, Democracy, and Ralph's Pretty Good Grocery.* Princeton, N.J.: Princeton University Press.

40. John Doble Research Associates (1996), *The Story of NIF.*

41. Gastil, J., and Dillard, J. P. (1999). "Increasing Political Sophistication Through Public Deliberation." *Political Communication, 16,* 3–23.

42. Heyser (1999). "Newspaper Gives More Emphasis to Citizens' Views," 9–14.

43. Coates, R. E., Sr. (ed.). (1995). "Quotations from the Writings of Thomas Jefferson." Electronic Text Center, Alderman Library, University of Virginia. [http://etext.lib.virginia.edu/jefferson/quotations/index.html]. Retrieved Feb. 16, 2005.

44. Kathy Christie, interview with Taylor Willingham, Jan. 2004.

45. Gastil, J., and Kelshaw, T. (2000). *Public Meetings: A Sampler of Deliberative Forums That Bring Officeholders and Citizens Together.* Dayton, Ohio: Charles F. Kettering Foundation, 34.

46. Fung, A., and Wright, E. O. (2001, March). "Deepening Democracy: Innovations in Empowered Participatory Governance." *Politics and Society, 29*(1), 18.

47. John Zickefoose, interviews with Taylor Willingham, Nov. 2000. The UNITY brochure credits the 1996 town hall forum as the impetus for the community to come together and form a coalition committed to promoting involvement of the full community in the positive development of children, youth, and families of the greater Corona-Norco area. Approximately one hundred people attended the first forum, and twenty-five people signed up to continue meeting. UNITY now boasts over seventy-five members. Jill Walker, UNITY's treasurer, says that the group has erased turf wars, and she marvels, "It's something I have never seen in my social work." See also Nichy, J. (2000). "Fighting Against Juvenile Crime." *Corona/Norco Independent,* Feb. 18, 2000.

48. See Grisham, V. L., Jr. (1999). *Tupelo: The Evolution of a Community.* Dayton, Ohio: Kettering Foundation Press.

49. Sirianni, C., and Friedland, L. (2001). *Civic Innovation in America.* Berkeley: University of California Press, 1.

50. Sirianni and Friedland (2001), *Civic Innovation in America,* 260.

51. Our concern here echoes Sirianni and Friedland's discussion in their 2001 book *Civic Innovation in America,* in the section entitled "Why is the civic renewal movement nonpartisan and why should it remain so?" (p. 261).

52. As Sirianni and Friedland (2001) note in *Civic Innovation in America,* there is reason for this perception. Many individuals and organizations in what they call the civic renewal movement trace their history to progressive and populist ideas, especially to leftist or liberal social movements such as the civil rights and women's movements.

53. There are notable exceptions. One participant in the spring 2004 taping of the public television program "A Public Voice" was Congressman Tim Murphy, who represents the Pittsburgh area in Pennsylvania. In the process of attending a series of local NIF forums, Murphy became an enthusiastic spokesperson for deliberative events. In Charleston, West

Virginia; Panama City, Florida; Grand Rapids, Michigan; and other communities, NIF conveners have established regular connections with public officials and plan regular briefings.

54. Sixty years ago, George Gallup and other pioneers in the field of public opinion—who held out high hopes for polls as a means of conveying public sentiments and preferences to officials—had to sell the concept of public opinion and its significance. Dan Yankelovich, among others, has persuasively made the case for moving beyond public opinion to more revealing and significant measures of public judgment. As we noted, Yankelovich's thinking in this regard and others has been a seminal influence in shaping the NIF approach. But the task of selling public deliberation and explaining the importance of the concept of public judgment to policymakers has just begun. See Yankelovich (1991), *Coming to Public Judgment.*

55. Harwood (1991), *Citizens and Politics.*

CHAPTER FOUR

ELECTORAL DELIBERATION AND PUBLIC JOURNALISM

Michelle Charles, Harris Sokoloff, Chris Satullo

On a sunny Saturday in May 1999, citizens streamed into an auditorium on the University of Pennsylvania campus, wending their way around television trucks and a maze of wires. Inside, seated on a stage, were the five candidates for the Democratic nomination for mayor of Philadelphia. The debate that was about to begin had produced some real buzz. This race to succeed the wildly popular Ed Rendell as mayor was generating tremendous interest and anxiety. Rendell had rescued the city from bankruptcy and near despair in the early 1990s, restoring a sense of forward civic momentum. Now, from the glass towers of Market Street to the row houses of Bustleton, a sense of urgency bubbled.

The candidates on stage were a diverse, accomplished group: two city council members; a state legislator; a former state and city cabinet member; and a rainmaking lawyer who'd been part of the inner ring of the legendary Frank Rizzo. Three were black, two white. Four men, one woman. None was a clear front-runner, a political fact that had forced all of them to accept dozens of invitations to appear at candidate forums and debates. This evening's event was one none dared shirk—a live televised debate cosponsored by the city's dominant newspaper, *The Philadelphia Inquirer,* and its dominant news station, WPVI-TV, the ABC affiliate.

The questioners this night would not be the usual blow-dried television anchors and print journalists in scruffy shoes. They would be citizens, clutching index cards in their hands. On each card was written a question that represented the fruit of four months of public deliberation involving over six hundred citizens and reaching into every corner of a city that is famed as a mosaic of neighborhoods.

It was time for the first question. Sidney Toombs, a short, shy security guard from Southwest Philadelphia, rose. His question concerned Philadelphia's public schools, a topic the Citizen Voices had chosen as the most important facing the city. That choice rewrote the conventional priority list dictated by the pollsters and consultants, which put crime first. Toombs spoke into the microphone: "Our group was divided over which is the bigger problem in the city schools. It's either (a) the schools don't have enough money to do the job, or (b) the schools misuse too much of the money they get. In your view, which is the bigger problem, and how, specifically, would you go about solving it?" The first candidate to reply launched into his set piece about his school plan, as if reading from an index card. Marc Howard, a WPVI anchor hosting the debate, turned back to Toombs. "Did that answer your question?" Toombs paused, swallowed, and said, "Well, not really. No, it didn't get at our question at all." A ripple of laughter washed over the auditorium. The candidate flushed; the other candidates exchanged glances, eyebrows raised. This would not be your usual televised debate.

The 1999 Philadelphia mayoral election was to end in a near dead heat between Democratic city council president John Street and Republican businessman Sam Katz. Street won, by the slimmest margin since 1911. The margin of victory would be provided by some of the usual pyrotechnics of urban politics: television attack ads financed by a record $27.5 million in overall spending; a late rousing visit by President Clinton to spur turnout for Street by reanimating entrenched racial divisions between black and white voters. Despite all that, the campaign struck observers as the most issues-oriented, forward-looking, and *civil* Philadelphia mayoral campaign in memory. Some credit for that goes to the political circumstance—an open seat sought by a large field of serious candidates. But much credit should go to a broad-based effort in the community to insist that the candidates present themselves all over the city, in a variety of formats, to talk substantively about what needed to be done and how they would do it. This insistence was conveyed by the business community, civic and neighborhood groups, and the media. The Citizen Voices project was a major component of that effort, but its success can only be weighed within that larger context.

Origin and Design of the Citizen Voices Project

Citizen Voices was one newspaper's attempt to engage a cross section of a diverse city in a yearlong civic conversation that was modeled on the National Issues Forums and aimed at amplifying the voice of the grass roots in the midst of a noisy, expensive political campaign.[1] From January through October, over six hundred citizens, recruited through a combination of polling, media announcements, and civic mapping, took part in a series of public forums. (The recruiting techniques are described in more detail later in this chapter.) More than sixty forums were held throughout the region. The forums—a combination of small local forums and larger regional sessions—were designed to help citizens work together to name the issues that mattered most to them in the election, to frame those issues as a set of richly detailed political choices, to deliberate about those frameworks, and to use their deliberations as a springboard for questioning the candidates.

Two televised candidate debates were held in conjunction with the local ABC affiliate, WPVI—one in the spring, before the primaries, and one in the fall, before the general election. The project acquired a second media partnership with the public radio and television station WHYY. WHYY broadcasted excerpts of the citizen deliberations from the issues conventions, expanding and broadening the listening audience for the discussions. WHYY twice broadcast town meetings after the debates, at which participants in Citizen Voices discussed what they'd heard from the candidates and how that meshed with their concerns. The station incorporated Citizen Voices participants as commentators on its election night coverage. No media outlet, though, derived more benefit from the Citizen Voices input than the *Inquirer.*

Civic journalism (also called *public journalism*) was a reform movement that sparked to life in the early to mid-1990s. Two of its early major institutional proponents were the Knight-Ridder newspaper chain, which owns the *Inquirer,* and The Pew Charitable Trusts, an activist philanthropy that is based in Philadelphia. Civic journalism[2] was based on the following logic: public life in America was broken; voting and volunteerism were down; apathy, cynicism, and alienation from electoral politics were rising. (Robert Putnam's *Bowling Alone* was a sacred text for civic journalists advancing this argument.)[3] Journalists were complicit in the problems of public life; their habitual focus on conflict rather than solutions and on elitist framing of issues left ordinary citizens cold. Thus, journalists had a duty to repair their ways and try more explicitly to help the nation's public life go well. If this meant breaking venerable journalistic rules against advocacy and entangling alliances, so be it. If this meant changing old habits about how to frame and present issues, so be it.[4]

Civic journalism was controversial within the business, to say the least. Traditionalist journalists derided civic journalists as shallow and reckless. Civic journalists returned fire, calling traditionalists arrogant and out of touch, clueless as to why they'd lost the respect and trust of their audiences. Despite its corporate parent's enthusiasm, the *Inquirer* was an early critic of civic journalism. The paper was a bastion of elite journalism and the winner of eighteen Pulitzer Prizes in the previous twenty-five years; most of its journalists were skeptical about civic journalism to the point of outright hostility. Added to that was the staff's feeling of embattlement in the face of cost-cutting pressure from Knight-Ridder. Among the staff of the paper, Knight-Ridder's advocacy of civic journalism was viewed as just another corporate "flavor of the month" that was being promoted by executives who were looking for ways *not* to fund serious journalism. So it was only in one small corner of a large newsroom—the editorial board—that such experiments took place, and even then, they were never acknowledged under the rubric of civic journalism.

The journalists on the editorial board, noticing the declining impact of the opinion pieces they wrote, were looking to refresh their work through closer contact with the citizens they sought to persuade. The editorial board had begun the Citizen Voices program of public forums in 1996, emulating the National Issues Convention organized by professor James Fishkin of the University of Texas and MacNeil/Lehrer Productions (see Chapter Three). This was the first collaboration between two of the authors of this chapter, Chris Satullo, then deputy editorial page editor (now editor of the page), and Harris Sokoloff, a professor at the Graduate School of Education at the University of Pennsylvania. That year, the editorial board convened local forums on national issues, using the materials that had been developed for Fishkin's National Issues Convention. The next year, Citizen Voices returned with an expanded, yearlong effort that focused on the New Jersey governor's race. That time, instead of using off-the-shelf materials as a framework for deliberation, the project experimented with having citizens name the key issues and develop their own issue frameworks.

By 1999, Citizen Voices had gained some notice in the community and some credibility among the newspaper staff. At the instigation of Robert Hall, the publisher of the paper, the editorial board developed a Citizen Voices project on the Philadelphia mayoral race. A budget of more than $100,000 was set, and Michelle Charles, the other author of this chapter, was hired to work with Satullo to coordinate the project, including community outreach.

The project gained an immensely important ally when Kathleen Hall Jamieson, then dean of the Annenberg School for Communication at the University of Pennsylvania, offered to partner with Citizen Voices. She was devising a project on the mayor's race, jointly funded by her school and by The Pew Charitable Trusts, called the Philadelphia Compact, whose intent was to promote a civil and issues-oriented mayoral campaign.[5] Jamieson, to avoid reinventing the wheel, asked Citizen Voices to partner with the Philadelphia Compact on the citizen engagement piece of the project. After some careful negotiations to ensure that the *Inquirer* did not directly receive any funds from two institutions (Pew and Penn) that it covered as major newsmakers, the deal was struck.

It was clear that the credibility of the project, in a city divided by race and in a campaign that would eventually pit a white Republican against a black Democrat, would hinge on how representative of the city the Citizen Voices group was. In 1999, Philadelphia was 48 percent white, 41.5 percent black, 6.8 percent Hispanic, and 3.4 percent Asian American. As for other meaningful criteria of diversity in an election, the city's registration breakdown was about 80 percent Democratic and 20 percent Republican, and the number of people without a college education far outnumbered those with degrees.

Recruitment began with a Satullo op-ed column explaining the project and accompanied by a registration coupon, which drew more than four hundred responses. Like the readership of the paper's opinion pages, this group skewed whiter, older, more affluent, and more educated than the city as a whole. To help repair that defect of diversity, Annenberg did a ten-minute phone survey of 2,300 Philadelphians asking baseline questions about issues in the coming election. The telephone survey recruitment effort produced a list of three hundred potential participants that was closer to a valid random sample of the city. Even then, however, the roster of possible participants was still not as diverse as it needed to be. Thus, the patient, hands-on work of civic mapping began.

Civic mapping is an effort to see the connections that create community across the various levels of people's lives. In 1999, the people working on this project were not fully conversant in the theory of this activity, but their efforts to diversify the sample took them willy-nilly into the field. In one view of civic mapping, there are five layers of civic life: the official (political); the quasi-official (well-organized associations and groups); third places (sites where people gather for specific purposes such as houses of worship, parks, recreation centers); the incidental (locations where people run into one another informally such as parking lots, storefronts); and the private (people's homes).[6] Philadelphia is a city of small communities, each with its own identity, which is often ethnically based. It is not unusual for communities to be isolated from one another, even when they are separated only by a back alley or street, nor is it unusual for members of one group to avoid a community meeting held at a site they perceive to belong to another group. Thus, the project's main recruitment challenge was to find the trusted "go-to" people and institutions in each neighborhood and across the layers of civic life. These people and places were the brokers who could relay our invitation to participate in effective ways; their sponsorship could overcome any distrust of the convening institutions or their motives. Civic mapping was vital to connecting with these brokers and to finding meeting places in twenty-two different neighborhoods for the first round of forums. The city's Human Relations Commission provided valuable advice in that effort. Efforts to use foreign-language media to promote the forums yielded disappointing results. Organizers learned to rely on personal contact as the only effective tool, but even then, results were spotty. Eventually, the list of locations included a Latino community center, a Korean Presbyterian Church, and several historically black churches. Contacts with local high schools and colleges were usually productive, providing enthusiastic participants.[7]

In planning the first round of forums, organizers were keenly aware of two potential pitfalls—one general and one a matter of local culture. The general concern was that some critics of the National Issues Forum–style deliberation (described in Chapter Three) view such forums as overly intellectualized and accessible only to middle-class, college-educated groups. The concern about the local culture was that Philadelphia has a reputation for being "Negadelphia." The desire to avoid those pitfalls led organizers to invent "The Oprah Show," an optimistic visioning exercise that was seeded with humor and theater in order to be inviting to people of all backgrounds and to coax them into thinking about solutions as well as problems.[8] An imaginary version of "The Oprah Winfrey Show" was going to do a show on a remarkable urban renaissance; the job of the group was to paint a detailed portrait of what a livable city looked like and what had been done in the last decade to get it there. In the final portion of the evening, a few of the citizens would serve as "expert panelists" and be questioned about the Philadelphia miracle by "Oprah" (the moderator), while the rest of the citizens, serving as the "studio audience," would chime in with their questions.

By the end of January 1999, "The Oprah Show" had elicited a rich, textured mix of observations and ideas from the citizens. Five issues had clearly risen to the fore: education, jobs, neighborhoods, public safety, and reforming city hall, in that order. A sixth issue, race, percolated through the other five. Unsure how to keep that topic from exploding in its face, the project team decided not to address it directly just then.

In February and March, the second round of forums asked citizens to draft a National Issues Forum–style discussion framework for the first five issues. Then, in May, about 250 citizens gathered at the University of Pennsylvania for an issues convention, each taking part in a deliberative forum on the issue of his or her choosing. Each forum used one of the frameworks drafted in February and March as the basis for a discussion. Then each group reviewed detailed position papers that the mayoral candidates had submitted to the Citizen Voices project. The citizens used the comparison of their deliberation and the candidate's positions to frame their questions for the May 8 debate.[9]

Throughout the year, Citizen Voices remained a frequent presence on the *Inquirer*'s opinion pages. Essays by Citizen Voices participants that flowed out of the forums were published on commentary pages. The editorial board framed its editorials on the campaign around the five issues picked by the Citizen Voices. (By the end of the project, there were six issues; the issue of race was added to the final mix as a result of a series of well-attended forums held between the primaries in the spring and the general election in the fall to discuss how race relations had complicated Philadelphia's effort to address its problems.) The issue frameworks were all published on the commentary page in striking full-page layouts. Candidates were asked to respond on the commentary page to questions on issues that were drafted by citizens.

Outcomes and Lessons Learned

The first question often asked about civic engagement projects is whether they increased voter turnout. In our view, that is the wrong question. Declining turnout is a complex phenomenon that has developed over decades; no single project, no matter how ambitious or well-meaning, can turn that trend around in one election year. Turnout in the mayoral election of 1999 was 44.5 percent—higher than in 1995, about the same as in 1991. By the end of the campaign, a civic consensus emerged that this had been an issues-oriented campaign that dealt intelligently with real problems. It had also been less nasty and racially divisive than feared, although such elements certainly appeared in the final weeks of an extremely close race.

Inside the *Inquirer*, there is no doubt that the Citizen Voices project deepened the journalism that was done by the editorial board on the mayoral race. The objective journalists in the newsroom began 1999 with an arm's-length attitude to this experiment, which we view as appropriate in light of the traditional wall between news and opinion at a newspaper. Some reporters covering the election never warmed to Citizen Voices, but by the fall, others were eagerly asking for information, insights, and sources churned up by the project.

But listening to citizens is a not a substitute for expert knowledge; it does no good merely to substitute the flawed wisdom of the masses for the flawed wisdom of the experts. The goal that the Citizen Voices program has pursued is a fruitful marriage of citizen *values* and expert knowledge. Citizens, by and large, do not naturally talk about issues in the same way that experts do, and they do not like to be forced to use expert discourse. Public talk is going to be driven as much by personal anecdote and values as by statistics, facts, and rational analysis. If more facts need to be introduced into the discussion, moderators should find ways that don't seem pedantic and lecturing. They should ask citizens what facts they feel they need to have a good discussion. Usually citizens will ask for everything the organizers wish they would, plus some interesting information that no one thought of beforehand.

An Annenberg study found encouraging, though by no means conclusive, evidence that taking part in the forums had made low-income participants more confident in their political views and more willing to express them.[10] Even in a city notorious for booing Santa Claus, hundreds of citizens responded enthusiastically to an invitation to think optimistically and productively about their city. Citizens care.

The project's main shortcoming occurred after the election. The concluding step in this project was supposed to be a handoff of "ownership" of the Citizen Voices franchise from the paper to the citizens themselves. Citizen Voices would then draft a citizens' agenda to present to the new mayor and city council. Despite an effort to bring in a new sponsoring institution for the citizens' agenda, this effort collapsed. Citizens mourned the loss of the *Inquirer*'s involvement and could not agree among themselves on whether Citizen Voices should live on as a city-wide discussion forum or as a more activist advocate. Citizens are prone to wanting to move too quickly from deliberation to action, but the role of a convener is to figure out how talk can lead to action. Sometimes the convener must first force citizens to slow down and build up the muscles needed to forge consensus around workable solutions. But be clear on this point: citizens are not content to let talk be an end in itself. You don't want to get citizens excited and engaged and then leave them with what might be called the Peggy Lee moment: "Is that all there is?"

The Citizen Voices project did not transform politics or voter turnout in Philadelphia, yet it still had more impact than the project team could have hoped for when they started out. It gave some journalists a new set of tools for understanding urban issues that remains useful to this day. It created a new civic expectation of what the role of a major newspaper would be in an election. Nowadays, when a high-profile election rolls around, Satullo gets calls from citizens and other media representatives, asking, "Are you guys doing a Citizen Voices on this one?" Most important, the project found a way to reinvigorate individuals' sense of commitment to their roles as citizens and voters. As Darcell Caldwell, a regular participant in the 1999 project, said about it: "It's one of the few times I've had even the smallest sense of feeling empowered. It was one of the few times in my life that I felt like a true citizen."

Notes

1. For more on the National Issues Forums model of deliberation, see www.nifi.org.
2. See, for example, Rosen, J. (2001), *What Are Journalists For?* New Haven, Conn.: Yale University Press, 2001.
3. The original piece was an article entitled "Bowling Alone: America's Declining Social Capital," which appeared in the *Journal of Democracy*, July 1995. Putnam (2000) extended the argument and answered many of his critics in a book entitled *Bowling Alone: The Collapse and Revival of American Community*. New York: Simon & Schuster.
4. Jay Rosen, one of the lead theoreticians and researchers of civic journalism, has argued that "every institution has within it an image of the public and that if you change that image

you change the mind of the institution" ("Where Has the 'Public' Gone and Why? Can We Have Institutions Without a Public?" Presentation by Jay Rosen to the Center for School Study Councils at the University of Pennsylvania, Sept. 2, 1998). The Citizen Voices project was founded on an image of citizens as capable of defining what issues they think most important and how those issues should be discussed. It is an image of a public capable of grappling with complexity, of identifying and perhaps building common ground across differences and the difficult trade-offs required by real-world solutions. These capacities of the public are enacted when individuals come together and work through different perspectives together. This working through can only happen when individuals come together in a public space to do this work. In the case of the Citizen Voices project, the goal of public engagement was to create a reciprocal relationship between journalists and citizen readers.

5. For a quick introduction to the Philadelphia Compact, see a brief article by Treglia, S. P. (1999, Dec.). "The Philadelphia Story." In *Campaigns & Elections, 19.* [http://www.findarticles.com/p/articles/mi_m2519/is_10_20/ai_60087722/print].

6. Harwood Institute for Public Innovation. (2000). *Tapping Civic Life: How to Report First, and Best, What's Happening in Your Community.* (2nd ed.) College Park, Md.: Pew Center for Civic Journalism. Each of these layers of civic life consists of valuable but often undervalued human resources—citizens who act formally and informally with one another in community. These cycles of interactions are what ultimately influence journalists' choice of stories to cover.

7. Phyllis Kaniss, at the Annenberg School for Communication, University of Pennsylvania, directed the project. See Kaniss, P. (1999, Sept.–Oct.). "Making Their Voices Heard." *Pennsylvania Gazette, 98*(1), 50-54; also available on the Web at http://www.upenn.edu/gazette/0999/kaniss.html.

8. The first round of "The Oprah Show" was an adaptation of a group technique entitled "History of the Future" that was developed by the Center for Applied Research (CFAR). See Gilmore, T. N., and Shea, G. (1997, Summer). "Organizational Learning and the Leadership Skill of Time Travel." *Journal of Management Development, 16*(4), 302–311. For more on CFAR, see www.cfar.com. Moderators for all of the forums in this project were trained through the Deliberative Democracy Workshops, the University of Pennsylvania Graduate School of Education's adaptation of National Issues Forums (NIF) training. We provided additional training to link the NIF training to the "History of the Future" technique. For more information on the University of Pennsylvania's NIF training, see the on-line conference brochure at http://www.gse.upenn.edu/cssc/conference.php.

9. For the general election in the fall, the issues convention was essentially repeated, producing questions that were posed to candidates in two broadcast debates. The one difference was that race was added as an issue for deliberation.

10. Dutwin, D. (2003). "The Character of Deliberation: Equality, Argument and the Formation of Public Opinion." *International Journal of Public Opinion Research, 15*, 239–264.

CHAPTER FIVE

DELIBERATIVE POLLING

From Experiment to Community Resource

James Fishkin, Cynthia Farrar

On a chilly Friday evening in March 2002, a group of people from various walks of life and from every town in the New Haven metropolitan area made their way to a registration desk outside Yale University's cavernous Commons. They spanned the full spectrum of ages and ethnicities; each was selected randomly so that together they would constitute a microcosm of the region. They were participating in a *deliberative poll*—a poll of citizens before and after they have had a chance to arrive at considered judgments based on information and exposure to the views of their fellow citizens.

After collecting their packets and moving into the hall, this group of strangers milled about a bit anxiously, relieved when the food appeared and they could busy themselves with trays and plates and proceed to assigned tables to meet their moderator and their fellow participants in small groups. The event organizers (the Community Foundation for Greater New Haven and the League of Women Voters of Connecticut, aided by Yale's Institution for Social and Policy Studies and the Center for Deliberative Polling at the University of Texas, Austin) were concerned about the relatively light turnout. The *New Haven Register* had provided advance publicity on the front page of the newspaper. The organizers had anticipated that 250 local residents would gather to discuss two issues: the future of the regional airport and the possibility of sharing property taxes across town lines. However, 133 individuals actually turned up.

The conversations that ensued, from the orientation that evening to the small-group discussions and question-and-answer sessions that took place on Saturday and half of Sunday, exposed participants to viewpoints that many of them had had no other occasion to encounter, such as the views of those who lived near the airport and would be directly affected by expansion. An observer reported that "a man from East Haven . . . spent the entire discussion making impassioned speeches about the burden [an expanded airport] would be to him and his neighbors." By Sunday, "he admitted that in light of new information he had received he had started to consider the possibility of the expansion," and "by the end of the day, he had pledged not only to go to his East Haven town meeting, but also to attend New Haven's in order to learn more about how people in areas other than his own felt about the issue." At a follow-up meeting with elected officials from his town, a participant commented, "I learned that everything that happens affects different people in different ways. . . . I hadn't thought about the airport before. Then I met some folks from East Haven. . . . That's the problem with separatism—you don't get to hear other people's perspectives."

On the question of sharing property taxes across town boundaries, individuals from across the region heard the views of residents of the wealthier towns, some of whom find themselves supporting expanded commercial development in order to meet rising school costs, and of attendees from less affluent urban and inner-ring communities that have been forced to impose higher taxes in order to meet the social service needs of families with few residential choices. In the small-group discussions, one participant remarked that "another way of saying revenue sharing is taxation without representation." Another expressed the view that "it's got to be a mutual benefit for both towns. Otherwise, forget about it."

Attendees changed their opinions considerably after exchanging views with one another and questioning a panel of experts. When first interviewed, 80 percent thought that towns should retain control of their own taxes, but after deliberation, only 42 percent held that view. At the same time, support increased substantially for voluntary agreements to share incremental tax revenue on commercial property (only the increased revenue would be shared) and for the use of state incentives to encourage this kind of cooperation. Although fewer people attended than the organizers had planned for, most of the changes of opinion were statistically significant. After the participants from New Haven met with their mayor, John DeStefano, Jr., he called one of the organizers and said, "What impressed me was that I did not know any of these individuals. They were not the people I see at meetings week after week. And they were passionate and engaged and informed on issues that had nothing to do with their immediate self-interest. That's unusual."

Like many other deliberative polls, this one was an experiment. The split-half design used on this occasion was the first rigorous experimental attempt to isolate the effect of face-to-face deliberation in small groups. In the morning, half the attendees discussed one issue (the airport), while half discussed the other (revenue sharing). Then each half took another round of the full questionnaire (on the issue they had discussed *and* the one they had not), thus serving as a control group for comparison with the other half of the attendees. The results demonstrated that a substantial portion of opinion change came from the discussion of the issue.[1]

Two years later, on May 8, 2004, the third annual Greater New Haven Citizens Forum was held in New Haven with a new group of residents. This time, based on previous experience, 175 participants were expected to show up; 242 actually came. Once again, the participants discussed two issues (prison overcrowding and the financing of K–12 public schools), but they did so in one long day instead of two and a half. The Community Foundation for Greater New Haven and the League of Women Voters were now officially sponsoring this annual event; all the funding was local. Costs had been cut substantially not only by shortening the length of the deliberation but also by using an in-state policy think tank to develop the background materials and by shrinking the length of the telephone survey that was administered before the event. Only a few items on the postdeliberation survey had been included in the pre-deliberation survey; the emphasis in reporting the results, therefore, was on the considered views of a randomly invited sample, not on change in those views. Twelve percent of participants said they had heard about the previous year's forum. Again, exposure to different views was a salient feature of the deliberation. In one group, for instance, sympathetic discussion of more lenient treatment for some offenders came to a temporary halt when a participant spoke up to say that her mother had been murdered by a paroled inmate. During the day, despite the simultaneous occurrence of the state Democratic and Republican conventions, several prominent state legislators and a handful of local elected officials came to listen; at the end, more arrived to host a reception for the participants.

In the weeks and months after the event, moderators have stayed in touch with participants and encouraged them to attend follow-up meetings with elected officials. Local organizations are convening additional conversations about the two issues that will bring 2004 participants together with alumni of the 2002 and 2003 events and other interested citizens.[2] The evolution from a one-time experiment to an annual event, the streamlined format, the larger number of elected officials who attended, and the doubling in the number of participants are all signs that what started as a thinking person's opinion poll may be taking root as a democratic practice in the New Haven community.

Roots of the Deliberative Poll

The deliberative poll is a distinctive form of public consultation. It combines two key values: political equality and deliberation. By political equality, we mean the equal consideration of everyone's preferences.[3] The root of the word *deliberation* means "weighing." So by *deliberation,* we mean a process of discussion in which people weigh competing arguments on their merits. The quality of deliberation depends on the degree to which four criteria are met:

1. *Completeness:* the extent to which arguments offered on one side of an issue are answered by arguments from another side that are then answered in turn
2. *Information:* the extent to which the information that people employ is reasonably accurate
3. *Conscientiousness:* the extent to which people participate so as to decide the issue on its merits
4. *Diversity:* the extent to which those who deliberate represent the diversity of viewpoints in the relevant population

A deliberative poll attempts to satisfy each of these criteria to a reasonably high degree. Balance is the hallmark of the briefing materials, the panels of experts, and the training of the moderators. Every effort is made to provide the participants with accurate information, which is usually reviewed by an advisory group (as it was in New Haven). Organizers also create an atmosphere of mutual respect so that participants will be interested in deciding the issue on its merits. Random sampling, when effective, produces a diversity of viewpoints and backgrounds. When it works well, the deliberative polling process requires citizens to take their real differences into account, sidesteps the distorting power of special interests, and mitigates polarization among the participants.

Deliberative polls use two features of ancient Athenian democracy: selection of decision makers by lot (that is, randomly) and payment of citizens who perform this role (to ensure a microcosm that is representative of the larger public). Athenian officeholders, including, for example, the five hundred members of the agenda-setting council, were selected by lot from among those who put themselves forward (*hoi boulomenoi*), and they were paid to serve. For a deliberative poll to change civic behavior and capacity, it needs to be embedded in an institutional context that shares some other features of ancient Athens. The principle of rotation of office permitted Athenians to serve as a councillor only twice in their life. As a result, everyone had an equal chance of playing this significant role, and a large proportion of the public took their turn. More than a third of all Athenian citizens[4] over the age of eighteen served as a councillor at least once in their life.[5]

The annual recurrence of deliberative polls in the New Haven region, a community not much larger than ancient Athens, may enable the process to take root, to acquire visibility and credibility, and, over time, to provide some of the civic benefits of rotation and regular exposure to difference. But can this process be taken to scale, and can it engage citizens in issues that transcend local concerns? The By the People Citizen Deliberations project, sponsored by MacNeil/Lehrer Productions, is designed to build infrastructure for local deliberation that is similar to New Haven's annual forum and also to link local interests to a national and international context. Using local affiliates of the national Public Broadcasting System as the scaffolding, By the People has been partnering with local coalitions of public television stations, civic groups, community foundations, and colleges and universities to convene and broadcast simultaneous deliberations on national issues as seen from a local perspective. Ten deliberations on national security and international trade were held on January 24, 2004, and seven of those communities participated in the seventeen-site Deliberation Day held in October 2004. New Haven convened its fourth deliberative poll as part of this multisite deliberation. The goal of By the People is to include a substantial proportion of these communities—and others—in an ongoing local and national conversation in 2005 and beyond.[6]

How a Deliberative Poll Works

Designing a Deliberative Event

Because its distinctive features include a random sample, balanced background materials, and a formal survey, a deliberative poll cannot occur spontaneously. Discussions that arise spontaneously tend to bring together people who already know each other and share an interest or a concern. By contrast, deliberative polls are organized and structured occasions, and the conveners (whether local or national) must have access to technical expertise (to recruit the participants, write the background materials, and enter and analyze the survey data) plus local civic resources (to ensure a nonpartisan approach, organize the event, facilitate media coverage, and disseminate the results, as well as keep participants engaged afterward). Financial resources are also required to pay the participants and cover the cost of their recruitment. Conveners, therefore, usually include some or all of the following groups: local and national funders, civic associations, universities, and the media. Sometimes, as in the utility polls that have been held in Texas periodically since 1996, one of the conveners is an entity that voluntarily seeks or has been required to secure public input and is in a position to make use of the survey results.

Although the length of the deliberation has been reduced since its inception and the order of elements varies from one event to another, the structure of a deliberative poll always includes small-group discussion; the opportunity to come together as a large group in a plenary session in order to ask questions of an expert panel; and the administration of a final survey. Ideally, participants will have an opportunity to digest what they have heard from the panel in the plenary session before completing the survey. The topics are generally chosen by the leading convener (for example, the Community Foundation for Greater New Haven, in consultation with local public officials and relevant civic groups). For the October 2004 By the People conversations, MacNeil/Lehrer Productions chose two topics: (1) national security and (2) American jobs in a global economy. Within that rubric, the specific national security issue was selected by MacNeil/Lehrer Productions, to promote uniformity across sites, while the economic issue was determined by the local partners, to facilitate local engagement. Media coverage connects the process to local or national policymaking. At the local level, as in New Haven in 2004, participants may be given opportunities to express their views directly to policymakers, and conveners may also undertake strategic dissemination of the results.

In advance of the event, prospective participants are sent background materials that present a range of information and perspectives on the questions under discussion. If the media is a key partner, as in the By the People project, the day's deliberations may begin with the screening of brief background videos that seek to convey the gist of the issue as well as a glimpse of competing viewpoints. In New Haven in 2004, an on-the-spot resource person was available to answer questions of fact that arose during discussions and were not addressed in the background materials or could not be resolved within the group. The challenge is to ensure that all groups get access to the answers.

Most deliberative polls are face-to-face conversations; two successful on-line versions have occurred, but even they take place in real time and use microphones so that participants can hear their fellow deliberators.[7] The deliberations have taken place in a variety of settings that offer assembly space as well as rooms for small-group meetings, from universities to high schools to community centers to television studios. Very little technology is required except audiovisual equipment for the plenary sessions.

Convening a Public Meeting

The deliberations are always facilitated by experienced group moderators. Moderators may be drawn from a variety of backgrounds, such as League of Women Voters volunteers, academics, individuals experienced in running National Issues Forums (see Chapter Three), mediation programs, or study circles (see Chapter

Fourteen). Sometimes moderators are paid, sometimes not, depending on local conventions, but they are rarely professional moderators. In every case, they receive training on the specific approach embodied in the deliberative poll, particularly on remaining neutral and not imparting information; encouraging broad participation; and refraining from promoting consensus among participants.

The participants are randomly invited, usually through a process of random-digit dialing but occasionally by sending a warm-up letter to a random sample of phone listings and following up with phone calls.[8] Several calls are made to each phone number to ensure that the sample does not just include those who are easiest to reach. Once a household is reached, the interviewer uses a device such as asking for the person with the next birthday in order to ensure that the sample is not skewed in favor of the people who tend to pick up the phone (who more often are women). Those who say yes or maybe receive follow-up mailings and phone calls. Additional targeted phone calls may be made—as they were in New Haven in 2004—to encourage participation by those who are less likely to attend (typically, this includes those with less formal education and those living in low-income or remote areas). Participants are paid ($200 for the two-and-a-half-day deliberation in New Haven in 2002; $100 for one day in 2004; $75 for the By the People Citizen Deliberations), which also encourages heterogeneity. In most instances, the participants have approximated the initial sample (and the larger target population) in both demographic characteristics and attitudes. However, the deliberative poll recruitment process, like most telephone polls,[9] does tend to skew toward older populations, who have land lines and are more likely to be home, and toward the better-educated, who are more likely to be willing to talk with the pollster. Those who decide to attend are usually somewhat more politically active and better educated than the initial sample. To this point, participation has for the most part been limited to English-speaking individuals, for logistical reasons.[10] The number of people who participate in a deliberative poll has ranged from about 130 to more than 450. There is, in principle, no upper limit except that all of the people must fit in the space available for the plenary session, but the small groups should ideally be limited to eighteen participants. Experience suggests that this is the largest group in which it is possible for everyone to participate actively; groups of twelve to fifteen participants are preferable. Participants are told that they are being assembled as a randomly invited cross section of a given public. The content of what they say is not restricted, nor is the kind of speech they use. They are not instructed to stick to arguments or to refrain from telling stories, nor are they asked to restrict themselves to appeals to the common good. Appealing to narrower interests is legitimate.[11] No formal limit is placed on how long individuals may speak, but the moderator actively encourages participation from all members of the group and tries to keep the group on task by systematically canvassing various perspectives and concerns identified in the background materials and represented by individual group members.

In the initial round of deliberative polls, many of which were national events, little attention was given to sustaining participant engagement afterward. Impact was sought through media coverage, by disseminating the survey results to relevant players, and in New Haven, through repeating the event annually with different participants. Sometimes the rest of the public was informed through national television broadcasts before a referendum (as in the deliberative polls in Australia and Denmark before referenda on whether to become a republic and whether to adopt the Euro, respectively) or before an election (as in deliberative polls before the 1997 British general election and before the 2004 presidential election in the United States).[12] After the first New Haven citizens forum, the names of participants were shared (with their permission) with local elected officials and with various local organizations that were interested in the topics they had discussed. More recently, moderators have been recruited (and paid a modest stipend) to maintain contact with participants after the event and to encourage ongoing involvement, and opportunities for continued discussion have been organized by groups whose mission is public education on the topics discussed. Civic coalitions involved in the By the People events are being encouraged to find ways to keep participants involved: in Rochester, for example, WXXI Public Television has involved both January and October deliberators in an ongoing initiative called Voice of the Voter.

Realizing Deliberative Democracy

So far, there have been more than fifty deliberative polls around the world. Eleven of the face-to-face deliberative polls have been national—five in Britain (on crime, Britain's future in Europe, the monarchy, the 1997 British general election, and the future of the National Health Service), one in Denmark (on the 2000 referendum on whether Denmark should adopt the Euro), one in Bulgaria (on crime), two in Australia (in 1999 on the referendum on Australia's becoming a republic and in 2001 on reconciliation with the Aboriginals), and two in the United States (the first on issues of foreign policy, the American family, and economics in 1996 at the beginning of the presidential primary season and the second on foreign policy in 2003 on the brink of the war with Iraq). Thirty-nine have been local or regional (all in the United States)—the twenty-seven By the People Citizen Deliberations sponsored by MacNeil/Lehrer Productions on America in the world, eight on integrated resource planning for electric utilities in and around Texas, as well as one on electric utility matters in Nebraska, and three regional deliberations thus far in New

Haven.[13] The two on-line deliberative polls, which were both national in scope and both held in the United States, have been on America's role in the world and on the American presidential primary process.

The results from deliberative polls have yielded a few core findings. First, deliberation makes a difference. Participants' opinions at the end of the process of deliberation are often substantially different from the beginning in comparison with control groups or other surveys of the population (when these are available or when the project can afford such comparison groups).[14] Second, participants in deliberative polls usually come away significantly better informed. This can be demonstrated through comparison of participants' responses to factual questions before and after deliberation.[15] Third, the changes in opinion are demonstrably associated with learning; it is those who gain information who change their views.[16] Fourth, deliberation is good for democracy in that the participants come away from the process with a greatly increased sense of efficacy and engagement. They are likely to continue learning and participating for many months afterward.[17] Finally, deliberative public opinion tends to be more collectively consistent. When there are ranking questions, these are less likely to produce the kind of cycle that would make our collective efforts at self-government incoherent. For example, when there are more than two options, it is possible for majority votes to prefer A to B, B to C, and then C to A, leading public decision into an unproductive cycle. But the kind of preference structure that results from deliberation is less likely to produce such a cycle.[18] The voice of the people revealed by these exercises is motivated by information and mutual understanding and is more likely to be collectively coherent and reflectively stable than the top-of-the-head attitudes presented as public opinion by conventional polls.

Like many of the forms of deliberation described in this book, the deliberative poll is in its infancy as a form of public consultation. It has been used now in many different ways, and each version has distinctive advantages and disadvantages. The national deliberative poll has the advantage of creating a microcosm of the entire country, ready to confront trade-offs and difficult issues, and providing a picture of informed and representative public opinion. When a national deliberative poll is combined with a national broadcast, it can spread the word to both policymakers and the public. Before a referendum (as in Australia or Denmark) or before a national election (as in Britain), the microcosm's conclusions and key concerns can be particularly useful to the rest of the voting public.

On the other hand, it is expensive to transport and to reimburse the time of enough people to create a microcosm of an entire nation. Hence, local deliberative polls also have advantages. First they are less expensive; few participants require transportation, and often there are no hotel costs. Second, engagement at the local level creates social capital; engaged citizens may meet again with other citizens and with policymakers, and regular, rotating participation in deliberative polls or other forums may create an expectation and a habit of informed discourse on the part of ordinary citizens. In this way, it is possible for local deliberative polls to have an effect on the character of a democratic community.

The advantage of deliberative polls in cyberspace is that they can be national in scope without the expense of transporting the microcosm to a single place. No airfares, no hotels, no catering are necessary—just computers. As access to computers spreads, the principal cost of holding deliberative polls in cyberspace will disappear, since the principal cost right now is that of providing computers to those who do not have them.[19] However, cyberspace deliberative polls lack the drama of television, the great moving force of political communication in the twentieth century (and maybe even the twenty-first). The deliberative poll is not just a poll of informed opinion. It is also a poll with a human face, and television has proven to be an excellent way to capture that potential.[20] Perhaps other technological developments will provide alternatives, but so far the Internet has not matched television as a medium for communicating the multifaceted human character of the public's concerns once the public has had a chance to think about an issue.

The most significant challenge ahead is to find ways to adapt, institutionalize, and take the deliberative poll to scale while preserving its defining elements (random selection and systematic exposure to different points of view). The simultaneous local and national structure of the By the People project may be a particularly fruitful way to approach this challenge. A number of By the People partners are pursuing adaptations of that method to address local or state issues.[21] The hope is that eventually, the incorporation of Athenian practices in many New Havens on many occasions may deepen and broaden democracy in America.

Notes

1. Other deliberative polls have had posttest-only control groups, and some have had predeliberation and postdeliberation control groups.

2. For further information about the Greater New Haven Citizens Forum, consult the Web site of the Community Foundation for Greater New Haven at http://www.cfgnh.org and of the Yale Institution for Social and Policy Studies at http://www.yale.edu/isps.

3. Consider a mechanism in which each voter is described anonymously, without reference to identity or past voting history, and in which each voter has an equal chance of being the decisive voter. This kind of political equality would be realized if everyone voted and we just counted the votes. It could just as well be realized by a lottery in which those chosen by lot voted and those votes were counted equally. Each person, in other words, has equal voting power. See Fishkin, J. S. (1991). *Democracy and Deliberation: New Directions for Democratic Reform*. New Haven, Conn.: Yale University Press.

4. As is well known, the Athenians excluded women and slaves from citizenship. The great and unprecedented democratic achievement of the Athenians was to expand full political membership to include individuals without property or social status. As a group, women and slaves were considered unsuited to the responsibilities of ruling and being ruled in turn. The comparison with modern liberal democracies indicates not only that modern citizenship is more inclusive but also that it is less demanding. See Farrar, C. (in press). "Power to the People." In K. A. Raaflaub, J. Ober, and R. Wallace, with chapters by P. Cartledge and C. Farrar. *The Origins of Democracy in Ancient Greece.* Berkeley: University of California Press.

5. Note that the structure of the council also prevented its members from consulting only with men from their own part of Attica: the groups of fifty who together served as the executive committee of the council were members of an artificial tribe comprising individuals from three different parts of Attica who were assigned to that tribe by lot, according to the democratic reforms introduced by Kleisthenes in 508–507 B.C. See Hansen, M. H. (1999). *The Athenian Democracy in the Age of Demosthenes: Structures, Principles, and Ideology.* (expanded ed.) Norman: University of Oklahoma Press.

6. For more on the strategy of extending deliberative polls to larger populations, see Ackerman, B., and Fishkin, J. S. (2004). *Deliberation Day.* New Haven, Conn.: Yale University Press. Information about MacNeil/Lehrer Productions' By the People project is available at http://www.by-the-people.org.

7. Iyengar, S., Luskin, R. C., and Fishkin, J. S. (2004, May). "Considered Opinions on U.S. Foreign Policy: Face to Face Versus Online Deliberative Polling." Paper presented at the annual meetings of the International Communication Association, New Orleans.

8. When the percentage of unlisted numbers is significant, the phone list sample should be supplemented by RDD to reflect that percentage.

9. See, for example, Traugott, M. W. (2003). "Can We Trust the Polls? It All Depends." *Brookings Review, 21*(3), 8–11. In the January 2004 By the People poll, for example, Democrats were overrepresented:

	Participants	Control Group
Democrat	37%	34%
Republican	28%	33%
Independent/No Preference	34%	33%

Democrats were also overrepresented in the October 2004 deliberations, which occurred just before the 2004 general election. In partisan contexts, we are considering the possibility of stratification by party or related demographic variables in order to ensure representativeness.

10. One of the Texas utility polls included Spanish speakers. In the October 2004 By the People citizen deliberations, four sites were given a chance to include individuals whose first language was Spanish but who were reasonably competent in English. Background materials were translated but not the surveys or the plenary sessions, although interpreters were on hand to assist these persons in understanding the survey and expressing themselves in small-group discussions.

11. Participants receive the following guidelines, which are also posted on the wall of each room:

Treat one another with respect.
Listen to other people's views; don't interrupt.
Explain your own perspective.
Focus on reasoned argument and relevant facts.

These guidelines suggest a focus on reasoned discussion, but the annotated agenda given to moderators encourages them to solicit stories as well as arguments from participants.

12. For the deliberative poll in Denmark, see Hansen, K. M. (2003). "Deliberative Democracy and Opinion Formation." Unpublished doctoral dissertation, Department of Political Science and Public Management, University of Southern Denmark. For the deliberative poll in Australia, see the Web site of Issues Deliberation Australia at http://www.ida.org.au. For other papers on relevant deliberative polls, see http://cdd.stanford.edu.

13. The results of the Texas Polls are summarized in a report from the National Renewables Laboratory: Lehr, R. L., Guild, W., Thomas, D. L., and Swezey, B. G. (2003, June). "Listening to Customers: How Deliberative Polling Helped Build 1,000 MW of New Renewable Projects in Texas." Report no. NREL/TP-620-33177. [http://www.nrel.gov/docs/fy03osti/33177.pdf]; the Nebraska project is reported in an article by Will and Robert Guild (Guild, W., Guild, R., and Thompson, F. [2004, March–April]. "21st Century Polling." *Public Power, 62*[2], 28–35.)

14. For an overview of evidence about deliberative polls, see Ackerman and Fishkin (2004), *Deliberation Day*, chap. 3.

15. Luskin, R. C., Fishkin, J. S., and Jowell, R. (2002). "Considered Opinions: Deliberative Polling in Britain." *British Journal of Political Science, 32*, 455–487; Farrar, C., Fishkin, J., Green, D., List, C., Luskin, R. C., and Paluck, E. L. (2003, Sept. 18–21). "Experimenting with Deliberative Democracy: Effects on Policy Preferences and Social Choice." Paper presented at the European Consortium for Political Research conference, Marburg, Germany.

16. Luskin, Fishkin, and Jowell (2002), "Considered Opinions."

17. Luskin, R. C., and Fishkin, J. S. (2002, Mar. 22–27). "Deliberation and 'Better Citizens.'" Paper presented at the annual joint sessions of workshops of the European Consortium for Political Research, Turin, Italy; Fishkin, J. S. (1997). *The Voice of the People: Public Opinion and Democracy.* (Rev. paperback ed.) New Haven, Conn.: Yale University Press.

18. Farrar and others (2003), "Experimenting with Deliberative Democracy," and McLean, I., List, C., Fishkin, J., and Luskin, R. C. (2000). "Does Deliberation Induce Preference Structuration? Evidence from the Deliberative Polls." Paper presented at the meetings of the American Political Science Association.

19. Iyengar, Luskin, and Fishkin (2004), "Considered Opinions on U.S. Foreign Policy"; Luskin, R. C., Fishkin, J. S., and Iyengar, S. (2004, Apr. 23–24). "Deliberative Public Opinion in Presidential Primaries: Evidence from the Online Deliberative Poll." Paper presented at the Voice and Citizenship: Re-thinking Theory and Practice in Political Communication conference, University of Washington.

20. Television coverage can be more difficult to secure at the local level without the national component; however, Louisiana Public Broadcasting has adapted the By the People approach for regular use in its Public Square series, and Nebraska Educational Television broadcast the public power deliberations. Citizens' access television can be a useful alternative or supplement to public television.

21. Examples of adaptations of the By the People model include Louisiana Public Broadcasting's Public Square; the University of Nebraska Public Policy Center's project with the *Lincoln Journal Star* and Leadership Lincoln; and the plans for regional deliberations being pursued by Case Western Reserve University in Cleveland and Carnegie Mellon University and the Carnegie Library in Pittsburgh in conjunction with their local public television stations.

CHAPTER SIX

CONSENSUS CONFERENCES AND PLANNING CELLS

Lay Citizen Deliberations

Carolyn M. Hendriks

Ladies and gentleman, some politicians say that democracy is far too important to leave to the people. Well, you've just proven them wrong. Looking at all of you, you come from different places, you look different, you speak differently—I know some of you were terrified of standing up and asking questions. And yet you've had the courage, drive, initiative to come here, and not only wish that someone would do something to bring about change, you have brought about change. This forum, and others that may come afterwards, are a direct way of involving the people in decision making. I think not only on behalf of everyone here, but on behalf of everyone in this marvelous nation in which we live, and to which we belong, thank you.

FATHER DES COATES, AN ETHICIST, SPEAKING AT AN
AUSTRALIAN CONSENSUS CONFERENCE IN 1999[1]

These words marked the end of Australia's first consensus conference, at which fourteen citizens from across the nation came together to deliberate on the issue of gene technology in the food chain. March 1999 was a busy time for such deliberations. On the other side of the globe, in Canada and Denmark, citizens were also participating in consensus conferences on the biotechnology of food.[2] The citizens at the Australian consensus conference came from diverse walks of

In addition to secondary sources, this chapter draws on interviews conducted with a number of consensus conference and planning cell conveners. For their time and insights, I would like to thank Lyn Carson, Carole Renouf, Ronnie Harding, Jane Palmer, Silke Schicktanz, Jörg Naumann, Christian Weilmeier, and Peter Dienel. I am especially grateful to Hilmar Sturm for sharing his knowledge on the planning cell model and for his comments on a draft version of this chapter. The empirical research referred to in this chapter is supported by research grants from Land & Water Australia, and the Deutscher Akademischer Austauschdienst.

life and included an artist, a stockbroker, an engineer, a tarot reader, and a furniture maker. As a panel, they confronted a barrage of information, difficult and incomplete science, and polarized partisan views. After two preparatory weekends and three days of deliberation, they presented their report, which stunned politicians, bureaucrats, and even the citizens themselves. As one citizen explained: "I just can't believe we did it; we finally achieved what we set out to do. It's the most important thing I've ever done in my whole life, I suppose."[3]

Background

Public deliberation can extend well beyond the most active and expert members of a community. In this chapter, I review two closely related deliberative models, planning cells and consensus conferences, which specifically aim to include "ordinary" citizens in policy deliberations. Both models are intended to complement rather than replace existing forms of democratic decision making. They provide meeting spaces where the politically unorganized can come together to develop an informed and considered public voice on issues of social relevance. To achieve this, consensus conferences and planning cells rely on a highly structured deliberative procedure.[4] They bring together a panel of randomly selected lay citizens for three to four days to deliberate on a particular matter. The panel is informed with briefing materials, field trips, and presentations from relevant government officials, academics, interest group representatives, and activists. With the assistance of independent facilitators, the citizens deliberate on the information put to them; after questioning presenters, they develop a series of policy recommendations. In the final stage, the citizens present their findings in the form of a report to decision makers. The report is then circulated to relevant policy elites in order to be considered alongside other forms of policy advice.[5]

The deliberative models considered in this chapter both emerged out of policy practice in Europe. In the early 1970s, Peter Dienel developed the planning cell model (Planungszelle®) with the aim of involving citizens in urban planning policy discussions.[6] Dienel's model is based on a series of concurrent four-day deliberative processes or planning cells, each involving around twenty-five participants. The total number of citizens engaged depends on the quantity of planning cells, with experiences to date varying from around one hundred to five hundred participants. Today, planning cells are primarily used to elicit citizens' preferences on a broad range of policy issues. Some researchers also suggest that planning cells are useful social research instruments that can help them to understand the origins of specific attitudes and beliefs or to assess the likely public response to a proposed policy measure.[7]

It wasn't until the late 1980s that the Danish Board of Technology (Teknologirådet) developed a different deliberative model as part of its move toward participatory technology assessment. Their approach was based on the consensus development conference, an expert-based model developed in the United States in 1977 for assessing medical technologies.[8] The Danes radically amended the American model by placing lay citizens at the center of the deliberations. This was done with two aims in mind: the deliberative output should provide policymakers with an improved understanding of the social context of emerging technologies, and the process should stimulate informed public debate on technology issues.[9]

What makes planning cells and consensus conferences so unusual but also so controversial is the nature of their participants. Lay citizens with no particular expertise or specialized knowledge regarding the issue are invited to sit at the policy table. Typically, the citizens are also unaffiliated in any substantial way with key interest groups involved in the debate.[10] This approach is the antithesis of elite, technocratic, and activist understandings of policymaking. Instead of engaging the extraordinarily specialized and the politically organized, consensus conferences and planning cells give priority to ordinary citizens.

How do disinterested citizens come to be involved in such projects?[11] Both models rely on random selection to choose who will be invited to attend. Participants are selected on the basis of chance, rather than on the basis of what they know or whom they represent. When sample sizes are small, as in consensus conferences, stratified random sampling is used to ensure that the sample reflects certain characteristics of the population; for example, an equal number of men and women are chosen. All those within each stratum or grouping have an equal chance of being selected.[12] When sample sizes are larger, as is the case in planning cell projects, simple random sampling is usually employed and no adjustments are made to the sample to meet predetermined quotas.

Whereas random selection in politics might seem a novel concept today, it was a core democratic principle in ancient Athens and in the Italian republics of the Middle Ages.[13] Contemporary advocates of random selection in politics are motivated by a desire "to incorporate greater political equality and better citizen deliberation in the process . . . [and] to make the decisions more responsive to the needs of constituents and more able to serve the public good."[14] Random selection is inclusive and fair to the extent that it provides everyone with an equal chance of being selected to participate. It also serves deliberation well because it is more likely to select nonpartisans with relatively open preferences than a process that relies entirely on self-selection.[15]

In this chapter, I explore the basic features of consensus conferences and planning cells, and I discuss some of their impacts and limitations. This discussion might generate more questions than it resolves, but my aim is to provide a starting point for further explorations. Over the years, the Danish consensus conference model and Dienel's planning cell model have evolved and been adapted to suit different issues and political contexts.[16] As far as possible, I will represent the core features of both models as they now stand, recognizing that in practice variations and exceptions to the "standard model" abound.

The Danish Consensus Conference

The consensus conference procedure is well documented,[17] so a brief outline will suffice here. The Danish model is based on a two-stage procedure that engages ten to twenty-five citizens in eight days of deliberation over a period of approximately three months. In the first stage, the citizens meet for two preparatory weekends to learn about the topic, the process, and the group. During these weekends, the panel also develops a series of questions for the conference to address and selects the conference presenters from a list of possible experts and interest group representatives.[18] In the second stage of the process, the actual four-day conference takes place.[19] On the first two days, various presenters appear before a plenary forum to respond to the questions set for the conference. Throughout this period, the citizens' panel retreats into nonpublic sessions to formulate further questions for the presenters and to clarify any misunderstandings or points of contention. On the last two days, the citizens work together to write a report outlining their key recommendations, which they then present to relevant decision makers before a public audience.[20] In some cases, the presenters have the right to reply, after which the citizens are free to reformulate their report.[21]

Facilitation is a central element of the consensus conference model. Facilitators must be impartial and, ideally, professionally trained, with good pedagogic skills. It is also important that the facilitators, like the lay citizens, not be experts on the issue under deliberation.[22] The facilitator's primary function is to help the citizens to deliberate together to achieve their task. The facilitator is also expected to manage the proceedings—for example, by ensuring that the presenters adhere to the rules of the process and answer the citizens' questions. In some conferences, these two roles are separated: a facilitator works with and for the citizens, and a chairperson manages procedural matters.[23]

Another important feature of consensus conferences is an external advisory committee. Apart from maintaining procedural integrity, an external advisory body adds legitimacy to the process.[24] The committee oversees a number of tasks, including selection of the citizens; compilation of the presenter list; development of briefing materials; selection of facilitators and evaluators; and relations with the media and the public. Advisory committee members typically include academics and practitioners of public participation, as well as the least partial experts on the issue under deliberation. In some cases, representatives from relevant stakeholder groups also sit on the advisory committee. This strategy does make the procedure more vulnerable to partisan interests, but experience suggests that the active engagement of groups and experts in process planning can facilitate an appreciation of public deliberation and foster a sense of stewardship of the process.[25]

Planning Cells

The planning cell model merits more attention in this chapter because there is relatively little English documentation on the procedure.[26] In general, planning cells are larger undertakings than most other deliberative processes considered in this book. They often include hundreds of citizens at multiple venues, although the model is quite flexible in terms of participant numbers as well as the length and intensity of the program.[27] On average, projects involve six to ten replicating planning cells, each containing around twenty-five citizens.[28] To simplify logistics, two planning cells are usually run one hour apart at the same location. This also maximizes the use of the presenters' time and reduces costs. Figure 6.1 shows the structure of a recent planning cell project conducted in Germany in 2001–2002 on the issue of consumer protection. The project was commissioned by the Bavarian minister for health, nutrition and consumer protection in the wake of 'mad cow' disease outbreaks in Germany.[29] Eighteen separate planning cells were conducted, involving 425 citizens in five different localities across Bavaria.[30]

Each four-day planning cell is divided into sixteen discrete work units involving a mix of information sessions, hearings (with presenters), site visits, and, most important, small-group discussions. To ensure consistency, the structure of each planning cell within a project is identical. Figure 6.2 shows the sixteen work units for the aforementioned Bavarian project.

In some respects, each planning cell is similar to a consensus conference. Over a four-day period, the twenty-five or so citizens in the planning cell are informed about an issue and have the opportunity to hear from a range of different experts and interest group representatives. Unlike in consensus conferences, however, the presenters and the specific topics for deliberation are determined in advance by the commissioning body and the conveners, not by the citizens. In more recent projects, experts and interest groups have been involved in determining the topics through a roundtable process.[31]

Facilitation is another point of difference between planning cells and consensus conferences. In each planning cell, there is a male and a female process

FIGURE 6.1. EIGHTEEN PLANNING CELLS
ON CONSUMER PROTECTION IN BAVARIA

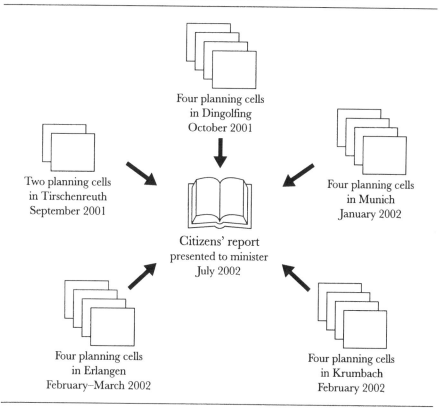

Four planning cells
in Dingolfing
October 2001

Two planning cells
in Tirschenreuth
September 2001

Four planning cells
in Munich
January 2002

Citizens' report
presented to minister
July 2002

Four planning cells
in Erlangen
February–March 2002

Four planning cells
in Krumbach
February 2002

steward (*Prozessbegleiter* or *Tagungsleiter*), whose role is more to manage and chair the proceedings than to facilitate discussions. One of their primary tasks is to collate the outputs from small group discussions; for this reason, it helps if they have a good understanding of the policy issue.[32] One planning cell project might involve up to forty different process stewards, much like the numerous group moderators in the deliberative polling model (discussed in Chapter Five). Rather than worrying about consistency, Dienel celebrates the use of multiple stewards because it arguably minimizes the effects of moderator bias.[33] In some urban planning projects, planners and technical experts also assist the citizens in their deliberations.[34]

When all the planning cells have been completed, the conveners collate and synthesize the citizens' outputs into a project report called the *citizens' report* (*Bürgergutachten*). Drafts are circulated and approved by a group of citizens nominated

FIGURE 6.2. SIXTEEN-UNIT PLANNING CELL STRUCTURE FOR BAVARIAN CONSUMER PROTECTION PROJECT

Day 1	Day 2	Day 3	Day 4
Unit 1: Introduction to consumer protection	Units 5 & 6: Food production, additives, and labeling	Unit 9: Product safety (for example, mobile phones)	Unit 13: Responsibilities of consumers
Unit 2: Health and environment		Unit 10: Needs of special groups	Unit 14: Consumer information and advice
Unit 3: Consumer protection in health	Unit 7: Food control and safety	Unit 11: Advertising	Unit 15: The meaning of consumption
Unit 4: Nutrition and agriculture	Unit 8: Product safety (for example, clothing)	Unit 12: Presentations from politicians	Unit 16: Summary and priority setting

from each planning cell. Once the report is finalized (usually weeks after the last planning cell), the citizens or representatives from the cells reconvene to formally hand the collective product of their deliberations to the decision makers. The report is published and made available to the broader public, and it is directly distributed to the presenters, politicians, and other relevant organizations and associations.

There are a number of distinctive features of the planning cell model; I will highlight four here. First, as in the deliberative poll (Chapter Five) and Citizens Jury (Chapter Seven) processes, citizens are remunerated for their commitment to the process, usually through a fixed honorarium. For example, in the Bavarian project mentioned earlier, the citizens all received about $165 (U.S. dollars) for participating.[35] Remuneration—an integral part of Dienel's model—was originally intended to motivate citizens to participate. However, years of experience have found that participants tend to place more value on the money's symbolic meaning than on the money itself. According to Dienel, it provides citizens with a sign that their contribution is valued by society and that the project is a serious political undertaking.[36]

A second notable feature of the planning cell model is its emphasis on small-group work. The bulk of the citizens' deliberations occurs in groups of five.[37] The principle here is that when citizens participate in small constellations, they have more opportunities to offer their opinions and to interact.[38] Small-group work also enables citizens to participate freely without the fear of having an audience.[39] Throughout a four-day planning cell, the citizens break into small groups to record their preferences on different scenarios, reach collective decisions, or develop written recommendations.[40] Group membership rotates for each exercise in order to enable direct dialogue between all participants and to minimize dysfunctional group dynamics, such as the formation of factions or hierarchies.[41]

Also worth noting is the minimal level of facilitation used in the planning cell process. For all their structure, the planning cells are surprisingly loose when it comes to managing group dynamics. Unlike the facilitators of consensus conferences, process stewards invest little or no time in preparatory empowerment or group-building exercises. The literature is ambiguous on this matter, but my discussions with practitioners suggest that facilitation of this kind is not viewed favorably. According to Dienel, facilitation and group building is intentionally avoided. He argues that such "games" only provide opportunities to manipulate the citizens.[42] Practitioners explain that the citizens learn to deliberate together as they work on their allocated tasks.[43]

A final noteworthy feature of planning cells is that the citizens' output is aggregated. In other deliberative processes, like the consensus conference, the citizens deliberate as one group and work together to write their collective report. This approach encounters problems in a planning cell project because the citizens are not privy to all the deliberations. In theory, each cell could prepare a written report, but eventually the recommendations, suggestions, and preferences would need to be collated and synthesized in some way. As Dienel himself admits, one downside of having so many cells and small working groups is that it produces enormous amounts of data that need to be aggregated by the conveners in some way.[44] The aggregated reports from planning cell projects tend to be more quantitative and less qualified than those prepared directly by citizens. When it comes to aggregative outputs, the planning cell model has some commonality with a deliberative polling process.[45]

Convening Activities

Despite their procedural differences, consensus conferences and planning cell projects require similar activities on the part of those who convene them. Both are highly planned one-time deliberative events that can take from six to eighteen months to prepare, depending on the complexity of the project. Conveners ideally are neutral bodies with the necessary resources and administrative capacity to conduct a range of activities, such as booking venues; organizing meetings; selecting citizens and presenters; and engaging politicians and the media. Conveners are commonly research institutes or consulting groups, but in some cases, they may be state-funded institutions, such as museums, or advisory bodies, such as the Danish Board of Technology. The steps involved in preparing for consensus conferences and planning cells are well documented;[46] here I focus on how such projects are instigated and where they are typically conducted.

The stimulus for consensus conferences varies from context to context. In Denmark, consensus conferences are just one of a number of participatory mechanisms employed by the Danish Board of Technology.[47] In general, topics are selected through an annual consultation process in which state and nongovernmental organizations, as well interested individuals, may contribute suggestions. In some cases, conferences have been directly instigated by a member of parliament or by a parliamentary committee.[48] Outside of Denmark, it is far more common for consensus conferences to be instigated by an organization other than the parliament or the central government, such as a university or an association working on an issue.[49] In these cases, the instigators or sponsors select topics on the basis of their immediate relevance to society.

Planning cells, by definition, are commissioned and sponsored by an organization with a concrete policy problem to address. The stimulus almost always comes from a government official—such as a mayor, minister, or senior bureaucrat—who is seeking public input on a particular administrative task. Advocates are quick to point out that planning cells engage citizens in real political problems, not hypotheticals.[50] This does, however, present a dilemma. On one hand, close ties to the state enable planning cells to directly influence policy, but on the other hand, it makes them more vulnerable to the imperatives of the state.[51]

Consensus conferences and planning cells demand slightly different kinds of venues, although both require enough space for plenary discussion and small-group work. Since one of the goals of consensus conferences is to stimulate public debate, they are typically high-profile public events, held at venues of great public significance, such as national or provincial parliaments. Consensus conferences also require enough space for an audience of fifty to a hundred people to attend the plenary sessions. Venues for planning cells are comparatively modest and are locally based. They are usually held in a public building such as a town hall, library, or school. The venue must also have the capacity to house at least two concurrent planning cells. It is also common for conveners to establish local project offices in the regions where planning cells are to take place. This provides a local presence for the project and a point of contact for interested citizens. It also takes advantage of local knowledge in arranging services such as caterers, child care facilities, and transportation and, if necessary, site visits.

Historical Uses of Consensus Conferences and Planning Cells

Planning cells and consensus conferences were each developed in a specific political context for particular kinds of issues. However, since they were first introduced some twenty to thirty years ago, their use has expanded considerably. Both models appear to travel sparingly but well outside their country of origin, with impacts varying in different contexts.

It is no accident that consensus conferences evolved in Denmark. Over the past 150 years, the country has developed a democratic tradition characterized by an active and informed public.[52] In response to rising public concern about the social consequences of technologies such as nuclear energy, the Danish parliament (*Folketinget*) established the Board of Technology in 1985 with a specific charter to stimulate public debate.[53] Whereas many countries prefer to restrict technology assessment to the scientific realm, the Danes emphasize the social context of technological development. Thus, the consensus conference is a product of Denmark's republican tradition and a particular participatory approach to technology assessment.[54] Since the model was first tested in 1987, it has been applied in Denmark in relation to at least twenty-two controversial technology issues, including gene technology in industry and agriculture (1987), air pollution (1990), infertility (1993), teleworking (1997), electronic surveillance (2000), and road pricing (2002).[55] Over the past decade, the model has generated significant international interest. To date, at least fifty consensus conferences have been conducted in sixteen different countries, including Argentina, New Zealand, Korea, Israel, Japan, Canada, and the United States.[56] The consensus conference model has also proven its adaptability in diverse political contexts—Western and non-Western, regional and national.[57] The most popular consensus conference topic worldwide is gene technology in food and medical testing.

Planning cells have enjoyed a slightly longer history than consensus conferences. Since Dienel first proposed his model in the early 1970s, most planning cell projects have been commissioned by local government agencies and concentrated on urban infrastructure problems.[58] A handful of projects have been sponsored by state and federal agencies on a broader range of policy issues, including information technology, energy, waste management, gene technology, and health. According to Dienel, it has only been in the last fifteen years that planning cells have "truly gained momentum."[59] Interest is growing outside of Germany, with experiences with planning cells occurring in Austria, Switzerland, Spain, and the

United States.[60] To date, there have been over fifty planning cell projects conducted worldwide, although the vast majority of these have been in Germany.
This amounts to an estimated three hundred separate planning cells, involving
about seven thousand citizens in 1,200 days of public deliberation.[61]

With each experience, the planning cell model continues to evolve. One dynamic element of the model is the length of the citizens' deliberations. In Dienel's
original proposal, planning cells were to be conducted over a twelve-week period.
This was reduced to three weeks, then to four days, which is now standard.[62]
Project experiences have shown that citizens cannot afford to devote large amounts
of time to planning cells; however, they have also revealed that citizens are fast
learners.[63] Another noteworthy development in Germany over the past few years
has been the substitution of the term *citizens' report* (*Bürgergutachten*) for *planning cells*
(*Planungszelle*).[64] Practitioners have found the "planning" label unnecessarily restrictive and have discovered that the reference to *cells* can evoke prison imagery.
Recent project experiences suggest that the term *citizens' report* provides a useful,
descriptive title that shifts the emphasis toward the outcomes.[65]

The Impacts of Consensus Conferences and Planning Cells

The consequences of any deliberative process are multidimensional. A deliberative process may have direct effects, for example, on substantive policy outcomes
or on the citizens involved. It might also have more indirect results by influencing
public discourse or the ideas of policy elites.[66] Space limitations do not allow me
to fully address and elaborate on the performance of consensus conferences and
planning cells along these sorts of impact dimensions. Instead, I will provide a flavor of some of the direct and indirect impacts that have been reported in various
evaluations. Before proceeding, it is important to note that while the impacts of
some specific projects have been evaluated, few comparative analyses exist.[67]

I will look first at the direct impact of these deliberative models on citizen
participants. Project evaluations report that when invited to attend a deliberative
forum, many randomly selected citizens in the community choose to participate.[68]
These citizens come from a broad range of social groups that roughly correspond
to local demographic patterns with respect to sex, age, education, occupation, and
household size.[69] Commentators explain that when citizens enter the deliberative
forum, they take their role very seriously and are willing to learn and discuss the
issue at hand.[70] As a result of their deliberations, citizens reportedly learn about
the broader dimensions of the policy issue under consideration, and many shift
their preferences.[71] Evaluations also indicate that consensus conferences and planning cells can have a profound impact on participants. Although the deliberations

are intense, most participants report the process to be a fulfilling experience, one that positively influences their self-confidence, knowledge of policy issues, and level of political awareness.[72] Some citizens have felt empowered to join associations and groups, while others have been invited to sit as lay representatives on committees and boards.[73] Studies have also found that participants can have an impact on their immediate social world as they share their experiences with family, friends, and work colleagues.[74] Overall, most participants who have been surveyed support the use of further deliberative processes such as planning cells and consensus conferences. They are, however, not uncritically accepting and are keen to offer constructive criticism on how the deliberative processes could be improved.[75]

The impacts of consensus conferences and planning cells on substantive policy outcomes and public debate is far more difficult to ascertain. Citizens' reports are conceived as advisory, and their recommendations invariably compete with other forms of advice from political parties, expert committees, and interest groups, for example. Moreover, when some of these other sources of policy advice happen to recommend the same policies and celebrate the same values articulated in the citizens' reports, it can be difficult to determine which recommendation held more sway.

In any case, the capacity for a citizens' report to influence actual policy outcomes and public debate is contingent on political circumstances. Such impacts are shaped by contextual factors, including the willingness of decision makers to listen to lay citizens; the salience and ferocity of competing agendas; and the nature of public discourse. Given the significance of context, I will first discuss the impacts of consensus conferences and planning cells in their respective countries of origin and then consider how they perform in other policy settings.

In Denmark, the impact of consensus conferences on substantive policy outcomes has varied. One common misconception is that Danish parliamentarians are bound to consider the citizens' recommendations.[76] Although this is not the case, the unique political position of the Board of Technology facilitates close and regular contact with parliamentarians and various parliamentary committees.[77] In some projects, these linkages have enabled consensus conferences to trigger the development or amendment of relevant legislation.[78] There are however, other consensus conferences in Denmark that have resulted in little or no direct policy impact.[79] Empirical studies suggest that consensus conferences stimulate public debate throughout Denmark, primarily through media dissemination, but also through related local and regional debates.[80] In the Danish context, then, consensus conferences provide a viable mechanism for participatory technology assessment, not only because they help to inform decision makers but also because they facilitate public discourse.[81]

When we look beyond Denmark, there is little evidence to suggest that consensus conferences result in substantive impacts on policy.[82] Institutional setting and political culture appear to be influential factors. Outside the Danish context, the model represents a dramatic shift away from the elite and technocratic models of conventional technology assessment. It is often the case that conferences lack an institutional anchor such as the Danish Board of Technology. Although some consensus conferences (for example, in the Netherlands and France) are convened by an equivalent institution, most are instigated by entities outside the legislature and central governmental agencies—for example, by research institutions (Canada); public museums (United Kingdom, Germany); foundations (United States); international development agencies (South Korea); and advocacy groups (Australia).[83] The advisory capacity of conferences convened by nonstate actors can be relatively weak, particularly when key decision makers are not engaged. Often, poor timing also limits impact. In some countries, consensus conferences have had minimal political or public resonance simply because they entered the political and public arena after decisions had been made or after the issue had reached its saturation point in the media.[84]

Although direct policy impacts might be rare, international experiences demonstrate that when lay citizens are given a voice, a chorus of indirect impacts on public discourse and policy elites can result. Some projects have resulted in subtle political impacts; for example, a few conferences have initiated public discourse on the issues under deliberation or provided support for reforms already in the pipeline.[85] Media coverage, though variable, is generally positive and in some projects equivalent to the levels experienced in Denmark.[86] In a number of cases, media coverage focused less on the issue under deliberation and more on the novelty of the participatory process.[87] In a similar vein, evaluations indicate that consensus conferences influence the way that different policy elites view lay citizens and public deliberation in general. Elites, however, rarely appear to shift their preferences on the policy issue itself as a result of lay citizen deliberations.[88]

The impacts of planning cells in Germany are positive, although independent evaluations are scarce. Early evaluations concluded that citizens produce outcomes oriented toward the common good.[89] According to Dienel, planning cells have "proved themselves to be a cost-effective means of resolving a range of urban planning problems. They have led to a significant reduction in the total costs of planning, statutory and legal processes."[90] Practitioners report that governments, especially at the local and community level, are willing to adopt the citizens' recommendations to the extent that they are technically feasible and economically viable.[91]

One of the most extensive evaluations of the planning cell model was conducted from 1982 to 1985 as part of a three-year project that examined the preferences of West German citizens on four energy scenarios that had originally been developed by a parliamentary advisory body.[92] An evaluation team comprising scientists, stakeholders, and administrators concluded that the planning cell model provides a suitable method of assessing preferences when citizens have a direct relationship or local experience with the issue. However, opinion was divided on the utility of planning cells for regional and national issues. It seems that at higher levels of the political system, planning cells provoke more controversy than their local equivalents. National and state-based projects tend to address broader issues and irritate more political actors. Under these circumstances, the recommending force of the citizens' report can be more easily weakened by the competing claims of different groups and advisory bodies. However, more recent experiences suggest that when politicians and administrators are committed to the project, planning cells have the potential to shape policy outcomes at all levels of government.[93]

Planning cells have traveled far less on the international scene than consensus conferences. The only known U.S. planning cell project was conducted in 1988 and 1989 in New Jersey on the issue of sewage sludge management.[94] This project sheds light on some of the unintended impacts that can result when planning cells are conducted in controversial political settings. In this case, the program was considerably altered when the selected citizens began to distrust a procedure run by an external third party. They rejected the organizers and the facilitators and developed their own report, which they then handed to the commissioning body. The project achieved its desired outcome in that it gave administrators a clearer idea of the citizens' preferences, but the panels' response highlights the fact that not all communities and stakeholders are willing to entrust a deliberative process to an external party.[95]

Experiences elsewhere have been more promising. For example, in Spain, planning cells have made a valuable contribution to resolving disputes over a freeway controversy in the volatile Basque region.[96] Like consensus conferences, the planning cell procedure appears to adapt well to different political contexts. For example, in one Swiss project, the commissioning body was concerned that random selection would not be perceived as legitimate in Switzerland. Instead of randomly selecting participants, the organizers ran a series of town hall meetings in different locations, from which a number of community representatives were nominated.[97]

Reflections on Consensus Conferences and Planning Cells

Consensus conferences and planning cells aim to elicit considered input from lay citizens on complex policy issues. While many people applaud the democratic goals of these deliberations, it is important to acknowledge that in practice, lay citizen engagement can be a demanding and challenging enterprise.

Cautionary Notes

Consensus conferences and planning cells are not simple events to convene. Practitioners report that although they are rewarding, these types of events are resource-intensive and administratively demanding.[98] As innovative processes, they require champions to instigate and foster their development. More significantly, they need strong financial support from a commissioning body.[99] Depending on travel and accommodation requirements, one consensus conference (including preparatory weekends) is estimated to cost between $70,000 and $200,000 (U.S. dollars). The cost of a project involving eight planning cells (approximately two hundred citizens) is estimated at $180,000–$240,000 (U.S. dollars).[100] While these figures might compare unfavorably with the costs of opinion polls, town hall meetings, or stakeholder roundtables, their outputs are qualitatively different. Further research would be well served by comparisons of these figures with the costs of running an expert advisory committee or parliamentary inquiry.

Consensus conferences and planning cells are not the participatory solution to all kinds of issues, nor are they appropriate in every context.[101] Both models are best suited to deal with issues that are publicly significant and relevant to the lives of lay citizens. Planning cells are considered appropriate when the problem is relatively urgent and when there are different options available, each posing different benefits and risks. They are less likely to be successful when the options are restricted to binary (yes-or-no) outcomes, when the issue is highly polarized, or when large inequalities may exist between different communities.[102] Consensus conferences are best suited to issues that pose a complex mix of social, ethical, and technical consequences for society.[103] The Danish Board of Technology finds appropriate consensus conference topics to be those that present unresolved issues of attitudes, applications, and regulation. The board finds that the model works best when the issue is of current interest, steeped in expert knowledge, well demarcated, and controversial.[104]

Context is also an important consideration, especially when lay citizen involvement is uncommon or likely to be controversial. Some settings are hostile to lay citizen deliberation. This may occur when distrust in organized public participation is high or when powerful interest groups have captured the issue. Some political contexts are unsuitable because there is insufficient support from decision makers and policy elites.[105] Consensus conferences are more flexible on this front, since they have been used successfully outside the state to stimulate public debate and policy reform.[106]

The highly planned nature of consensus conferences and planning cells may also mean that these processes are not always suitable or welcome. As well-choreographed events, they may not be as spontaneous or flexible as some policy issues and groups demand. There are several issues to consider here. First, consensus conferences and planning cells are one-time events that rarely sustain any contact with citizens after the process.[107] Second, the planned nature of consensus conferences and planning cells provides opportunities for organizers to manipulate the process, especially if the procedure is not transparent and inclusive of the broader public. In terms of flexibility and transparency, consensus conferences are likely to fare better than planning cells because citizens in a consensus conference are given more autonomy to frame the problem in their own terms and select the presenters whom they believe are relevant to the issue. The presence of an external advisory committee can also ensure that procedural matters of a consensus conference or planning cell project are transparent and open to scrutiny. Third, structure does not always fit well with the more informal kinds of deliberation in the public sphere.[108] This is a limitation of which some advocates of consensus conferences are well aware. Joss, for example, warns that the model's "relatively rigid" format "could have its drawbacks: for example, it might not relate or contribute to wider public debate, and it might be perceived by the public as just another remote administrative institution."[109]

Challenges

Planning cells and consensus conferences seek to create a workable deliberative forum by limiting participation to a group of randomly selected lay citizens. Given that not everyone who wants to participate can, how legitimate is the process to those outside the forum? This is a question that continues to plague theories of deliberative democracy. The legitimacy of consensus conferences and planning cells is rarely a given, and conveners work hard to demonstrate their impartiality and rigor.[110] Despite such efforts, these processes fly in the face of technocratic and elite forms of policymaking and thus may fuel resentment among powerful policy actors.[111] There will almost always be politicians who are reluctant to open up an issue to public debate; experts who worry about the competence of lay citizens; and stakeholders and "expert activists" who feel excluded from the process.[112]

Skepticism toward consensus conferences and planning cells is heightened in contexts in which public participation is unfamiliar or in which experts or interest groups have long since captured the issue. My comparative research, which draws on interviews with more than seventy different policy actors, suggests that these sorts of deliberative models have at least three controversial features.[113] First, some technocrats and elites reject the idea that nonexperts and unaffiliated citizens can make legitimate contributions to public policy. They raise concerns about the capacity of lay citizens to comprehend complex material, and they criticize lay citizens' accountability, authority, and representativeness as a microcosm of the community. Second, deliberative designs assign policy actors a new role as presenters and, in doing so, change the use of power in the policy arena. This role serves to contain and expose coercive forms of power by encouraging experts and representatives of interest groups to use communicative and collective power. A number of policy actors resist taking up this new role because it constrains their control of and influence on the policy debate and their ability to participate freely in policy discussions. Third, deliberative designs seek to transform communicative conditions from a state of competition to one based on reasoned argument and reflection. Skeptics tend to understand public opinion as the sum of individual static preferences and are therefore challenged by the notion of collective will formation. Also unfamiliar and contentious is the notion that deliberation is a social process that promotes learning and collective outcomes.

Not only can these challenges undermine the perceived procedural legitimacy of planning cells and consensus conferences, but they can also affect how such deliberative events function. On one hand, the models rely on policy actors to present their perspectives to the forum; on the other hand, they insulate these same players from actively participating in the citizens' deliberations. This tension between partial involvement and insulation makes securing commitment from policy actors no straightforward matter.[114]

This is not to say that policy actors always resist deliberative forums involving lay citizens. Evidence suggests that experts, elites, and interest groups willingly engage when there are incentives to participate.[115] For example, some interest groups welcome the opportunity to publicly advocate their message; a few commercial organizations appreciate consumer feedback; and in some cases, scientists feel the need to publicly defend their technology. In order for stakeholders and policy elites to appreciate the benefits of public deliberation, practitioners have found that it is important to involve them at an early stage—for example, through project briefings or as members of an advisory committee. It is also important to accurately communicate to them what the process is seeking to achieve, as well as its limits.

An often-misunderstood aspect of consensus conferences and planning cells is their claim to representativeness. The relatively small sample of citizens in a consensus conference is not expected to be statistically representative, but it is designed to be demographically diverse.[116] Since the sample sizes used in planning cells are much larger, they can make more legitimate claims to representativeness, but even so, assertions that participants are statistically representative of the population are exaggerated.[117] Misconceptions about what and whom the citizens represent distract attention from the citizens' deliberative role in the forum. It is for this reason that commentators on deliberative designs caution against describing citizens' panels as 'representative microcosms'.[118] In the end, it is diversity that appears to matter most in these processes. When a group of deliberators are heterogeneous, it is less likely that they will enter into enclave deliberation and reinforce their own positions.[119]

Areas for Further Development

The participatory models discussed in this chapter supplement the various ways in which public voices enter the policymaking process. They provide an avenue for unaffiliated citizens to express their ideas, and in doing so, they add a further dimension to existing forms of policy advice such as expert opinions or polling data. The challenge for practitioners and decision makers is how to integrate these different kinds of policy inputs, especially when they pose competing claims.

An important first step would be to further integrate lay citizen models with other forms of public deliberation. The three-stage cooperative discourse model, developed by Ortwin Renn and his colleagues, provides a useful starting point.[120] Under this model, stakeholders, experts, and the lay public are sequentially involved in policy deliberations. Stakeholder groups are involved initially to elicit values and criteria. Experts are then brought in to develop performance profiles of different policy options. In the third stage, randomly selected citizens evaluate and design policies. Carson proposes a fourth stage in which feedback is sought from the broader community for purposes of accountability and public education.[121] This three- or four-stage discourse model aims to increase the accountability of policy elites by sandwiching their involvement between input from randomly selected citizens and the broader public.

Consensus conferences and planning cells could easily be hybridized with other deliberative methods. Network technology may open up some interesting options by enabling deliberative designs to be convened simultaneously at different locations. Such networking could overcome the isolation that exists between separate planning cells in the current planning cell model. Such technology could also be used to increase the numbers involved in consensus conference events. Greater use of the media and the Internet would also expand the impacts of a deliberative forum on public awareness and discourse. Although some deliberative projects have successfully used Internet discussion forums, they could be improved by using on-line facilitation and by integrating Web-based input with lay citizens' deliberations.[122] A step is this direction has been taken by a group of researchers from North Carolina State University who studied the differences between participants in a face-to-face consensus conference and participants in an on-line consensus conference on the topic of genetically modified foods.[123]

Where to from Here?

Planning cells and consensus conferences are not participatory panaceas. Like all forms of public involvement, they are open to the dangers of manipulation, paternalism, and "alibi participation" (using token citizen involvement as an alibi to justify autocratic decision making).[124] Certain elements of these processes are likely to be more controversial in some political and cultural settings than others, but on the whole, experiences in Denmark, Germany, and elsewhere demonstrate that lay citizens are willing, capable, and valuable deliberators. Planning cells are especially appealing because they can engage a large number of citizens while still maintaining deliberative conditions through small-group work. This is a useful approach, especially when citizens are widely dispersed across a given region or nation. What consensus conferences cannot offer in terms of numbers, they make up for in deliberative quality. Through a two-stage procedure, citizens are empowered to think critically about the information that they receive and are free to determine the questions and presenters for the final conference. Apart from providing policy advice, consensus conferences can stimulate public debate outside the forum through media and audience involvement.

Skeptics may continue to wonder whether public deliberation, especially among lay citizens, is a possibility, yet prospects do exist even in the most unlikely of places. For example, in December 2003, the U.S. Congress passed the 21st Century Nanotechnology Research and Development Act, which requires that the newly established National Nanotechnology Program provide opportunities for "regular and ongoing public discussions, through mechanisms such as citizens' panels, consensus conferences, and educational events, as appropriate." While the legislation does not necessarily ensure that public concerns will be taken on board, it at least formally stipulates that policymakers provide spaces for citizens to meet and voice their perspectives.[125]

With their tentative beginnings more or less behind us, it is no longer a question of what consensus conferences and planning cells can achieve. More pertinent now are questions about finding their optimal location within a larger democratic system and discovering how to secure their legitimacy and funding for the long term.

Notes

1. Father Des Coates presented at the 1999 Australian consensus conference on gene technology in the food chain. This quote is taken from the Australian Broadcasting Corporation's Radio National program "Life Matters," which aired a story on the consensus conference May 3–7, 1999. Recordings are available from http://www.abc.net.au/rn/contact.htm. See

also Australian Broadcasting Corporation. (1999). "Waiter, There Is a Gene in My Food..."
[http://www.abc.net.au/science/slab/consconf/forum.htm]. Retrieved May 28, 2004.

2. Einsiedel, E. F., Jelsøe, E., and Breck, T. (2001). "Publics and the Technology Table: The Australian, Canadian and Danish Consensus Conferences on Food Biotechnology." *Public Understanding of Science, 10*(1), 83–98.

3. Lay citizen participant, 1999 Australian consensus conference on gene technology in the food chain, quoted on the "Life Matters" radio program. See note 1 for more information on how to obtain a copy of this program.

4. Planning cells and consensus conferences share a number of common features with the Citizens Jury (see Chapter Seven of this volume). There are, however, important differences between the three models, especially with respect to participant numbers and small-group work.

5. See Dienel, P. C., and Renn, O. (1995). "Planning Cells: A Gate to 'Fractal' Mediation." In O. Renn, T. Webler, and P. Wiedemann (eds.), *Fairness and Competence in Citizen Participation.* Dordrecht, Netherlands: Kluwer, 127; Joss, S. (1998). "Danish Consensus Conferences as a Model of Participatory Technology Assessment: An Impact Study of Consensus Conferences on Danish Parliament and Danish Public Debate." *Science and Public Policy, 25*(1), 21.

6. Peter Dienel is based at the Bergische Universität Wuppertal in Germany. He first published his ideas on planning cells in 1971. See Dienel, P. C. (1971). "Wie können die Bürger an Planungsprozessen beteiligt werden? Planwahl und Planungszelle als Beteiligungsverfahren" [How can citizens participate in planning processes? Plan choice and planning cells as methods for public participation]. *Der Bürger im Staat* [The citizen in the state], *3,* 151–156. To standardize the methodology and ensure quality, *Planungszelle* was registered as a trademark by CitCon Citizen Consult, an independent self-financing institute in Germany. See Dienel, P. C. (1999). "Planning Cells: The German Experience." In U. Khan (ed.), *Participation Beyond the Ballot Box: European Case Studies in State-Citizen Political Dialogue.* London: UCL Press, 87.

7. Renn, O., Stegelmann, H. U., Albrecht, G., Kotte, U., and Peters, H. P. (1984). "An Empirical Investigation of Citizens' Preferences Among Four Energy Scenarios." *Technological Forecasting and Social Change, 26*(1), 43.

8. Jørgensen, T. (1995). "Consensus Conferences in the Health Care Sector." In S. Joss and J. Durant (eds.), *Public Participation in Science: The Role of Consensus Conferences in Europe.* London: Science Museum, 17–29.

9. Joss (1998), "Danish Consensus Conferences," 5, 19.

10. This characteristic of lay citizens is sometimes described with the term *non-committed* (for example, in Dienel and Renn [1995], "Planning Cells," 126).

11. By *disinterested,* I mean impartial, not holding a particular position.

12. If stratified random sampling is used, citizens in smaller stratum groups—for example, ethnic minorities—are more likely to be selected than citizens in larger stratum groups.

13. See Carson, L., and Martin, B. (1999). *Random Selection in Politics.* Westport, Conn.: Praeger, 31–33; Manin, B. (1997). *The Principles of Representative Government.* Cambridge, U.K.: Cambridge University Press, 42–93.

14. Mansbridge, J. (2000). "What Does a Representative Do? Descriptive Representation in Communicative Settings of Distrust, Uncrystallized Interests, and Historically Denigrated Status." In W. Kymlicka and W. Norman (eds.), *Citizenship in Diverse Societies.* Oxford, U.K.: Oxford University Press, 106. Some contemporary advocates of random selection include Burnheim, J. (1985). *Is Democracy Possible?* Cambridge, U.K.: Polity Press; Carson and Martin

(1999), *Random Selection in Politics*; Dahl, R. (1985). *Controlling Nuclear Weapons: Democracy Versus Guardianship.* Syracuse, N.Y.: Syracuse University Press; Fishkin, J. (1997). *The Voice of the People: Public Opinion and Democracy.* (2nd ed.) New Haven, Conn.: Yale University Press; Goodwin, B. (1992). *Justice by Lottery.* New York: Harvester Wheatsheaf.

15. Self-selection occurs when participation is open to anyone willing to volunteer. It is a common form of selection for many community consultation events and tends to attract partisan members of the community who have a particular interest in the issue, such as activists and representatives from interest groups. Of course, the deliberative procedures discussed in this chapter are not devoid of the effects of self-selection, since even those selected at random have to be willing to participate and volunteer their time. However, conveners of planning cells and consensus conferences try to reduce the effects of self-selection—for example, by following up with reluctant citizens to encourage them to participate. As I discuss later in this chapter, in some projects, participating citizens are remunerated for their time.

16. For variations of the consensus conference model in different contexts, see Einsiedel, Jelsøe, and Breck (2001), "Publics and the Technology Table"; Guston, D. H. (1999). "Evaluating the First U.S. Consensus Conference: The Impact of the Citizens' Panel on Telecommunications and the Future of Democracy." *Science, Technology & Human Values, 24*(4), 451–482; Joss, S. (2000). *Die Konsensuskonferenz in Theorie und Anwendung* [The consensus conference in theory and practice]. Stuttgart, Germany: Center for Technology Assessment. Less comparative research has been conducted on planning cells, but see Dienel, P. C. (2002). *Die Planungszelle. Die Bürger als Chance* [The planning cells: The citizen as chance]. (5th ed. with status report). Opladen, Germany: Westdeutscher Verlag, 291–293; Renn, O., Webler, T., Rakel, H., Dienel, P. C., and Johnson, B. (1993). "Public Participation in Decision Making: A Three-Step Procedure." *Policy Sciences, 26,* 204–205.

17. See Anderson, I.-E., Klüver, L., Bilderbeck, R., and Danielsen, O. (eds.). (1995). "Feasibility Study on New Awareness Initiatives: Studying the Possibilities to Implement Consensus Conferences and Scenario Workshops." [http://www.cordis.lu/interfaces/src/feasibil.htm]. Retrieved Oct. 31, 2003]; Grundahl, J. (1995). "The Danish Consensus Conference Model." In S. Joss and J. Durant (eds.), *Public Participation in Science: The Role of Consensus Conferences in Europe.* London: Science Museum; Joss (1998), "Danish Consensus Conferences"; Joss (2000), *Die Konsensuskonferenz in Theorie und Anwendung;* Joss, S., and Durant, J. (eds.). (1995). *Public Participation in Science: The Role of Consensus Conferences in Europe.* London: Science Museum.

18. Citizens select the presenters from a list of potential speakers developed by the conveners in conjunction with a steering committee. Commentators point out that in practice, citizens find this a difficult task, so conveners usually provide some assistance. See Grundahl (1995), "The Danish Consensus Conference Model," 39; Mayer, I., and Geurts, J. (1998). "Consensus Conference as Participatory Policy Analysis: A Methodological Contribution to the Social Management of Technology." In P. Wheale, R. von Schomberg, and P. Glasner (eds.), *Social Management of Genetic Engineering.* Aldershot, U.K.: Ashgate, 291.

19. Three-day consensus conferences are also common. See Klüver, L. (1995). "Consensus Conferences at the Danish Board of Technology." In S. Joss and J. Durant (eds.), *Public Participation in Science: The Role of Consensus Conferences in Europe.* London: Science Museum.

20. In the report-writing process, the citizens are not expected to reach a unanimous decision. The term *consensus* is a somewhat misleading descriptor of this model, because there is room for dissent. In Denmark, the idea is to see how close the panel can come to consensus, but it is not forced on them (Klüver [1995], "Consensus Conferences at the Danish Board of Technology," 46–47). Elsewhere, differences in opinion are recorded in the form

of majority and minority statements. In some cases, dissent provides interesting insights into potential social or demographic differences. For example, in the 2001 consensus conference in Germany on genetic diagnostics, all of the eleven female participants were against the introduction of pre-implantation genetic diagnostics (genetic testing performed on embryos in vitro before implantation). All the males except one supported the technology. Interestingly, this was a gender difference that had not yet surfaced in all of the expert committees and broader public discourse on the issue. See Schicktanz, S., and Naumann, J. (eds.). (2003). *Bürgerkonferenz: Streitfall Gendiagnostik* [Citizens' conference: Conflict over genetic diagnostics]. Opladen, Germany: Leske & Budrich.

21. Renn, O., and Webler, T. (1998). "Der kooperative Diskurs—Theoretische Grundlagen, Anforderungen, Möglichkeiten" [The cooperative discourse—Theoretical foundations, requirements, and opportunities]. In O. Renn, H. Kastenholz, P. Schild, and U. Wilhelm (eds.), *Abfall Politik im kooperativen Diskurs: Bürgerbeteiligung bei der Standortsuche für eine Deponie im Kanton Aargau* [Waste policy in cooperative discourse: Public participation in the search for a landfill site in Canton Aargau]. Zurich, Switzerland: VDF, 33–34.

22. Grundahl (1995), "The Danish Consensus Conference Model," 34.

23. In Denmark, facilitation and chairing are usually combined into one role, whereas in other countries, such as the United Kingdom and Australia, these roles are separated. See Grundahl (1995), "The Danish Consensus Conference Model," 34; Joss (2000), *Die Konsensuskonferenz in Theorie und Anwendung*, 24.

24. See Joss (2000), *Die Konsensuskonferenz in Theorie und Anwendung*, 22.

25. This was the case for the 1999 Australian consensus conference on gene technology in the food chain, according to interviews conducted by the author with steering committee members between November 2002 and March 2003. In the planning stages of the conference, various stakeholders on the steering committee championed the project within their own organizations and policy networks. See also Crombie, A., and Ducker, C. (2000). *Evaluation Report: Phase 2.* Report commissioned by the Consensus Conference Steering Committee of the First Australian Consensus Conference: Gene Technology in the Food Chain, Canberra, March 10–12, 1999. Available at http://genetechnology.chirp.com.au/concon.html.

26. The majority of literature on planning cells is in German, with the most detailed accounts provided by Dienel, P. C. (1997). *Die Planungszelle. Eine Alternative zur Establishment-Demokratie* [The planning cells: An alternative to establishment-democracy]. (4th ed. with status report.) Opladen, Germany: Westdeutscher Verlag; and Bongardt, H. (1999). *Die Planungszelle in Theorie und Anwendung* [The planning cell conference in theory and practice]. Stuttgart, Germany: Center for Technology Assessment. English articles on planning cells include Dienel, P. C. (1989). "Contributing to Social Decision Methodology: Citizens Reports on Technology Projects." In C. Vlek and G. Cvetkovich (eds.), *Social Decision Methodology for Technical Projects.* Dordrecht, Netherlands: Kluwer, 113–155; Dienel (1999), "Planning Cells"; Dienel and Renn (1995), "Planning Cells"; Renn and others (1984), "An Empirical Investigation of Citizens' Preferences"; Renn and others (1993), "Public Participation in Decision Making."

27. Dienel (1997), *Die Planungszelle*, 108.

28. Dienel (1999), "Planning Cells," 88.

29. 'Mad cow' disease (bovine spongiform encephalopathy, or BSE) is a fatal cattle disease that emerged in Britain in the mid-1980s. The consumption of affected meat has been linked to a new variant of the human neurological disease Creutzfeldt-Jacob disease (vCJD).

30. For more details on the Bavarian planning cells on consumer protection, see Bavarian Ministry for Environment, Health and Consumer Protection. (2002). "Bürgergutachten zum Verbraucherschutz" [Citizens' report on consumer protection]. [http://www.stmugv.bayern.de/de/verbraucherschutz/buergergutachten/buergergutachten.htm].

31. Hilmar Sturm, planning cells practitioner, Munich, personal communication, May 30, 2004.

32. Bongardt (1999), *Die Planungszelle in Theorie und Anwendung*, 9–10.

33. Dienel (1999), "Planning Cells," 88.

34. Dienel (1997), *Die Planungszelle*, 98.

35. The citizens received 130 Euro each for participating in a four-day planning cell on the topic of consumer protection in Bavaria (Englisch, R. [2002, Mar. 6] "Begeisterung ist unerwartet groß" [Enthusiasm is unexpectedly large]. *Erlanger Nachrichten*).

36. Dienel (1997), *Die Planungszelle*, 82.

37. Dienel (1999), "Planning Cells," 85–86.

38. Dienel (2002), *Die Planungszelle*, 279.

39. Hilmar Sturm, planning cell practitioner, Munich, personal communication, May 30, 2004.

40. Dienel (1989). "Contributing to Social Decision Methodology," 144–149.

41. Dienel (1999), "Planning Cells," 86. See also Thompson, S., and Hoggett, P. (2000). "The Emotional Dynamics of Deliberative Democracy." *Policy and Politics, 29*(3), 351–364.

42. Peter Dienel, interview with author, Wuppertal, Germany, Feb. 26, 2002.

43. Author interviews with planning cell practitioners Peter Dienel (Feb. 26, 2002, Wuppertal); Christian Weilmeier (Jan. 22, 2003, Munich); and Hilmar Sturm (Jan. 23, 2003, Munich).

44. In contrast, deliberative democrats usually promote collective rather than aggregated political outputs from a deliberative forum.

45. For a comparative discussion of planning cells and deliberative polls, see Price, V., and Neijens, P. (1998). "Deliberative Polls: Toward Improved Measures of 'Informed' Public Opinion?" *International Journal of Public Opinion Research, 10*(2), 145–176.

46. Details on how to plan both types of events are well documented. For planning cells, see Bongardt (1999), *Die Planungszelle in Theorie und Anwendung;* Dienel (1997), *Die Planungszelle;* Dienel (1999), "Planning Cells"; and Renn and others (1984), "An Empirical Investigation of Citizens' Preferences." For consensus conferences, see Einsiedel, E. F. (2000). "Consensus Conferences as Deliberative Democracy." *Science Communication, 21*(4), 323–343; Grundahl (1995), "The Danish Consensus Conference Model"; Joss (1998), "Danish Consensus Conferences"; Joss (2000), *Die Konsensuskonferenz in Theorie und Anwendung.*

47. The Danish Board of Technology also uses committees of experts, scenario workshops, and voting conferences. See Anderson, I.-E., and Jæger, B. (1999). "Scenario Workshops and Consensus Conferences: Towards More Democratic Decision Making." *Science and Public Policy, 26*(5), 331–340; and Klüver (1995), "Consensus Conferences at the Danish Board of Technology." See also Teknologirådet [The Danish Board of Technology]. (2005). "Methods." [http://www.tekno.dk/subpage.php3?survey=16&language=uk].

48. Joss (2000), *Die Konsensuskonferenz in Theorie und Anwendung,* 18–19.

49. Joss (2000), *Die Konsensuskonferenz in Theorie und Anwendung,* 21, states that outside of Denmark, consensus conferences have been conducted by a number of private and public institutions.

50. Author interviews with planning cell practitioners Peter Dienel (Feb. 26, 2002, Wuppertal); Christian Weilmeier (Jan. 22, 2003, Munich); and Hilmar Sturm (Jan. 23, 2003, Munich).

51. According to Dryzek, J. S., Downes, D., Hunold, C., Schlosberg, D., and Hernes, H.-K. (2003). *Green States and Social Movements: Environmentalism in the United States, United Kingdom,*

Germany and Norway. Oxford, U.K.: Oxford University Press, 1–2, the imperatives of the modern state include domestic order, survival, revenue generation, securing economic growth (accumulation), and legitimation.

52. Danish political culture has been strongly influenced by Danish priest, poet and philosopher Nicolai Grundtvig (1783–1872). Grundtvig encouraged a "people's enlightenment" (*folkeoplysning*) in which ordinary citizens participate in cooperatives and "folk high schools" to learn about public issues. See Cronberg, T. (1995). "Do Marginal Voices Shape Technology?" In S. Joss and J. Durant (eds.), *Public Participation in Science: The Role of Consensus Conferences in Europe.* London: Science Museum, 125; Klüver (1995), "Consensus Conferences at the Danish Board of Technology," 41.

53. Klüver (1995), "Consensus Conferences at the Danish Board of Technology," 43.

54. Joss (1998), "Danish Consensus Conferences."

55. Danish Board of Technology. (2002). "Consensus Conference." [http://www.tekno.dk/subpage.php3?article=468]. Retrieved May 15, 2004.

56. See The Loka Institute. (2004). "Danish-Style, Citizen-Based Deliberative 'Consensus Conferences' on Science & Technology Policy Worldwide." [http://www.loka.org/pages/worldpanels.htm]. Retrieved May 15, 2004.

57. For details on Western and non-Western experiences with consensus conferences, see note 56. On a regional experience with consensus conferencing in Canada, see Einsiedel, Jelsøe, and Breck (2001), "Publics and the Technology Table," 88.

58. According to Dienel (2002b), *Die Planungszelle,* 282–283, decision makers at the local government level are most willing to engage with the public.

59. Dienel (1999), "Planning Cells," 92.

60. For a discussion of the only U.S. experience with planning cells, see Dienel and Renn (1995), "Planning Cells"; Renn and others (1993), "Public Participation in Decision Making."

61. These figures represent averages drawn from Dienel's list of processes in Dienel (2002), *Die Planungszelle,* 280–282. See also Dienel, P. (2004). "Bisherige Bürgergutachten" [Previous citizens' reports]. [http://www2.uni-wuppertal.de/FB1/planungszelle/liste.html].

62. See Dienel (1997), *Die Planungszelle,* 83; Dienel (1999), "Planning Cells," 88.

63. Dienel, P. C. (2002, Apr.). "Die Planungszelle—Zur Praxis der Bürgerbeteiligung" [The planning cells—On the practice of public participation]. *FES-Analyse,* 6, observes that the learning that takes place in planning cells is much faster than that in schools or universities. He accounts for this by observing that the citizens take their task seriously, like they would if they were in a commercial situation, in love, or faced with a life-threatening situation.

64. The term *citizens' panel* is also used in some English publications; see for example Renn and others (1993), "Public Participation in Decision Making." Planning cells are also often incorrectly equated with citizens' juries; see note 4.

65. Hilmar Sturm, planning cells practitioner, Munich, personal communication, May 30, 2004. In German, the term *citizens' report* (*Bürgergutachten*), can refer to both the process and its outcomes.

66. This list is adapted from Guston's categories of impact in Guston (1999), "Evaluating the First U.S. Consensus Conference," 457–461—a schema he developed to evaluate the impact of the first U.S. consensus conference.

67. More analysis of impacts has been conducted on consensus conferences than on planning cells. See Einsiedel, Jelsøe, and Breck (2001), "Publics and the Technology Table"; Joss, S., and Bellucci, S. (eds.). (2002). *Participatory Technology Assessment: European Perspectives.* London: Centre for the Study of Democracy.

68. Citizen response rates vary from project to project. Consensus conference evaluations report response rates of 3 percent in Germany from random mailings (Zimmer, R. [2002, Feb.]. *Begleitende Evaluation der Bürgerkonferenz "Streitfall Gendiagnostik"* [Accompanying evaluation of the "Conflict over Genetic Diagnostics" citizens' conference]. Karlsruhe, Germany: Fraunhofer-Institut für Systemtechnik und Innovationsforschung, 11); about 6 percent in Denmark from random mailings (Anderson and Jæger [1999], "Scenario Workshops and Consensus Conferences," 335); and 12.5 percent in the United States from random phone calls (Guston [1999]. "Evaluating the First U.S. Consensus Conference," 455). For consensus conference recruitment via newspaper advertisements, response rates are reported as follows: 200 citizens in Australia (McKay, E. [1999]. *Evaluation Report: Phase 1.* Report commissioned by the Consensus Conference Steering Committee of the First Australian Consensus Conference: Gene Technology in the Food Chain, Canberra, March 10–12, 1999. Canberra: P. J. Dawson & Associates, 20); 323 citizens and 111 citizens for two different projects in the Netherlands (Mayer, I., de Vries, J., and Geurts, J. [1995]. "An Evaluation of the Effects of Participation in a Consensus Conference." In S. Joss and D. John [eds.], *Public Participation in Science: The Role of Consensus Conferences in Europe.* London: Science Museum, 112); and over 400 citizens in the United Kingdom (Joss, S. [1995]. "Evaluating Consensus Conferences: Necessity or Luxury?" In S. Joss and J. Durant [eds.], *Public Participation in Science: The Role of Consensus Conferences in Europe.* London: Science Museum, 101). For planning cell projects involving random mailings, response rates vary, for example, from 8 percent (Sturm, H., Weilmeier, C., and Roßkopf, K. [2002]. *Bürgergutachten zum Verbraucherschutz in Bayern* [Citizens' report for consumer protection in Bavaria]. Munich, Germany: Bayerisches Staatsministerium für Gesundheit, Ernährung und Verbraucherschutz, 29) to 20 percent (Renn and others [1984], "An Empirical Investigation of Citizens' Preferences," 27).

69. In neither the consensus conference nor planning cell model are the samples intended to be statistically representative of the community—an issue I explore later in this chapter. However, this is a claim that advocates tend to make more for planning cells than for consensus conferences. The literature reports that participants in planning cells come from a wide variety of social groups, even in the absence of stratified sampling. See Dienel (2002), "Die Planungszelle," 15–16; Dienel and Renn (1995), "Planning Cells"; Garbe, D. (1992). "Social Compatibility of Telecommunication Technologies." *Telecommunications Policy, 16*(8), 646–656; Renn and others (1984), "An Empirical Investigation of Citizens' Preferences," 27–29; Sturm, Weilmeier, and Roßkopf (2002), *Bürgergutachten zum Verbraucherschutz in Bayern,* 48–54. The only reported sampling bias is in relation to participants' occupations. One project reported overrepresentation of white-collar workers and also found that more students and retired people attended than self-employed people (Renn and others [1984], "An Empirical Investigation of Citizens' Preferences," 27–29). More recent projects however, report a diverse range of occupations (see for example, Sturm, Weilmeier, and Roßkopf [2002], *Bürgergutachten zum Verbraucherschutz in Bayern,* 249–254).

70. See Dienel (2002), "Die Planungszelle"; Einsiedel (2000), "Consensus Conferences as Deliberative Democracy"; Joss (1995), "Evaluating Consensus Conferences," 101–104; Zimmer (2002), *Begleitende Evaluation der Bürgerkonferenz "Streitfall Gendiagnostik,"* 14–18.

71. Several evaluations report how after participation in consensus conferences or planning cells, citizens have an increased awareness of the uncertainties and risks associated with policymaking as well as the limitations of expert knowledge. Citizens also report greater appreciation of the policymaking process and its social ramifications. See, for example,

Einsiedel (2000), "Consensus Conferences as Deliberative Democracy"; Guston (1999), "Evaluating the First U.S. Consensus Conference," 469–471; Mayer, de Vries, and Geurts (1995), "An Evaluation of the Effects of Participation in a Consensus Conference"; McKay (1999), *Evaluation Report: Phase 1*. Some studies report how citizens' preferences shift as a result of deliberation. See, for example, Dienel (2002), *Die Planungszelle*, 279; Mayer, de Vries, and Geurts (1995), "An Evaluation of the Effects of Participation in a Consensus Conference"; McKay (1999), *Evaluation Report: Phase 1*; Zimmer (2002), *Begleitende Evaluation der Bürgerkonferenz "Streitfall Gendiagnostik,"* 40–46.

72. See, for example, Einsiedel (2000), "Consensus Conferences as Deliberative Democracy"; Guston (1999), "Evaluating the First U.S. Consensus Conference"; Mayer and Geurts (1998), "Consensus Conference as Participatory Policy Analysis."

73. See, for example, Crombie and Ducker (2000), *Evaluation Report*, 24; Einsiedel (2000), "Consensus Conferences as Deliberative Democracy," 337.

74. See, for example, Einsiedel (2000), "Consensus Conferences as Deliberative Democracy," 336; Garbe, D. (1980). *Die Planungszelle und ihre Umwelt: Analyse des Beziehungsgefüges zwischen Verfahren, Teilnehmern und Planern* [Planning cells and their environment: Analysis of networks between processes, participants and planners]. Frankfurt am Main, Germany: Lang, 272–279; Zimmer (2002), *Begleitende Evaluation der Bürgerkonferenz "Streitfall Gendiagnostik,"* 47–48.

75. Several evaluations report overall positive feedback from participants. See, for example, Einsiedel (2000), "Consensus Conferences as Deliberative Democracy," 337–338; Garbe (1980), *Die Planungszelle und ihre Umwelt*, 257–266; Mayer, de Vries, and Geurts (1995), "An Evaluation of the Effects of Participation in a Consensus Conference," 293; McKay (1999), *Evaluation Report: Phase 1*. In some projects, citizens are overwhelmingly supportive of future deliberative forums. For example, after the 2001–2002 Bavarian planning cell project on consumer protection, 99.5 percent of participants said that they would recommend participating in such a process to others (Sturm, Weilmeier, and Roßkopf [2002], *Bürgergutachten zum Verbraucherschutz in Bayern*, 31–32). In other cases, where the involvement and commitment from decision makers was minimal, citizens conditioned their support for future deliberative forums by adding "if the government listened to the panel and acted on what we did" (Guston [1999], "Evaluating the First U.S. Consensus Conference," 471).

76. For a detailed discussion of the role of consensus conferences in the Danish parliament, see Joss (1998), "Danish Consensus Conferences."

77. See Einsiedel, Jelsøe, and Breck (2001), "Publics and the Technology Table"; Joss (1998), "Danish Consensus Conferences"; Joss (2000), *Die Konsensuskonferenz in Theorie und Anwendung*, 19.

78. This is the overall conclusion reached by Joss (1998), "Danish Consensus Conferences," who conducted extensive empirical research on the effects of consensus conferences on policy decisions and public debates in Denmark.

79. See, for example, Klüver (1995), "Consensus Conferences at the Danish Board of Technology," 44.

80. See Joss (1998), "Danish Consensus Conferences," 16–18; Klüver (1995), "Consensus Conferences at the Danish Board of Technology," 44–45. One Danish opinion poll revealed that 17 percent of the surveyed population ($n = 1000$) had heard of consensus conferences and could cite a number of different topics that the conferences had addressed (see Joss [1998], "Danish Consensus Conferences," 16–17).

81. See Joss (1998), "Danish Consensus Conferences."

82. This conclusion is drawn in evaluations in the United States (Guston [1999], "Evaluating the First U.S. Consensus Conference"); the Netherlands (Mayer and Geurts [1998], "Consensus Conference as Participatory Policy Analysis"); the United Kingdom (Joss [1995],

"Evaluating Consensus Conferences"); and in Australia and Canada (Einsiedel, Jelsøe, and Breck [2001],"Publics and the Technology Table").

83. For details on these and other international experiences with consensus conferences, see The Loka Institute (2004), "Danish-Style, Citizen-Based Deliberative 'Consensus Conferences.'"

84. This was the case for consensus conferences conducted in the United Kingdom on plant biotechnology; in the Netherlands on predictive human genetics (Mayer and Geurts, [1998], "Consensus Conference as Participatory Policy Analysis," 296); and in Germany on genetic diagnostics (interviews conducted by the author with several policy actors associated with this project in Berlin, Munich, Dresden, and Stuttgart between January and March 2003); see also Schicktanz and Naumann (2003), *Bürgerkonferenz;* Zimmer (2002), *Begleitende Evaluation der Bürgerkonferenz "Streitfall Gendiagnostik,"* 52–53.

85. This was the case for the Australian and Canadian consensus conferences on gene technology. See Crombie and Ducker (2000), *Evaluation Report,* v; Einsiedel, Jelsøe, and Breck (2001), "Publics and the Technology Table," 93–94; McDonald, J. (1999). "Mechanisms for Public Participation in Environmental Policy Development: Lessons from Australia's First Consensus Conference." *Environmental and Planning Law Journal, 16*(3), 258–266.

86. In Denmark, consensus conferences often result in "more than a hundred press clippings" (Klüver [1995], "Consensus Conferences at the Danish Board of Technology," 44). This figure has been matched by some experiences outside of Denmark. For example, the 1994 U.K. consensus conference on plant biotechnology resulted in 152 news items (including 128 newspaper articles) (Joss [1995], "Evaluating Consensus Conferences," 95); the 1999 Australian consensus conference on gene technology in the food chain resulted in 287 media items (including 53 newspaper articles) (Crombie and Ducker [2000], *Evaluation Report,* 37). Other consensus conferences have struggled to attract media attention—for example, the 2001 German consensus conference on genetic diagnostics was covered by only 37 news items (Zimmer [2002], *Begleitende Evaluation der Bürgerkonferenz "Streitfall Gendiagnostik"*). Media coverage was also very poor for the U.S. conference on telecommunications and the future of democracy in 1997; only 5 news items were recorded (Guston, [1999], "Evaluating the First U.S. Consensus Conference," 472–473).

87. See, for example, Guston (1999), "Evaluating the First U.S. Consensus Conference," 473; and Mayer and Geurts (1998), "Consensus Conference as Participatory Policy Analysis," 295–296.

88. See, for example, Guston (1999), "Evaluating the First U.S. Consensus Conference," 464–469; and Crombie and Ducker (2000), *Evaluation Report,* 21–24.

89. See, for example, Garbe (1980), *Die Planungszelle und ihre Umwelt.*

90. Dienel (1999), "Planning Cells," 91.

91. Dienel and Renn (1995), "Planning Cells," 130–131.

92. See Renn and others (1984), "An Empirical Investigation of Citizens' Preferences."

93. Practitioners in Germany report that since the mid-1990s, there has been increasing interest in planning cells from politicians and agencies at federal and state levels (author interviews with planning cell practitioners Peter Dienel [Feb. 26, 2002, Wuppertal]; Christian Weilmeier [Jan. 22, 2003, Munich]; and Hilmar Sturm [Jan. 23, 2003, Munich]). Since 2000, a number of state governments in Germany have committed resources to planning cell projects. For example, the Bavarian state government has commissioned two large planning cell projects, each involving over four hundred citizens. One of the projects, undertaken in 2001–2002, was on consumer protection; the other project, completed in 2004, was on health reform (see Bavarian Ministry for Environment, Health and Con-

sumer Protection. [2004]. "Bürgergutachten für Gesundheit" [Citizens' report for health]. [http://www.stmugv.bayern.de/de/gesundheit/buergergut_ges.htm]). Similarly, in the state of Rhineland-Pfalz, the Ministry for Work, Social Affairs, Family and Health has commissioned a series of planning cells to address the issue of demographic change in an aging society (see Rhineland-Pfalz Ministry for Work, Social Issues, Family and Health. [2004]. "Bürgergutachten: Miteinander der Generationen in einer alternden Gesellschaft" [Citizens' report: Together as generations in an aging society]. [http://www.masfg.rlp.de/Funktionsnavigation/Dokumente/Buergergutachten/Gutachten_Inhalt.htm]).

94. Dienel and Renn (1995), "Planning Cells," 135–136; Renn and others (1993), "Public Participation in Decision Making," 204–205.

95. Whereas citizens in German planning cell projects tend to welcome the idea of a structured participatory process, the citizens in the U.S. project "distrust[ed] prefabricated participation models and suspected[ed] hidden agendas" (Renn and others [1993], "Public Participation in Decision Making," 205).

96. See Dienel (2002), *Die Planungszelle*, 291–293; Dienel and Renn (1995), "Planning Cells," 134–135.

97. Dienel and Renn (1995), "Planning Cells," 132–134.

98. See Joss (2000), *Die Konsensuskonferenz in Theorie und Anwendung*, 15; Renn and others (1984), "An Empirical Investigation of Citizens' Preferences," 43.

99. Cost is one of the largest impediments to further expansion of planning cells and consensus conferences (Dienel [1999], "Planning Cells," 91; Zimmer (2002), *Begleitende Evaluation der Bürgerkonferenz "Streitfall Gendiagnostik,"* 61). According to Dienel (2002b), *Die Planungszelle*, 280, a number of planning cell projects have collapsed during preparations due to a sudden lack of resources from the commissioning body.

100. These figures do not include the salaries of the project conveners, who may work on preparations for six to eighteen months. They represent averages from figures found in the literature. For consensus conferences, see Guston (1999), "Evaluating the First U.S. Consensus Conference," 454; Klüver (1995), "Consensus Conferences at the Danish Board of Technology," 47; Zimmer (2002), *Begleitende Evaluation der Bürgerkonferenz "Streitfall Gendiagnostik,"* 34–35. For planning cells, see Bongardt (1999), *Die Planungszelle in Theorie und Anwendung*, 18–21; Dienel (1999), "Planning Cells," 91. Costs vary significantly, depending on the travel distances. In the case of planning cells, costs are reduced when there are fewer planning cell locations (Hilmar Sturm, planning cell practitioner, personal communication, Munich, May 14, 2004).

101. For more discussion on the limitations of the models discussed in this chapter, see Hennen, L. (1999). "Participatory Technology Assessment: A Response to Technical Modernity?" *Science and Public Policy, 26*(5), 303–312; Renn and others (1984), "An Empirical Investigation of Citizens' Preferences," 45; Rippe, K. P., and Schaber, P. (1999). "Democracy and Environmental Decision Making." *Environmental Values, 8*(1), 75–88; Seiler, H.-J. (1995). "Review of Planning Cells: Problems of Legitimation." In O. Renn, T. Webler, and P. Wiedemann (eds.), *Fairness and Competence in Citizen Participation*. Dordrecht, Netherlands: Kluwer, 141–155.

102. Dienel and Renn (1995), "Planning Cells," 128–129; Renn and others (1993), "Public Participation in Decision Making," 207.

103. Mayer and Geurts (1998), "Consensus Conference as Participatory Policy Analysis," 290.

104. Anderson and Jæger (1999), "Scenario Workshops and Consensus Conferences," 334.

105. Dienel and Renn (1995), "Planning Cells," 129–130.

106. For example, the 1999 Australian consensus conference on gene technology in the food chain was instigated by a not-for-profit community organization, the Australian Consumers' Association. See Renouf, C. (1999). "Rebirthing Democracy: The Experience of the First Australian Consensus Conference." *Consuming Interest, 79,* 16–19.

107. There have been some instances in which citizens have maintained informal contact among themselves (author interviews with planning cell practitioners Peter Dienel [Feb. 26, 2002, Wuppertal]; Christian Weilmeier [Jan. 22, 2003, Munich]; and Hilmar Sturm [Jan. 23, 2003, Munich]). In the case of the 2001–2002 Bavarian planning cell project, a group of citizens has been formally reactivated to provide further advice to the Bavarian government on consumer protection issues. See Gesellschaft für Bürgergutachten [Society for Citizens Report]. (2003). "Detail-Bürgergutachten zur Lebensmittelqualität im erweiterten Europa" [Detailed citizens' report on food quality in a broader Europe].[http://www .buergergutachten.com/Buergergutachten/DetailBG%20Lebensmittelqualit%E4t.pdf]. Retrieved Feb. 5, 2005.

108. Several democratic theorists have drawn attention to the tensions between deliberation in structured procedures and deliberation in the public sphere. Some argue that deliberation in formal venues can ostracize those unfamiliar with structured debate or poised speech (Sanders, L. M. [1997]. "Against Deliberation." *Political Theory, 25*(3), 347–376; Young, I. M. [1996]. "Communication and the Other: Beyond Deliberative Democracy." In S. Benhabib (ed.), *Democracy and Difference: Contesting Boundaries of the Political.* Princeton, N.J.: Princeton University Press, 120–135), or it can exclude oppressed groups who may need to assert their self-interest (Mansbridge, J. [2003]. "Practice-Thought-Practice." In A. Fung and E. O. Wright (eds.), *Deepening Democracy: Institutional Innovation in Empowered Participatory Governance.* London: Verso, 175–199. For a good overview of the tensions and differences between deliberation in formal procedures and deliberation in the public sphere, see Fraser, N. (1992). "Rethinking the Public Sphere: A Contribution to the Critique of Actually Existing Democracy." In C. Calhoun (ed.), *Habermas and the Public Sphere.* Cambridge, Mass.: MIT Press, 109–142; Young, I. M. (2001). "Activist Challenges to Deliberative Democracy." *Political Theory, 29*(5), 670–690.

109. Joss (1998), "Danish Consensus Conferences," 21.

110. On legitimacy problems with planning cells, see Renn and others (1984), "An Empirical Investigation of Citizens' Preferences"; Renn and others (1993), "Public Participation in Decision Making"; Seiler (1995), "Review of Planning Cells"; on legitimacy issues in relation to consensus conferences, see Cronberg (1995), "Do Marginal Voices Shape Technology?" For a discussion on legitimacy problems in deliberative democracy and deliberative designs in general, see Parkinson, J. (2003). "Legitimacy Problems in Deliberative Democracy." *Political Studies, 51*(1), 180–196; Parkinson, J. (2003). "The Legitimation of Deliberative Democracy." Unpublished doctoral dissertation, Australian National University, Canberra.

111. The reactions of different policy actors to planning cell projects are discussed by Dienel and Renn (1995), "Planning Cells"; Renn and others (1993), "Public Participation in Decision Making"; and Garbe (1980), *Die Planungszelle und ihre Umwelt,* chaps. 7 and 8.

112. The term *expert activist* is borrowed from Bang, H., and Sørenson, E. (2001). "The Everyday Maker: Building Political Rather Than Social Capital." In P. Dekker and E. Uslaner (eds.), *Social Capital and Participation in Everyday Life.* London: Routledge, 148–161.

113. This research draws on my doctoral dissertation, which investigated the responses of stakeholders and policy elites to four different deliberative designs (two in Germany and two

in Australia): two consensus conferences, one planning cell project, and a citizens' jury (Hendriks, C. M. [2004]. "Public Deliberation and Interest Organisations: A Study of Responses to Lay Citizen Engagement in Public Policy." Unpublished doctoral dissertation, Australian National University, Canberra). Other researchers who have touched on similar issues include Dienel (2002), "Die Planungszelle," 19–20; Dienel and Renn (1995), "Planning Cells," 27–28; Garbe (1980), *Die Planungszelle und ihre Umwelt*, 215–221.

114. For more on this tension, see Hendriks (2004), "Public Deliberation and Interest Organisations"; Hendriks, C. M. (2002). "Institutions of Deliberative Democratic Processes and Interest Groups: Roles, Tensions and Incentives." *Australian Journal of Public Administration, 61*(1), 64–75.

115. See Hendriks (2004), "Public Deliberation and Interest Organisations," chap. 9.

116. Grundahl (1995), "The Danish Consensus Conference Model," 39; Klüver (1995), "Consensus Conferences at the Danish Board of Technology," 46.

117. According to Parkinson (2003), "The Legitimation of Deliberative Democracy," 108, a sample size of at least 399 is required in order to achieve a statistically representative sample that reflects gender proportions at a 95 percent confidence level. This is to say nothing of the sample sizes needed to achieve the same confidence level for other demographic characteristics such as age, education, occupation, and ethnicity.

118. For example, Smith and Wales prefer to highlight the panel's inclusivity as opposed to its representativeness (Smith, G., and Wales, C. [2000]. "Citizens' Juries and Deliberative Democracy." *Political Studies, 48*(1), 56–57). Elsewhere, Smith argues, "It is important that citizens are not necessarily seen as representing 'people like them' in any strong sense" (Smith, G. [2000]. "Toward Deliberative Institutions." In M. Saward (ed.), *Democratic Innovation: Deliberation, Representation and Association.* London: Routledge, 34).

119. Sunstein, C. (2002, June). "The Law of Group Polarization." *Journal of Political Philosophy,* pp. 175–195; Sunstein, C. R. (2000). "Deliberative Trouble? Why Groups Go to Extremes." *Yale Law Journal, 110*(1), 71–119.

120. Renn, O. (1999). "A Model for an Analytic-Deliberative Process in Risk Management." *Environmental Science & Technology, 33*(18), 3049–3055; Renn and others (1993), "Public Participation in Decision Making."

121. Carson, L. (1999, Aug. 31). "Random Selection: Achieving Representation in Planning." Paper presented at the Alison Burton Memorial Lecture, Royal Australian Planning Institute, Canberra. [http://activedemocracy.net/articles.htm]. Retrieved Jan. 4, 2005.

122. In some projects, Web sites have been used to promote a particular deliberative project—for example, the 1999 Canadian consensus conference on food biotechnology (Einsiedel, Jelsøe, and Breck [2001], "Publics and the Technology Table," 330). Web forums have also been used in conjunction with some projects; for example, during the weeks before and after the 1999 Australian consensus conference on gene technology in the food chain, an unfacilitated on-line discussion forum was hosted on the Australian Broadcasting Corporation's Web site for the conference. This forum provided an on-line deliberative space in which members of the broader public could interact with the conference speakers and the lay citizens. See Australian Broadcasting Corporation (1999), *"Waiter, There Is a Gene in My Food. . . . "*

123. For more on the North Carolina Citizens' Technology Forum, see Center for Information Society Studies, North Carolina State University. (2002). "Sponsored Research." [http://www.ncsu.edu/chass/communication/ciss/sponsored.html#ncctf]. Retrieved Feb. 7, 2005.

124. The expression *alibi participation* is adapted from the word *Alibiveranstaltung*, which was used by one of my German interviewees.

125. The "21st Century Nanotechnology Research and Development Act" establishes the National Nanotechnology Program and charges it with ensuring that "ethical, legal, environmental, and other appropriate societal concerns, including the potential use of nanotechnology in enhancing human intelligence and in developing artificial intelligence which exceeds human capacity, are considered during the development of nanotechnology by . . . providing . . . for public input and outreach to be integrated into the Program by the convening of regular and ongoing public discussions, through mechanisms such as citizens' panels, consensus conferences, and educational events, as appropriate" (Public Law 108–153, Dec. 3, 2003). See Library of Congress. (2004). "Thomas: Legislative Information on the Internet." [http://thomas.loc.gov].

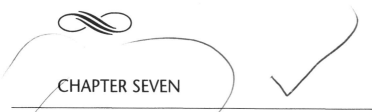

CHAPTER SEVEN

CITIZENS JURIES

Creating a Trustworthy Voice of the People

Ned Crosby, Doug Nethercut

On the morning of January 14, 1993, twenty-four randomly selected people from all over the United States were meeting for the fifth day in Washington, D.C., to discuss the federal budget. They had heard from a variety of conservative witnesses gathered by former congressman Vin Weber and liberal witnesses gathered by Robert Kuttner, editor of *The American Prospect*. The participants' task was to balance the budget. They had cut spending by $44 billion from what incoming President Clinton proposed, but they wanted to keep the deficit at less than $200 billion. To do this, they voted 17 to 7 for a $70 billion tax increase.

"I never dreamed that I'd make the choice of raising my taxes," said Philip Grant, a commercial vehicle inspector from Klamath Falls, Oregon. "But we have to sacrifice now for the sake of our kids."[1]

The twenty-four people were meeting in the first national Citizens Jury, conducted by the Jefferson Center, a nonprofit organization based in Minneapolis, Minnesota. As in all such projects, the jurors had been stratified in order to be a microcosm of the population from which they were drawn. A national survey that was used as a basis for selecting the jurors showed that 45 percent of the public wanted federal taxes and spending to go down; thus, juror selection ensured that eleven of the twenty-four participants held that attitude, with only four of the jurors at the start of the project favoring raises in taxes and spending. Such stratification by attitude does not determine the final result, since a Citizens Jury gives jurors the opportunity to explore deeply held views and change them in light of evidence presented at the hearings.

Washington Post columnist William Raspberry commented that by deliberating carefully on a matter of public importance, "this Citizens Jury has done what the Founding Fathers intended the Congress to do." He added, "The politicians can't do what has to be done. The people can't afford not to."[2]

Origins and Features of Citizens Juries

The Citizens Jury® process was invented by Ned Crosby in 1971 while writing a doctoral dissertation on social ethics. By 1974, he had given up on most of the moral philosophy but decided that the "citizens committees," as he originally called them, were worth testing to see whether they could empower a microcosm of the public to deal effectively with complex issues.[3] Crosby set up the Jefferson Center in 1974 to do research and development on new democratic processes. By 2002, the center had conducted thirty-one Citizens Jury projects in the United States. Over two hundred citizens juries have been conducted in Britain, Australia, and a few other countries since 1996. The center maintains quality control over the process in the United States through a trademark of the name. This trademark does not apply abroad, and the citizens juries run there have been of variable quality.[4] This chapter deals only with the Citizens Jury process as conducted by the Jefferson Center.

Crosby's original aim was to create a process that would enhance reason and empathy among citizens as they discussed a public policy matter or evaluated candidates. Over the ensuing years, the Jefferson Center board and staff aimed at conducting a high-quality process, even when this made it expensive and difficult to sell to decision makers.

Basic Elements of the Citizens Jury Process

In the 1970s, the Jefferson Center staff hoped that high-quality evaluations could be done of different methods for promoting reasonable discussions and creating empathy among the participants. Unfortunately, the center was never able to raise sufficient funds to set up rigorous quantitative evaluations. Instead, staff used common sense and the comments of the randomly selected participants to create what appeared to them to be the best process. Years of innovation and refinement have made clear that seven elements go into the design of any successful Citizens Jury process:

Microcosm of the community. The goal in bringing randomly selected citizens together is to construct a microcosm of the community (for example, a city, county, or nation) from which they were drawn. What evolved is a method for stratifying those selected so that they resemble their community in terms of age, education, gender, geographic location of their residence, and race. Participants were often stratified by political attitudes as well. To get a good acceptance rate from those approached, it is necessary to pay a decent day's wages. For a project in 2001, for example, the jurors were paid $150 a day for their participation.

As large a group as possible, consistent with good deliberation. Small groups are not as impressive to policymakers as large ones, but the center was determined not to let good deliberation suffer. It was decided that twenty-four people is the largest group that is still able to have good deliberation at the plenary level. Small-group discussions of four to six people are also an integral part of the Citizens Jury process. Multiple juries are also possible as part of a single project. In the 1980s, the Jefferson Center conducted one project with five twelve-person juries and another with eight twelve-person juries.[5]

High-quality information. During the first ten years of experimentation, it became clear that the best way to present information to the randomly selected jurors is to have witnesses express their own views, rather than relying on written information or even on staff presentations summarizing different points of view. It is also important to give jurors ample time to question the witnesses directly.

High-quality deliberation. The Jefferson Center developed a practice in which skilled facilitation is central, in order to ensure a good dialogue. The facilitators aim to strike a balance between a discussion open enough for the jurors to express themselves freely yet controlled enough so that jurors focus on the question at hand and no juror dominates the discussions. Witnesses are required to reserve ample time to answer jurors' questions and are helped to give brief and direct answers. Facilitators must be carefully trained in order to perform their tasks properly.

Minimizing staff biases and avoiding outside manipulations. Considerable effort was given to minimizing staff biases, even to the point of controlling the body language of the facilitators. A critical element in monitoring staff bias is to have the jurors evaluate staff at the end of the project.[6] Also, efforts were made to be sure that jurors were able to express their final recommendations in their own words and review the final report before it was made public.

Fair agenda and hearings. The Jefferson Center came to rely on outside advisory committees that represented a broad range of views to help set the agenda for a Citizens Jury and to advise on selecting witnesses. The center also learned through trial and error how to train facilitators to enhance dialogue among the participants without introducing biases.

Sufficient time to study the matter. By the end of the 1980s, the typical Citizens Jury was a five-day event. Virtually no jurors in any project have complained that five days is too long, whereas many have complained that it is too short. We would have liked to try out projects lasting longer than a week, but it was clear from juror comments that most of them would not have accepted an invitation to participate for more than a week. We did not want to conduct projects in which the jurors were largely students, unemployed, or retired. If deliberative methods become more widely used and more influential, longer projects may become possible with groups that still are a microcosm of their community.

Additional Considerations When Designing a Citizens Jury

The central dilemma in designing a Citizens Jury is how to structure the event so that it can both have an impact on public policy and empower a microcosm of the public to do its best job of producing sound policy recommendations in the public interest.[7] To influence public policy, an event should either have a commitment from policymakers or receive wide media coverage, or both. The steps taken to gain influence, however, may conflict with what is needed to produce high-quality results. The media are much more likely to pay attention to an event with one thousand or more citizens that lasts a day than a five-day event with twenty-four citizens. Sometimes a day is enough to produce a solid result, but many public policy questions are so complex that even five days are barely enough. Public officials are often tempted to require agendas and witness lists that avoid policy questions that might embarrass them or their major supporters.

Convening a Citizens Jury project is also a balancing act. Not only must there be an agenda that is satisfactory to the primary stakeholders (most or all of whom should be represented on the advisory committee), but it is also important to make sure that the jurors have some say over the conduct of the hearings. Jurors should be given enough of a say over how the event is conducted that they are sure the public interest is served, without their having so much control that they can overturn the fair balance of witnesses worked out in advance of the hearings.

Jurors should have some control over the style of facilitation, which can range from one that is rather tightly controlled in terms of who talks and for how long to one where the facilitator is much more relaxed about how long jurors can take in asking their questions, how often one can speak up during any session, and how long witnesses can take in answering questions. Jurors should also be able to request an additional witness or two or ask that a few witnesses be recalled.

Jurors must be welcomed to the process and made to feel at home. It takes an hour or more to explain the basics of the process, outline the issue to be studied, and allow the jurors to introduce themselves and ask questions. For the two national Citizens Jury projects, in which all the jurors arrived the evening before the event started, this introduction took place at that time so that the full five days could be devoted to the issue under consideration.

The Jefferson Center tried in the 1980s to figure out steps that could be taken to ensure that the recommendations of the jurors would be acted on by those sponsoring the Citizens Jury project. It is very difficult, however, to lobby for the recommendations of a Citizens Jury. The center's staff was not well trained to do this, the nonprofit status of the center was a hindrance, and the jurors' recommendations were too static to fit in well with the quick moves needed to lobby effectively for a bill. As spokespeople for a cause, jurors with no ax to grind could not do nearly as well as the "poster children" that play a large role in the media and legislative discussions of public policy. Recommendations to agencies or local governments failed to have much impact for similar reasons.[8]

History and Impact of Citizens Juries

There were four main stages in the work of the Jefferson Center. The first was from 1974 through 1983, when the basics of the Citizens Jury process were tested and refined. Crosby worked alone for half of this time and with part-time staff for the rest. The first Citizens Jury project that was used to evaluate candidates based on their stands on issues was tested in a low-profile project in 1976 in which jurors evaluated Ford versus Carter. Two mature law students acted as advocates for the two candidates.[9]

The second stage was the growth of Citizens Jury projects on issues. These included a 1984 project on agriculture and its impact on water quality (conducted for a sponsoring group of eleven Minnesota state agencies and nonprofit organizations) and two national Citizens Juries in 1993, one on the federal budget and the other on the Clinton health care plan. Both of the national juries took place in Washington, D.C., and featured prominent advocates and witnesses (for example, Ira Magaziner, director of health care planning under Clinton, testified for an hour). The White House informed the center through back channels that if the jurors "did a good job" in considering the Clinton health care plan, they would be invited to the White House. Apparently, a 19–5 vote against the Clinton health care plan did not constitute a good job. In spite of significant efforts to get extensive media coverage, the national projects failed to attract much media attention. William Raspberry wrote an op-ed article for the *Washington Post,* praising the federal budget project, and Roger Mudd hosted an hour-long public television show on the health care project. Beyond that, however, there was scant coverage.

The third stage, from 1989 through 1994, overlapped the second stage and was marked by the growth of interest in Citizens Jury projects to evaluate candidates based on their stands on issues. The Jefferson Center teamed with the League of Women Voters to conduct Citizens Jury projects to evaluate candidates in the 1989 mayoral race in St. Paul, Minnesota; the 1990 gubernatorial race in Minnesota; and the 1992 U.S. Senate race in Pennsylvania between Lynn Yaekel and Arlen Specter. The 1992 project attracted a great deal of media attention and was highly praised in editorials and op-ed pieces in the *Pittsburgh Post-Gazette*, *Philadelphia Inquirer*, and *Washington Post*.

Unfortunately, the Internal Revenue Service (IRS) intervened in 1993 and claimed that the Jefferson Center was in violation of rules regarding the involvement of 501(c)(3) nonprofit organizations in electoral activities. The center fought the claim vigorously, but in 1996, the IRS finally ruled that the center could no longer conduct projects to evaluate candidates. This was a considerable blow, since it was clear that voters found the findings and recommendations of Citizens Juries useful. Research on the 1990 project showed that it had the potential to change 5 to 10 percent of the votes cast in that election.[10] Regrettably, this potential response by voters was precisely what concerned the IRS. Electoral relevance, it appears, is taxable.

The final stage of the Jefferson Center's activities was from 1994 through 2002. During this time, sixteen projects were conducted on topics ranging from welfare reform (sponsored by congressman Tim Penny) to property tax reform (sponsored by the Minnesota Department of Revenue), hog farming (sponsored by Carleton and St. Olaf colleges), school bonding (sponsored by the Orono [Minnesota] School District), and global climate change (sponsored by the U.S. Environmental Protection Agency).

Although many of these were high-quality projects, it became clear over time that the center was not getting repeat customers. In spite of considerable marketing efforts and the development of additional services besides the Citizens Jury process, it was clear that the work of the center was not having a large enough impact on public policy to warrant its continuation. By 2002, the Citizens Jury process was alive and well in other nations but not in the United States. One reason for this was the determination of the Jefferson Center not to water down the process by running inexpensive versions of it.[11] Therefore, the center closed its offices and let its staff go, although it has kept its Web site in order to provide a historical archive, guidelines for conducting juries, and highlights of interesting Citizens Jury projects in other countries.

The closing of the Jefferson Center was not the end of the Citizens Jury process in the United States. Efforts are now under way to institutionalize the Citizens Jury model in order to bring trustworthy information to voters. Unlike the projects of the 1990s, this new effort will focus on the evaluation of ballot initiatives rather than candidates (see www.cirwa.com). This is discussed in more detail in the next section.

Future Directions

In the United States, a Citizens Jury should be used to make recommendations on specific policies only when there are sponsors who clearly want such input and are willing and able to act on the citizens' findings. Thus, a challenge for the Citizens Jury process—and, indeed, for any deliberative method—is to find powerful sponsors who are committed to a high-quality participatory process.

The 2004 Citizens' Assembly on Electoral Reform in British Columbia shows what can be done when there is a powerful and committed sponsor (see http://www.citizensassembly.bc.ca/public). The Citizens' Assembly consisted of 160 randomly selected voters who spent ten weekends in 2004 learning about different voting systems. After hearing public commentary, they discussed several voting methods and decided by a vote of 146 to 7 to recommend a novel kind of single transferable vote, adapted to the needs of British Columbia. The method they recommended is a proportional voting system that is a variation of the single transferable vote method. Rather than marking an x beside one name, voters number all candidates from most favorite to least favorite. If a voter's top choice is not elected or has more votes than necessary to be elected, the votes are redistributed to the second choice. The aim of this method is to make all votes count. This recommendation will be placed before the voters in British Columbia in May 2005 as a referendum. Although the Canadian project might be improved by using some of the methods of the Citizens Jury process to examine key questions that arise during deliberation, the project as it stands is breaking new ground in empowering citizens who meet in a deliberative format.

For those who care about significantly changing the American political system, the most important aspect of the Citizens Jury process is bringing trustworthy information to voters in a way that has a significant impact on election results. Since 1997, Crosby has been designing ways to institutionalize the Citizens Jury process to do this.[12] The main method under consideration is the Citizens Initiative Review, which is designed to use citizens panels (the generic name for the Citizens Jury process) to review initiatives in any of the twenty-four states that allow voter initiatives and referenda. Activities are now under way to put Citizens Initiative Review in place in Washington state (or possibly just in King County, where Seattle is located). The Citizens Initiative Review would operate as an independent commission working out of the Office of the Secretary of State. Each initiative that is placed on the ballot would be reviewed by a separate citizens panel, conducted according to the Citizens Jury model. It is intended that this commission be funded through a specific amount taken out of the interest on Washington state's general fund.

If the evaluation of ballot initiatives is successful, then efforts should be made to institutionalize the evaluation of candidates based on their stands on issues. A method for doing this has been designed so that it will be more powerful than the Citizens Jury projects on elections that were conducted by the Jefferson Center, yet conducted in a way that meets the objections of the IRS.[13] This proposal is several years away from being enacted, but it holds the potential for powerfully influencing the election of governors and, ultimately, U.S. senators. This means that more than thirty years after its invention, there is exciting potential for the Citizens Jury process to form the basis of a powerful new electoral reform.

Notes

1. Citizens Jury 1993. (1993). *America's Tough Choices.* Minneapolis, Minn.: Jefferson Center, 2. This is the report on the 1993 Citizens Jury project on the federal budget.
2. Raspberry, W. *Washington Post,* Jan. 23, 1993, op-ed article.
3. Crosby's original goal was to create a social ethics based on the approach of negative utilitarianism (the view in ethics that we should help first those who hurt the most). He hoped to create a more sophisticated measure of well-being than those used by most utilitarian philosophers, given the knowledge of psychometrics that he had gained from writing what was essentially a master's thesis for Paul Meehl, the creator of one of the four methods for validating a psychological test. But Crosby was unable to find measures that were both cost-effective and valid. At the same time, he became taken with the ordinary language philosophy of Wittgenstein. This led him to believe that those using ordinary language with an eye to justifying their positions could come up with reasonable positions on public policy matters. Why not, therefore, randomly select a small group of people and have them dialogue about public policy matters in a reasonable way? Also, there are many studies in social psychology that show the irrationality of small groups of people under certain group dynamics. Accordingly, the discussions were structured to minimize such dynamics.
4. The planning cell, invented by Peter Dienel in 1969 or 1970, is remarkably similar to the Citizens Jury process and has been run under fairly good quality control (see Chapter Six). Over 150 planning cells have been run in Germany, with as many as 24 cells convened under one project. The spread of citizens' juries in Britain came about when the Institute for Public Policy Research of London issued a booklet on it in 1994, after visits by its staff to Dienel and the Jefferson Center. The trademark on Citizens Jury® was useful in 2002 in preventing a movie named *Citizens Jury,* starring Jerry Springer, from being made.

5. In 1984, the Jefferson Center used five twelve-person Citizens Juries to examine the impacts of agriculture on water quality for a steering committee of eleven state agencies and nongovernmental organizations. In 1986–1987, the center used eight twelve-person Citizens Juries to examine the question of whether there should be clinics in high schools to help prevent teen pregnancy and AIDS. This project was requested by the Health and Human Services Committee of the Minnesota Senate.

6. The Jefferson Center's evaluations go back to 1981, one of the longest records of participant evaluation that exists. See www.jefferson-center.org.

7. Those wishing to learn more about design can download a detailed handbook from the Jefferson Center Web site at www.jefferson-center.org. Since 1996, many people around the world have designed citizens' juries on their own, with no reference to the Jefferson Center model.

8. It would be interesting to see a careful analysis of the attempts in the last half of the twentieth century to get recommendations from deliberative methods implemented. The Center for the Study of Democratic Institutions was established by prominent people in the 1960s yet was essentially out of business by the end of the 1970s. (It did not have much interest in deliberative methods, but was the first think tank on democracy to be set up in the United States). The Public Agenda Foundation and the Roosevelt Center were major players in the 1980s. But over the years, the former turned more to doing focus groups and polls for various interest groups. The latter spent $17 million in seven years and then went out of business. Was the relative lack of influence of these efforts due to an unfriendly political climate, or were there opportunities that were missed?

9. During this time, the center also experimented with extended policy discussions, which were intended to clarify areas of agreement and disagreement among experts on key policy issues. Prominent legislators sponsored two projects: one on U.S. government–held grain reserves (sponsored by congressmen Paul Findley and Bob Bergland) and the other on serious juvenile offenders (sponsored by key legislators from the Minnesota legislature). This process succeeded in terms of the interesting dialogues that were developed between experts but turned out to be sophisticated enough so that it was of little use to legislators, who were too busy to ponder the results. It was also too slow for the rapidly evolving legislative scene, and the center had too little clout to get attention paid to the results.

10. These findings were based on a survey of 450 individuals who were sent the jurors' recommendations before the election and then surveyed after. For details, see www.jefferson-center.org.

11. The success of the Planungszelle (planning cell), especially in projects conducted in the last decade in Hanover and Regensburg, raises the question of whether Germany has a political culture that is more friendly to processes such as the Citizens Jury and Planungszelle or whether Peter Dienel and his associates simply did a better job of marketing.

12. Crosby has received significant help in this from Nethercut in 1997 and 2001 and from many people in Washington state from 1999 to the present.

13. For more about this proposal, see www.healthydemocracy.org.

CHAPTER EIGHT

ADAPTING AND COMBINING DELIBERATIVE DESIGNS

Juries, Polls, and Forums

Lyn Carson, Janette Hartz-Karp

I was a facilitator for a massive consultation called Dialogue with the City *in Perth, Western Australia, in September 2003. The event was like no other I'd experienced. I'd been at Australia's first deliberative poll in 1999, where 350 people wandered around Old Parliament House in Canberra, and I considered that to be an impressively large consultation. But this Dialogue with the City event drew 1,100 people into a single room—a huge, cavernous passenger terminal at the Fremantle port. The minister for planning and infrastructure stayed involved during the entire day, reiterating that the outcomes of this dialogue process would guide the future planning of Perth and result in "action on the ground."*

I was part of one small group linked, like all the other groups, to a central computer via individual laptops. I recall at one stage the collective frustration and excitement of our table of eight people, who had come from such disparate backgrounds, each with their strong views. They were standing over a one-meter-by-two-meter colored map of Perth and its environs. In their hands, each person held rectangular and square stickers representing different urban forms, housing densities, commercial and industrial centers. Together, they had to address the challenge of finding a place for the 750,000 new people, 370,000 new homes, and employment opportunities that will be needed over the next twenty years. They had to place future residents somewhere and get their fellow team members to go along with it. So, for example, they couldn't oppose medium density in one area without finding a place elsewhere for these people to live. They had to deal with the consequences of each of their decisions in terms of urban form, potential loss of green space, and transport. It was a fabulous real-world puzzle with real-world consequences.

STUART WHITE[1]

This vignette from a volunteer moderator involved with Perth's Dialogue in the City encapsulates our story. We both have been driven by a desire to strengthen democracy—to include the missing voices, to improve the communicative competence of citizens, and to ensure that the recommendations they make are sound and influential. We have separately experimented with deliberative democratic processes for the past fifteen years and, in doing so, have made many mistakes and experienced many successes. We crossed paths several years ago and have been influencing each other ever since. Coauthoring this chapter gives us an opportunity to compare experiences and make sense of our learning.

In the pages that follow, we explore the origins of deliberative processes in Australia. We then describe three deliberative processes that typify our experience. We believe that the Australian experience provides an example of one country's unique response to experiments that have occurred elsewhere. Australia has imported many deliberative methods, but practitioners also have recognized that these methods can be adapted and combined to suit the issues facing us. We evaluate the extent to which these adaptations have been effective, using a set of criteria that underpin deliberative theory and our own practice. Finally, we draw conclusions about adaptation and the need to constantly address the challenge of maximizing inclusion, deliberation, and influence.

Arriving at Criteria for Public Deliberation

Lyn Carson's path along the deliberative highway began when she was elected to local government in 1991. She was a frustrated councillor with democratic ideals who was obstructed by a wall of constraints. She decided to complete a doctoral degree to help unravel the contradictions she encountered and to enable her to experiment with alternative forms of decision making. She was influenced by the writings of John Burnheim and Fred Emery, two Australians who were tackling the problems of a democratic deficit in very different ways.[2] With Brian Martin, she later synthesized the ideas of Burnheim and Emery with the practices of Ted Mack (a passionate Australian politician), Ned Crosby[3] (the originator of the Citizens Jury and coauthor of Chapter Seven), Peter Dienel[4] (the originator of planning cells, described in Chapter Six), and others.[5]

Carson noted the local government's nonparticipatory style and hungered for change. She experimented with deliberative, inclusive processes to give voice to the voiceless, hoping that their views could be heard effectively. She became wary of the incensed and the articulate, the people who routinely participated in public meetings or advisory committees. Carson also advocated a combination of techniques to ensure that the weaknesses of one would be overcome by the strengths of another. After her period in office, this idea found expression in 2001 in a process that combined a citizens' jury with a televote.[6]

Janette Hartz-Karp's journey into deliberative democracy started as an academic and later as a change agent consultant. It became clear to her that in order for real change to happen, all those involved needed to be engaged in a different way. For her, it was all about building people's capacity to deliberate and then having their voices heard in decisions that would affect them. When the Australian Labor Party came to power in Western Australia in 2001, Hartz-Karp was asked by Alannah MacTiernan, the new Labor minister for planning and infrastructure, to work as a consultant to find innovative ways to engage citizens in joint decision making with government. It was the minister's view that Australian government was becoming increasingly dysfunctional, partly as a result of its endemic cynicism and a media focused on infotainment.[7] It was time to reverse the trend.

In an interesting practitioner-politician partnership, Hartz-Karp and MacTiernan have been working together since 2001 to engage citizens in joint decision making with government. Techniques such as citizens' juries, consensus conferences, consensus forums, multicriteria analysis conferences, deliberative polls, and 21st Century Town Meetings have been adapted and combined in order to deal with complex, often contentious issues. Citizens have been engaged with experts, industry, and government from the inception of each process through its implementation, often taking several years. Some of these processes have changed the face of Perth, Western Australia's capital city.

What we have in common, clearly, is a history of adapting, inventing, and combining different deliberative processes such as those described in the other chapters of this book. Our varied experiences with these mixed designs have clarified for us the essential elements of an effective deliberative process. These can be thought of as three criteria for a fully democratic deliberative process:

1. *Influence:* The process should have the ability to influence policy and decision making.
2. *Inclusion:* The process should be representative of the population and inclusive of diverse viewpoints and values, providing equal opportunity for all to participate.
3. *Deliberation:* The process should provide open dialogue, access to information, respect, space to understand and reframe issues, and movement toward consensus.

All consultation methods attempt to meet these three criteria, albeit to varying degrees, and we believe that performance on these three criteria indicates a method's success as a democratic process.[8] Each is a necessary criterion for success, and only the combination of all three is sufficient for an event to be fully democratic. For example, a referendum or a deliberative poll could be extremely *influential* (if mandated by a nation's constitution or commissioned by a decision maker) and highly representative or *inclusive* (especially if voting is compulsory or if random selection is used), but it might be flawed by its inability to allow participants to wrestle with the issue's complexity due to limited opportunities for moderated, in-depth dialogue and reflection. So it would be deficient in terms of its dialogic potential or *deliberative* capacity.[9]

Similarly, a community-initiated citizens' jury might be highly *inclusive* if steps have been taken to select randomly (usually via a stratified sample that matches a demographic profile), and it might be deeply *deliberative* because its skilled, neutral moderator fosters dialogue and positive group processes. Nonetheless, it could be seriously flawed in terms of its ability to *influence* decision makers.

Further, these three criteria are interdependent and interrelated. For example, without an evident pathway from consultation to *influence*, it is difficult to attract a highly *inclusive* sample to engage in *deliberation*. Without a very *inclusive* sample, the process will lack credibility amongst those who should be *influenced*, and so on. Failure to meet any of these three criteria typically causes the process to founder, and it can have a compounding, negative effect on the other criteria.

This does not mean that suboptimal practices are always a waste of time. Indeed, depending on the question being considered, a deliberative poll might not need more than a limited amount of dialogue, or a citizens' jury that has inclusive opportunities for dialogue but not much influence with decision makers might nonetheless change the lives of its participants. Progress and change are still possible and probable. What is important for us, as practitioners, is maintaining awareness of a process's performance in relation to these criteria and measuring that performance against realistic standards, given the circumstances.

Having clarified the criteria by which we evaluate public meetings, we will briefly examine three attempts to create the best possible public discussion process. For each case study, we describe the purpose of the discussion and how different methods were combined to meet that purpose. In each case, an attempt was made to compensate for the weakness of one process by pairing it with another that had a complementary strength. In the final section of the chapter, we will evaluate the extent to which inclusiveness, deliberation, and influence were achieved in these cases.

Container Deposit Legislation in New South Wales: Televote and Citizens Jury

Conveners

In 2000, Lyn Carson designed Australia's first combined televote and citizens' jury in collaboration with the Institute for Sustainable Futures. The minister for the environment in New South Wales (NSW) commissioned Stuart White from the Institute for Sustainable Futures to undertake an independent review of container deposit legislation (also called a *bottle bill*) as part of a statutory requirement to review the Waste Act in New South Wales. The policy environment was hostile,[10] with packaging and beverage industries pitted against local government and environmental groups because of the absence of container deposit legislation in New South Wales. Such legislation would unequivocally place responsibility for container collection in the hands of producers: the beverage and packaging industry.

Meeting Design

Extensive analytical work was undertaken, supported by extensive social research. The combined televote and citizens' jury represented an important part of the social research, which consisted of a "combination of qualitative and quantitative methods of stakeholder consultation and public participations,"[11] including a call for written public comment and interviews with stakeholders. White, the reviewer, wanted to test some deliberative innovations to ensure that the citizens who offered opinions were highly informed. All of the earlier opinion polls that had been conducted—some of them by the industries that opposed container deposit legislation—showed overwhelming support for the legislation. This consumer support, however, was often dismissed as being uninformed.[12]

Had only a citizens' jury been convened, the findings would have been dismissed as being too small a sample. Had only a televote been conducted, the findings would have been dismissed as being too uninformed, even though a televote overcomes some of the weaknesses of standard opinion polling.[13] It was hoped that the weakness of the citizens' jury (its small number of just eleven participants) would be overcome by the strength of the televote (which employed a statistically representative sample of four hundred people. We also believed that the deeply deliberative nature of the citizens' jury (intensive, discussion-based inquiry over three days) would compensate for the unfocused deliberation of the televote (see Table 8.1).[14]

TABLE 8.1. COMPARATIVE AND COMPLEMENTARY CHARACTERISTICS OF TELEVOTE AND CITIZENS JURY ON CONTAINER DEPOSIT LEGISLATION

Televote	Citizens Jury
Randomly selected	Randomly selected (The time commitment required may have resulted in greater self-selection than in the televote.)
Contacted by telephone	Contacted by mail
Representative	Diverse group reflecting a cross section of the New South Wales community

TABLE 8.1. COMPARATIVE AND COMPLEMENTARY CHARACTERISTICS OF TELEVOTE AND CITIZENS JURY ON CONTAINER DEPOSIT LEGISLATION, Cont'd.

Televote	Citizens Jury
$n = 400$ citizens of rural and urban New South Wales	$n = 11$ citizens of rural and urban New South Wales
Large number of people involved (directly and indirectly) means that potential for raising community awareness of an issue is significant.	Limited number of people involved but can generate media interest and thus stimulate community learning and awareness
Cost: $15,500-$39,000 (U.S. dollars) for 400 people	Cost: $8,000-12,000 (U.S. dollars) for 11 people
Quantitative output; sample size is sufficient to yield statistically significant results.	Qualitative output; recommendations in the form of a report prepared by the panel
Process may be perceived to have greater legitimacy due to the number of people involved.	Process may be perceived by key decision makers as illegitimate because it only involves a handful of people and because the deliberative component is not quantifiable.
More informed than an opinion survey	Highly informed
Individual deliberation, though participants were encouraged to discuss the issue with friends, family, and colleagues	Group deliberation: face-to-face questioning of experts, facilitated discussion, exposure to a variety of opinions and arguments, opportunities for experiential learning and social interaction (for example, could involve field trips)
Access to summarized, printed information avoids persuasive power of experts but allows some exposure to opinions of others. (The process could have incorporated computers, which would have enabled more interactivity and greater access to information.)	Initial access to summarized, printed information, then more detailed, printed information and other media (for example, videos, slides) throughout the process. Exposure to the persuasion, motivations, and characteristics of those who dominate the debate; in this way, participants can sense the values inherent in "facts" and can use their own judgment to separate fact from rhetoric.
Decision based on self-interest, modified through discussion with others	Deliberation tends to steer people toward outcomes in the interest of the community. Dialogue and exposure to other positions and opinions allows for learning and consensus building.

Source: Carson, L., White, S., Hendriks, C., and Palmer, J. (2002, July). "Community Consultation in Environmental Policy Making." *The Drawing Board: An Australian Review of Public Affairs, 3*(1).

The topic of container deposit legislation was predetermined by the terms for the independent review of container deposit legislation. Therefore, the Institute for Sustainable Futures determined the citizens' jury charge and the televote questions. A stakeholder group of disparate parties vetted the briefing document and agreed on the accuracy and fairness of its contents before it was distributed to all televote and citizens' jury participants.

Setting

The televote included a random sample of telephone users that had been selected via random-digit dialing. The citizens' jury participants had responded to an invitation sent to two thousand New South Wales households that had been selected from an electronic telephone directory; 143 people had expressed interest in participating without knowing the topic; these citizens came from across the state. The residential citizens' jury took place at the Women's College at the University of Sydney on February 9–11, 2001. The televote took place in January 2001.[15]

Facilitation

The citizens' jury was facilitated by two professional facilitators. One was designated chair of proceedings; the other, facilitator for the jury. This distinction became irrelevant when the expert presenters from the beverage and packaging industry withdrew at the eleventh hour in what the organizers perceived as an orchestrated attempt to undermine the process. The citizens' jury went ahead without expert presenters from local government or environmental groups. Instead, public officials and academics presented the information, to avoid the accusation of bias. The potential accusation of bias was also addressed by having an independent evaluation of the citizens' jury.

Participants

Thanks to random selection, participants in both the televote and the citizens' jury were extremely diverse. There was no attempt to stratify the televote sample because of its large size, and it conformed well to census data in New South Wales.[16] By contrast, the citizens' jury was carefully stratified to guarantee a diverse mix of participants in relation to the sociodemographic differences that influence beverage use and waste collection (for example, age, location, household structure).

Information and Activities

The televote participants were asked to complete a survey, then asked if they would complete another survey after receiving information about container deposit legislation and discussing that information with family or friends. Those who agreed were phoned back one week later and surveyed again. On the key question of whether container deposit legislation should be introduced, the original survey yielded a result of 71 percent support, while the follow-up survey yielded a result of only 59 percent support. This did not mean that 12 percent dropped their support; the televote results indicated that there was considerable movement in attitudes both away from and toward support for container deposit legislation. However, the largest proportion shifted from yes to no or from don't know to no.

The eleven citizens' jury participants received the same information as the televote participants. Then, over the weekend of the citizens' jury, they heard presentations and had access to a substantial library and Web sites on the subject of container deposit legislation. They worked mostly as one group and were encouraged to investigate and discuss the topic using a variety of group processes, which occasionally involved working more intensively in small subgroups. Deliberating intensively, the citizens' jury slowly shifted from seven supporters (with four unsure) to unanimous support for the legislation.

We concluded that the more people learned about this topic, the more they supported the introduction of container deposit legislation. The televote provided further evidence for this conclusion: those who discussed the subject with household members or others between the first and the second televote were more likely by a factor of two to support container deposit legislation than not. Those who did not discuss it had views on the legislation that were consistent with the original views of the sample as a whole, that is, lower support for container deposit legislation.[17]

Sustainability

There was no attempt to sustain deliberation after the project, since the aim was to discover what citizens thought when given access to comprehensive information on a reasonably complex topic. A contract was signed with citizens' jury participants, guaranteeing that its recommendations would be given to the minister without any interference from the Institute for Sustainable Futures, and this occurred. We believe that the strength of the citizens' jury was its in-depth discussion, which led to unanimity, while the televote demonstrated majority support without having the benefit of such deliberation. The televote had strengths that the jury lacked— for example, its statistically representative sample. The televote had the advantage of briefing documents that had been agreed to by all parties, while the jury experienced a stakeholder boycott (although this was not communicated to the jury). Other comparisons can be found in Table 8.2. We concluded that overall, the combination of the two events improved the credibility of the findings.

TABLE 8.2. INCLUSION, DELIBERATION, AND INFLUENCE OF DELIBERATIVE PROCESSES

Consultation Method	Inclusion	Deliberation	Influence
Combined citizens jury and televote	3, 3	5, 2	1
Dialogue with the City	4	4	4
Citizens jury alone	5	4	5
Multi Criteria Analysis Conference	3	4	4
Consensus forum and deliberative survey	4, 4	4, 3	4, 3

Note: 0 = not at all/none; 1 = a little; 2 = some/more than a little; 3 = adequate; 4 = more than adequate; 5 = exemplary. When two methods have been combined, each method was evaluated separately, resulting in two numbers.

Source: Adapted from Coote, A., and Lenaghan, J. (1997). *Citizens' Juries: Theory into Practice.* London: Institute for Public Policy Research, 11.

Freight Network Review: Consensus Forum, Multicriteria Analysis Conference, Deliberative Poll, and Stakeholder Implementation

As in most capital cities, the transport of freight around metropolitan Perth has become critical, not just to the economics of the state but to its quality of life. The aim of the Freight Network Review, which was designed, coordinated, and facilitated by Janette Hartz-Karp, was to bring the community, industry, and state and local government into the heart of the freight planning process. This was important for the development of a mutually acceptable and sustainable freight network plan (involving transport via road, rail, sea, and air) and key strategies to achieve it.

Conveners

The state minister for planning and infrastructure of the state of Western Australia convened the Freight Network Review, with the assistance of her departmental chief executive officers (CEOs). A series of techniques were used to maximize the three key elements of inclusiveness, deliberation, and influence.

To maximize inclusiveness, considerable effort was made to ensure that all voices were heard, including those without specific interests. At each consensus forum, experts, public officials, interested parties, and a random sample of the community sat together at tables to deliberate and seek common ground. A random-sample survey and a deliberative poll[18] were incorporated in order to ensure broad community input. A community advisory group oversaw the process from inception to conclusion, to increase transparency.

Effective deliberation depends on access to comprehensive information and opportunities for dialogue. In phase 1, stakeholder working groups developed the forum briefing papers. A telephone survey of a random sample of one thousand people (five hundred metropolitan residents and five hundred who lived on freight routes that caused community concern) was conducted in order to determine public attitudes and issues, providing input to the process. The first two-day forum, with 130 participants, was designed to maximize opportunities for deliberation on the broad policy directions needed and a methodology for designating freight routes.

Phase 2 aimed at incorporating the outcomes of the forum in actionable solutions. An implementation policy team of community, industry, and state and local government representatives developed a comprehensive policy for freight planning that was based on the outcomes of the first forum. After the policy framework had been set, six working groups were convened to develop the plan to put the policy into effect. The working groups involved all stakeholders, and each was chaired by an agency CEO. Two of the working groups conducted separate community engagement exercises: a deliberative poll, to determine the limits on growth of the Fremantle harbor, and a multicriteria analysis conference, to determine the best east-west freight link. The final forum, which brought together 120 of the original participants, reviewed the outcomes of the working groups, determined the level of support, the gaps that still needed to be addressed, and the priorities.

In phase 3, a comprehensive six-point plan was developed by the implementation policy team, based on the second forum's priorities. An agency CEO is now responsible for each point, and a quarterly report, disseminated to all forum participants, outlines progress toward the targets set. The agency CEOs have regular meetings with the minister to ensure that the process is on track and on time. This implementation process has aimed to maximize the influence of the consensus forums on the decision-making process.

Participants

There were approximately 130 participants at the first forum: one-third came from a broad range of invited stakeholder groups from the community, industry, and state and local government; one-third were respondents to advertisements in statewide and local newspapers and professional journals; and the remaining third came from a random sample of residents, stratified by area. (The sample represented approximately a 12 percent response rate to the invitation.)

Forum representatives formed the implementation policy team and the working groups. All forum participants were invited to the two-day multicriteria analysis conference, and 80 attended. They were invited again to the final one-day forum, and 120 attended.

Information

Briefing papers were disseminated to participants more than a week before the first forum, along with a request to read them carefully prior to the event. The information reflected different viewpoints, was comprehensive, and was easy to read. The papers were developed by key issues work groups that consisted of representatives from government agencies, industry, and community groups. Participants also received the report summarizing the findings of the initial survey, and these were discussed during the forum proceedings. Within two weeks of the first forum, the outcomes were disseminated.

Prior to the final forum, the working group papers were sent to all participants and then were discussed during the forum. Following the final forum, the outcomes were disseminated to all participants. Quarterly progress reports of implementation have been submitted to the minister and sent to participants.

Setting

The first and final forums were held at the same venue—a large passenger terminal. Participants were seated at round tables in groups of ten. For all other events, participants were seated purposefully, to ensure a mix at each table of random-sample, industry, community, and local and state government participants.

Facilitation

A lead facilitator orchestrated each of the forums. Each table was facilitated either by a member of parliament or a member of the executive group from each of the government departments. All facilitators received a two-hour training session prior to the forums and took part in a two-hour debriefing session afterward. Each table recorded its findings on a flipchart. The implementation team and working groups were facilitated, to maximize group interaction. They were chaired by agency CEOs or directors, to ensure agency backup and cooperation.

Activities

The first two-day forum included a half day of presentations of papers, questioning, and exploration of key issues through an expert panel. The remaining day and a half was spent in interactive small-group sessions. Deliberation focused on finding common ground—a vision for an ideal freight system and the elements, "drivers," and key strategies needed to realize it. Techniques included empathetic listening, to encourage each person to understand the others' points of view; mind mapping,[19] to capture the visions and key strategies; a series of affinity diagrams,[20] to ensure that every person's ideas were captured and included; and a multicriteria analysis prioritization matrix,[21] to highlight the key issues.

Six working groups were created, comprising community, industry, and government representatives, to develop an implementation plan for each of the key areas. One working group held a deliberative poll to find out what an informed public thought about limits on growth of the Fremantle Port. A random sample of 1,600 residents of the port catchment area was sent surveys, together with balanced background information developed by the disparate stakeholders. Respondents were asked to read the papers, ring a toll-free number if they needed additional information, and discuss the issues with colleagues and family before filling out the survey and returning it. There was a 31 percent response rate,[22] and the survey findings were used by the working group to develop their recommendations.

A multicriteria analysis conference was held to determine the best east-west freight route. An initial community conference of eighty participants developed the options and the social, economic, and environmental criteria against which the options would be measured. An expert panel of ten then assessed each option against each criterion, using quantitative and qualitative data. Results were fed into a computer. The community group reassembled at a second conference to weight the criteria by attaching a measure of importance to each. This information was fed into the computer and in front of the community, the program ranked the alternatives based on how well they satisfied the criteria. The working group used the rankings to support their recommendations.

The final Freight Network Review forum was held in 2002, with 120 of the original 130 forum participants. The reports of each of the working groups were sent to participants beforehand and then presented briefly at the forum. Issues were explored, using a panel of representatives from each working group. During the interactive session, groups discussed gaps, verified how well the reports addressed the first forum outcomes, and then focused on the prioritization and timing of the implementation.

The stakeholder implementation team was charged with developing the recommendations from the forum and submitting them to the minister. They were accepted in total, and new teams were formed to oversee their implementation.

Sustainability

Both in terms of content and process, the Freight Network Review focused on sustainability. In terms of content, the six-point plan adopted by the government in response to the consensus forum aims to make the current freight system more sustainable. In terms of process, the aim of engaging the community in joint decision making was achieved. By focusing on optimizing inclusion, deliberation, and influence, community participation and trust was enhanced. Participant feedback highlighted the willingness of the great majority to participate in community engagement such as this in the future. The Freight Network Review built on the learning of a prior community engagement—the Road Train Summit, and opened the way to broader deliberation—the Dialogue with the City—which we will now discuss.

Dialogue with the City: 21st Century Town Meeting, Regional Planning Game, Interactive Web Site, Multimedia Involvement, and Stakeholder Implementation

Since the early 1990s, the Perth metropolitan area had been spreading in an unsustainable way. Although a minority of residents were involved in local planning disputes and localized lobbying groups were proliferating, there was little public understanding of the broader issues. Media coverage, focusing on infotainment, only exacerbated the lack of understanding and community ownership of the issues.

Conveners

Dialogue with the City was convened by the minister for planning and infrastructure of the state of Western Australia, together with the Western Australia Planning Commission and her departmental CEOs of road, rail, ports, land development, redevelopment authorities, and planning and infrastructure. In addition, strategic partnerships—for example, with a commercial television station, the major newspaper, several computer companies, and a key mining company—were sought, in order to broaden ownership and lessen the financial burden on the state.

Design, Participation, Setting, Facilitation, and Activities

Like the Freight Network Review, Dialogue with the City was not an event but a process. The process, which was designed, facilitated, and coordinated by Janette Hartz-Karp, began by focusing on what could be learned from the Freight Network Review. As a result, additional effort was placed on optimizing inclusiveness, deliberation, and influence. The design attempted to engage the whole community; thus, it included a survey of eight thousand residents, an interactive Web site, a one-hour television broadcast, a series of full-page stories about planning issues in the major newspaper, art and essay competitions in schools on the future of the city, and additional listening sessions for those who are frequently not heard—youth, Indigenous people, and those from a non-English-speaking background.

The process culminated in a 21st Century Town Meeting of 1,100 participants, held in September 2003. One-third of the attendees were stakeholder invitees, one-third were respondents to advertisements, and one-third were respondents to a mail invitation that was sent to a random sample of the population. Opportunities for deliberation were provided in innovative ways. The forum combined interactive computer technology, designed to determine key themes, with a planning game that enabled each participant to take the role of a planner and determine where and how the future growth of the city would occur. Participants were purposefully seated at tables of ten to maximize the mix of expertise and views. A lead facilitator moderated, and there was a volunteer facilitator and a scribe at each table. In all, there were 250 volunteers that day, all of whom had undergone a full day's training prior to the event. At the close of the forum, all participants received a preliminary report of the key outcomes. The outcomes of the forum highlighted the key themes that participants had developed and prioritized through polling. Themes included the key hopes for the future, what participants wanted to keep and change, their preferred model for the city, and specifically how that model could be achieved.

Over the next eight months, one hundred participants from the Dialogue with the City forum were involved with developing the plan for the metropolis. At each critical stage, the plan was reviewed by all 1,100 Dialogue with the City participants. Additional community members were also invited to offer comments. The end result, a new planning strategy for metropolitan Perth, was accepted by the Western Australia government.

Sustainability

The aim of the Dialogue with the City was to create the world's most livable city by 2030. It was clear that broad community support was needed if a new direction was to be successfully implemented. The new planning strategy for Perth is not only a change of planning direction that has sustainability at its core but a change in how we plan, a change that has deliberative democracy at its center.

The feedback from the forum was overwhelmingly positive, with 98 percent stating they were willing to participate in a similar community engagement in the future. Over a third stated that they changed or significantly broadened their views as a result of the dialogue.

Many participants requested local dialogues to determine how the plans could be implemented at a local level. In response, the minister for planning and infrastructure has announced a half-million-dollar package this year that will allow local governments to run local dialogues that are representative, deliberative, and influential, to be followed by one million dollars next year to fund the initiatives that emanate from the dialogues.

Reflections

Our experience has not been one of repeating single deliberative techniques, and we have wondered whether this is unique to Australia. We have found ourselves engaged in experimentation, combining and adapting techniques to maximize the possibilities for inclusion, deliberation, and influence in order to best serve the purpose at hand. In the Western Australian planning and infrastructure portfolio, an initiative is currently under way to institutionalize deliberative democracy within planning processes. Commitment has been weaker in other states.

The impact of these deliberative processes has varied according to the extent to which they were inclusive, deliberative, and influential. When all three characteristics have been present and intertwined, the impact has been significant. Not only have the deliberative events affected the community's engagement and support of a particular initiative, but they have increased the community's willingness to participate in addressing other issues in the future.

From our frame of reference, inclusion, deliberation, and influence are the key challenges of democratic process and hence the critical performance indicators. In Table 8.2, we have measured the performance of some of our processes against these indicators. Despite our focus on optimizing each element, this has been extremely difficult to achieve. It is clear to us that when performance has been exemplary or more than adequate on all indicators, we have made the most profound impacts. When *all* three performance criteria have been satisfied at a high level, the impact has been exponential, far more than the sum of the parts. The result has been that decision makers have felt more comfortable that they have the mandate to act. Participants have been able to reframe the issues, enabling them to find common ground, and consequently, they have felt ownership of the end results. As a result, agreed-on outcomes have been implemented, and community capacity and trust have been increased.

In terms of systems thinking, the interaction of the three elements acts as a "virtuous cycle,"[23] in which the reinforcing feedback loop ensures that a small change builds on itself, increasing trust and hence social capital (see Figure 8.1).[24] Such a virtuous cycle builds a cooperative civic environment for citizen engagement and policy change. In terms of building sustainable processes, it will not be until we have reversed the trend toward community disengagement that we will be able to enlist sufficient social capital for deliberative democracy to thrive.

We do not believe that achieving this dynamic is possible through any one formula or technique; it will require constant innovation, constant combining, adapting, and creating ways to improve what we do. Indeed, it is only after years of experience that we have come to understand how difficult it is to maximize each element. Issues that previously were of peripheral concern are now our focal points. These include engaging the disinterested,[25] creating designs that provide

FIGURE 8.1. VIRTUOUS CYCLE OF COMMUNITY ENGAGEMENT THROUGH DELIBERATIVE DEMOCRACY

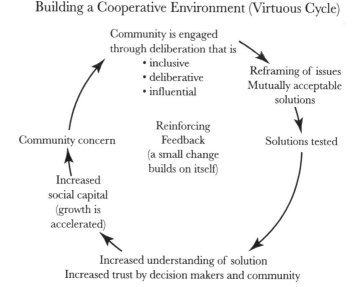

Building a Cooperative Environment (Virtuous Cycle)

opportunities and build capacities to engage in real dialogue, and creating processes to broaden and strengthen community engagement in any implementation of outcomes.

Community consultation in Australia has been institutionalized through legislation, regulation, policy, and accepted practice; however, less-than-effective implementation has resulted in the unintended consequences of increasing cynicism and reducing trust in both communities and government agencies. With the growing momentum toward community engagement and deliberative democracy, there are already signs that some are repackaging traditional community consultation techniques to incorporate the language but none of the practices of deliberative, inclusive processes. This is a worrying trend that could easily undermine trust in the nascent movement.

In our view, the key challenge is to use contentious and complex issues as opportunities to use (and adapt and combine) deliberative, inclusive processes. If we are to reverse the trend of civic disengagement, it will require a paradigm shift— a fundamental change in the way policymakers and policy experts consult with citizens. And making that change will involve continually innovating to find ways to optimize the degree of inclusiveness, deliberation, and influence in our processes.

Notes

1. Professor Stuart White from the Institute for Sustainable Futures, University of Technology, Sydney, was interviewed a month after the event took place.
2. Burnheim, J. (1985). *Is Democracy Possible? The Alternative to Electoral Politics*. Cambridge, U.K.: Polity Press; Emery, F. E. (1989). *Toward Real Democracy and Toward Real Democracy: Further Problems*. Toronto, Canada: Ontario Ministry for Labour.
3. Crosby, N. (2003). *Healthy Democracy: Empowering a Clear and Informed Voice of the People*. Edina, Minn.: Beaver's Pond Press.
4. Dienel, P., and Renn, O. (1995). "Planning Cells: A Gate to 'Fractal' Mediation." In O. Renn, T. Webler, and P. Wiedemann (eds.), *Fairness and Competence in Citizen Participation: Evaluating Models for Environmental Discourse*. Dordrecht, Netherlands: Kluwer.
5. Carson, L., and Martin, B. (1999). *Random Selection in Politics*. Westport, Conn.: Praeger.
6. Carson, L., White, S., Hendriks, C., and Palmer, J. (2002, July). "Community Consultation in Environmental Policy Making." *The Drawing Board: An Australian Review of Public Affairs*, 3(1), 1–13.
7. Australian cultural commentator Catharine Lumby (1999) describes "infotainment" as products that blur the "boundaries between information and entertainment" in *Gotcha: Life in a Tabloid World*. St. Leonards, Australia: Allen & Unwin, 50. Australia is following in the footsteps of the United States and has a dumbed-down media that would be familiar to American author Neil Postman (1985). *Amusing Ourselves to Death: Public Discourse in the Age of Show Business*. New York: Viking.

8. These terms were coined by Carolyn Hendriks (2002) in "The Ambiguous Role of Civil Society in Deliberative Democracy" (Paper presented at the Jubilee Conference of the Australasian Political Studies Association, Australian National University, Canberra. [http://arts.anu.edu.au/sss/apsa/default.htm]), following the concepts of John S. Dryzek's (2000) discursive designs in *Deliberative Democracy and Beyond: Liberals, Critics, Contestations.* Oxford, U.K.: Oxford University Press.

9. Blaug, R. (1999). *Democracy, Real and Ideal: Discourse Ethics and Radical Politics.* Albany: State University of New York Press.

10. Carolyn Hendriks, in her doctoral research, notes one Australian television journalist's claim that this thirty-year-old dispute is "a toxic mix of spin, rubbish and a great deal of money" (Ticky Fullerton [2003, Sept. 8], "The Waste Club," a segment on "Four Corners." Sydney: Australian Broadcasting Corporation).

11. White, S. (2001, Nov.). *Independent Review of Container Deposit Legislation in New South Wales.* Report prepared for Bob Debus, Australian minister for the environment. Vol. 3. Sydney: Institute for Sustainable Futures, 2. [http://www.isf.uts.edu.au/publications/white.html]. Retrieved May 16, 2004.

12. One of the polls was conducted in South Australia, where container deposit legislation has been in force since 1976. The respondents were, arguably, highly informed because container deposit legislation is part of their daily lives, and 95 percent of those surveyed supported it. However, there is also truth to the claim that citizens' preferences can be unreliable. The beverage industry has demonstrated this via its "litter spies" approach, which uncovers the gap between espoused and demonstrated behavior. See Beverage Industry Environment Council. (2001). "A New Method for Measuring Littering Behaviour in Australia." [http://www.biec.com.au/litterspies.html]. Retrieved Jan. 28, 2005.

13. Becker, T., and Slaton, C. (2000). *The Future of Teledemocracy.* Westport, Conn.: Praeger.

14. Precise details of the two consultation methods can be found in Volume 3 of the report that followed the review (White [2001], *Independent Review of Container Deposit Legislation*), and abbreviated information can be found on the Institute for Sustainable Futures' Web site at http://www.isf.uts.edu.au/CDL_Report/.

15. Full details of this case study can be found on the Institute for Sustainable Futures' Web site, in Volume 3 of the final report to the minister at http://www.isf.uts.edu.au/CDL_Report.

16. White 2001, *Independent Review of Container Deposit Legislation,* vol. 3, 23.

17. White 2001, *Independent Review of Container Deposit Legislation,* vol. 3, 26.

18. The term *deliberative survey* rather than *deliberative poll* was used in Western Australia to avoid connotations of a single-solution poll and to emphasize the complexity of the issues under deliberation.

19. See, for example, http://cmap.coginst.uwf.edu/info/ and http://www.columbia.k12.mo .us/she/cncptmap.html for links to concept-mapping resources. A mind map or concept map is a device that allows its creator to make sense of concepts by linking them or relating them in a spatial or hierarchical manner.

20. Brassard, M. (1989). *The Memory Jogger Plus: Featuring the Seven Management and Planning Tools.* Methuen, Mass.: Goal QPC. An affinity diagram is a method used to organize large amounts of data that have been generated; it is a collaborative, usually silent activity that enables the group to match similar ideas.

21. Brassard (1989), *The Memory Jogger Plus.* Multicriteria analysis is a method of integrating different criteria that are relevant to a decision, in which each criterion is assigned a different relative importance; a matrix is used in the process of prioritizing.

22. This response rate was higher than that of other surveys conducted by Hartz-Karp, which typically had a 15–20 percent response rate.

23. Senge, P. M. (1990). *The Fifth Discipline: The Art and Practice of the Learning Organization.* New York: Doubleday.

24. Hartz-Karp, J. (2004, May 14). "Harmonising Divergent Voices: Sharing the Challenge of Decision Making." Keynote address at the New South Wales State Conference of the Institute of Public Administration Australia. [http://www.nsw.ipaa.org.au/07_publications/2004_conf_papers.htm]. Retrieved Jan. 31, 2005.

25. Ralston Saul, J. (1997). *The Unconscious Civilization.* Maryborough, Victoria, Australia: Penguin Books.

PART THREE

DELIBERATIVE GOVERNANCE

CHAPTER NINE

BRINGING THE PUBLIC AND THE GOVERNMENT TOGETHER THROUGH ON-LINE DIALOGUES

Patricia A. Bonner, Robert Carlitz, Rosemary Gunn, Laurie E. Maak, Charles A. Ratliff

Five authors in five different places[1] wrote this chapter. We coordinated our efforts by e-mail, serendipitously recreating the dynamic we're trying to describe. A few paraphrased excerpts capture the spirit of the conversation:

> "How do we begin? What's a good way to illustrate what happens in an on-line dialogue?"

> "There was the Senator in the California dialogue who used all-caps everywhere. We worried about whether to change to lowercase—because people could read that as shouting. It shows that a lot needs to be done behind the scenes."

> "Yes, but that example emphasizes the technology! The 'feeling' is what's unique and compelling—the enthusiastic, pleasant, and courteous exchange of ideas and information. People don't 'feel' the technology, they feel part of something special and interesting. They listen and learn and become more open to each other's ideas."

> "Even though I'm less of a 'feeling' person, I think it's true that participants were most positive about the experience of communicating with a broader community. But I believe the technology is worth a sentence or two. For example, the participant profiles helped me interpret some people's perspectives when I was a moderator."

"Yes, and we should use the comment, 'Most contributors began by addressing their personal needs from their own backgrounds and/or schools. As time went on, they began to develop the *big picture* idea and saw everything as a whole. That was great!' That about sums it up, doesn't it?"

"How about quotes to show how ideas build, how hosts, participants and panelists all interact—there's action and energy—it's really <u>alive</u>!"

"Good idea. I like, 'I felt that participants were listened to and given credence. I commented on a thread that I thought was very important, but that had not been discussed very much, and I got more responses. Everyone had something worthwhile to contribute.'"

"We could go on for days! But we need to describe how the pieces come together to result in these great comments!"

This was a conversation among collaborators who know each other and have worked together for some time—incisive, friendly, and spiced with occasional disagreement. The on-line events that we describe in this chapter involve 500 to 1,200 people, most of whom had not previously met, yet the dynamic of the conversations is similar. These groups are able to address complex issues, come to an understanding of essential underlying points, and move to specific questions and recommendations. And they don't feel like strangers.

Participants in structured on-line dialogues see problems and solutions from widely different perspectives and bring knowledge and passion to the conversation. They may disagree, but more often than not, they respond to disagreement with politeness and constructive discourse. As information and ideas are added to the discussion, participants often make specific recommendations aimed at solving the problem that led to the initial disagreement or misunderstanding. In light of our experiences, we present our model of on-line dialogue as an excellent mechanism for large-scale discussions of public policy and as a valuable supplement to conventional public hearings and solicitations for written comments.

Origins and Purpose of the Dialogues

Information Renaissance's on-line dialogues grew out of direct experience with government mechanisms for handling public input. The first dialogue was held in 1996 in response to the Federal Communications Commission's proposed E-rate initiative to subsidize the cost of connecting schools and libraries to the Internet.[2] Information Renaissance, a nonprofit corporation that facilitates public involvement with government via the Internet, created an electronic docket that included background materials and all of the written comments that had been submitted to the Federal Communications Commission (FCC).[3] Information Renaissance then provided a forum for public involvement by conducting a six-week on-line dialogue for five hundred teachers, librarians, telecommunications industry people, and agency staff.[4]

In 1999, Information Renaissance worked with Americans Discuss Social Security[5] to produce a dialogue that brought policymakers and subject specialists more directly into the discussion, including them as on-line panelists. Subsequent events experimented with different styles of on-line moderation and more extensive involvement of agency staff. In 2003, WestEd simplified the model to allow sponsors to produce their own dialogues less expensively.[6]

This chapter reflects our experience with dialogues held in 2001 on public involvement in EPA decisions,[7] sponsored by the U.S. Environmental Protection Agency (EPA); in 2002 on the draft Master Plan for California Education (CAMP),[8] involving members of the joint legislative committee that created the plan; and in 2003 on legislation intended to guide plan implementation, sponsored and produced by the Office of the Education Master Plan.[9] Each dialogue involved approximately one thousand people.

On-line dialogues seek to provide a new sort of public space, enabling a conversation between government policymakers and members of the public. This broad, interactive, and accessible venue can increase citizen involvement in policy development and facilitate a nonadversarial exchange of information and ideas that goes far beyond traditional hearings and written comments.[10] The dialogue Web site encourages an informed exchange: participants can learn enough about the topic on the site to discuss it in depth with others, including policymakers, subject experts, and implementers.

Distinctive Features

On-line dialogues have a number of advantages: (1) They are less formal than many other public involvement processes, with adequate time for participants to understand others' comments and make their case; (2) participants can join in at their convenience; (3) extensive resource materials are readily available and help level the playing field by informing the public; (4) all participants, including policymakers, take part on an equal footing; and (5) the discussion is more deliberative, more an interchange among participants than mere testimony to policymakers. As one dialogue participant noted, "It was helpful . . . to see the different points of view represented and to gain a better understanding of those that differ from mine."[11] Even though on-line forums can handle large groups, the experience feels direct and personal; a dialogue "reads like a real conversation between individuals who care about the topic."[12]

The Internet is a malleable medium, so a common framework can yield events with varying styles and content. Certain features, however, are essential. The sponsor, which can be any entity seeking informed public involvement, must buy into the activity at least to the extent of contributing staff time and understanding the consequences of their public commitment. Greater visibility on the part of policymakers and their staff makes the public more likely to participate, to take the activity seriously, and to expect that their voices will be heard. Further, while participants will be self-selected, key stakeholders should be identified at the outset, and explicit outreach should be conducted to increase the diversity of participants.

Other important features include panelists (invited participants who bring a range of knowledge and viewpoints to the discussions) and a moderator who can pose discussion points and help with the flow of the conversation. A behind-the-scenes facilitator can provide assistance and encourage hesitant individuals to share their views. Daily summaries, e-mailed early the next morning to all registrants, make it easy for busy participants and latecomers to catch up, and provide policymakers with an overview of the discussion.

The on-line conversation is structured to encourage a thoughtful and constructive exchange. Participants, panelists, and hosts interact freely and rapidly with one another, exchanging information and ideas in the nonthreatening environment of their office or home. Reflection on the issues is encouraged, and people can read and respond to messages on the Web site.

To encourage personal interaction, participants can be asked to register, identify themselves by name, and provide some individual background information on themselves, their interests, and their involvement with the topic. This provides a useful context for the ideas and perspectives presented in the discussion. We also introduce staff and panelists. In federal dialogues, the Privacy Act[13] prohibits requesting individual information and the Paperwork Reduction Act[14] discourages collecting it; these regulations may also inhibit evaluation and analysis of conversations.[15] Also, in some federal agencies, legal counsel may interpret First Amendment rights as prohibiting a moderator from questioning an inappropriate message. In our experience, however, this is almost never necessary, because socialization among participants promotes civility and a genuine desire to hear and be heard by others.

Designing and Conducting an On-Line Dialogue

Decisions must be made about how the dialogue will be organized and who will carry out specific tasks. The sponsor is accountable for the event and should participate on-line: dialogue participants believe their views and priorities will be better understood by decision makers and staff when they are present, and give high marks to officials who take part.[16] The sponsor's tasks may range from the minimal involvement of participating on-line to the large task of creating the whole event. Often a producer will build the Web site, prepare staff and panelists, and coordinate all the elements of the dialogue. For a politically sensitive topic or when trust among potential participants is low, the sponsor might prefer that a nonpartisan contractor develop materials and host the dialogue. The sponsor should be involved in the decision making if activities such as defining stakeholders, recruiting participants, developing content (agenda, panelists, and library), and conducting the event are carried out by others.

A dialogue typically takes place over one to two weeks. Discussions focus on one major theme, with specific topics addressed each day. This format allows participants time to consult resources, reflect on the conversation, discuss ideas with others, and compose their contributions at a convenient time, day or night. Once introduced, topics remain open for additional comments throughout the dialogue so that participants can continue to exchange ideas.

Organizations with interests related to the dialogue are asked to help announce the event. They distribute invitations in electronic discussions, place links on relevant Web sites, include articles promoting the dialogue in print and electronic newsletters, hand out flyers at meetings and conferences, and send out media advisories. Interested individuals visit the dialogue Web site and register to participate; if demographic information is collected, it provides a profile of the dialogue participants.

During the dialogue, participants can prepare by reviewing the day's agenda, background resources, panelist information, summaries from previous days, and discussion guidelines. The moderator introduces a topic and calls for clarification or additional views throughout the day. The style and extent of moderation for the discussion depends on the issue, the purpose, and the desired outcome. Panelists' messages also help frame the discussion. Participants add their views and discuss those of others, strongly influencing the flow of the conversation. The sponsor's staff clarifies information and responds to inquiries, and the facilitator provides support, answering questions and encouraging participation. On-line surveys can capture and quantify participants' aggregate views.

At the conclusion of the dialogue, participants are asked to complete an evaluation form to provide feedback to the sponsors and producers. The Web site archive is maintained for a period arranged with the sponsor.[17]

The Impact of On-Line Dialogues

On-line dialogues like those described here have been carried out roughly once a year since 1996. The model described in this chapter is a result of this experience.

Our experience has been that these on-line policy dialogues can bring a public audience together with government officials and can have an impact on both groups. The precise impact is hard to quantify, because a dialogue is typically part of a larger process, and implementation of the decision under discussion may take place long after the dialogue. However, we have gathered information from participants through on-line surveys, reviews of individual comments, and interviews with selected individuals. Participants consistently express high satisfaction and would like to participate in such events in the future; they see the communication as respectful and constructive, and they report learning a great deal about how others view the topic under discussion.[18] Many CAMP dialogue participants left the discussions more interested in government and politics.[19] Dialogue participants appreciate the effort put forth by the sponsoring agency and recognize the individuals who contribute to the agency's performance during the dialogue. In the long term, dialogues can help create an active, engaged citizenry that pays attention to its government and expects to be involved in open discussions of policy.

Discussion affects government, too. For example, in the CAMP dialogue, a joint committee staffer told a participant, "Your comments have challenged some of my own thinking." Staff also reported that the dialogue had direct policy effects on the master plan, and an animated discussion of adult education in the 2002 CAMP dialogue prompted additional actions by the joint committee. The California Senate Office of Research produced a report on adult education programs nationwide, and a new select committee was formed by an assemblymember who had taken part in the dialogue. To increase impact within government, future efforts should ensure agencywide involvement and carefully time the dialogues.

Agencywide Involvement

Convening 1,166 members of the public in an on-line dialogue[20] was more cost-effective for the EPA and less time-consuming for field staff than sponsoring a series of public meetings nationwide. The 2001 dialogue involved a far larger and more representative group of stakeholders than would have been able to provide feedback through more conventional methods. The event provided an opportunity to combine the intensive interaction of small-group discussions with broad, national participation, resulting in rich discussion of more varied viewpoints and experiences. It also enabled more field staff as well as headquarters personnel to participate, because they could drop in on the discussion for short periods without leaving their desk.

Many EPA staff nationwide helped in planning, in recruiting participants and panelists, and by responding directly to questions or statements that applied to their activities. Ten EPA offices each hosted a day of the discussion. Public involvement staff monitored all messages and referred questions or erroneous information to personnel across the agency. During and after the event, every region and most headquarters offices responded to something that was relevant to their programs.

This was a learning event for the EPA as well as for the public. The many EPA staffers who sent messages or looked in on the discussion were able to directly "hear" the participants' voices, making the abstract concepts of public involvement more real. Non-EPA participants expressed surprise that EPA was open to hearing from them and risking criticism and were very positive about EPA staff responsiveness as well as their openness to exploring suggestions for improvement.

Since the dialogue, the lessons from the experience and some of the material that was gathered have been incorporated in a series of training brochures designed to improve public involvement practices at the EPA.[21] The EPA issued the final Public Involvement Policy in June 2003.[22]

Timing a Dialogue to Increase Impact

Public involvement can have an impact on policy only when decision makers are committed to listening and intend to take comments into account. It is also important for involvement to occur before essential decisions have been made. Conducting a dialogue during the formative phase of policymaking indicates that public opinion is valued, generates more useful information for policymakers, and avoids criticism for being after the fact.

Timing is critical to securing lawmakers' involvement. For example, in California, a dialogue between April and June—the busiest part of the legislative calendar—will not attract much attention. Equally important, a dialogue that is too close to deadlines for moving bills out of committees reduces the likelihood that participants' comments will lead to substantive revisions.

The two dialogues related to the California Master Plan for Education offer a perspective on how timing can make public participation more effective for both the public and the government entities involved. The first dialogue[23] provided an opportunity for participants to review and offer suggestions for revisions to the plan before it was finalized. Many of these ideas were incorporated in later versions, which helped to broaden support for the plan. The second dialogue[24] sought comments on legislation that had been introduced to implement some of the master plan's recommendations; in this case, participant suggestions were received after bill text had already been drafted and had little impact.

Both California dialogues were scheduled to fit the legislative calendar, and both were held at the end of the school year. In each case, there were about one thousand participants, but their responses made clear that many others would have taken part and more messages would have been contributed at another time.

Ideally, public involvement and discussion would start at a much earlier stage of policy development. For education issues, we can imagine a two-part process involving many organizations and secondary and postsecondary students. The first part would be a general exploration of policy goals, intentions, and vision. This dialogue could be built into community programs, courses, and media. A subsequent dialogue on a proposed plan could then include many who are already familiar with the goals and issues. Early involvement could increase impact in several ways: public feedback would be received while policy is in a formative phase; more informed, in-depth public discussion with policymakers could occur; an expanded range of alternatives could be considered; and discussions would lead to greater public understanding over time and greater public attention to resulting legislation.

Reflections

We close this chapter by offering some cautions about on-line dialogue, challenges to doing it well, and opportunities for future extensions of the technique.

Cautions

On-line participatory processes may be used for many reasons—to meet statutory requirements, interact with the public, educate stakeholder groups, or achieve better procedures and results. A successful event can produce gains in trust and goodwill. Like any public involvement process, however, on-line dialogue creates responsibilities; failure to meet these responsibilities entails risks for the sponsoring agency.

Prerequisites for positive results include an approach that is genuinely open to public involvement (thus, the earlier in the policy development process the better); forthright statements to participants about the purpose of the discussion,[25] what is open to change, how comments will be used, and how participants will learn about outcomes; and nonpartisanship, balance, and diversity in every aspect of preparing and conducting the dialogue, including selection of library resources and panelists, identification and notification of stakeholders, moderation of the discussion, and staff involvement.

Producers and service providers for on-line dialogues have a responsibility to discuss with a sponsor the capabilities, staff time, and resources required, so that the sponsor can accurately assess the amount of outside help that might be necessary. In addition to the resources required to complete preparatory tasks, support will be needed by participants during the event, and there must be a plan for processing, sharing, and putting to use the significant amount of material from the dialogue when the event is over.[26] A sponsor that is experienced in public participation will be best prepared to handle these tasks independently.[27]

Challenges

On-line events present both challenges and opportunities for public involvement. Since the Internet eliminates distances, it is possible to identify and reach out to a geographically diverse set of stakeholders. At the same time, it is a challenge to recruit minority groups, tribal representatives, low-income populations, and young people; to interest those who are new to policy discussions or uncomfortable interacting in public; and to suggest access points for those who do not have on-line access at hand. In the short term, care should be taken to include advocacy groups and other intermediaries. In the long term, Internet access may be more widespread. Nevertheless, this will not lower other barriers to participation in policymaking, including unfamiliarity with the lawmaking process, lack of trust, and illiteracy.[28]

On-line public involvement will challenge government practices at all levels. The medium is intrinsically more transparent than traditional options. Legal guidelines established for hearings or written comments may require new interpretations to make sense in the on-line environment, and laws such as the Paperwork Reduction Act may inadvertently discourage innovative means of data collection and presentation. For policymakers, even with decades of experience in public hearings, some adjustment to the demands and opportunities of on-line dialogue may be needed. The public may deal harshly with a defensive response. On the other hand, good listening skills, openness to criticism, and genuine responses are rewarded, and one can take time to think through an answer and ask others to help when needed.

Extensions and Opportunities

On-line dialogue provides a mechanism for simultaneously educating and engaging the public in discussions of policy questions. If applied early in the process of policy formulation and accompanied by balanced and accessible information, dialogues can deepen and broaden public discussion, expand the range of options considered, and help the public appreciate trade-offs. Extensions of the model we have used might allow on-line dialogues that support negotiation or move toward group agreements.

Success in broad engagement will also create a new challenge: How does one orchestrate public discussions on an even larger scale? We have had success with groups of about a thousand people. Computer technology can facilitate effective direct interactions of much larger groups, but it will be a challenge to do this in a way that meets the needs of government and satisfies the majority of participants.

Dialogues with thoughtful and diverse participants have the potential to influence a broader group than just those who contribute messages to the discussion. Participants often report that they have refrained from submitting messages when they feel others have already spoken for them. This is not unlike proxy dialogue,[29] in which viewers take part vicariously by watching a learning process involving people with whom they can identify.

We believe that the audience for on-line policy dialogues will grow and that, ultimately, this will become a part of public involvement that is routinely embedded in government planning. Institutionalization will simplify many steps of the process: notification of potential participants will become a simple matter; production will be straightforward and inexpensive due to reusable components; ethical standards will be codified; public expectations will be clarified; laws will have standardized interpretations for Internet applications; and agencies will expect public comments and use the information they receive.[30] On-line civic engagement offers an exciting addition to the methods discussed in the other chapters of this volume, and the future possibilities are bright.

Notes

1. The five authors of this chapter are Patricia Bonner, U.S. Environmental Protection Agency, Washington, D.C.; Robert Carlitz and Rosemary Gunn, Information Renaissance, Pittsburgh, Pennsylvania; Laurie Maak, WestEd, San Francisco; and Charles A. Ratliff, Office of the Education Master Plan, Sacramento, California.

2. Before the on-line dialogue, only two of the nation's sixteen thousand school districts had responded to an FCC request for written comments on the proposed initiative, presumably because the commission's announcement in the Federal Register did not reach these stakeholders.

3. Information Renaissance. (1996, Aug.). "Comments, Reply Comments and Ex Parte Presentations." FCC Docket No. 96–45 In the Matter of Universal Service. [http://www.info-ren.org/projects/universal-service/repository-index.html]. Retrieved June 8, 2004.

4. Information Renaissance. (1996, Aug.). "Universal Service/Network Democracy On-Line Seminar." [http://www.info-ren.org/projects/universal-service/]. Retrieved June 8, 2004.

5. Information Renaissance. (1999, Mar.). "National Dialogue on Social Security." [http://www.network-democracy.org/social-security/]. Retrieved June 8, 2004.

6. See http://www.webdialogues.net/masterplan. The Office of the Education Master Plan (known at that time as the California Education Master Plan Alliance, or CEMPA) independently produced this dialogue using a hosted service from WestEd, a nonprofit research, development, and service organization. WestEd guided CEMPA staff through building the

Web site, involving panelists, recruiting participants, and conducting the discussions. WestEd also licenses their software to customers who prefer to run their own server.

7. Information Renaissance. (2001, June). "Dialogue on Public Involvement in EPA Decisions." [http://www.network-democracy.org/epa-pip/]. Retrieved June 8, 2004. See also Langlois, G. (2001, Aug. 6). "Online and Involved." *Federal Computer Week, 15*(26), 38 [http://www.fcw.com/fcw/articles/2001/0806/pol-epa-08-06-01.asp]. Retrieved June 10, 2004; and Visishtha, P. (2001, July 30). "EPA Takes a People Approach to E-Gov." *Government Computer News, 20*(21), 1, 14. [http://www.gcn.com/vol20_no21/news/4764-1.html]. Retrieved June 8, 2004.

8. Information Renaissance. (2002, May). "California Education Master Plan Dialogue." [http://www.network-democracy.org/camp]. Retrieved June 8, 2004.

9. California Education Master Plan Alliance. (2003, Apr.). "California Education Master Plan Dialogue." [http://www.webdialogues.net/masterplan]. Retrieved June 8, 2004.

10. In interviews after the California dialogue, legislative staff portrayed dialogue as far more interactive than other venues for public comment. They pointed out that for many participants, this was the first time that they had been able to address a legislator directly. Public hearings were contrasted as relatively structured and formal; most who testify at such hearings are lobbyists, union representatives, or spokespeople from professional associations, appearing on behalf of an organization. Also, public hearings are a one-shot format; once you have spoken, there is no opportunity to reply to another person's comments. See Gunn, R. W., and Carlitz, R. D. (2003). *Online Dialogue in a Political Context: The California Master Plan for Education.* Pittsburgh, Pa.: Information Renaissance, 64. [http://www.network-democracy.org/camp/report.shtml]. Retrieved June 7, 2004.

11. California Education Master Plan Alliance. (2003, Apr.). "California Education Master Plan Dialogue, Wrap-Up Evaluation." [http://www.webdialogues.net/cs/emp/download/dlib/183/alliance_eval.doc?x-r=pcfile_d]. Retrieved June 8, 2004.

12. California Education Master Plan Alliance (2003), "California Education Master Plan Dialogue, Wrap-Up Evaluation."

13. U.S. Department of Justice. (2002). "Overview of the Privacy Act of 1974." [http://www.usdoj.gov/04foia/04_7_1.html]. Retrieved June 10, 2004.

14. U.S. Fish and Wildlife Service. (1998). "Overview of the Paperwork Reduction Act of 1995." [http://www.fws.gov/pdm/opra.html]. Retrieved June 10, 2004.

15. A dialogue conducted with state government may also encounter legal or procedural obstacles, including laws similar to those at the federal level or perhaps a requirement that legislators review their statements before they are made public. (Such a requirement could make interactions extremely slow, which would significantly alter the nature of a dialogue.) An inquiry about laws or procedures that apply to interactions with the public is therefore an important part of preparation for a successful dialogue with a government entity.

16. Of the participants who completed wrap-up evaluations following the 2003 California Education Master Plan dialogue, 88 percent reported that they would definitely or probably view more favorably lawmakers who solicit the general public's opinion through similar on-line dialogues. See California Education Master Plan Alliance (2003), "California Education Master Plan Dialogue, Wrap-Up Evaluation."

17. Archives for dialogues discussed in this chapter are available on-line: Information Renaissance. "Dialogue Archives." [http://www.info-ren.org/what/dialogues_projects.shtml]. Retrieved June 10, 2004; and WebDialogues. "Dialogue Archive." [http://www.webdialogues.net]. Retrieved June 8, 2004.

18. Beierle, T. C. (2002). *Democracy On-Line: An Evaluation of the National Dialogue on Public Involvement in EPA Decisions*, chap. 4. Washington D.C.: Resources for the Future. [http://www.rff.org/Documents/RFF-RPT-demonline.pdf]. Retrieved June 8, 2004; Gunn and Carlitz (2003), *Online Dialogue in a Political Context*, chap. 5.

19. Gunn and Carlitz (2003), *Online Dialogue in a Political Context*, 7: After the CAMP dialogue, more than one-third of all evaluation respondents—and 50 percent of those who had been less active—reported that the dialogue had increased their interest in "government and politics."

20. See Information Renaissance (2001), "Dialogue on Public Involvement in EPA Decisions."

21. Brochures on public involvement (EPA Numbers 233F03005-233F03012 and 233F03014), published by the Office of Environmental Policy Innovation, U.S. Environmental Protection Agency, Washington, D.C., from August 2003 to July 2004, are available from the National Service Center for Environmental Publications, P.O. Box 42419, Cincinnati, OH 45242-2419. The series includes information on how to plan and budget, identify people to involve, provide technical and financial assistance, do outreach, consult with and involve the public, review and use public input and provide feedback, evaluate, improve public meetings and hearings, and involve environmental justice communities.

22. Office of Policy, Economics and Innovation, U.S. Environmental Protection Agency. (2003, May). "Public Involvement Policy of the U.S. Environmental Protection Agency." EPA 233-B-03-002. Washington, D.C.: U.S. Environmental Protection Agency. [http://www.epa.gov/publicinvolvement/policy2003]. Retrieved June 6, 2004. The EPA sponsored the 2001 dialogue to gather ideas for inclusion in a plan for improving public involvement practice at the EPA. That input is reflected in the information sharing, training, and evaluation tasks and tools in the "Framework" document on the same Web page: Office of Policy, Economics and Innovation, U.S. Environmental Protection Agency. (2003, May). "Framework for Implementing EPA's Public Involvement Policy." EPA 233-F-03-001. Washington, D.C.: U.S. Environmental Protection Agency. [http://www.epa.gov/publicinvolvement/policy2003].

23. See Information Renaissance (2002), "California Master Plan for Education Dialogue."

24. See California Education Master Plan Alliance (2003), "California Education Master Plan Dialogue."

25. The 2001 EPA dialogue, for instance, took place alongside a more formal procedure for submitting written comments to the agency. Staff tried to make this very clear in the publicity and during the dialogue: the messages would be useful in developing the implementation strategy for the policy and materials to support that strategy; however, due to legal restrictions, formal comments on the policy draft had to be sent in separately.

26. For example, the two EPA staff members who developed the 2001 dialogue read every message for the first two days and realized how difficult it would be to organize all the messages after the event. Working with Information Renaissance staff, they developed a list of topic themes and began sorting the messages. These later became searchable tables, which are posted on the dialogue Web site: Information Renaissance. (2001, Aug.). "Dialogue on Public Involvement in EPA Decisions: Summary Data Tables." [http://www.network-democracy.org/cgi-bin/epa-pip/show_tables.pl]. Retrieved June 9, 2004. EPA has since mined the tables many times for ideas to include in the training materials described in note 22.

27. The production of the 2003 dialogue by California's Office of the Education Master Plan demonstrates the viability of a sponsor owning its own dialogue process. This group benefited from their involvement in the 2002 CAMP dialogue and their close association with the Joint Committee to Develop the Master Plan for Education.

28. Kirsch, I. S., Jungeblut, A., Jenkins, L., and Kolstad, A. (1993). *Executive Summary of Adult Literacy in America: A First Look at the Results of the National Adult Literacy Survey.* Washington, D.C.: National Center for Education Statistics. [http://nces.ed.gov/naal/resources/execsumm.asp]. Retrieved June 10, 2004. (Also available in Kirsch, I. S., Jungeblut, A., Jenkins, L., and Kolstad, A. [1993, Aug. 30]. *Adult Literacy in America: A First Look at the Findings of the National Adult Literacy Survey.* NCES 93275. Washington, D.C.: National Center for Education Statistics.) According to Kirsch and his colleagues, up to 23 percent of the population have only "level one" literacy skills. Simple, routine tasks involving brief and uncomplicated texts can be performed by many at this level, but some have extremely limited reading skills.

29. Yankelovich, D. (1999). *The Magic of Dialogue.* New York: Simon & Schuster, 164–168.

30. Gunn and Carlitz (2003), *Online Dialogue in a Political Context,* 85ff.

CHAPTER TEN

A TOWN MEETING FOR THE TWENTY-FIRST CENTURY

Carolyn J. Lukensmeyer, Joe Goldman, Steven Brigham

More than three thousand Washington, D.C., residents joined Mayor Anthony Williams at the Washington Convention Center in the fall of 1999 for his first Citizen Summit. They had come together from across the city at the invitation of their new mayor to help create the district's budget and strategic plan. Many were skeptical of the new effort, and they had every right to be. For years, local leaders had asked residents to take part in planning for the city's future. Hours and hours of time spent at community meetings had produced enough plans and reports to fill a small library, but these efforts rarely led to any meaningful actions or outcomes.

Mayor Williams promised that his Neighborhood Action initiative was something different. At Williams's request, America*Speaks*[1] had designed a new process through which the community's priorities would drive the programs and services provided by the city (see Figure 10.1). Williams believed that he could regain the public's trust by engaging thousands of people in setting the city's direction. Their priorities would guide the development of the district's budget. Implementation of public priorities would be tracked through a sophisticated performance management process and public scorecard.

At the heart of Williams' promise to transform governance in the District of Columbia is the Citizen Summit. Every two years since 1999, Williams has presented a draft strategic plan for comment to the thousands of residents who attend the unique public forum. At the summit, citizens spend the day seated at

FIGURE 10.1. STRATEGIC MANAGEMENT CYCLE
FOR THE DISTRICT OF COLUMBIA

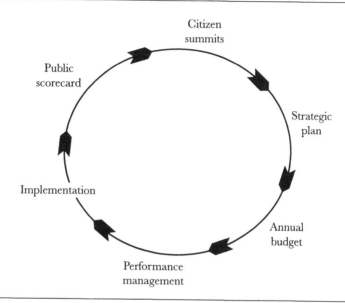

tables of ten people, where they review programs proposed by the mayor and wrestle with the city's problems. People from every walk of life attend the summit, representing the rich diversity of the community.[2] As they tackle each issue put before them, roomwide themes, collected through a networked computer system at each table, emerge from across the massive convention center. The themes are presented back to the group on large screens at the front of the room. Participants then use polling keypads to send a clear signal to the mayor about their highest priorities for the future.

Priorities articulated by the public at the Citizen Summit are used by the mayor to revise his strategic plan, which he then presents back to citizens at another forum two months later. The final strategic plan is used to develop the city's budget. A performance management system that is aligned with the strategic plan holds government accountable through an on-line scorecard and performance contracts for agency directors.

Williams has delivered on his promise to the residents of Washington, D.C. By creating a transparent link between public input and public accountability, the mayor has created a new paradigm for local government in a city that had been plagued by mismanagement for decades. Over the past five years, Neighborhood

Action has engaged more than ten thousand people in the governance of the city. At the end of each Citizen Summit, participants have overwhelmingly given the process high marks.[3] More important, Neighborhood Action has shifted millions of dollars of public funds to programs prioritized by the public. For example, the mayor and his agency directors earmarked over $700 million in new programming to match public priorities as part of the mayor's budget request to the city council after the first Citizen Summit in 1999.[4]

Overview

Most Americans would agree that there is something deeply wrong with the way our democracy is working. Over the past few decades, politics has become far more partisan, elections far more expensive, and policymaking far more beholden to special interests. In the process, one key voice continually gets squeezed out: the citizen's. A recent poll conducted by The Pew Charitable Trusts found that fewer than four in ten Americans believed that "most elected officials care what people like me think."[5] Another poll found that the percentage of Americans who "think they can trust the government in Washington to do what is right" always or most of the time dropped to 18 percent in 1995. After September 11, 2001, this number rebounded to 55 percent, but it has since fallen back to 36 percent as of the summer of 2004.[6]

While a healthy democracy depends on the ability of citizens to directly influence the public policies that deeply affect their lives, the current system has little room for genuine citizen input and impact. Unfortunately, the usual strategies for gathering input do not engage and sustain citizen interest or generate much useful information for decision makers. As a result, they do little to reinvigorate and expand participation in civic life. In this climate of high distrust between citizens and their government, we need new ways to involve citizens.

At America*Speaks,* we set out to design new mechanisms to address this challenge. How could we help decision makers go beyond polling to connect quickly and authentically with citizens and listen to their voices? How could we tap into the value of informal citizen conversation and make sure that the wisdom was heard and citizen voices respected? How could we deepen the relationship between decision makers and the public so that citizens could have a tangible impact on policymaking and resource planning? How could we take this process to a larger scale and meet the time demands of political officials? The 21st Century Town Meeting was first implemented in 1998 to respond to these questions.[7]

There is something magical about a 21st Century Town Meeting. Thousands of people arrive at a forum as distinct individuals, each with his or her own unique interests and point of view. As the day begins, individuals at each of the hundreds of tables across the room start to discuss critical issues facing the community. With the help of skilled facilitators, participants at each table learn that they care about many of the same things. They type their common ideas into a computer and send them off to the front of the room. Then, minutes later, participants look up and see that the ideas supported by their table are shared throughout the entire room. Some words have changed and a few new items have been added, but the essential ideas are there. The process of moving from "I" to "we" has begun.

A 21st Century Town Meeting enables thousands of citizens to simultaneously participate in intimate deliberation and contribute to the collective wisdom of everyone who has been convened. By engaging large, demographically representative groups in public deliberation, a 21st Century Town Meeting ensures that (1) all voices are at the table (those of the general public and those of key stakeholders); (2) the priorities of the public get the attention of decision makers and the media; and (3) a substantial segment of the public supports the results of the forum and has a stake in its implementation. Each meeting is strategically designed to create an immediate and transparent link between citizen voices and actual decision making.

Description of the Town Meeting Process

21st Century Town Meetings are convened by America*Speaks* and a sponsor organization or organizations in order to address a critical issue facing a community. In most cases, the sponsor of a 21st Century Town Meeting is the actual public official or institution that has decision-making authority on a given topic. For example, Mayor Williams has convened the public as part of the process of developing his city's budget and strategic plan for the past five years. Regional planning agencies in Chicago and Cincinnati have convened the public to participate in the development of comprehensive land-use plans for those regions. In other instances, civic organizations sponsor 21st Century Town Meetings as neutral conveners on an issue. In New York City, for example, a coalition of almost a hundred civic organizations convened three 21st Century Town Meetings as part of the redevelopment of the World Trade Center site after the September 11 attacks. In cases where a forum is convened by civic organizations, decision makers are brought into the process as partners, to ensure that they are committed to responding to the outcomes of the forum.

America*Speaks* works with sponsors to ensure that public input is integrated into a larger planning or decision-making process. For some initiatives, like those in Chicago, Cincinnati, and Washington, D.C., the 21st Century Town Meeting becomes a formal component of the institution's ongoing management and decision-making processes. When the convener of a town meeting is a civic organization, the process tends to rely more heavily on securing commitments from stakeholders and decision makers to participate in and respond to the process. The large scale of the event also pressures decision makers to heed the results of the forum.

A 21st Century Town Meeting convenes hundreds or thousands of people at a time, to ensure that all sorts of voices are part of the process and to increase the influence of the priorities that emerge from the discussions. The scale of a given meeting is planned with the sponsor on the basis of how many people must participate in order for the event to have sufficient credibility with three audiences: the public, decision makers, and the media. While there is no scientific way to set a target size for a forum, several criteria are considered, including the size of the community, the profile of the issue, and the past track record of public engagement in the community. Once the size of the meeting is established, America-*Speaks* works with the sponsor to determine the demographic composition of the forum. Generally, we start with the demographic reality of a community as measured by the U.S. Census and then consider what special groups may need additional representation—for example, victims' family members, for the forums to redevelop Ground Zero in New York.

America*Speaks* ensures that 21st Century Town Meetings are demographically representative of the community by actively recruiting participants to meet demographic targets. Outreach strategies are specifically tailored for each project, but they generally include some combination of grassroots organizing and a sophisticated media campaign. Members of hard-to-reach groups, like young people or low-income residents, receive personal invitations from people whom they know and trust. As participants register to attend a forum, America*Speaks* compares registration numbers to its demographic targets and modifies the recruitment strategy as needed. If, for example, registration numbers are low for a certain ward or demographic of a city, resources are shifted to increase recruitment of that group.

To ensure that participants have adequate information to participate in the deliberations, America*Speaks* works with sponsors to develop highly accessible participant guides. These guides are written to help people understand the context surrounding an issue and the diverse menu of options that policymakers are considering. In most cases, materials are translated into multiple languages. Whenever possible, these educational materials are mailed to participants prior to a forum and, in some cases, are distributed to the whole community through local newspapers and at popular community locales, such as grocery stores and libraries. Written materials are supplemented by presentations and videos at the forum. In addition, neutral issue experts are available to answer questions that come up at tables.

The architecture of the 21st Century Town Meeting itself has several critical components:

Facilitated deliberation. Demographically diverse groups of ten to twelve participants come together with the support of a trained facilitator for in-depth discussion of the issue under consideration. The size of the group creates a safe, intimate space in which participants arrive at a collective view that represents the best integration of individual perspectives.

Networked computers. Computers at each table serve as electronic flipcharts, creating an instant record of the ideas generated at tables and ensuring that all voices are heard and no idea is lost. Through a wireless network, citizens transmit their ideas to a central database, setting the stage for distillation of themes from every table.

Theming. Members of a "theme team" read participants' comments from every table in real time and distill them into key themes or messages. The themes are then presented back to the room to build collective ownership of the entire group's work.

Polling keypads. Each participant in a 21st Century Town Meeting has a wireless keypad for voting on issues and measuring his or her position with respect to other participants. Keypads also are used to establish the demographics of the event so that participants get a sense of the larger group of which they are a part. Keypad polling yields volumes of demographically sortable data that can be of great value to decision makers.

Using technology to gather, distill, and project themes allows a 21st Century Town Meeting to move back and forth between intimate small-group dialogue and the collective work of thousands of people. This back-and-forth between the small-scale and large-scale dialogues can occur as many times as needed to develop recommendations on which decision makers can take action.

What does a 21st Century Town Meeting actually look like from start to finish? The day begins with brief opening comments from key political leaders, to set the context for the issues under discussion. Participants begin by answering a series of demographic questions, using polling keypads, both to get oriented to the technology and to find out who is in the room. Before any deliberation on key content, there is a vision- or values-based discussion to allow participants to learn what is important to them regarding the issues at hand. The critical vision or values identified by participants lay the foundation for the next four to five hours of discussion on key issues and policy options. As already described, in each segment of the agenda, discussion begins at individual tables, is themed in real time, then presented back to the whole for clarification and modification and, finally, for voting.

The last twenty minutes of a forum are used to evaluate the day, review next steps, and allow time for decision makers to comment on what they have heard from participants. A report that summarizes the day's outcomes is developed during the day and distributed to participants as they leave. The same information is made available to the public that is provided to decision makers and the media. By the end of the day, decision makers, the media, and citizens have heard the collective wisdom of a large, demographically representative cross section of the public. Because decision makers have participated in the event and committed to act on the recommendations, the voices that come together at a 21st Century Town Meeting have a lasting impact. Whenever possible, ongoing mechanisms are put in place to support continued public participation. For example, Mayor Williams created neighborhood processes to provide citizens with an ongoing role, linking them to neighborhood planners and agency service delivery.

History and Impact of Town Meetings

America*Speaks* has convened more than forty 21st Century Town Meetings in more than thirty states across the country. The organization has produced a track record of creating meaningful results, ranging from influencing the terms of the Social Security debate to shifting the plans for the redevelopment of the World Trade Center site after the September 11 attacks.

What evidence is there that 21st Century Town Meetings have made a difference? First, 21st Century Town Meetings educate participants and change how individuals relate to the issue in question. Routinely, America*Speaks* uses keypad polling to ask participants whether they have learned something at a forum, whether any of their opinions have shifted, and whether they plan to remain involved with the issue. Invariably, the response is overwhelmingly positive for each of these questions. An evaluation of a series of 21st Century Town Meetings on Social Security reform that was written by researchers at Northwestern University's Institute for Policy Research in 1998 confirmed these findings. According to the report, participants' understanding of the issues of Social Security reform increased significantly as a result of their participation in the deliberations: "Not only did attendees say their understanding of facts of Social Security increased as a result of their participation in the forum, but also their responses to a series of six factual questions showed their overall knowledge really did increase."[8] The evaluation went on to say, "The salience of Social Security increased dramatically for those people who attended the forum as compared to the random sample and to those who were invited and did not attend. After the forum, attendees were dramatically more likely than others to say they spent time thinking about, talking about, and reading about Social Security."[9] The evaluation also found that support for certain policy options increased as a result of their participation, as did their enthusiasm for remaining involved with the issue.

The impact that a 21st Century Town Meeting can have on public decision making can be even more dramatic. For example, America*Speaks'* work in New York City had a substantial effect on the World Trade Center redevelopment. More than two hundred media outlets, along with representatives of the governor, the mayor, and local planning agencies, looked on as thousands of participants at the forum overwhelmingly rejected several critical elements of each of the six plans. Most notably, a substantial portion of the public was unhappy with the density of the site plans and a requirement that each of the plans replace all of the office and retail space that had been in the former World Trade Center. The next day, newspapers across the country ran stories with headlines like this one from the *New York Daily News:* "Plans for WTC Ripped: So, Back to the Drawing Board."[10]

Within days of the forum, state and city leaders agreed to reassess several unpopular assumptions underlying the plans. Less than two weeks later, a *New York Times* editorial reported that Governor Pataki had decided that it was "time to go back to the drawing board" on the plans in response to "a wave of public dismay over the first designs for rebuilding Lower Manhattan." The editorial continued: "The governor, like Mayor Michael Bloomberg, now seems committed to creating a better mix of uses for ground zero, and a 24-hour community in Manhattan's downtown. . . . Mr. Pataki openly questioned the Port Authority's requirement that any plan for the site must replace all the office, hotel and retail square footage lost in the attack on Sept. 11."[11]

In October, officials responsible for the redevelopment process created a new program that cut the amount of office space mandated for the plans by one million square feet and permitted them to reduce the amount of office space that had to be on the site itself by about 40 percent. The new program and the request for proposals for new plans included many of the detailed recommendations that had been produced by the public, including constructing at least one tall tower to add visual interest to the skyline and depressing West Street under a promenade.[12]

Reflections

The dramatic outcomes that were produced in New York were not unique. Every 21st Century Town Meeting is designed to respond to the political realities of contemporary policymaking in order to produce real results. America*Speaks'* approach uses scale, diversity, transparency, and strong relationships with decision makers to ensure that the voices of the public are heard and that the experience of participation is an empowering one. It is our hope that as applications of the 21st

Century Town Meeting increase, we can rebuild the public's faith in its role in the governance process.

Critics of deliberative democracy often argue that claims of the positive impacts of deliberative participation are unsupported by hard data. There is some validity to this criticism. We at America*Speaks* have only just begun to research the effects of 21st Century Town Meetings in relation to how individuals and policymaking are influenced over the long term. However, based on our seven years of experience and the limited data that is available to us, we remain confident that the benefits of providing the public with a greater voice through 21st Century Town Meetings will withstand scrutiny.

The field of deliberative democracy and citizen engagement is young, and many of the leading models for engaging the public remain works in progress. The 21st Century Town Meeting is no different. With each process that we organize, America*Speaks* learns more about how to create diverse, high-quality forums that provide the public with a stronger voice in decision making. Three concerns stand out as areas in which America*Speaks* continues to work to improve:

Diversity. While America*Speaks* has made considerable strides in the development of outreach strategies that generate demographically representative groups of participants, the recruitment of certain hard-to-reach groups—most notably youth and low-income residents—remains a challenge.

Sustainability. Whereas America*Speaks* has had considerable success in bringing very large numbers of people into governance processes, we have struggled with the creation of systems that will sustain large-scale citizen participation after a 21st Century Town Meeting is over.

Cost. The cost of engaging hundreds or thousands of citizens can be quite significant and is often beyond the reach of many small to midsize communities. We are always looking for ways to reduce the cost of engaging the public without sacrificing the quality of the process.

As America*Speaks* looks to the future, our highest priority is taking what we have learned about engaging the public and applying those lessons to national policymaking. The public needs a greater voice in governance at all levels, but it is at the national level that there is the greatest disconnection between citizens and decision makers. Recently, America*Speaks* convened a coalition of a dozen leaders in the field of citizen engagement to develop a blueprint for a national discussion that would involve millions of people in a deliberation that could influence both Congress and the executive branch of the federal government. We must find ways to incorporate these national discussions into more effective governing mechanisms, linking the public's voice to the nation's governance processes in order to restore the health of our democratic institutions.

The path to revitalizing our democracy will no doubt be a long one. It is heartening, however, to see the recent progress that has been made in demonstrating new approaches to involving the public. With each step forward, we come closer to a nation truly of the people, by the people, and for the people.

Notes

1. America*Speaks*, founded in 1995, is a nonprofit organization based in Washington, D.C. America*Speaks*' mission is to engage citizens in the most important public decisions that affect their lives, at every level of government.

2. For example, at the first Citizen Summit in 1999, the demographics of participants were measured by gender, geography, age, household income, and ethnicity through anonymous keypad polling at the beginning of the day. Sixty-one percent of participants were female, and 39 percent were male. Of the city's eight wards, no ward was represented by more than 15 percent of the participants or less than 9 percent of the participants. Annual household income was measured in five categories: less than $25,000 (22 percent), $25,001–$40,000 (19 percent), $40,001–$60,000 (20 percent), $60,001–$100,000 (21 percent), and more than $100,000 (18 percent). Twelve percent of participants were under the age of 18, 12 percent were aged 19–34, 35 percent were 35–54, 19 percent were 55–64, and 22 percent were 65 or older. Sixty-one percent of participants were African American, 5 percent were Asian, 22 percent were Caucasian, 3 percent were Hispanic, 2 percent were Native American, 5 percent were multicultural, and 1 percent preferred not to reveal their ethnicity.

3. At the first Citizen Summit, participants were asked to evaluate the process through an anonymous keypad poll. Ninety-one percent said the summit was "excellent" or "good." Only four percent rated the summit as "fair" or "poor." Ninety-four percent of participants said they "had the chance to fully participate today." Ninety-one percent said the Neighborhood Action initiative was "a very important program," and 8 percent said it was a "somewhat important program."

4. Potapchuk, W. (2002). "Neighborhood Action Initiative: Engaging Citizens in Real Change." In D. D. Chrislip (ed.), *The Collaborative Leadership Fieldbook*. San Francisco: Jossey-Bass.

5. Pew Research Center for the People and the Press. (2003, Nov. 5). *Evenly Divided and Increasingly Polarized: 2004 Political Landscape*. Washington, D.C.: Pew Research Center for the People and the Press.

6. CBS News/*New York Times* Poll, July 11–15, 2004. $N = 955$ adults nationwide; margin of error: ± 3 percentage points.

7. The 21st Century Town Meeting™ is a trademarked process of America*Speaks*.

8. Cook, F. L., and Jacobs, L. R. (1998, Sept.). *Evaluation of Americans Discuss Social Security: Deliberative Democracy in Action*. Philadelphia: Pew Charitable Trusts, 27.

9. Cook and Jacobs (1998), *Evaluation of Americans Discuss Social Security*, 26.

10. Gittrich, G. (2002, July 21). "Plans for WTC Ripped: So, Back to the Drawing Board." *New York Daily News*, 7.

11. "Governor Pataki Weighs In." (2002, July 31). Editorial. *New York Times*, A18.

12. Rosegrant, S. (2003, Apr. 1). *Listening to the City: Rebuilding at New York's World Trade Center Site (Epilogue)*. Cambridge, Mass.: John F. Kennedy School of Government Case Program, Harvard University.

CHAPTER ELEVEN

COLLABORATIVE LEARNING AND THE PUBLIC'S STEWARDSHIP OF ITS FORESTS

Antony S. Cheng, Janet D. Fiero

Technical experts met recently to discuss the contentious issue of water storage projects in western Colorado. The conveners set the tone by explaining that each party was expected to represent his or her interest area. One of the participants had been involved in a Collaborative Learning project and argued with the facilitator, saying, "We are used to *collaborating* here on the Western Slope. We look at the big picture of all the interests and not just our own."

Collaborative Learning[1] is a recent innovation in public participation that breaks away from traditional issue-based processes. Collaborative Learning is grounded in theories of conflict management, systems thinking, and adult learning. The approach was specifically formulated to address both the complexity and the rancorous conflict that characterizes the management of U.S. public lands and resources, such as the national forests managed by the U.S. Department of Agriculture's Forest Service.

Public participation in decisions on how to manage the national forests is mandated by the National Forest Management Act of 1976, which requires the development and updating of a forest plan every ten to fifteen years for each national forest. The last plan for the Grand Mesa, Uncompahgre, and Gunnison National Forest (GMUG) in western Colorado was developed in 1983, and much had changed in the intervening years. Given the demographic, economic, and political transformation of the GMUG region, setting the strategic priorities for managing the GMUG posed enormous challenges. The leadership of the GMUG chose Collaborative Learning because they wanted to explore positive, collaborative methods that encouraged place-based deliberation.

One key aspect of the Collaborative Learning process is sustaining public participation throughout the planning process in order to produce a forest plan that is understood and supported by a broad range of stakeholders and therefore has a high probability of being implemented. In the case of the GMUG, the process was divided into five phases, beginning with a series of assessments for each of the five geographic areas of the forest and continuing with a draft plan, a final plan, an appeals period, and the implementation. This chapter focuses on the up-front assessment phase of GMUG forest planning, which was conducted from Spring 2002 through Summer 2004. Each assessment identified key issues facing the area, defined current and desired conditions, pointed out important trends, and provided interpretations and recommendations for plan development. Because the assessments laid the groundwork for potential GMUG forest plan decisions, stakeholder involvement was essential. The format for stakeholder involvement in the assessment phase was a series of landscape working groups that were organized for each geographic area. The working group participants interacted with the GMUG planning team and district staff, using a Collaborative Learning approach to develop vision statements, clarify current conditions, and identify desired future conditions that would be incorporated in draft geographic area assessments developed by the GMUG planning team.

Background on the Collaborative Learning Approach

The Collaborative Learning approach had its beginnings in the seemingly intractable resource management controversies of the Pacific Northwest in the early 1990s. Steve Daniels, formerly a professor of forest policy at Oregon State University and currently director of the Western Rural Development Center at Utah State University, and Gregg Walker, a speech communication professor at Oregon State University, adapted theories, frameworks, and practices that were used in negotiation, conflict management, adult learning, and soft systems methodology. The Collaborative Learning approach was first applied in two field settings: recreation management planning for the Oregon Dunes National Recreation Area[2] and postfire recovery in the Wenatchee National Forest in Washington.[3] Both processes generated remarkable progress and received high satisfaction ratings from public participants.[4]

Natural resource issues are both complex and controversial. The complexity is due to the interrelationships of the ecological, economic, and social dimensions of a resource situation. Efforts to simplify a natural resource issue into linear cause-and-effect relationships inevitably leave out many linkages. The soft-systems methodology in Collaborative Learning is employed to foster and enhance stakeholders' capacity to think about and therefore deliberate about issues systemically, instead of focusing on the "single-devil syndrome" associated with linear cause-and-effect approaches. Even stakeholders who have thought systemically about a resource issue may have deep conflicts about values. Frameworks and practices from experiential social learning, negotiation, and dispute resolution are applied to address the inherent value conflicts that people have about natural resources. The goal is for stakeholders to explore a situation as a system and from multiple perspectives. In doing so, stakeholders may discover ways of dealing with the issue that go beyond their own visions of what is possible.

The underlying premise of Collaborative Learning is that before making decisions that affect real pieces of land and real people's lives, it is necessary to learn a great deal about the surrounding issues, various stakeholders' values and concerns, scientific information, and ways of looking at a resource management situation from multiple angles. Both resource management agencies and stakeholders (for example, users, advocacy groups, and community members) can benefit from such learning.

Collaborative Learning has three essential characteristics: systems thinking, constructive dialogue, and a focus on feasible improvements. Although there are many other important features of Collaborative Learning that are similar to those described in other chapters, each of these three aspects helps distinguish this process from its deliberative cousins.

Systems thinking. Rarely can natural resource management situations be explained by using a linear cause-and-effect model. More commonly, there are multiple and often unknown natural and human forces acting on a natural resource system. There are also multiple and overlapping uses and values associated with a natural resource system, making precise measurement of causes and impacts exceedingly difficult. Stakeholders who view a natural resource situation as a complex system with interrelationships, feedback loops, and multiple linkages tend to be better equipped to move forward on making feasible improvements to the situation (and less likely to focus mistakenly on removing single causes). Specific techniques include situation or concept mapping, geographic mapping (using paper or digital maps), social network mapping, multidisciplinary panel presentations, and field trips.

Constructive dialogue about differences and commonalities. Many controversial natural resource management situations can be managed effectively once stakeholders begin to communicate respectfully with one another. Dialogue leads to understanding, and understanding opens doors to new perspectives on a situation. Constructive dialogue can be facilitated by a neutral third party. The Collaborative Learning approach makes liberal use of a variety of small-group and large-group techniques. One specific technique is for individuals to write down concerns and ideas for ten minutes, then share them with one other person for ten minutes. The pair joins with another pair for ten minutes before meeting in a group of eight individuals. This 1–2–4–8 discussion technique ensures that everyone has a chance to give voice to their own concerns and ideas as well as come up with a set of group concerns and ideas.

Focus on feasible improvements. In a typical stakeholder involvement process, individuals and groups are invited to provide input on a proposed agency action either through written comments or oral presentations at a public meeting. Stakeholders generally articulate what they want (or don't want), and the agency shoulders the responsibility for making all of these desires feasible. In a Collaborative Learning process, all stakeholders shoulder the responsibility for making feasible improvements to the situation, not just declaring what they want. In addition, in Collaborative Learning, the emphasis on improvements replaces problem solving as a key concept. Rarely are natural resource situations wholly solved, but they can be improved. Improvements can be measured and provide indicators of meaningful progress. Under Collaborative Learning, natural resource situations are best improved through marginal changes rather than wholesale disruptions.

This last observation was a critical starting point for the landscape working groups discussed in the following section. With diverse stakeholders at the table, it is unrealistic to resolve all issues for all time. It is also important not to focus attention exclusively on the on-the-ground substantive issues. Instead, Collaborative Learning recognizes that there are three dimensions to every collaborative process: substance, procedure, and relationships. Sustainable collaborative outcomes turn on making progress on all three dimensions, because the dimensions are interrelated. Hence, a collaborative process should provide opportunities to work on improving the fairness and rigor of the process and foster respectful working relationships in addition to tackling the on-the-ground situation.

Landscape Working Groups as Illustrations of Collaborative Learning

Each landscape working group was an open-invitation public process that was facilitated by a neutral third party under contract with the U.S. Institute for Environmental Conflict Resolution. In addition to sending postcards and e-mail and posting Web site announcements of group meetings, the neutral third party and public affairs staff for the GMUG planning team often personally contacted stakeholders. Participants in the groups included recreation enthusiasts, ranchers, environmental activists, local elected officials, timber industry representatives, Native

American tribal representatives, and citizens concerned with the sustainability of the local forest environment and community. Working group meetings were held in different communities around each geographic area to ensure that community stakeholders had ample access to the process. Forty-two meetings were held, and 1,035 individuals participated. The meetings took place in public meeting rooms ranging from fire hall lofts to formal rooms on college campuses. The number of participants was limited by the space available in the small towns of western Colorado.

The landscape working group process also had an evaluation research component, which used postmeeting interviews and surveys to measure indicators of progress. The indicators were based on the three dimensions of a collaborative process described earlier (substance, procedure, and relationships). The monitoring and evaluation were critical to the adaptation and refinement of the deliberative approaches used in the groups.

At the outset, the GMUG planning team introduced the landscape working group participants to the goal of the GMUG forest plan and the role of the public in contributing to the plan. Included in this introduction were clear expectations of what the public could and could not influence in the plan. Elements that could not be influenced were those required by statute, court order, or administrative rules. This introduction was vital because it clarified the "decision space" available to the public. The neutral third party also played an important role by presenting ground rules by which the group would operate. All participants in the group process were expected to abide by the rules and remind others of the rules when they saw violations.

After the introduction, the landscape working group process was divided into two phases—a landscape visioning process and a mapping process that focused on the desired future condition of the landscape. To develop the landscape vision, participants were divided into small groups of six to eight individuals. Each individual was asked to identify the features and values that made the geographic area unique—what the geographic area had that cannot be found anyplace else on Earth. This exercise allowed individuals to express their values—their full appreciation for the land, natural resources, and human communities in the area. Each individual was also asked to identify what actions had to happen to maintain or enhance these features and values, as well as what barriers stood in the way. Each individual was then asked to share ideas with the others in the small group, and each small group produced a comprehensive list of unique features and values, plus the opportunities for and barriers to maintaining or enhancing them. After thirty minutes of small-group discussion, the same discussion occurred with the entire large group. The discussion produced key words and phrases that were eventually incorporated into a draft vision statement that explained why the geographic area was unique and valuable and what actions were needed to sustain or improve it.

The vision statement provided the focal point for what all participants had in common—why they valued their geographic place. In the mapping phase, the participants worked together to identify what they would like their landscape to look like in the future. Again, the process broke participants into small groups of six to eight individuals. Forest Service personnel, who had received training in small-group facilitation prior to each meeting, sat at each table to clarify technical questions and encourage open dialogue. Each small-group table was equipped with three-by-five-foot maps of the geographic area divided into smaller landscape units; a landscape theme reference guide; data summaries for each landscape unit; and a desired condition worksheet.

The maps and data summaries had been generated by the planning team, working with district staff. The maps were digital replicas of maps that were commonly used for recreation pursuits, such as hiking, motorcycling, and car touring. Hence, the maps were of places and at a geographic scale that were familiar to stakeholders. The landscape units on the maps were color-coded by theme. Landscape themes classified landscape conditions on a continuum from pristine wilderness (theme 1) to permanent human-altered developments (theme 8). In essence, the themes described what kinds of disturbances may affect a landscape, from purely natural to purely human alterations. The purpose of the themes was to provide stakeholders with a common language for communicating the current and desired conditions and alterations of the landscape units.

The data summaries included tables of key information about the area, such as vegetation types, extent of roads and trails, recreation opportunities, potential for timber and other resource production activities, and unique ecological and social values, such as endangered species or historical landmarks.

The first stage of the mapping process was to affirm, adjust, and amend the information for each landscape unit on the map. In doing so, participants drew on their own and one another's knowledge of the landscape, resources, and uses, and matched it with the information provided by the Forest Service. This was a unique opportunity for local stakeholders to contribute to the production of information and knowledge about the local landscape. Changes were noted on the map and on the data summaries.

The second stage of the mapping process was to define the desired condition of the landscape. This was a highly deliberative process because it required people to integrate individual visions for how the land should look in the future and the role of people in achieving this vision. Diverse individuals had to confront their differences, weigh the relevant technical information about environmental conditions, consider diverse values concerning the landscape, and arrive at a common vision that would be subject to further change. A desired condition worksheet was formatted to encourage stakeholders to use the landscape themes to describe the findings of small-group deliberations. Specific comments and concerns were written on the worksheets to give voice to dissenting viewpoints.

History of Collaborative Learning

Collaborative Learning as a deliberative approach has been applied in numerous situations, such as recreation area planning,[5] postfire recovery planning,[6] and several small-scale land management planning contexts.[7] However, the large-scale landscape working group framework is unique to the Grand Mesa, Uncompahgre, and Gunnison National Forest and has not been applied in other national forest planning processes to date. In sum, 1,035 individuals participated in the group process across the five geographic areas of the GMUG, with an average meeting attendance of twenty-nine to fifty-two participants. The two-stage visioning and mapping process described earlier was implemented in the remaining three of the five geographic areas based on a critical lesson that had been learned: the need to be more efficient in engaging stakeholders. Thus, the first two landscape working groups (the Uncompahgre and North Fork Valley groups) had a total of seventeen and eight meetings, respectively, whereas the last three groups (Grand Mesa, San Juans, and Gunnison Basin) had fewer meetings: six, six, and four meetings, respectively.

Postmeeting evaluation surveys provide a quantitative indication of the impact of the deliberative process on participants. Table 11.1 shows mean scores of the responses to selected statements focused on learning. As the table indicates, almost all participants appreciated the opportunity to deliberate early in the planning process. The average response to the statement "It is important that the public is being involved at this early stage of the Forest Plan Revision" was 4.59 on a scale of 1 ("strongly disagree") to 5 ("strongly agree"). Using the same response scale, participants also indicated that they valued the knowledge that others possessed (mean = 4.30), including the Forest Service (mean = 4.22). Participants generally valued the small-group discussions (mean = 4.29) and the mapping process (mean = 4.36), but they were somewhat less comfortable with the large-group discussions (mean = 3.96). It is important to note that participants who attended the landscape working groups were already well-versed in deliberative processes, having been a part of two or three previous collaborative groups.

Reflections and Recommendations

To successfully apply Collaborative Learning to different places and purposes, conveners need to carefully adapt the discussion methods used in each meeting, based on local culture and the complexity of the public issue. Conveners must

TABLE 11.1. MEAN RESPONSES TO LEARNING-BASED STATEMENTS FROM POSTMEETING SURVEYS OF THE GRAND MESA, SAN JUANS, AND GUNNISON BASIN LANDSCAPE WORKING GROUPS

Evaluation Question	Mean	Standard Deviation
I understand how this evening's meeting fits into the GMUG forest plan revision.	3.81	1.05
My knowledge of the area provided important contributions to this meeting.	4.06	1.05
Other citizens' knowledge of the area provided important contributions to this meeting.	4.30	0.98
The district staff's knowledge of the area provided important contributions to this meeting.	4.22	0.98
It is important that the public is being involved at this early stage of the Forest Plan Revision.	4.59	0.91
Presentations by Forest Service staff help me better understand various issues affecting the area.	4.11	1.04
I was comfortable discussing public land issues with people I don't know. ($n = 273$)	4.11	0.00
I was comfortable discussing public land issues with people who hold different viewpoints. ($n = 273$)	4.11	1.02
I was comfortable contributing to discussions during the large-group activity.	3.96	1.10
I was comfortable contributing to discussions during the small-group activity.	4.29	0.95
I felt comfortable using maps during the landscape management activity.	4.36	0.95
I am comfortable talking to Forest Service staff about issues in the area. ($n = 273$)	4.34	1.03
How many collaborative processes have you participated in over the past 5 years?	2.55	1.10
How many of these involved the GMUG forest?	2.16	1.14

Note: Responses were recorded on a scale ranging from 1 ("strongly disagree") to 5 ("strongly agree"). Total sample size (*n*) was 329, except when otherwise noted.

fully understand the underlying theories and frameworks of this process in order to design activities that ensure that collaborative learning will occur. Typically, government agencies such as the Forest Service lack adequate training, skills, time, and personnel and financial resources to convene such an intensive process. Even if there is understanding and support for a Collaborative Learning approach, it is simply not feasible without the necessary skills and resources. Designing meetings is not like following a step-by-step recipe from a cookbook. When the conveners and facilitators design site-specific meetings and respond to the changing needs of the local community, they are using the Collaborative Learning model adaptively and to its best advantage.

An ongoing challenge is to manage the expectations of stakeholders. The choice of language is fateful. Contentious, complex public issues cannot be solved, but they can be improved. Expecting collaboration will help collaboration happen. Likewise, expecting special interests to focus on their personal gains or losses will ensure that they fail to struggle with the complexity of the whole situation, including the larger systemic context in which particular disagreements and disputes are taking place. Honoring and embracing differences is altogether distinct from merely tolerating differences. Strategic behaviors among stakeholders—such as waiting to file administrative appeals and lawsuits or seeking legislative actions instead of engaging in deliberations from the beginning of the planning process—will persist.

Another ongoing challenge is taking the time for assessment and not jumping into developing recommendations or actions. During the assessment phase, studying the social, economic, and ecological history of the place allows neighbors and adversaries to develop a common picture of the current situation; they learn one another's perspectives and values. This common ground and mutual respect enables richer dialogue when they begin to develop suggestions for change and improvement.

High-quality assessment and the building of civic fabric requires representation of all of the diverse stakeholders. Ensuring demographic representation of all parties continues to be a challenge.

As the public learns more about the intrinsic satisfaction of well-designed public forums, more people will want to participate in public processes such as those discussed in this and the other chapters of this book. Designing meetings of one hundred or more people will require that activities and methods adapt. It will also be beneficial to experiment with technology as described in Chapters Nine, Ten, and Fifteen. The Internet offers on-line opportunities for broader participation, but it may sacrifice the relationship-building aspect of face-to-face meetings. Using modeling simulations to depict the probable results of decisions will also assist the public in making more informed input. As new meeting technologies evolve, the challenge will be to find ways to build the capacity of the community to address future issues together.

Notes

1. Daniels, S. E., and Walker, G. B. (2001). *Working Through Environmental Conflict: The Collaborative Learning Approach.* Westport, Conn.: Praeger, 328.
2. Daniels, S. E., and Walker, G. B. (1996). "Collaborative Learning: Improving Public Deliberation in Ecosystem-Based Management." *Environmental Impact Assessment Review, 16,* 71–102.
3. Daniels, S. E., and Walker, G. B. (1996). "Using Collaborative Learning in Fire Recovery Planning." *Journal of Forestry, 94*(8), 4–9.
4. Blatner, K. A., Carroll, M. S., Daniels, S. E., and Walker, G. B. (2001). "Evaluating the Application of Collaborative Learning to the Wenatchee Fire Recovery Planning Effort." *Environmental Impact Assessment Review, 21,* 241–270.
5. Daniels and Walker (1996), "Using Collaborative Learning in Fire Recovery Planning."
6. Daniels and Walker (1996), "Using Collaborative Learning in Fire Recovery Planning."
7. Daniels, S. E., and Walker, G. B. (1997). "Collaborative Learning and Land Management Conflict." In B. Solberg and S. Miina (eds.), *Conflict Management and Public Participation in Land Management.* Joensuu, Finland: European Forest Institute.

CHAPTER TWELVE

PARTICIPATION AND PUBLIC POLICIES IN BRAZIL

Vera Schattan P. Coelho, Barbara Pozzoni,
Mariana Cifuentes Montoya

The 1988 Brazilian Constitution, which established the formal transition to democracy, sanctioned the decentralization of policymaking and established mechanisms for citizens to participate in the formulation, management, and monitoring of social policies. Hundreds of thousands of interest groups worked throughout the country as the constitution was being drafted and collected half a million signatures to demand the creation of participatory democratic mechanisms. Underpinning such demand was the belief that by opening spaces for citizens to participate, the policymaking process would become more transparent and accountable and social policies would better reflect the needs of the citizens.

This legal foundation promoted the development of an extensive institutional framework for participation by citizens, including management councils, public hearings, conferences, participatory budgeting, and deliberative mechanisms within regulatory agencies. Of the plethora of participatory mechanisms in Brazil, participatory budgeting and management councils gained the greatest momentum in the 1990s. These two participatory mechanisms are linked to the executive branch and stress transparency, local control, and the redistribution of resources to underserved areas.

This chapter presents results of research carried out by the Brazilian Centre of Analysis and Planning and the Development Research Centre on Citizenship, Participation and Accountability at the Institute of Development Studies and supported by the Department for International Development/United Kingdom.

Since 1989, 250 of the 5,507 Brazilian municipalities have adopted the participatory budgeting process, which enables the participation of citizens in setting priorities for government investment in infrastructure and basic social services. Participatory budgeting is a local practice of public deliberation on budget issues. The participatory budgeting assemblies facilitate public scrutiny of government performance, and they provide a space in which citizens negotiate priorities on public investment. The final document of the participatory budgeting process is the plan of work and services; this plan is sent to the executive as an integral part of the budget, then submitted to the legislature for review and a final vote. In Porto Alegre, the city of 1.3 million inhabitants where participatory budgeting was first established, close to 100,000 people have taken part in the participatory budgeting process.[1]

Over 28,000 management councils have been established for health policy, education, the environment, and other matters. These councils are organized at all levels of government, from local to federal, and they provide forums in which citizens join service providers and the government in defining public policies and overseeing their implementation. Management councils enable citizens to have a voice in policymaking and provide a mechanism for greater downward accountability.

Of these two participatory mechanisms, the management councils are much more important, at least in terms of their scale. Previous research, however, has raised questions about how effective these councils are at promoting effective citizen participation. In this view, the democratic promise of these councils has been compromised by the authoritarian tradition within the Brazilian state and, more generally, a lingering authoritarian political culture, fragile associational life, and resistance from both society and state actors.[2] Even when councils are implemented, the poorest remain excluded and continue to lack sufficient resources to articulate their demands, while the costs of participation continue to be lower for those with more resources.

In this chapter, we take a different perspective. We acknowledge that a management council's organizational structure can reinforce existing inequalities among the actors involved, but they can be addressed, at least partially, through improving the deliberation that is part of the council process. Thus, it is necessary to review the process through which councillors are chosen and devise appropriate rules and procedures to ensure that those citizens with relatively little technical expertise and communicative resources are included as effective participants in the deliberative decision-making process.

In making our case, we focus on the Municipal Health Council of São Paulo, a council that works in a favorable environment with a strongly committed government and citizenry.[3] Health councils such as this one make for a good case study because they have been established for a longer period than most councils and are perceived as more consolidated. Before discussing the particulars of the São Paulo case, we review the legal context of health councils.

The Legal Context of Health Councils

The 1988 constitution defined health as a right of all citizens and the responsibility of the state and established the Unified Health System (SUS)—the Brazilian public health system—based on the principles of universality and equity of health care provision. The SUS introduced the notion of accountability (*controle social*) and popular participation; it stated that the health system had to be democratically governed and that the participation of civil society in policymaking was fundamental for attaining its democratization.[4] Health councils emerged within the legal framework as the institutions responsible for enabling citizen participation in health governance. Health councils have been established at federal, state, and municipal levels of the government.

The health council is a permanent collective body that consists of citizens, health professionals, governmental institutions, and providers and producers of health services (Federal Law 8,142). There are currently more than 5,500 health councils involving almost 100,000 citizens and a vast number of associations. Health councils are political forums in which participants discuss issues and may make alliances to help the health secretariat plan and define priorities and policies. The strength of these councils largely lies in the law that grants them veto power over the plans and accounts of the health secretariat. If the council rejects the plan and budget that the health secretariat is required to present annually, the Health Ministry does not transfer funds.

Municipal health councils, such as the one in São Paulo, are of particular importance in health governance because one of the principles of the SUS was decentralization of the health system. Through the process of decentralization, both health planning and the provision of health services became the responsibility of municipal governments.[5] This process turned the municipality into a key political space for the definition of health policies and municipal health councils into an important arena for participation in policymaking. In order to implement this constitutional provision, enabling legislation was enacted to change the distribution of resources between federal, state, and municipal governments, greatly strengthening the municipal governments. The Basic Operational Norms, which regulate the SUS, make the transfers of resources within the health sector from the federal government—which manages 60 percent of the public health budget—to the municipalities, conditioned on the existence of the municipal health councils. The enforcement of this legal framework has led to the rapid institution of municipal health councils throughout Brazil. The Basic Operational Norms also stipulate that representation in these councils be based on a parity principle that states that the number of representatives of civil society (citizens) must be equal to that of service providers, health professionals, and government institutions added together.

How the São Paulo Council Works

The Municipal Health Council of São Paulo is located at the headquarters of the municipal health secretariat in downtown São Paulo, a city of ten million inhabitants. The council is made up of three bodies: the Deliberative Assembly, the Executive Commission, and the General Secretariat (Municipal Decree 38,576/99). Deliberative Assemblies, or plenary meetings, are held monthly (ordinary meetings) and every time the president or the majority of its members deem it necessary (extraordinary meetings) at the headquarters of the municipal health secretariat. Deliberative Assemblies are open to the public and make final decisions on council matters. The quorum required for the meetings of the Deliberative Assembly is half of its members plus one. The council has sixty-four members—thirty-two titular members and thirty-two substitutes. Councillors are elected for a two-year term and may be reelected for another term. The law establishes that they cannot be paid, because their participation constitutes a public service. The municipal health secretary is by law a member of the council and its president; he or she has the right to voice opinions but not vote in the Deliberative Assembly, except in cases where his or her vote is needed to break a tie.

The municipal decree that formally constitutes the council establishes the general profile of the associations and organizations within each of the four membership groups that have the right to be represented in the council and the number of seats they hold (see Table 12.1).[6] The responsibility of electing or otherwise choosing their representatives to the council lies with these four sectors.[7] The parity principle guarantees organizations from civil society half of the seats on the council. Health professionals make up one quarter of the seats, while representatives of governmental institutions, together with representatives of public and private providers of health services, account for the remaining quarter.

Previous research points out that in São Paulo, the majority of organizations from civil society that are represented on the council work closely with citizens who have historically been marginalized or excluded from the policymaking process and suffered discrimination from mainstream society. These marginalized groups include poor dwellers on the depressed peripheries of the city, the black population, disabled people, and the elderly.[8] Most of the seats reserved for citizen organizations (eleven out of sixteen) have been assigned to popular health movements and social movements, and an additional three are occupied by associations that represent disabled citizens (one seat) and people affected by diseases such as AIDS (two seats). The remaining two seats are reserved for representatives of trade unions. The role played by social movements in the transition to democracy and in the institutionalization of health councils explains the large number of seats they occupy on the council. In São Paulo in particular, popular health

TABLE 12.1. COMPOSITION OF THE
MUNICIPAL HEALTH COUNCIL OF SÃO PAULO

Institutions Represented in the Municipal Health Council	Number of Seats
Civil society (16 total seats)	
Popular health movements	6
Social movements	5
Associations of people with pathologies	2
Associations of disabled people	1
General workers' unions	1
General corporate unions	1
Health professionals (8 total seats)	
Health professionals' unions	2
General unions	2
Supervisory councils of professionals involved in direct service to patients	2
Supervisory councils of professionals involved in the supervision and production inputs (such as blood banks or pharmaceuticals)	1
Associations for professionals such as physicians and engineers	1
Governmental institutions (6 total seats)	
Municipal health secretariat	4
Public universities and research institutes	1
Private universities and research institutes	1
Suppliers and producers of health products (2 total seats)	
Corporate entities supplying or producing health services or products	1
Nonprofit entities supplying health services	1

Source: Municipal Decree 38,576/99.

movements played an important role in the struggle for the improvement of the health and living conditions of poor and marginalized people.

Little is known about the process through which the council's member organizations choose their representatives. On March 2002, a councillor summoned an extraordinary meeting of the council, denouncing the "partisan appropriation" of the council on the part of the Workers' Party. The councillor alleged that the Workers' Party controls the process through which some of the councillors are chosen, especially those connected with social movements and unions. This issue generated a heated discussion within the council, but it did not result in any change.

To exemplify the process through which some of the councillors are chosen, we recount briefly the election of the representative of the Popular Health Movement of the Eastern Zone, which took place in July 2001.[9] The meeting was held on a weekday, in the afternoon, and was attended by sixty-four people from the thirteen health districts comprised in the Eastern Zone of the city, as well as a public official nominated by the municipal council.[10] There were three candidates for the post of councillor, and no explanation was given as to how these names had been chosen. After the candidates had presented and discussed their proposals, participants were asked to vote by raising their hands. The winner got thirty-nine votes. We were unable to obtain information on the identity of the participants and the organizations they represented; these details had not been documented. This description should not be taken as paradigmatic; it is likely that other organizations on the council (and other health councils in the country) adopt different methods for choosing their representatives. Nevertheless, it illustrates the dearth of information on the processes through which such choices are made, as well as the difficulties in shedding light on such processes.

Research on the socioeconomic and political profile of the council has found that 45 percent of citizen representatives began participating in social movements during the 1970s and 1980s, and the rest were connected to left-wing parties. Seventy-five percent of civil society representatives in the 2000–2001 term were women; 78 percent were over fifty years old; and many of the elderly councillors were retired. Citizen representatives have lower levels of education and are less well-off compared with the other groups represented on the council. Forty-three percent of citizen representatives declared that they earned an income equivalent to four or less minimum wages, which is much lower than that earned by representatives of the other groups.

Although being granted the right of membership on the council by decree is a prerequisite for the inclusion of citizens in policymaking, this in itself is not sufficient. Inclusion can only be secured to the extent that citizen representatives are able and willing to attend the meetings of the council. The meetings are scheduled on weekdays at two o'clock in the afternoon, which means that employed councillors need to take time off from work to attend. For the representatives of governmental institutions and most health professionals, this does not present a difficulty, for the nature of their employment facilitates their participation. In contrast, citizen representatives have to request permission from their employers and negotiate with them in order to obtain time off from work, and some of them do not get paid for the hours of work forgone. For them, therefore, attendance at council meetings entails a considerable opportunity cost.[11] In view of these considerations, it would not be surprising if only a few representatives of civil society were able or willing to attend the council meetings. However, a review of the lists of attendance at the Municipal Health Council plenary meetings during the 2001–2002 term reveals that the majority of citizen representatives *do* attend the council meetings. Moreover, because their level of attendance tends to be slightly higher than that of the other groups on the council, they always constituted at least half of the participants, and they often outnumbered the other groups.[12]

The data on the socioeconomic profile of the councillors and their level of attendance suggest that the Municipal Health Council has succeeded in opening a space for dialogue between social groups that do not usually meet in other forums and that have historically lacked the opportunity to debate and define health policies collectively. In spite of this achievement, it is important to not to lose sight of the fact that the poorest sectors of society are still not participating and that a significant number of citizen organizations represented on the council have historically been linked to the Workers' Party, while numerous other organizations that are working to improve provision of health services to the poor have been excluded from the formal composition of the council.[13]

This situation can be largely attributed to the council's internal regulations, which reserve seats for specific associations and organizations. The rules regulating citizens' access to the council mean that only some groups have access to it (that is, those that were mobilized when the rules were created), thus reinforcing the exclusion of social groups that lack representation. To counter this trend, it would be necessary to devise more appropriate ways to organize representation in participatory institutions so as to ensure the inclusion of less mobilized and more vulnerable groups. Several authors have proposed ways of doing so, and we expect that some of these alternatives will be tested in participatory forums in the coming years.[14]

Assessing the Impact of the São Paulo Council

The council's formal structure is horizontal, assuring the full freedom of its members to participate in face-to-face discussions and bring their own views and preferences into the debates. The council plenary meetings are chaired by an elected councillor, who plays the role of facilitator. It is expected that this horizontal structure will bring the voices of different social actors into health governance.

Our review of the minutes of the council plenary meetings shows, however, that fostering an exchange of information among participants can be difficult. Only some interventions succeed in provoking a response from other participants, thereby generating a debate, whereas other interventions are silently ignored. When interviewed, most of the councillors agreed that an argument that goes straight to the point and keeps to the issue under discussion, avoiding digressions, is an effective way to advance one's position within the council. Mastering the technical language of the health sector enables councillors to convey their views in a way that resonates with current policy discourses, thereby conferring greater weight and legitimacy to the positions they advance. The tendency of citizen representatives to construct their arguments in a way that is regarded as unstructured, combined with their focus on highly localized issues, makes their speeches appear unclear, emotional, disruptive, or irrelevant to most representatives of the other sectors. Moreover, this style of speech tends to be associated with poorer and less educated people, and it is regarded as not only ineffective but also virtually unintelligible.

When debates were about important political issues, such as changes in administrative rules or health programs, numerous councillors found that the arguments they advanced failed to modify in any meaningful way the proposals advanced by the government. Even when the majority of the councillors held views that were opposed to that of the government, the council proved unable to develop and put forward coherent alternative policy proposals. Interviews with the councillors reveal that they are aware of the limited influence that the council exerts within the health system. They say that they are always denouncing problems of the everyday functioning of the system but rarely find ways to organize themselves to solve them. This implies that although it is meant to be a mechanism for citizen participation, the council has failed to legitimize new concerns and practices, which puts it in a weak negotiating position vis-à-vis the government. In spite of these limitations, many councillors describe their experience as a member of the Municipal Health Council as rewarding. This is so for at least two reasons. First, being a councillor grants them access to new information that they previously did not have access to. Second, they find the council a friendly space where they meet other people who are committed to improving the health system.[15]

Our analysis of the dynamics of participation in the Municipal Health Council of São Paulo suggests that significant advances have been made in terms of institutionalizing a political space in which the views of hitherto excluded groups can be expressed. Nevertheless, much remains to be done if the voices of these groups are to be heard. One of the main challenges is fostering an inclusive dialogue between different socioeconomic groups. Relying on a councillor to facilitate the discussion during plenary meetings and to foster the participation of all participants has not proved be an efficacious strategy because the councillors don't have the necessary skills to perform these tasks. Several authors argue that to enable underprivileged groups to express themselves effectively in participatory forums, specific methodologies aimed at fostering the abilities of participants with less technical expertise and communicative resources need to be devised and adopted.[16]

On the other hand, the council's inability to exert influence over the policies and programs defined by the health secretariat calls for a more careful selection of the issues discussed in the council. Some areas are likely to benefit little from citizen participation because they require highly specialized knowledge or because citizens lack expertise and information.[17] On the other hand, significant benefits can be expected in those areas in which citizens have an advantage over politicians and administrators—that is, when local knowledge and citizens' preferences play an important role.

Reflections

The experience of municipal health councils is part of a movement that should be carefully examined—a movement in which civil society and political actors have joined forces to institutionalize political spaces for citizen participation in policymaking. As the experience of the Municipal Health Council of São Paulo shows, the challenges for attaining effective citizen inclusion in health governance are many, even in a favorable context. As we saw, these challenges arise from inequalities in the distribution of political and communicative resources between the actors involved, as well as from the rules that define how citizen representatives are chosen, how issues for discussion are selected, and how the process of deliberation is organized. Unless these challenges are addressed, they will reproduce and reinforce the exclusion of groups that lack political ties as well as communicative and technical resources.

A participatory institution such as a municipal health council is expected to provide resources to at least partially mitigate these inequalities. Our recommendation is that these resources be invested to make the selection of citizen representatives more transparent and democratic and to strengthen the council's organizational capacity so as to render the deliberation process more inclusive. It remains to be seen whether the actors involved will feel sufficiently capable and motivated to promote such changes. Whereas the response to these challenges is likely to come from the political sphere, the considerable efforts devoted to the promotion of participatory forums during the last few years suggest that a wide range of social, state, and political actors will contribute to its realization.

Notes

1. Souza Santos, B. (1998). "Participatory Budgeting in Porto Alegre: Toward a Redistributive Democracy." [http://www.ssc.wisc.edu/~wright/santosweb.html].

2. Brazilian Association of Collective Health. (1993). *Relatório final da oficina: incentivo à participação popular e controle social em saúde* [Final report: Popular participation and social control in health]. Série Saúde e movimento [Health and movement series]. Vol. 1. Brasília: Brazil-

ian Association of Collective Health; Andrade, I. (1998). "Descentralização e poder municipal no nordeste: os dois lados da moeda" [Decentralization and municipal power in the North East: Two sides of the coin]. In J. A. Soares (ed.), *O orçamento dos municípios do Nordeste brasileiro* [The municipal budget in the Brazilian Northeast]. Brasília: Paralelo15; Carneiro, C. (2002, March). "Conselhos: Uma reflexão sobre os condicionantes de sua atuação e os desafios de sua efetivação" [Councils: Challenges for their implementation]. *Informativo CEPAM* [CEPAM Bulletin], *1*(3), 62–70. São Paulo: Fundação Prefeito Faria Lima; Carvalho, A. (1995). "Conselhos de Saúde No Brasil" [Health Councils in Brazil]. In *Política, Planejamento e Gestao em Saúde*. Série Estudos [Study series: Politics, planning, and health management], no. 3. Rio de Janeiro: Ibam/Fase, 5–41.

3. The Workers' Party (*Partido dos Trabalhadores*) won the municipal elections for the 2000–2004 term. In the first two years of this term, the health secretary was Eduardo Jorge, an enthusiastic promoter of civil society participation.

4. Lobato, L. (1998, Sept. 24–26). "Stress and Contradictions in the Brazilian Healthcare Reform." Paper presented at the annual meeting of the Latin American Studies Association, Chicago.

5. Lobato, (1998). "Stress and Contradictions in the Brazilian Healthcare Reform." The federal government retained responsibility for developing national policies, controlling national regulation through the SUS, and providing technical and financial support to states and municipalities. The states became responsible for controlling the health network and hierarchy within the state and for supervising and providing technical and financial support to municipalities.

6. To our knowledge, no study has examined how or why these organizations and associations have been chosen instead of others. While it is highly likely that the list in Table 12.1 is the result of an intense process of political negotiation among a number of different actors, light has yet to be shed on the ways in which this negotiation took place.

7. To appoint councillors, a list of nominees is presented to the health secretariat, which in turn gives tenure to the new councillors during the municipal health conference.

8. Pozzoni, B. (2002). "Citizen Participation and Deliberation in Brazil." Unpublished master's thesis, Institute of Development Studies, University of Sussex, Brighton, U.K.; Coelho, V. (2004, Apr.). "Brazil's Health Councils: The Challenge of Building Participatory Political Institutions." *IDS* [Institute of Development Studies] *Bulletin, 35*(2), 33–39.

9. Pozzoni (2002), "Citizen Participation and Deliberation in Brazil." In São Paulo, there are six organizations associated with the popular health movement—one for each of the six regions of the city—and each of them holds one seat on the Municipal Health Council.

10. Health districts comprise a population of approximately 250,000 inhabitants each.

11. For citizen representatives who are either unemployed or retired, attending the meetings is an activity carried out on their own time. While this is not likely to entail an opportunity cost comparable to that paid by those who are employed, it does constitute an extra demand on their otherwise free time.

12. Pozzoni (2002), "Citizen Participation and Deliberation in Brazil."

13. Coelho, V. (2004). "Conselhos de saúde enquanto instituições políticas: o que está faltando?" [Health councils as political institutions: What is lacking?]. In V.S.P. Coelho and M. Nobre (eds.), *Deliberação e Participação no Brasil* [Deliberation and participation in Brazil]. São Paulo: Editora 34 Letras.

14. Fishkin, J. (1995). *The Voice of the People.* New Haven, Conn.: Yale University Press; Cornwall, A. (2004, Apr.). "New Democratic Spaces? The Politics and Dynamics of Institutionalised Participation." *IDS* [Institute of Development Studies] *Bulletin, 35*(2), 1–10; Fung, A. (2003).

"Recipes for Public Spheres: Eight Institutional Design Choices and Their Consequences." *Journal of Political Philosophy, 11*, 1–30; Font, J. (2004). "Participación ciudadana y decisions públicas: conceptos, experiencias y metodologias" [Citizen participation and public decisions: Concepts, experiences, and methodologies]. In A. Ziccardi (ed.), *Participación ciudadana y políticas socials en el ámbito local* [Citizen participation and social policies in local government]. Mexico: Instituto Nacional de Desarrollo Social [National Institute of Social Development].

15. Interviews of the councillors who were in office in 2000–2001 and 2002–2003 were part of the "Participation and Social Inclusion in Brazil" project carried out by the Brazilian Center of Analysis and Planning with the support of the Citizenship Development Research Centre on Citizenship, Participation and Accountability, Institute of Development Studies, University of Sussex.

16. Carvalho (1995). "Conselhos de Saúde No Brasil"; Fung (2003). "Recipes for Public Spheres"; Gaventa, J. (2004). "Strengthening Participatory Approaches to Local Governance: Learning the Lessons from Abroad," *National Civic Review, 3*(4), 16–27; Cifuentes, M. (2002). "Political Legitimacy of Deliberative Institutions." Unpublished master's thesis, Institute of Development Studies, University of Sussex, Brighton, U.K.; Delli Carpini, M. X., Cook, F. L., and Jacobs, L. R. (2003). "Talking Together: Discursive Capital and Civil Deliberation in America." Paper presented at the meeting of the Midwest Political Science Association, Chicago.

17. Fung (2003), "Recipes for Public Spheres."

CHAPTER THIRTEEN

DELIBERATIVE CITY PLANNING ON THE PHILADELPHIA WATERFRONT

Harris Sokoloff, Harris M. Steinberg, Steven N. Pyser

Development and revitalization in Philadelphia has suffered for years under the weight of a political culture that discourages public input. Backroom deals and personal relationships have often seemed to define the "public interest." This is the story of one attempt to give the public a voice in city planning and development.

For over thirty years, the Philadelphia waterfront at Penn's Landing has been stuck at the intersection of public interest and private development. A landfill built in 1976 as public space on the Delaware River, Penn's Landing was conceived as a major destination that would bring visitors to the region.[1] The intervening years have seen many attempts to develop the site. Still, Penn's Landing remains a mere vestige of urban renewal's best intentions. Disconnected from the city by ten lanes of highway, the site has continually defied development.

The summer of 2002 saw the sixth failed development proposal,[2] and Mayor John F. Street and his development team quickly set about finding a new developer for the site. This process brought Penn Praxis (a special program in the University of Pennsylvania School of Design) into a partnership with the editorial board of *The Philadelphia Inquirer* (the region's largest daily newspaper), the Center for School Study Councils (at the University of Pennsylvania Graduate School of Education), and the Design Advocacy Group of Philadelphia, which provided program support. Together, the partners crafted a public process to engage the people of Philadelphia in a public conversation about the future of their waterfront.[3]

For fifty days in the winter of 2003, Philadelphians engaged in a robust public dialogue about the future of the Philadelphia waterfront at Penn's Landing. Held with the participation and support of Mayor Street's administration, the Penn's Landing Forums consisted of a series of four events on the future of the landing that included expert presentations on waterfront development, facilitated citizen deliberations on the landing's future, and a design charrette.[4] Over eight hundred people participated in this mutually respectful civic relationship between expert knowledge and citizen response, resulting in the Penn's Landing Principles, a fundamental set of values that any development on Penn's Landing must honor. The forums allowed Philadelphians to be a constructive voice in a city where public opinion is all too often viewed as an opportunity to say "No" rather than "What if?"

Background on the Penn's Landing Forums

The Penn's Landing Forums grew out of a desire to create more public engagement in Philadelphia's isolated political and development culture.

Origins and Purpose

Given the history of failed development efforts at Penn's landing, Philadelphians had reason to feel largely ignored in matters of civic design and planning. In the past, the "pay-to-play" power structure of the city had demonstrated little tolerance for listening to citizen expressions of what to build at Penn's Landing or elsewhere. City leaders and powerful developers were not about to relinquish control over how to determine who should receive development rights and public subsidies at important sites. Thus, this project sought to give citizens a formative, not a determinative role in shaping the future of Philadelphia's central waterfront. With the active participation of the editorial board of the *Inquirer*, the public's voice was ensured a platform. The design principles were published both in the *Inquirer*'s editorial pages and on its Web site.

This project acknowledges that the role of a citizen in a representative democracy is to be informed and then, in turn, to inform the work of policymakers.[5] Typically, citizens educate themselves by referring to newspapers and other print and electronic media and attending lectures and other information sessions. Citizens then inform their elected representatives by contacting them directly or through an intermediary, such as a special-interest or lobbying group. Often, representatives conduct polls to find out what the public is thinking.

Each of these modes of becoming informed and informing has weaknesses. Individual learning can be isolated and limited to one or two narrow perspectives on an issue. Often, individual citizens fail to recognize how their positions conflict with the positions of other citizens. Polling suffers from problems of inconsistency and variability of responses over time and thus provides scant or inaccurate information on underlying public opinions.[6]

Distinctive Features

The Penn's Landing Forums overcame the failings of individual learning and polling by creating opportunities for citizens with different perspectives to come together, learn from experts, share concerns and hopes, and develop a coherent direction. The process was designed to enable them to work together to coproduce[7] a unified voice that might inform the work of developers and policymakers.

The Penn's Landing Forums had much in common with the deliberation processes described in the preceding chapters, but it had two distinctive features. One was the role of the design community in coming up with design ideas for the site. The other was the important role of the newspaper in convening the public gatherings, disseminating the results, and linking the broader public with the issue.

In regard to the first of these features, the Penn's Landing Principles served as the foundation for a daylong visioning workshop or design charrette held at the Independence Seaport Museum at Penn's Landing. Three teams composed of planners, architects, designers, engineers, economists, students, artists, and citizens each explored a different design approach for the site; each approach was drawn from the civic discussion. The teams were charged with abiding by the Penn's Landing Principles. The designs produced during the charrette reflected the values and tensions inherent in the principles and framed a values-based civic conversation about the waterfront.

Second, the role played by the *Philadelphia Inquirer* was critical to the success of the forums. The *Inquirer* has the largest daily circulation in the region, and the invitation to participate was posted on its editorial page. This enabled the forum organizers to reach a wide prospective audience. In addition, the paper chronicled the course of the forums through editorials, opinion pieces, a dedicated Web page, and a special Sunday editorial section that published the results of the charrette. By actively and repeatedly engaging readers with the topic of waterfront development over the course of the forums, the *Inquirer* played a unique role as both convener and reporter.[8]

Designing and Convening the Forums

Given this background, we adapted our work in other settings to meet the needs of this project in Philadelphia. Each of the three main partners brought different backgrounds and objectives to the forum design process. The resulting forums were a collaborative effort that reflected the strengths and values of the different disciplines involved.

Meeting Design

The process consisted of four sessions designed to alternate between expert-driven and citizen-driven work. The forums began with a panel presentation that featured experts knowledgeable in real estate, waterfront design and development, the history of development on the Penn's Landing site, and successful designs at other waterfronts around the world.[9] Their presentations, along with a series of concurrent articles in the *Inquirer* and a Web site that the newspaper dedicated to the project, created a common base of knowledge for the public deliberation.

The second public meeting was dedicated to small-group public deliberations in which citizens connected the expert information to their personal experiences of the waterfront. The meeting began with an overview of the site that augmented the prior presentations and articles, ensuring that participants in the deliberations had a rich sense of the key design issues at Penn's Landing.[10]

The second meeting was designed to develop a set of fundamental principles for developing Penn's Landing. Participants were randomly divided into ten small groups. Each group worked with a trained facilitator, focusing on four question areas: (1) Who uses Penn's Landing? Who are the past, present, and future users? Who isn't at the table? (2) What do people do at Penn's Landing? How do people currently use it, and what other uses do you think would work on that site? (3) What constrains people (from question 1) from engaging in those uses (from question 2)? (4) Based on the group's answers to questions 1–3, what principles does the group think ought to guide the development of Penn's Landing?

The last question made an essential move from the concrete to the abstract, from the particular to the universal. It recognized elected officials' responsibility to listen to public input while also recognizing the public's responsibility to provide informed input to their policymakers. This enabled individual citizens to look beyond their own interests to recognize the tensions that might exist between their interests and the interests of others. Coproducing a set of principles that embraced those tensions created common ground on which developers could build.

The small-group work led to the development of the following Penn's Landing Principles, which any development on the site must honor.[11]

Distinctively Philadelphia, with pride. Create a signature space for Philadelphia, a "front door" to the world to which its citizens can point with pride.

It's the river, stupid. Enhance citizens' enjoyment of the Delaware River. Make Penn's Landing the focal point of a growing Philadelphia identity as a "river city."

Get the connections right. Master the connections with Center City, Camden, and the scattered amenities along the Philadelphia waterfront. Address the Interstate 95 barrier, parking, and mass transit.

Bolster "Destination Philadelphia." Treat Penn's Landing as a regional attraction as well as a local park.

Make it affordable and sustainable. Be realistic about the economic potential and environmental limitations of Penn's Landing.

Keep it a public space. Preserve Penn's Landing as a fundamentally public space.

Use a public process. Ensure that the region's taxpayers have a timely say in its future.

The order of the principles does not imply any ranking. Tensions exist among the principles; therefore, no single plan could honor them all equally.

The ideas and values discussed in the expert presentations and in the citizen deliberations were used to develop three design scenarios that became the basis for the third meeting, the design charrette. The charrette was not open to the public and was organized with the aid of the Design Advocacy Group of Philadelphia. Participants included well-known local architects, planners, landscape architects, engineers, economists, artists, students, and faculty members.

Scenario 1: A respite from the city. Show how to update Penn's Landing as a truly public place, one providing both daily access to the river for nearby residents and workers and a venue where the region can gather for big civic events.

Scenario 2: A vibrant new neighborhood. Explore how, if the barriers between the river and Center City neighborhoods could be eased, Penn's Landing might become the heart of a new riverfront neighborhood.

Scenario 3: Making Independence Harbor work. Consider how Penn's Landing could complement Center City's historic sites, as well as Camden's waterfront attractions, to achieve the goal of Independence Harbor, a regional tourist attraction that embraces both sides of the river.

The results of the charrette were published the weekend before the final public meeting in the Sunday editorial section of the *Inquirer* and posted on their Web site. The design scenarios were conceptual and schematic, intended to reflect how the principles might be translated into development scenarios. The design principles, on the other hand, were intended to provide advice to policymakers. Indeed, the principles continued to be used after the project ended.

The final public meeting was announced on the editorial pages of the *Inquirer,* and all participants in previous meetings were invited via e-mail. Over 350 Philadelphians attended the final session, which was held at the Independence

Seaport Museum at Penn's Landing. Following a presentation of each of the three design scenarios and a recap of the principles, participants were randomly assigned to small groups. Each group discussed each scenario in terms of its fidelity to the principles. The small-group work ended with each participant rating each scenario in terms of how it honored the principles as well as what he or she wanted to see built at Penn's Landing. At the end of the evening, the final ratings were reported to the assembled group.

All of the meetings and deliberative sessions were face-to-face encounters and were supported by a special Web site that was created by the *Inquirer* and devoted to Penn's Landing. The Web site included a three-week poll of the design suggestions put forth by the charrette. The poll received over five thousand responses. In addition, the newspaper received over three hundred letters about Penn's Landing during the forums, a number that was second only to the number of letters received about the pending war in Iraq.

Meeting places for forums such as the Penn's Landing Forums are important for their symbolic value. The first two forums were held at the University of Pennsylvania, which the public viewed as an independent convener of the process. The final forum was held on the site of Penn's Landing and drew the largest crowd.

Convening the Public Meetings

The Penn's Landing Forums were an adaptation of the National Issues Forums approach (see Chapter Three). In this case, the common ground was a set of planning principles and designs that incorporated public deliberation. The process was tightly structured, with clearly stated goals and a fixed schedule of tasks, events, and products.

The protocols for this public process were customized for the task and structured to elicit fact finding, reflective dialogue, and evaluation. All facilitators were experienced dialogue practitioners, with specialties in conflict resolution, dialogue and deliberation, education, political science, or law. Many drew from their experience as faculty for the National Issues Forums, the Public Policy Institute at the University of Pennsylvania, and elsewhere around the county.

The facilitation team carefully prepared for the forums by studying the subject of waterfront development at Penn's Landing and imagining the broad range of stakeholders who might attend, with the expectation that the forums would be emotionally charged. Guidelines and ground rules to cover contingencies were prepared and shared with the participants. As it turned out, all the public dialogue was respectful and productive. The high level of preparation and the group guidelines played an important role in the success of the events.

An open call for forum participants was part of a series of editorials and news stories published in the fall of 2003 by the *Inquirer*.[12] The articles provided a historical context in order to help identify the interests of all stakeholders. This public call to action was met with interest and commitment to participate from a broad range of citizens, developers, policymakers, topic experts, and interest groups from Pennsylvania and New Jersey, all of whom completed a simple registration form.[13] Whereas participants represented broad diversity in ages and roles, including students and senior citizens, an overwhelming number of the participants were white and lived near the site. Thus, the group did not come close to matching the demographics of the 2000 Philadelphia census.[14] The lack of minority participation suggests the need for more targeted recruitment in the future.

Forum participants were invited to attend three public events over the fifty-day period of the project. Before the meeting, all participants received an e-mail that clearly spelled out stated goals and the problem-solving mission of the forums. The process, timing, and sequence of the forums were also explained at the beginning of each event, and they were explained by facilitators when the participants moved into their small-group dialogues.

Although the forum process followed a specific protocol, facilitators were flexible in leading the dialogue, in order to encourage full participation.[15] The dialogue groups used a poster of the National Issues Forums guidelines, and some facilitators supplemented those ground rules with additional rules. Facilitators worked with their groups to clarify what public participation and involvement meant, discussing the nature of the ideal actions of participants.

Participants were invited to contribute to the forum through various forms of talk, including personal recollections and stories. Participants were encouraged to share stories about personal experiences at Penn's Landing and their own thoughts about future development. The pace was fast, groups were energized, and the dialogue was lively and passionate. Focus and a definiteness of purpose were needed because of the ambitious agenda and the limited time to deliberate.

Facilitators used time-tested techniques for checking for tensions between different ideas and clarifying differences. In retrospect, part of the success of the forums flowed from inviting participants to work with one another by sharing information. This created fertile ground for the participants to integrate their values and ideals with other types of expertise provided by the organizers.

The Impact of the Forums

The Penn's Landing Forums had an immediate and significant impact that has implications for how Philadelphia will engage in civic conversations about public planning in the future. Previously, the history of Penn's Landing had consisted of closed-door, politically driven development deals. The Penn's Landing Forums provided the first opportunity for real civic engagement and feedback about the future of the waterfront. In response, Philadelphians expressed their interest and appreciation through letters to the editor of the *Inquirer*, e-mails to the organizers, and participation in an on-line survey.

Most significantly, the project had an immediate and important impact on the selection and design process for the Penn's Landing site. As Mayor Street and his development team sought proposals to develop the site, they stopped their process to allow the Penn's Landing Forums to run their course.[16] Key members of the administration participated in all of the public events. A report was delivered to the mayor at the culmination of the process, and the organizers were invited to brief the mayor on the outcomes and recommendations. The Street administration included the Penn's Landing Principles in the material given to developers who were interested in bidding on the site and required developers to use the principles to explain their projects. Once proposals were submitted, Harris Steinberg and Harris Sokoloff responded to the design proposals in an *Inquirer* commentary article that reviewed the proposals in accordance with their compliance with the principles.[17]

The Penn's Landing Forums created the expectation that Philadelphians should be included in a constructive civic dialogue with their public officials about how to design the public realm. The discussion about the site continues to this day, and Mayor Street recently announced plans to invest $500 million to spur development of new waterfront communities in Philadelphia[18] and has rejected all development proposals for the site. Penn's Landing remains the keystone of this "river city" concept, and the Penn's Landing Forums have helped Philadelphians communicate with their elected officials about the importance of a public planning process in the pursuit of excellence in urban design.

In addition, the forums captured the imagination of the public and created the opportunity for additional forums on other significant planning issues. Praxis and the Center for School Study Councils have since employed the expert-citizen deliberative process for a community and high school project focusing on the Bensalem waterfront,[19] which is just north of Philadelphia on the Delaware River, and in West Philadelphia in the creation of planning principles for the evolution of the main street that joins the University of Pennsylvania and the local community.[20] The team of Praxis, the *Inquirer*, the Center for School Study Councils, and the Design Advocacy Group has been asked by a local foundation to lead a series of forums, deliberative sessions, and design charrettes on the future of school design in Philadelphia.[21]

The significance of the forums has also been recognized by professional associations. The project received a 2003 Citation for Architectural Excellence from the Pennsylvania chapter of the American Institute of Architects[22] and the 2004 Clearwater Award from the Waterfront Center.[23] In March 2004, the project was presented as a best practice at Grassroots 2004, the national American Institute of Architects leadership conference.[24] In addition, the project was a finalist for a 2003 Batten Award for Civic Journalism and was presented in Washington, D.C., at the Press Club in September 2003.[25]

Reflections

Participants in the Penn's Landing Forums worked through an ambitious set of tasks. The need for productive dialogue was measured against the political reality that the city had put the Penn's Landing development on a fast track. Therefore, it was necessary to move to dialogue in a single evening. A more sustained conversation over time would have allowed for richer discussions.

Basic contact information was collected when citizens registered to participate. To make the registration process seamless and easy, detailed demographic information was not collected. When participants arrived for the events, they were assigned to groups based solely on their arrival time. On further reflection, we see that more detailed registration information could have enabled more purposeful assignment to work groups.

There are challenges in bringing this model of dialogue and deliberation into more frequent use. The first barrier is citizen alienation and moving people to step out of their individual comfort zone to share their perspectives in a public dialogue. At the same time, we should note that these forums and subsequent forums on urban design underscore a thirst for this kind of public dialogue in Philadelphia. The second challenge is educating the public about how citizen voices can influence public decisions about their future. Most people feel powerless against well-organized lobbies, and many are currently disconnected from representative government. Against this backdrop, formal government continues to operate from a position of strength in comparison with a traditionally silent electorate.

The Penn's Landing Forum process can be seen as a form of generative dialogue and deliberation, in which a deliberative public process generated principles and designs. Traditional governmental agencies may be reluctant to engage in such deliberation because it exposes them to public review and accountability, although it does hold the potential for generating broad public support. The Penn's Landing Forums provide a model process in which experts and citizens work together to inform public policy. Most important, the principles generated during the forums create common ground for ongoing deliberation.

Notes

1. Ed Bacon, Philadelphia's legendary post–World War II city planner, in collaboration with Oskar Stonorov, first proposed the idea for a revitalized waterfront park in 1947.

2. The 2002 development proposal was for a 600,000-square-foot entertainment complex with above-ground parking proposed by the Simon Property Group of Indianapolis.

3. This partnership was inspired, in part, by the landmark *Listening to the City* event that had been convened in New York City during the summer of 2002, in which over four thousand citizens responded to preliminary plans put forward to replace the decimated World Trade Center. See Chapter Ten and Pyser, S., and Figallo, C. (2004, Spring). "The 'Listening to the City' Online Dialogues Experience: The Impact of a Full Value Contract." *Conflict Resolution Quarterly, 21*(3), 382.

4. See the Web site that the *Inquirer* dedicated to the Penn's Landing Forums and other related material at http://go.philly.com/pennslanding.

5. David Mathews has suggested that there are four roles that only the public can play in a democracy: (1) defining the public interest; (2) building common ground for action; (3) supporting consistent government over the long term; and (4) transforming private individuals into public citizens.

6. Yankelovich, D. (1991). *Coming to Public Judgment: Making Democracy Work in a Complex World.* Syracuse, N.Y.: Syracuse University Press.

7. Susskind, L. (1983). *Paternalism, Conflict, and Coproduction: Learning from Citizen Action and Citizen Participation in Western Europe.* New York: Plenum Press.

8. On the news side, Inga Saffron wrote a series entitled "Lost Waterfront" that preceded the charrette and established an excellent platform for the forums. Saffron was a finalist for a Pulitzer Prize for this series. In addition, the news department of the *Inquirer* actively reported ongoing news stories about the development process as well as the forums. All of this can be accessed through the *Philadelphia Inquirer* Web site: http://gophilly.com/penslanding.

9. The five experts were James Corner (professor and chair, Department of Landscape Architecture, University of Pennsylvania), Witold Rybczynski (Martin & Margy Meyerson Professor of Urbanism and professor of real estate, University of Pennsylvania), Peter D. Linneman (Albert Sussman Professor of Real Estate and professor of finance and business and public policy, University of Pennsylvania), James Cuorato (commerce director, City of Philadelphia), and Gary Hack (Paley Professor and dean of the School of Design, University of Pennsylvania).

10. Denise Scott-Brown, an internationally renowned architect and planner and a principal in the firm of Venturi Scott Brown and Associates, gave this presentation and focused on such topics as access, land use, transportation, symbolism, imagery, and context.

11. The full version of the principles is as follows: (1) *Distinctively Philadelphia, with pride:* Create a signature space for Philadelphia, a "front door" to the world to which its citizens can point with pride. Do not ape any other city's riverfront plan. Penn's Landing should not be a "chain store" place, but a Philadelphia place. This means it should reflect the city's virtues, such as: Center City's human scale and walkability; a sense of history (particularly on this spot where the seed was planted for William Penn's great experiment); a tradition of first-class urban design; and diverse populations. There is a public thirst for the site to include an "iconic" building or gesture—some item that could join the Liberty Bell, Billy Penn's hat, and the Art Museum steps as a signature image of the city. (2) *It's the river, stupid:* Enhance, do not diminish, citizens' enjoyment of the Delaware River. Give people more ways to connect with the water—looking at it, walking alongside it, doing things in it (fishing, boating, etc.). Penn's Landing should become a focal point of a growing Philadelphia identity as a "river city," with a network of riverside walkways and parks. But do this with respect for the Delaware as a "serious" river; Philadelphia's status as a hard-working port

city should not be ignored or sanitized. (3) *Get the connections right*: Understand that Penn's Landing is the key to mastering two sets of vital connections: (1) east-west, between Camden's burgeoning waterfront and Center City; (2) north-south, among Philadelphia's now-fragmented waterfront amenities. Get the connections right, and the whole can become greater than the parts. Get the connections right, and a proper balance of public, commercial and residential uses becomes easier to achieve. Conversely, any plan for Penn's Landing that doesn't address the site's isolation is doomed. A good plan must include strategies for dealing with the Interstate 95 barrier, parking, mass transit, and links to the Camden waterfront and the scattered amenities along the Philadelphia waterfront. (4) *Bolster "Destination Philadelphia"*: Treat Penn's Landing as a regional attraction as well as a local park. Use it to consolidate the visitor appeal generated in recent years by impressive cultural and entertainment investments on Camden's riverfront and in historic Philadelphia. Make Penn's Landing a transition point where the multigenerational appeal of Camden meshes with the historic riches of Philadelphia. (5) *Make it affordable and sustainable*: Don't fall into the grandiose overreaching that doomed three decades of plans for Penn's Landing. Be realistic about its economic potential and environmental limitations. To avoid the pitfall of cramming more onto the site than it can bear, treat it as one piece of a broader plan for the central waterfront. Don't approach riverfront development as a once-and-done event, but as a patient, generational enterprise. Learn from and capitalize on existing successes along the riverfront. Anticipate I-95's likely obsolescence within 15 years. (6) *Keep it a public space*: Preserve Penn's Landing as a fundamentally public space. Commercial uses should not overwhelm or preclude public uses. Citizens place high value on the site's role as a gathering place for major public events along the river, preferring it to the Festival Pier. The current design of the Great Plaza need not be maintained, but its function must be. City residents also value Penn's Landing highly as a safe spot where individuals and families can connect daily with the river. So the event space should not intimidate or prevent individuals from enjoying the river on ordinary days. (7) *Use a public process*: Ensure that the region's taxpayers, who paid to create Penn's Landing, have a timely, genuine say in its future. The public clearly does not want the fate of Penn's Landing to be determined by the city's habitual "pay-to-play" wheeling and dealing. Plans based on an authentic public process are more likely to generate community pride and support.

12. The Inquirer Web site at http://go.philly.com/pennslanding contains an archive of stories and editorials.

13. Although it was never statistically evaluated, we feel that word-of-mouth promotion by participants also generated participation in the forums. Electronic listservs of organizations such as the Philadelphia City Planning Commission, the local chapter of the Urban Land Institute, the Philadelphia chapter of the American Institute of Architects, and the Design Advocacy Group of Philadelphia greatly aided the organizers in reaching specific constituencies.

14. Ethnically, Philadelphia is 40 percent white, 44 percent black, 9 percent Hispanic, 5 percent Asian American, and 2 percent other. Source: American Community Survey 2003 data file.

15. The facilitators met before each of the deliberative sessions, to help ensure a productive environment.

16. Indeed, one of our goals as forum organizers was to slow down fast-track "politics as usual" in order to allow meaningful public engagement to be incorporated as part of the decision-making process.

17. Steinberg, H., and Sokoloff, H. (2003, Oct. 23). "Developers Plans and the Public Voice." *Philadelphia Inquirer.* [http://www.philly.com/mld/inquirer/news/editorial/7079394.htm].

18. Mayor Street's budget address of March 18, 2004 (http://www.phila.gov/pdfs/budget _04_speech.pdf) refers to a $500 million investment fund that will underwrite an unprecedented investment in the thirty-eight miles of waterfront along the Delaware and Schuylkill Rivers.

19. See McGinnis, J. (2003, Oct. 10). "Students Present Riverfront Dreams." *The Intelligencer.* [http://www.phillyburbs.com/pb-dyn/news/113-10102003-175392.html].

20. See the Friends of 40th Street Web site on the community planning process at www.40thSt.org.

21. Building on the success of the Penn's Landing Forums, the William Penn Foundation is funding a series of forums intended to foster a civic dialogue about the Philadelphia School District's proposed $1.5 billion plan to build and renovate schools over the next decade.

22. AIA Pennsylvania. (2003). "AIA Pennsylvania 2003 Design Awards." [http://www.aiapa.org/ special_events/honor_award/2003Winners.htm].

23. Waterfront Center. (2004). "2004 Excellence on the Water Awards." [http://www.water frontcenter.org/awards/awards2004.html#clearwater].

24. In March 2004, Harris Steinberg and Chris Satullo presented "Giving the Public a Voice: The Penn's Landing Forums" at Grassroots 2004, a national architectural leadership conference of the American Institute of Architects in Washington, D.C.

25. J-Lab: The Institute for Interactive Journalism. (2003). "Batten Awards—2003 Selected Entries." [http://www.j-lab.org/coolb2003.html].

PART FOUR

COMMUNITIES AND DELIBERATIVE CULTURE

STUDY CIRCLES

Local Deliberation as the Cornerstone of Deliberative Democracy

Patrick L. Scully, Martha L. McCoy

Portsmouth, New Hampshire, is well on its way to making deliberative dialogue an integral part of its civic culture. Over the past several years, diverse community groups have organized several rounds of study circles that have involved hundreds of residents. Each success has inspired a new group of leaders to organize deliberation on a different issue.[1]

In 1999, *Days of Dialogue: Respectful Schools* gave Portsmouth residents their first taste of study circles when two hundred sixth graders from Portsmouth Middle School and seventy-five adults met several times to discuss bullying and other school safety issues. Following the circles, students presented recommendations to a joint meeting of the school board and the city council. These circles led to new school policies and a decline in bullying. Furthermore, they helped different community factions to connect. School and community leaders now communicate more frequently and view public deliberation as a pathway to positive change.

A year later, a school board member who had taken part in the circles recommended the same process to address a school redistricting issue. Prior attempts to resolve the schools' enrollment and space problems had failed in the wake of bitter public argument. More than one hundred people took part in the circles, with equal representation from each school. Holding sessions at different elementary schools helped participants appreciate the schools and see the effects of

The authors would like to thank Molly Holme Barrett for her invaluable editorial advice.

A study circle

- is a small, diverse group of eight to twelve people.
- meets for several two-hour sessions.
- sets its own ground rules. This helps the group share responsibility for the quality of the discussion.
- is led by an impartial facilitator who helps manage the discussion. He or she is not there to teach the group about the issue.
- starts with personal stories, then helps the group look at a problem from many points of view. Next, the group explores possible solutions. Finally, they make plans for action and change.

A study circle program

- is organized by a diverse group of people from the whole community.
- includes a large number of people from all walks of life.
- has easy-to-use, fair-minded discussion materials.
- uses trained facilitators who reflect the community's diversity.
- moves a community to action when the study circles conclude.

overcrowding. The final report from the circles, *Rethinking Instead of Redistricting*, provided ten recommendations for the redistricting plan, and it resulted in limiting relocation to only sixty-five students. Compared with previous redistricting efforts, the level of community acceptance was striking.

In 2002, responding to allegations of racial profiling and harassment of young black males, the city police department, the local chapter of the National Association for the Advancement of Colored People (NAACP), and the school district sponsored study circles on racism and race relations. The discussions included police officers, school leaders, community members, and high school students. No specific policy changes have resulted, but communication between the police and the community is improving.

Later in 2002, the city planning board—backed by the mayor, the city manager, the planning department, and city council members—endorsed study circles to generate citizen input for the city's master plan. Leaders created an informal organization, Portsmouth Listens, to spearhead the study circles. Organizers made sure that people from all parts of the community planned the program and joined the deliberations. The program unfolded in three stages. Phase 1, in January 2003, involved nearly three hundred people. They defined what *quality of life* means to Portsmouth residents, recommended ways to sustain it, then reported back to the city's planning board at an unusually constructive and well-attended public meeting. In April 2003, Portsmouth Listens kicked off phase 2 of deliberation on the master plan. This time, the circles emphasized action. Seven groups each identified an issue affecting quality of life, discussed potential actions, and made recommendations to the planning board. When the revised plan was released, it was clear that the city had incorporated advice from the circles.[2] During the summer of 2004, phase 3 participants met in both small and large groups to discuss findings, set priorities, address final comments to the city, and explore ways to partner with the city to influence and enable changes.

Using study circles to address multiple issues, Portsmouth residents are creating a public space in which they can air their differences constructively and work together productively (see Table 14.1). As one researcher says, "Study circles have proven themselves in Portsmouth to be a powerful tool for resolving community conflict and producing meaningful change."

Origins, Purpose, and Essential Principles of Study Circles

Study circles as practiced in the United States today originated with the vision of Paul Aicher, an industrialist and philanthropist who started the Study Circles Resource Center in 1989. He created the center to help make face-to-face deliberation a regular part of public life.[3] The study circle concept appealed to Aicher because of its populist history and principles. Study circles had emerged in the United States in the late nineteenth century; soon after, they flourished in Sweden,

TABLE 14.1. STUDY CIRCLES IN PORTSMOUTH, NEW HAMPSHIRE

Date	Lead Organizers	Issue	Number of Participants
1999	Portsmouth Middle School	Bullying, school safety	275
2000	School board	Redistricting elementary schools	100
Spring 2002	Police department, NAACP, school district	Racism and race relations	50
Fall 2002– Summer 2004	Portsmouth Listens (city government, Citywide Neighborhoods Committee, Chamber of Commerce, and volunteer residents)	City's master plan (three phases): 1. Setting direction 2. In-depth exploration of specific plan elements 3. Review of the master plan in light of input from the circles	Phase 1: 300 Phase 2: 100 Phase 3: 40

where they are credited with making Swedish democracy more participatory.[4] Although for some people, the term *study circle* may connote an educational process, in the United States it is increasingly being associated with a practice of active citizenship. Study circles, as they have evolved since 1989, have played a leading role in connecting deliberation to all kinds of change—individual, community, institutional, and policy.

The ultimate purpose of study circle work is to provide *everyone* with routine opportunities for meaningful participation. The Study Circles Resource Center has concentrated on learning what works—in both the deliberation process itself and in putting deliberation in the context of community.

Our work at the Study Circles Resource Center is based on two "marriages." First, study circles are a marriage of dialogue and deliberation. Dialogue encourages constructive communication, the dispelling of stereotypes, honesty, and the intention to listen to and understand the other.[5] Deliberation encourages critical thinking and reasoned argument as a way for citizens to grapple with and make decisions on public policy.[6] Second, study circles are a marriage of deliberative dialogue and community organizing, thereby attempting to ensure large-scale, diverse participation and meaningful outcomes on all levels.[7]

We find it useful to articulate the essential features of study circles in terms of principles rather than specific processes or methods. Although there is benefit in giving specific advice about process, principles are the driving force behind good decisions about process design. Briefly, the principles are as follows:

- Involve *everyone*. Demonstrate that the whole community is welcome and needed.
- Embrace diversity. Reach out to all kinds of people.
- Share knowledge, resources, power, and decision making.
- Combine dialogue and deliberation. Create public talk that builds understanding and explores a range of solutions.
- Connect deliberative dialogue to social, political, and policy change.

Based on these principles, we advise many different kinds of communities—neighborhoods, cities and towns, states, school districts, schools, and college campuses—that are organizing dialogue. Learning with them, we create and revise tools and processes, and disseminate lessons through technical assistance and training. Our process advice helps organizers to create strategies for organizing communitywide deliberation; develop issue-specific discussion materials to structure the deliberations; recruit and train facilitators; connect deliberation to measurable change; and communicate the value and outcomes of deliberative dialogue.

Distinctive to Paul Aicher's vision was his desire to see communities make the practice of deliberation their own. He wanted them to have ready access to deliberative principles and tools so that people could work together democratically to solve public problems. In the process, they would provide models that could be replicated and adapted by others. Aicher also hoped that this local work would be the cornerstone of a nationwide network that would be prepared to address social and political issues of national importance. These aims remain the goals of the Study Circles Resource Center and the community programs that we advise.

Designing and Planning Deliberative Dialogue

Since democracy is constantly evolving, innovation and experimentation at the grass roots are essential. National organizations, such as the Study Circles Resource Center, play an important role in creating networks, learning from many cases, and disseminating lessons. We offer a flexible framework for deliberation as a starting point—a process that communities can adapt to their own circumstances and goals.

Organizing

The impetus for organizing study circles usually is concern about a specific issue. The driving force is seldom an explicit interest in improving civic life or promoting deliberative democracy.[8] Organizers contact us because a public problem is persisting, and they believe that they could make headway in solving it if their community had productive ways for people to hear one another and work together.

The best strategy for engaging significant numbers of people from every sector of the community is to build a diverse group of community leaders to plan and organize the effort.[9] Often, a single organization takes the lead and provides staff. Typical organizational homes for study circle programs are local governments, social service agencies, nonprofit organizations, religious congregations or associations, schools and school districts, and neighborhood associations. In some situations, such as in some neighborhoods or small communities, programs are organized by informal ad hoc groups.

Program Design and Support

The goals and resources of the local community drive the program design. When people come to us, we help them assess whether a deliberative process will enable them to achieve the kinds of change they are seeking. After organizers initiate a program, we advise them as they build a strong, diverse sponsoring coalition; articulate their goals; clarify the issue and decide on discussion materials; and develop communication strategies. To ensure optimal community participation, we also help them define the scope and size of the program (for example, by specifying the number of participants and the geographic boundaries desired); develop participant recruitment strategies (emphasizing diversity); and recruit, train, and support facilitators. Finally, we give them advice about how to provide program support (for example, staff, financial resources, and program coordination); create and support structures for connecting the deliberative dialogue to action and change; and document and evaluate the entire program.[10]

Generally, organizers plan large-scale rounds of deliberative dialogue that include a range of organizational players and decision makers, along with everyday people. Holding the meetings in accessible public spaces increases the likelihood that people from every sector of the community will participate. Each round includes many small-group meetings all across the community, deliberating on the same issue at the same time.

Each circle follows the same structure, progressing through a series of three to five two-hour sessions, each guided by trained facilitators. The initial session helps people set ground rules, get to know one another, and establish their personal connection to the issue. In subsequent meetings, participants explore the issue, consider solutions, and establish priorities for action and change. Typically, a round concludes with a large-scale event in which participants, public officials, and other leaders gather to consider ideas generated in the circles and set priorities for action. Some people may choose to establish and join action task forces. In an ideal situation, the organizers provide staff to help the action teams move forward. The most successful task forces continue to employ the deliberative skills and democratic practices that they learned in the circles.[11]

If the goal of the dialogue is to make changes in public policy, there are several important strategies to employ:

- Involve public officials in leadership roles at every stage of the program
- Recruit officials into the dialogues
- Incorporate the main ideas from the deliberations into reports for officials
- Engage officials in setting action priorities and in working with citizens to implement action ideas[12]

Discussion Materials and Facilitation

Effective discussion materials provide a baseline of information about the issue. They also provide a candid and balanced statement of the main arguments about the causes of the problem and what should be done. The best discussion guides are easy to read, simple to use, and help all kinds of people feel comfortable in expressing their ideas.[13] Many communities use or adapt discussion materials that were developed by the Study Circles Resource Center. When no discussion guide is available on a particular topic, the center often helps a community to develop its own. We provide Spanish translations of many of our guides, and several communities have translated the materials into other languages.

Just as the discussion materials provide substance, facilitators help to ensure a sound process. The essence of good facilitation is managing the deliberation process impartially, not acting as an expert or teacher. Large-scale study circle programs depend on trained volunteer facilitators drawn from the community; this expands the capacity of the community for deliberation and develops leadership at the grass roots. New facilitators typically attend one or two days of training to learn the principles and techniques of effective small-group deliberative dialogue and how the dialogue is connected to the program goals and the broader civic context. At the training, the new facilitators also learn how the discussion materials and the guiding principles of study circles make the process effective.[14]

Profile and Role of Participants

To generate meaningful outcomes, organizers must engage a critical mass of people. Successful efforts have involved numbers of people ranging from seventy-five to five hundred participants in a single round. Limiting the size of individual groups (eight to twelve people) allows everyone to contribute.

In addition to scale, diversity of participants is critical. Effective programs involve people of all racial and ethnic backgrounds, men and women, public officials and ordinary citizens, and people of all educational backgrounds, income levels, and ages—including people who are not usually involved in public life.[15]

Organizing deliberative dialogue *across* a community creates new opportunities for community building and public problem solving. Building a strong, diverse sponsoring coalition is the most effective way to engage a large, inclusive, and diverse pool of participants. Although collaboration and coalition building can be time-consuming, they are well worth the effort. The broader the coalition, the greater its capacity to effect change.

Study circles enable everyone to participate on an equal basis, with the assurance that the discussion will be both civil and productive. To ensure that all kinds of people have a real voice, the process uses devices such as ground rules, reflection on personal experiences, storytelling, brainstorming, and active listening.[16] In addition, participants agree to attend every session and to share responsibility for the quality of the discussion. It is also important for participants to consider whether they are willing to help implement some of the ideas for change that emerge from the discussions.

Sustainability

We encourage people to think of their study circle work not as an isolated event but rather as a first step toward creating a more democratic community. Whereas a single event may produce better informed and considered public opinions, it is not likely to develop the trust, understanding, and new working relationships that create the foundation for many forms of social and political change.

Another way of thinking about sustainability is to consider how deliberative dialogue might embed itself in *all* facets of a public engagement process. For example, in effective study circle efforts, deliberation is essential at every stage of program development: among the program sponsors as they set goals and make plans; among participants in their small groups; and in the action and change initiatives that emerge.

Evidence of change sustains deliberative dialogue programs over the long haul. As was shown in our opening illustration of Portsmouth, New Hampshire, when people see the concrete results of large-scale, inclusive deliberation, they will apply the process to all kinds of issues.

How Study Circles Have Been Used Across the United States

The following information focuses on participant numbers and program duration because they are some of the best raw indicators of a program's ability to foster collective change, especially changes in public policy and institutions.[17]

In 1993, the city of Lima, Ohio, launched the first communitywide study circle program, involving hundreds of people in deliberative dialogue on racism and race relations. Since then, at least 130 communities throughout the United States have engaged seventy-five or more participants in discrete rounds of study circles.[18] Twenty-nine of these communities organized rounds with two hundred or more people; four organized rounds involving at least five hundred participants. At least forty-three communities have organized rounds of study circles for three or more years (see Table 14.2).

Several states have organized statewide programs. Table 14.3 profiles efforts to influence state-level policy; in these programs, hundreds of people in communities across a state deliberated on the same issue during the same period.[19] In addition, some programs combine this approach with decentralized efforts to address issues at the local level. For example, in 2002, the Arkansas School Boards Association engaged about six thousand Arkansans in deliberations that informed a state education commission.[20] Since 1998, the Arkansas School Boards Association has also helped over a dozen communities use deliberative dialogue to improve their schools.[21] Maine has applied study circle principles to a variety of topics, engaging over ten thousand people (including four thousand young people) since 1991.[22]

TABLE 14.2. SOME COMMUNITIES THAT HAVE ENGAGED LARGE NUMBERS OF PEOPLE IN STUDY CIRCLES

Community	Duration	Issue	Number of Participants
Aurora, Illinois	1995–2004	Racism and race relations; youth concerns	4,000
Greater Hartford, Connecticut	1997–2004	Racism and race relations; education	3,000
Kansas City, Kansas	1999–2004	Education; neighborhood concerns	1,300
Lima, Ohio	1992–2004	Racism and race relations	3,000
Los Angeles, California[a]	1995–2003	Racism and race relations	5,000
New Castle County, Delaware	1996–2004	Racism and race relations	8,000
Racine and Kenosha, Wisconsin	1999–2004	Racism and race relations	1,600
Syracuse, New York	1996–2004	Racism and race relations	1,200
Twin Cities, Minnesota	1995–1999	Racial segregation, education, and housing	1,200
Wake County, North Carolina	1998–2004	Racism and race relations	2,500

[a]The Los Angeles program has organized primarily single-session dialogues, at times in rounds.

TABLE 14.3. A SAMPLE OF STATEWIDE STUDY CIRCLE PROGRAMS

State	Time Period	Issue	Number of Communities	Number of Participants
Arkansas	1998	Education reform	10	374
Maine	1998	Alcohol abuse	50	1,000
Minnesota	2000	Immigration and community change	17	961
New York	1999–2001	Criminal justice and corrections	71	2,200
Oklahoma	1996–1997	Criminal justice and corrections	13	972
Oklahoma	1998	Education reform	5	500

About 60 percent of all programs tracked by the Study Circles Resource Center since 1993 have addressed racism and race relations; roughly 20 percent of the programs have focused on K–12 education reform. Other programs have focused on issues such as community-police relations, growth and development, neighborhood revitalization, and immigration.

Impact

A two-year study of seventeen programs documented the ways in which study circles contribute to changes in people, organizations, communities, and institutions. Many outcomes cited in the research suggest that study circles build social capital and the capacity to solve public problems. (Typical of the social capital outcomes cited in the report is increased volunteerism from the African American community for the YWCA's governing board as a result of study circles in New Castle County, Delaware.)[23] We are currently looking at the influence of large-scale deliberative dialogue on institutions and public policy.[24] Table 14.4 uses examples

TABLE 14.4. ACTION AND CHANGE RESULTING FROM STUDY CIRCLE PROGRAMS IN PORTSMOUTH, NEW HAMPSHIRE

Kind of Change	Portsmouth Example
Changes in individual behavior and attitudes	As a participant in a study circle on school redistricting, one resident who consistently opposes tax increases saw the cramped conditions in three schools, heard the concerns and commitment of parents and teachers, and publicly supported a $1.7 million plan for school improvements that entailed a tax increase.
New relationships and networks	After circles on racism, the deputy chief of the police department commented that now when an issue or question comes up, it is easier for someone from the NAACP to simply call him or another officer rather than go through formal procedures.
Institutional changes	After the circles on school safety, new plans included the following student recommendations: cameras on buses, a peer mediation program, and increased adult supervision at school events. Since the plans have been implemented, school bullying appears to have declined.
Changes in public policy	After playing a leading role in organizing study circles on Portsmouth's ten-year master plan and meeting with participants, the planning board used input from the circles to learn about residents' priorities. Resulting changes to the plan included approval to purchase ten acres of green space for conservation and rezoning to gear waterfront residences and studios to artists' needs.

from Portsmouth, New Hampshire, to illustrate typical forms of action and change generated by study circles.[25]

Other Applications

Some small-scale efforts engage no more than thirty or forty people. These programs can be effective if the goal is to change individual attitudes and behaviors. While we do not track these programs closely, hundreds have occurred since 1993.

Middle schools and high schools also use and adapt study circle principles and processes. To support this work, the Study Circles Resource Center collaborates with the Southern Poverty Law Center on their Tolerance.org and Teaching Tolerance projects, providing resources to help teenagers address issues of social boundaries in their schools.[26] By June 2004, at least five hundred schools and ten thousand students had participated in Mix It Up deliberative dialogues.[27] In addition, at least twenty-five college campuses have used study circles to address a range of issues.[28]

Looking to the Future

The case of Portsmouth, New Hampshire, shows what can happen in communities across the country. With little outside assistance, Portsmouth is making deliberation a central part of its civic infrastructure and culture. This building of local capacity to solve public problems is what the Study Circles Resource Center wants to see happen everywhere.

The growing number of communities like Portsmouth can become the foundation for a nationwide infrastructure that supports deliberative democracy at all levels of society and government. Building this infrastructure may be essential for national deliberation on issues such as health care or foreign policy to have sufficient local support and national impact. Such an ambitious project surely will encounter many obstacles. As they build their local programs, study circle organizers across the country face a number of common challenges: engaging those with low incomes and education levels is especially difficult; communities are increasingly multilingual and multicultural; organizing is labor-intensive, and resources are limited; public officials and advocates may see deliberation as too costly, politically risky, or ineffective; and linking deliberation to institutional and policy change is more difficult than linking it to individual or small-group change.

Some of the largest challenges we perceive apply not only to the study circle approach to large-scale deliberative dialogue but also to the deliberative democracy movement as a whole:

Resources. Hundreds of study circle programs depend on local volunteers, in-kind contributions from local nonprofit organizations, and funding from local government and philanthropic foundations. For these local efforts to replicate and contribute to nationally coordinated initiatives, they will require substantial and sustained support at both local and national levels.

Research and evaluation. Local support depends on organizers' ability to demonstrate that deliberative dialogue fosters progress on difficult public issues. To this end, we need to demystify the practice of program evaluation so that local organizers can set goals and measure success on their own terms. Support for national initiatives will depend on scholarly researchers' comparing many local efforts and making sense of patterns and implications.

Communication. We must create a vocabulary that both inspires people to see deliberative dialogue as a way to reinvigorate and reclaim their democracy and communicates the practical benefits of public deliberation. We need to do a better job of telling the stories of how deliberation is helping people make progress on issues at all levels of society and governance.

Although much work remains to be done to strengthen local deliberation, we must also focus our attention on linking local efforts to a movement to place public deliberation at the heart of a reinvigorated national democracy. The obstacles we foresee are formidable, but they can be surmounted.

Notes

1. Goldman, J. (2004). "Draft Case Study of Portsmouth Study Circles." Cambridge, Mass.: Kennedy School of Government, Harvard University. This case study is part of a larger research effort led by Archon Fung at Harvard University's Kennedy School of Government. The case in this chapter was based on Goldman's case study and Mengual, G. (2003, Summer). "Portsmouth, N.H.—Where Public Dialogue is a Hallmark of Community Life." *Focus on Study Circles, 14*(2), 1, 7.

2. City of Portsmouth. (2004, May). *Portsmouth Master Plan: Vision Statement, Priorities for Action, Goals, Objectives, and Strategies—Draft.* Portsmouth, N.H.: City of Portsmouth.

3. The Study Circles Resource Center is a project of The Paul J. Aicher Foundation, formerly the Topsfield Foundation, Inc. For a history of the foundation and the Study Circles Resource Center, see Fanselow, J. (2002). *What Democracy Feels Like.* Pomfret, Conn.: Topsfield Foundation; or the Study Circles Resource Center home page at http://www.studycircles.org.

4. Oliver, L. P. (1987). *To Understand Is to Act: Study Circles, Coming Together for Personal Growth and Social Change.* Washington, D.C.: Seven Locks Press.

5. Daniel Yankelovich (1999) provides a useful overview of the many uses of dialogue in *The Magic of Dialogue: Transforming Conflict into Cooperation.* New York: Simon & Schuster.

6. Mathews, D. (1998, Dec.) "Dialogue and Deliberation: 'Meaning Making' Is Essential to Decision Making." *Connections, 9*(2), 24–27.

7. McCoy, M. L., and Scully, P. L. (2002, Summer). "Deliberative Dialogue to Expand Civic Engagement: What Kind of Talk Does Democracy Need?" *National Civic Review, 91*(2), 117–135.

8. In 1999, the League of Women Voters of the United States commissioned Lake Snell Perry & Associates and The Tarrance Group to conduct a multiphase project on civic participation. The report on the project, "How to Be Politically Effective: Working Together: Community Involvement in America," is based on one-on-one interviews with local activists, small-group interviews with citizens in four cities around the country, and a national survey. This study found that civic participation is frequently motivated by the opportunity to make a tangible difference on a community problem. (League of Women Voters. [1999]. "How to Be Politically Effective: Working Together: Community Involvement in America." [http://www.lwv.org/elibrary/pub/cp_survey/cp_1.html].) See also Michael X. Delli Carpini's comments in Dionne, E. J. (2000, Summer). "The State of the Movement." *National Civic Review, 89*(2), 122–126.

9. Mengual, G. (2003). *What Works: Study Circles in the Real World.* (2003). Adapted from a report by Rona Roberts of Roberts & Kay, Inc. Pomfret, Conn.: Topsfield Foundation, 6–13.

10. For our how-to advice and research on best practices in organizing study circles, see Campbell, S. vL., Malick, A., Landesman, J., Barrett, M. H., Leighninger, M., McCoy, M. L., and Scully, P. L. (2001). *Organizing Community-Wide Dialogue for Action and Change.* Pomfret, Conn.: Topsfield Foundation. Also see Mengual (2003), *What Works.*

11. Campbell and others (2001), *Organizing Community-Wide Dialogue,* 89–98.

12. Campbell and others (2001), *Organizing Community-Wide Dialogue,* 133–136.

13. Campbell and others (2001), *Organizing Community-Wide Dialogue,* 13–18.

14. Campbell, S. vL. (1998). *A Guide for Training Study Circle Facilitators.* Pomfret, Conn.: Topsfield Foundation, 1998.

15. Some of our research has focused on best practices for recruitment of diverse participants. See Mengual (2003), *What Works,* 20–27.

16. Combining process design and facilitation techniques yields a practical set of solutions that address some of the dilemmas posed in Lynn Sanders' critique of deliberation. She notes that deliberation as it is often idealized or practiced excludes many voices and perspectives. See Sanders, L. M. (1997, June). "Against Deliberation." *Political Theory, 25*(3), 347–376. This coincides with Iris Marion Young's call for a "communicative democracy" that values "greeting, rhetoric, and storytelling," in addition to critical argument. See Young, I. M. (1996). "Communication and the Other: Beyond Deliberative Democracy." *Democracy and Difference.* Princeton, N.J.: Princeton University Press, 120–135; Young, I. M. (2000). *Inclusion and Democracy.* London: Oxford University Press, chap. 2.

17. The frequency counts noted here are conservative estimates. Our practice of providing free access to discussion guides and how-to manuals on the Study Circles Resource Center's Web site may have resulted in the development of programs that we are not aware of. In addition to measuring important indicators such as number of participants and duration of programs, we are improving our capacity to measure other indicators, such as the extent to which study circle programs embody the principles identified in this chapter.

18. A *round* refers to large-scale study circle activity within a finite time period (three to four months). Some programs prefer a serial approach, convening a few circles at a time throughout the year. Both approaches can engage large numbers of participants. Although serial programs foster many positive effects, such as changes in individual behavior and attitudes, or new relationships, we hypothesize that they are less likely to lead to collective change.

19. Leighninger, M. (2002, Summer). "Enlisting Citizens: Building Political Legitimacy." *National Civic Review, 91*(2), 137–148.

20. While these "Speak Up Arkansas" conversations convened for only one meeting, their approach was guided by the same principles that inform study circles. See Arkansas Blue Ribbon Commission on Public Education. (2002). *Arkansans Speak Up! on Education.* Little Rock: Institute of Government, University of Arkansas at Little Rock.

21. Pan, D. T., and Mutchler, S. E. (2000). *Calling the Roll: Study Circles for Better Schools: Policy Research Report.* Austin, Tex.: Southwest Educational Development Laboratory; Metzler, D., McManus, M., Davis, P., Cook, J., and Best, H. (2003). *Schools and Communities Working Together: Helping Arkansas Students Succeed.* Little Rock: Institute of Economic Advancement, College of Business, University of Arkansas at Little Rock.

22. Houlé, K., and Roberts, R. (2000). *Toward Competent Communities: Best Practices for Producing Community-wide Study Circles.* Lexington, Ky.: Roberts & Kay, Inc., 63; Clary, B. (2000). *Program Evaluation: Maine Youth Study Circles, Project of the Maine Council of Churches, Funded by the Lilly Endowment.* Portland: University of Southern Maine.

23. Houlé and Roberts (2000), *Toward Competent Communities,* chaps. 8 and 9. For other examples of outcomes from study circle programs, see Leighninger, M. (1998, Fall). "How Have Study Circles Made an Impact?" *Focus on Study Circles, 9*(4), 2, 7; "How Have Study Circles Made an Impact? Organizers Report on Their Successes." (2000, Fall). *Focus on Study Circles, 11*(4), 1, 7.

24. A team of researchers led by Archon Fung at Harvard University's Kennedy School of Government is conducting a two-year study of the institutional and policy impacts of study circles and National Issues Forums. The study was commissioned by the Charles F. Kettering Foundation and partially funded by the William and Flora Hewlett Foundation.

25. An earlier version of this table first appeared in Mengual (2003), "Portsmouth, N.H."

26. Wulff, B., Campbell, S. vL. McCoy, M., and Holladay, J. (2003). *Reaching Across Boundaries: Talk to Create Change, A Mix It Up Handbook.* (2nd ed.) Montgomery, Ala.: Mix It Up.

27. Numbers are based on a 2004 survey of about 8,000 people who ordered the *Mix It Up Handbook.* Of the 1,200 people who responded to the survey, over 500 said that they had organized a dialogue process during the 2003–2004 school year. Assuming that people who responded to the survey were more likely to have organized dialogues, we estimate that Mix It Up dialogues took place this year in at least one thousand schools, engaging between 15,000 and 30,000 students.

28. For discussions of how study circle principles can be applied in middle and high schools, as well as in higher education, see Wulff, B. (2003, Fall). "Creating a Sandlot for Democracy: The Study Circles Resource Center's Approach to Youth Civic Engagement." *National Civic Review, 92*(3), 12–19; Mallory, B., and Thomas, N. (2003, Sept.–Oct.). "When the Medium Is the Message: Promoting Ethical Action Through Democratic Dialogue." *Change,* 11–17.

CHAPTER FIFTEEN

E-THEPEOPLE.ORG

Large-Scale, Ongoing Deliberation

G. Michael Weiksner

In mid-March 2003, during the weeks leading up to the war in Iraq, tensions among supporters and opponents of the war were high. e-thePeople was a place where both sides could come together to understand better the other's perspective. In one case, a twenty-one-year-old American soldier stationed in Kuwait started a conversation on whether protesting can be patriotic. After registering for an account on e-thePeople, he was able to post an article titled "I'm Serving in the Gulf," in which he writes, "We see demonstrations and anger, violence from peace protesters and view faithful Iraqis. Why is it that Iraqis can stand behind a leader who starves them, tortures them, and steals from them yet our own people can't stand behind our leader? We see stronger feelings for Iraqi casualties than we do for ours. Protestors who think they are doing a service for us are delusional. The time for peace protests is over. You are either with us or against us."

Using an on-line rating system, e-thePeople members voted overwhelmingly to encourage this conversation, and within hours it became the top-rated conversation. As the top-rated conversation, it appeared prominently on the front page of e-thePeople. In addition to regular e-thePeople users, thousands of others observed or participated in this conversation. They learned about it in one of two ways: either they came from their local newspaper Web sites, hundreds of which link to e-thePeople from their home page or politics section, or they were directed by Google and other search engines that included a link to this conversation among their top results for searches on the phrase *peace protesters*.

Anyone who wanted to participate was able to do so. To join the conversation, they registered on-line, creating a user name and entering their e-mail address. Responses came from people around the world, including Larry Beck, a Vietnam vet, married father of two, working as a new home warranty manager in Dallas; Donald Grbac, a retired computer analyst from Pennsylvania and a Kucinich for President supporter; "mariettagirl," a Southern Baptist and a self-described "Republican Conservative all the way"; and Sandra Kay, a Reform party member from California.

When people responded to the soldier's initial posting, their comments became the start of new conversation threads, allowing members to discuss multiple issues in as much depth as desired. For example, "Can you support the troops but not the war?" was the key issue raised. But many other issues were introduced and discussed in detail. For example, does the professed support of troops by protesters provide solace to our soldiers? Is protest and dissent a patriotic duty of every citizen? Does protesting embolden our enemies?

This conversation lasted four days, with members posting at their convenience and responding to the comments of others. This asynchronous quality of the conversation gave members the opportunity to reflect before posting, taking an average of forty-five minutes to compose a typical 120-word post. But every conversation, no matter how popular, falls eventually from the top spot due to the exponential decay of the relevance function, which ensures that the topics are always timely and relevant.

At the end of the week, e-thePeople administrators featured this conversation in the weekly newsletter that was e-mailed to fifteen thousand recipients. A 716-word essay used excerpts and summaries of thirteen members' comments to create a narrative that reflected the diverse range of viewpoints expressed in the 238 comments posted. This narrative provided a synthesis of the conversation for those who participated and an easily readable summary for those who did not. This narrative was also posted to a searchable archive on the e-thePeople Web site.[1]

Hundreds of conversations similar to this one emerged in the months that followed, addressing issues such as the handling of the war, the postwar occupation, presidential candidate Howard Dean's e-fundraising success, health care reform, the 9-11 commission, Iraqi prisoner abuse, Reagan's legacy, and Michael Moore's film *Fahrenheit 911*.

Origins and Purpose of e-thePeople

A key inspiration for the founding of e-thePeople in 1999 was the prediction that the Internet would transform the power dynamics of the political marketplace as profoundly as it was changing the power dynamics of commercial marketplaces. Just as businesses were becoming more "consumer-centric," government and politicians would eventually become more "citizen-centric." Just as eBay had created a competitive marketplace in which goods are sold to the highest bidder, e-thePeople could be a competitive marketplace of ideas in which the best proposals for governing our society would gain the most credibility and support.

Another important inspiration was the observation that the Internet encouraged more natural, open, and engaging communication than other media. Because a Web site is only powerful if people visit it, it needs to be authentic and useful, not manipulative. It needs to give people an experience they feel good about. It needs to treat them with respect. Without these things, people will simply click away. This concept, when applied to the political realm, implied a more authentic political conversation. Everyone hates political ads on television. What if the dominant information medium made such deceptive messages obsolete? Could it encourage political actors to engage one another on terms of mutual respect?

The mission of e-thePeople is to improve civic participation through the use of the Internet. To accomplish this mission, e-thePeople provides a free on-line forum for public discussion and political action. A distinctive characteristic of the forum is the degree to which the participants themselves govern the forum, creating and enforcing the rules, deciding on the topics of discussion, and framing those discussions; it's an attempt at a citizen-driven town hall.

There are already many discussion Web sites and software products out there, many available for free. What makes e-thePeople different is the combination of the following characteristics:

Deliberative. The rating system encourages people to write open, thoughtful pieces, because other members can strictly limit the exposure of articles that are uninformative, inaccurate, or seen as offensive.

Reflects consensus. The rating system allows the participants collectively to communicate what they believe to be important. This allows observers—politicians, journalists, and other participants—to get a "sense of the room" without having to read everything or conduct exhaustive studies of the participants.

Upholds community standards. Giving participants the ability to act as moderators of the discussion allows them to filter out inappropriate discussion without resorting to outright censorship. This self-moderation also gives participants a sense of ownership in the discussion, tempering suspicions that there is an outside agenda or bias.

Reflects diversity. Every article is subject to comment from other site users, allowing a diverse set of viewpoints to be represented.

Reader-friendly. Most discussion sites are designed with the person who posts messages in mind. Those who casually browse such sites often find them confusing and overwhelming. Recognizing that listeners are as important as talkers in any conversation, e-thePeople is designed to look like a reader-friendly news site, with headlines of self-contained articles and an intelligent filter that points readers to the most active and timely conversations.

Inclusive. Many people feel uncomfortable participating in Internet discussions, perhaps because they do not feel qualified or worry about how others might react. Thus, we have created several levels at which people can participate on e-thePeople, from simply reading to rating, to commenting, to posting articles themselves.

Deliberation at e-thePeople

E-thePeople deliberations develop from a collective, self-organizing process.[2]

Designing a Deliberative Event

Anyone with an e-mail account can register as a member. Members can participate in any conversation or start one of their own. Conversations on e-thePeople are structured according to an enhanced threaded discussion model. In a threaded discussion, you can reply directly to any post. (By contrast, in a linear discussion model, all posts are ordered chronologically.) We have enhanced the threaded discussion model by adding a rating system that enables members to prioritize posts.

Typically, conversations discuss policy directly or have significant policy implications. These conversations are not directly linked to a policymaking process. They may indirectly affect policymaking insofar as they affect the viewpoints of the tens of thousands of people who participate in e-thePeople conversations or read the weekly newsletter. From time to time, policymakers and experts are invited to participate on specific topics in the same forum as other members.

Information outside of the posts is not provided to discussion participants on the e-thePeople Web site. Because members can directly link to other Internet sites or background materials, however, participants may and do reply to any comment directly to ask for or provide supporting or contradictory evidence to claims made in the forum.

All conversations take place on-line. Members make posts using Web forms, and these posts appear immediately on the site without administrator review. All posts are linked to members' biographies, which may help other members to understand where another member may be coming from. Members can also share e-mail or instant message addresses in order to send private messages to each other.

Convening a Public Meeting

The principle behind e-thePeople is to allow participants to act as moderators of their own discussions. Participants begin by publishing articles for the rest of the community to read and respond to. As participants read an article, they provide feedback by rating the article as something they would encourage others to read or discourage others from reading (see Figure 15.1). This article, together with the comments that respond to it, form a conversation.

There are specific guidelines for rating articles. Members are asked to consider, "Was this article informative? Was it stimulating?" Members are asked to use voting to encourage civility and other deliberative norms rather than to signal what they agree or disagree with. These collective ratings help determine the relative prominence of articles on the e-thePeople home page (see Figure 15.2). The home page and the Conversations section contain the articles with the highest relevance score—a figure based on numbers of encourages, discourages, and the posting date. The more encourages and fewer discourages an article has, the higher is its relevance score. This relevance score decreases exponentially over time such that no article can have the highest relevance score forever, no matter how many encourages it receives. This ensures that featured articles are timely and do not crowd out new topics for too long.

In addition, there is a section that features new articles that have only very recently been posted to e-thePeople and have not been seen by very many people

FIGURE 15.1. VOTING MECHANISM FOR CONVERSATIONS ON E-THEPEOPLE.ORG

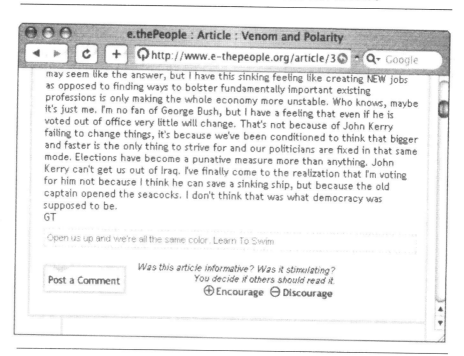

FIGURE 15.2. E-THEPEOPLE.ORG'S HOME PAGE

yet. The presence of this section ensures that all articles have an equal chance of being rated.

In addition to the information they introduce, articles are a starting point for people to respond. One responds to articles with comments, and comments show up alongside the article. For example, in Figure 15.3, the topic of the conversation is introduced by Paul Miller, who asks whether the costs of the drug war exceed its benefits. In response, "Socrates Thinks" states a belief that the costs do exceed the benefits based on the circumstances that resulted in his or her own daughter's death. This response is the highest-rated reply, so it appears immediately beneath the original topic. This comment alone elicits another seventeen replies, some which are highlighted. Based on reader feedback, an additional click is required to access Ralph Reckamp's reply entitled "Legalizing Drugs," whereas Paul Miller's rejoinder is shown in full because more readers found it worth recommending to others. This format allows participants to weigh in on a given article, answering a question it poses, offering new information, or challenging the assumptions it makes. As more and more comments appear next to an article, they

FIGURE 15.3. COMMENTS ON E-THEPEOPLE.ORG

become a rich and textured record of the diverse perspectives of participants on the site. Comments, like articles, can be encouraged and discouraged; the comments that resonate best appear at the top of the list and those that don't resonate as well appear at the bottom (or even on another page). This allows participants to collectively moderate content that violates the standards for discussion on the site. This also encourages participants to post thoughtful and respectful comments.

Participation in the Forum

Anyone can participate in e-thePeople's open forum. Participation can be as minimal as reading the weekly newsletter summary of activity or reading posts on the e-thePeople Web site. More involved members start or sign petitions, start or take polls, begin or join ongoing conversations, and vote on which posts to feature on the site.

In the twelve months from July 2003 through June 2004, e-thePeople had 1.8 million unique visitors who performed 16 million page-views; 300 electronic petitions were created, attracting 18,000 signatures; 16,000 articles and 75,000 comments were posted; 2,900 polls were created, eliciting 266,000 responses.[3] All petitions, articles, comments, and polls are written and prioritized solely by members on the site (that is, not by paid authors, editors, or administrators).

Policymakers and experts may freely participate as citizens. In addition, we occasionally invite them to participate in specific conversations. Because e-thePeople's conversations appear in newspapers across the country, editors and writers may read them.

Because e-thePeople is open to anyone who wants to participate, diversity cannot be strictly enforced; it can only be encouraged through broad promotion. One measure of success in this regard is the degree to which participants view the overall forum as ideologically balanced. Forty percent of members view a plurality of other members as being ideologically balanced, while 28 percent view others as liberal and 16 percent view them as conservative (see Figure 15.4). Figure 15.4 also shows that members are also more likely to view others as intelligent and respectful than mean-spirited or obscene.[4] e-thePeople is perhaps less diverse in demographic terms than the general population. Figure 15.5 shows members skewing toward ages 45–54, better educated than the general population, and disproportionately male.[5]

On average, top conversations last one to two days, attract sixty-four replies, and are read by 1,900 people. However, these figures vary considerably, depending on attractiveness of the topic and other factors. The most popular conversations will solicit comments from hundreds of individuals and be read by ten thousand people or more.

FIGURE 15.4. RESULTS OF E-THEPEOPLE SURVEY: USER PERCEPTIONS OF OTHER USERS

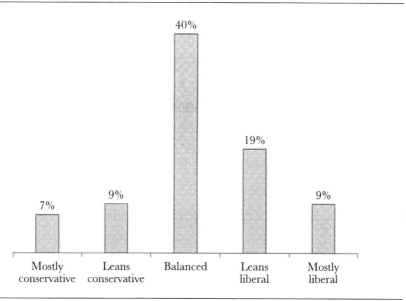

Note: Sixteen percent of the respondents answered "Don't know" or "No opinion."

e-thePeople users view other users as . . .

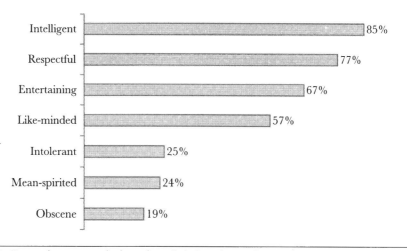

Note: Respondents were asked to select all choices that apply.

FIGURE 15.5. DEMOGRAPHICS OF E-THEPEOPLE USERS

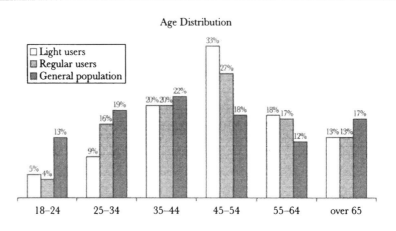

Age Distribution

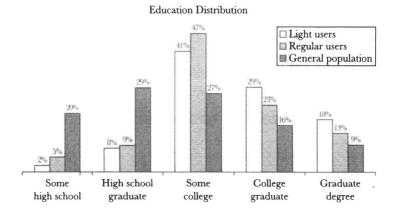

Education Distribution

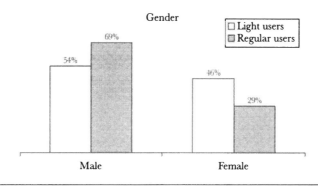

Gender

Note: Totals do not add up to 100 percent due to rounding.

What is the capacity of e-thePeople? The e-thePeople threaded discussion model can handle hundreds but probably not thousands of comments. We currently have one vibrant discussion a day, but based on the experiences of other successful discussion sites, it is likely that we could have six to eight vibrant discussions a day at most. As the conversations are currently structured, e-thePeople can probably operate at ten times our current participation levels.

On an annual basis, we currently have 30,000 regular visitors, 130,000 light users, and 1 million readers. Therefore, we can envision e-thePeople as it is currently structured handling 300,000 regular visitors, 1 million light users, and 10 million readers. Beyond these levels of participation, e-thePeople would likely require some or all of the extensions mentioned in the final section of this chapter.

Participants are responsible for almost all aspects of running the forum. These responsibilities include framing and promoting conversations, enforcing deliberation standards, and responding to other members. The only administrative functions provided by e-thePeople are technical support of the site, fraud detection and handling, and writing and sending the weekly e-mail newsletter. When making administrative, technical, and strategic decisions, e-thePeople administrators confer closely with the members through a metaconversation space about e-thePeople itself.

History and Impact of e-thePeople

e-thePeople has been in continual use since August 2000. From November 2000 to July 2004, the ninety-day moving average of articles and comments posted increased from 10 to 270 per day.[6] (In May 2002, the number of posts increased eightfold when the Quorum.org and e-thePeople Web sites were integrated.)

Posting on e-thePeople is growing but volatile. External events, like the Florida recount, the September 11 terrorist attack, and the war in Iraq, cause unusually high levels of posting. Other topics unrelated to the news that have generated unusually high levels of discussion include Social Security, equality and opportunity, race and the media, drug legalization, and immigration.

Because deliberations are not directly linked to a policymaking process, any impacts of e-thePeople are a consequence of impacts on participants themselves. To investigate this issue, a December 2002 site intercept study of e-thePeople asked who uses e-thePeople, why they participate, and what impact participation has had on them. According to this study, the two most frequently cited goals of participants were "to voice my opinion" and "to influence policymakers" (see Figure 15.6). At the next tier of goals, participants said they want "to listen to others" and "to get information not available in other media."[7] Nearly nine in ten regular users (87 percent) and two of three light users (67 percent) said that e-thePeople is

FIGURE 15.6. GOALS FOR USING E-THEPEOPLE.ORG

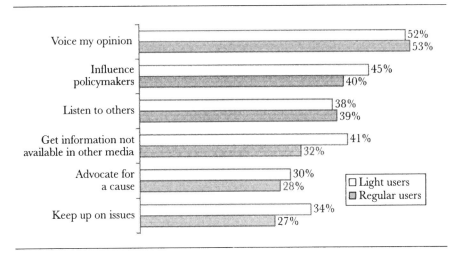

FIGURE 15.7. RESULTS OF E-THEPEOPLE SURVEY: IMPACT ON USERS

Users report that e-thePeople.org has had a "very positive" impact in the following areas:

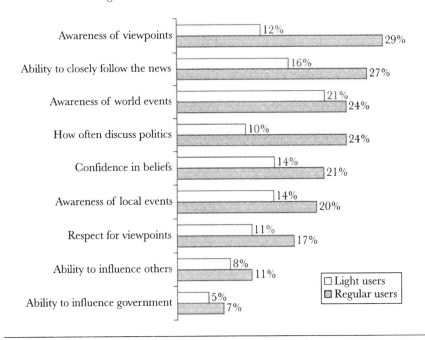

"somewhat" or "very" successful in meeting their goals for using the site. In fact, nearly one in two regular users (47 percent) say that e-thePeople was "very successful" in meeting their goals.[8]

As one might expect, self-reported impacts were strongest among regular users. Among regular users, the most frequently cited "very positive" impact was an increase in their "awareness of viewpoints" (see Figure 15.7). Among light users, the most frequently cited impact was increased "awareness of world events."[9] Given the emphasis that participants placed on the goals of being heard and influencing government officials, we interpret the low relative and absolute levels of such impacts as "ability to influence others" and "ability to influence government" as indicating that these areas deserve more attention.[10] On the other hand, it is reasonable to expect that direct impacts on users themselves (for example, increased awareness) would be more common and recognizable than indirect effects on other people and policymakers.

Limitations and Future Extensions of On-Line Deliberation

One limitation of the e-thePeople model is that the majority of conversations fail. By one definition of success (popularity of 10 or higher, with twenty or more replies), only 7 percent of the 9,000 conversations in the past year were successful.[11] Perhaps half of those failed for obvious reasons (for example, they were poorly written or addressed a redundant topic); however, a significant portion that were earnest attempts to follow best practices still did not manage to capture the attention of the other members. Perhaps the wasted effort by posters could be avoided if readers and writers had better ways to express interest. For example, if members had access to chat rooms, authors could propose ideas informally before investing the time to post an article.

Another limitation clearly is that e-thePeople requires Internet access, which means that for some potential users, it is only accessible through public libraries and Internet cafés. Computers also require a level of literacy that may exclude some citizens, and currently e-thePeople is available only in English.

Credibility and anonymity are also barriers that need to be overcome, and they are linked. Discussions on the Internet are portrayed by the media as either divisive and rancorous or homogeneous and one-sided; either way, Internet discussions lack credibility. The anonymity of participation also impedes credibility. Elected officials are unlikely to take a forum seriously unless they can know something about the people taking part—in particular, how many of the participants are their constituents. Similarly, media and other observers want demographic information about participants, perhaps to an even greater degree than they would if the participants took part in a face-to-face forum. Within the e-thePeople site, members talk about the positive and negative aspects of writing political commentary behind a computer screen. We have seen that a virtuous cycle is possible, in which members provide more personal information, which in turns build more trust among the members and encourages other members to open up. Nonetheless, building trust and respect remains a greater challenge than it is in face-to-face forums.

Many other challenges and limitations are worth mentioning. One is how to turn talk into action. As demonstrated by groups like MoveOn.org, "one-click activism" has popular appeal. But making one-click activism meaningful by linking it to deliberative processes is a challenge, both for on-line and face-to-face deliberative facilitators. Another challenge is motivating broad-based participation. Currently, only 0.5 percent of e-thePeople site visitors register to become members, suggesting that the value proposition for participating in e-thePeople deliberations is, for many, not compelling. This may be a reflection of the belief that just talking about politics has little effect and is not worth the time required to participate. Additional challenges, some not unique to on-line deliberation, are divisiveness, cliques, and the amount of time and energy required to participate.

Beyond these limitations, there are many promising ideas for extending e-thePeople beyond its current reach. Prioritizing (and funding) these ideas is the hard part. I conclude by highlighting three exciting possibilities:

Increasing trust through personal tools. Services like friendster.com, a popular site that connects people through networks of friends, are scratching the surface of the potential for linked personal political profiles. Services like moveabletype.com and bloglines.com are demonstrating the power of self-publishing with a more personal rather than a shared or public bent. Integrating these services could radically improve e-thePeople by building trust, accelerating member growth, and making activism more effective. For example, members could publish diaries and create profiles of their political causes to help draw attention to them.

Reaching a broader audience by strengthening the link to government. MoveOn.org and the Howard Dean campaign have demonstrated the power of one-click activism. e-thePeople can contribute by trying to make those tools more deliberative while tapping into the viral nature of political action. For example, on-line petitions could be linked to discussion spaces.

Increasing accessibility of the deliberations. Language translating tools could allow citizens to read and post in their native language and to interact with citizens in other countries or within the United States who don't speak English. In addition, e-thePeople could combine its conversations with face-to-face and other real-world initiatives to provide alternatives for those who can't use computers or aren't comfortable using them.

Notes

1. E-thePeople.org. (2003). "Is Protesting Patriotic? Domestic Dissent, Troop Morale and Collateral Damage." [http://www.e-thepeople.org/about/news/91802386].
2. The discussion technology that powers e-thePeople is proprietary and was developed by an in-house team.
3. Figures are from operational data stored on e-thePeople's Oracle™ database and from e-thePeople analysis of that data.
4. e-thePeople. (2003). "Emailing Alone." Research for the Rockefeller Brothers Fund. We randomly intercepted site visitors to e-thePeople.org during the period December 13–30, 2002. Two hundred sixty-four visitors voluntarily took a short on-line survey. We linked the survey data to operational data and compared it with the results of a focus group that we did in parallel. To understand the site dynamics better, we compared light and regular users of e-thePeople. Although light users outnumber regulars by better than four to one in the population, they constituted only 64 percent of the survey sample after we excluded marginal users. We did not study the marginal users, since they are likely to be first-time or very infrequent users of e-thePeople.
5. e-thePeople (2003), "Emailing Alone."
6. e-thePeople operational data and analysis.
7. e-thePeople (2003), "Emailing Alone."
8. e-thePeople (2003), "Emailing Alone."
9. e-thePeople (2003), "Emailing Alone."
10. e-thePeople (2003), "Emailing Alone."
11. e-thePeople operational data and analysis.

CHAPTER SIXTEEN

LEARNING DEMOCRACY CENTERS

Where the Public Works

Carole J. Schwinn, John T. Kesler, David R. Schwinn

While academics, politicians, and pundits wrangle over the relative power of federal, state, and local governments, a growing number of civic organizations are helping to put power back into the hands of ordinary citizens. In this chapter, we refer to these as *learning democracy centers*. These associations and initiatives are trusted, neutral, institutionalized conveners that have the capacity to engage diverse members of their communities in solving their most pressing social, economic, and environmental problems.

Each of these organizations helps its community master the competencies required in an inclusive, participatory democracy: valuing diversity in all of its dimensions; engaging in meaningful public dialogue; understanding the systemic nature of complex problems; collaborating across organizational and sectoral boundaries; generating and implementing innovative solutions; seeking out new sources of funding and support; providing evidence that their actions are making a difference in the community's well-being; and, finally, learning from experience.

Learning democracy centers exist in a growing number of communities in the United States. One example is the Lower Outer Cape Community Coalition of Eastham, Massachusetts. The coalition organizes task forces of diverse stakeholders to find local solutions to locally identified needs.[1] Over its fifteen-year history, the coalition has evolved into a social incubator of sorts that convenes stakeholders to work on broad-based community issues and facilitates their work through a standardized planning process. When ongoing programs or services result from the work of these task forces, they are either spun off as freestanding organizations or find a home in a related organization. The coalition's initiatives have included the Interfaith Council for the Homeless, the Cape Cod Children's Place, Healthy Connections, the Ellen Jones Community Dental Center, and many others.

The coalition began in 1987 as a network of health and human service agencies in response to a need to increase access to services. Given its location on a rather isolated peninsula, the area was frequently overlooked in terms of services and resources. Many people had to drive thirty or even sixty miles to obtain satisfactory care. The coalition has been instrumental in improving access and quality, but it has also embraced a much broader and more systemic definition of what it means for a community to care about its people, its economy, and its environment. Coalition members, for example, created a local community development corporation that focuses on economic development and affordable housing and are now forming a community roundtable that will foster collaboration by encouraging a "think regionally, act locally" approach.

The coalition's greatest success, however, is evidenced by a dramatic culture shift in how public work is accomplished in the region. In the fall of 2003, for example, the coalition organized a local response to the elimination of dental coverage from Medicaid in Massachusetts, in a geographic area where thirty thousand people lacked access to dental care, had no fluoridated water, and often suffered from extremely poor oral health. The education, prevention, screening, and dental care program that the coalition helped to develop now provides services in four schools and is entirely staffed by volunteers who operate on a shoestring budget. Reflecting on this initiative, the coalition's executive director, B. L. Hathaway, commented, "Most people would have rolled their eyes and said, 'There's nothing we can do about this huge issue.' But now there is this sense of capability and capacity, such that we hardly even think about limitations any more. I am so immersed in this sense of the possible that when I move outside of this group or geographic area and go to other places where I hear the negativity, cynicism, and all of the barriers about why things can't get done, I am reminded that the world still operates from that mentality."

Recently, the coalition has stepped up its proactive approach to increasing citizen engagement, competency, and capacity for leadership and participation in public work. In the coalition's Self-Training for Empowerment Program, participants are truly learning democracy through experiential training in dialogue and deliberation, conflict resolution, leading meetings, and focusing efforts for change. Participants also learn to use and facilitate the coalition's standard strategic planning process for task forces, which has become simply "the way things get done." According to Hathaway, the coalition's only full-time staff person, "The community has really honed that process over the years, because we've learned how to be successful. Part of the reason that we're able to do this work with so few resources is because of the nature of the coalition. Our role is to continue to get the right people to the table with the right process for working together."

Background

What we call the learning democracy centers movement comes from a variety of community-based change initiatives, including Sustainable Communities, Safe Communities, Community Building, Civic Democracy, Livable Communities, Smart Growth, and others. In 2000, the National Civic League and the Coalition for Healthier Cities and Communities received a grant from the W. K. Kellogg Foundation to evaluate the potential for converging these initiatives into a communities movement. The project conducted dialogues with organizations in five locations around the country: Des Moines, Iowa; White River Junction, Vermont; Jacksonville, Florida; Salt Lake City, Utah; and Washington, D.C. The project designers—including one of the coauthors of this chapter, John Kesler—were interested in each organization's purpose, alignment with other community-based movements, areas of emphasis, and underlying values. As reported by Kesler and Drew O'Connor, most participants agreed that there are "a set of underlying values, tools, and goals that the community movements share and that integration among the movements could serve to maximize resources and enhance the impact of community transformation projects." They also affirmed the importance of the civic sector in communities, "that notional place where dialogue and deliberation occur, where trust is built, and where the foundation for community problem solving is developed."[2]

As a follow-up to the communities movement research, we interviewed the leaders of a dozen learning democracy centers in 2003 and 2004. We wanted to learn more about how they function, how they are sponsored and funded, how they are organized, how they measure success, what they are learning, and, most important, what participatory and deliberative processes and practices they use to help people learn democracy through direct engagement in public work. Among other things, we discovered that these centers share a common goal of lifting the voices and mobilizing the creative energies of diverse community members to improve the quality of life across all sectors and in all its dimensions, including social, economic, and environmental dimensions. In short, these centers and many others like them are "community incubators" that are helping individuals, organizations, and institutions to learn democracy. They are giving birth to the new systems and structures through which ordinary people are taking responsibility for their own and their community's future.

Description

The deliberative practices used by the centers we interviewed are far more similar than they are different. A typical example is Partners for a Healthy Community, a grassroots, nonprofit organization that serves a three-county area that includes 30,000 people in the city of Anderson, South Carolina, and 150,000 people in the county.[3] Longtime president and chief executive officer Russell Harris reports that the organization's role is to help the community identify critical, systemic issues; bring the people together who can address them; provide facilitation and planning assistance; incubate new organizations and initiatives; and hand them off to stewards who will carry them forward and ensure their sustainability. Although the processes and practices vary across the centers, each uses most or all of the following elements to create positive social, economic, and environmental change in their communities.

Envisioning a Desired Future

The Champlain Initiative of Chittenden County, Vermont, launched its work in 1996 by engaging community members in crafting a twenty-year vision.[4] The process spawned groups that worked on specific issues that addressed the vision, including a sustainability initiative that has become a statewide organization, a racism study circle project (see Chapter Fourteen for a discussion of study circles), and many others. From those beginnings, the initiative has evolved into a "community innovation lab" that focuses on a wide array of social, environmental, and economic issues.

Likewise, Vision 2020 of Greater Lafayette, Indiana, was initially established to create a vision and a strategic plan for the region.[5] The organization now leads an ongoing process of convening citizens from the broad diversity of the community, updating the strategic plan, and making sure that all voices are heard. Managing director Kathy Dale reports that involving the community at large and increasing civic capacity has been just as important as reaching substantive goals.

Establishing Community Indicators

Many of the learning democracy center staff members whom we interviewed attribute a great deal of their success to the collaborative development, publication, and monitoring of community indicators. Most centers, including the Champlain Initiative of Chittenden County, Vermont, use indicators that are comprehensive and multidimensional, measuring the factors that contribute to a broad definition of their community's quality of life. The Boulder County (Colorado) Civic Forum tracks fifty indicators in four interrelated areas: people; the environment; the economy; and culture and civil society. These indicators are used as an information resource and planning tool by public officials, business leaders, grantmakers, community organizations, and the general public. The Boulder County Civic Forum's comprehensive view of these interrelated facets of community health enable the forum to "shed light rather than heat on complex community issues, many of which cross over the narrow limits of traditional issue advocacy and geopolitical boundaries."[6]

In another example, the annual indicators report published by Colorado's Yampa Valley Partners is the driving force for convening community conversations, identifying critical issues, forming working partnerships, and fostering collaboration and resource sharing.[7] To executive director Audrey Danner, however, it is not the report itself that is important. Rather, it is the meaning and shared understanding behind the indicators that emerges as community members come together to talk about who they are, what they value, and how they need to address these issues. Danner describes the participants' deliberations in one such conversation about creating a measure of the health of a community's children: "When we say we want healthy children, do we mean good test scores, immunization, prenatal care, family wages above the poverty level? How do those measures link together so that we all understand and continue to use them in our roles, whether as a small business owner downtown, a mining company, or other enterprise? How do we put all of that information together so that people realize that they contribute to it by most everything they do in the community? How can we educate people about the indicator? How do we get folks to participate in this process?"

Identifying Critical Issues

Critical issues come to the fore in a variety of ways, including the previously described processes of creating a vision and establishing community indicators. Other sources of information used by learning democracy centers include, for example, a human condition study conducted by the Lower Outer Cape Community Coalition and communitywide health assessments, forums, and summits organized by the Healthy York County (Pennsylvania) Coalition.[8] President Ruth Scott of Innovation Partners of Portland, Oregon, reports that her organization uses a fact-based research and development process to identify regional priorities in the areas of education, community building, and economic vitality.[9]

Among the more sophisticated processes for identifying critical issues and moving them onto the public agenda is the Jacksonville (Florida) Community Council Inc.'s study process. Each year, according to associate director Ben Warner, through a citizen participation process, the council identifies a number of significant community problems and selects issues for concentrated study.

Diverse study committees meet weekly for six to nine months, gain a thorough understanding of each study issue, reach consensus on key findings, and publish a report. Next, a citizens' implementation task force takes the report to the community and seeks to place issues on the community agenda. The goal is to seek further deliberation, increased public awareness, and, ultimately, action by appropriate officials. Jacksonville's initiative has developed publicly available guides for all phases of this process: selection of issues, study of issues, and implementation of actions to place issues before the community.[10]

Mobilizing Creative Energies

Once critical issues are identified, learning democracy centers have the capacity and competence to mobilize the creative energies of the community to address them. Katie Bell, executive director of the Healthy York County Coalition, notes that the coalition is viewed by the community as "the one neutral organization that can bring all facets of the community together, including businesses, government, and nonprofits." Executive director Hathaway of the Lower Outer Cape Community Coalition agrees that a diverse approach is important. "Over time," she says, "it became evident that if you're talking about basic needs—child care, housing, economic development issues—you have to engage multiple sectors of the community, in order to come up with broad-based solutions."

Learning democracy centers have been remarkably successful in mobilizing large numbers of diverse volunteers in their communities. One example is a program to reduce teenage pregnancies that has been initiated by Community-Building Community in Midvale City, Utah.[11] Based on statistics that reflected a rising rate of teenage pregnancy and an inclusive discussion of this concern, Community-Building Community decided to partner with all of the religious groups in the community. Executive director Hillary Evans reports that leaders from all denominations in the community were brought together to reach consensus on their shared concern. Basic information was provided, and each church group is working on this issue with its youth in the context of its own beliefs and value systems.

Leveraging Sponsorship and Resources

Sponsorship and support for learning democracy centers comes from a wide variety of sources, including local, state, and national government; public, private, and community foundations; colleges and universities; health care systems; donor gifts; membership fees; fund drives; and others. The centers' approaches to leveraging sponsorship and resources, like their approaches to other activities, are highly transparent and collaborative. Vision 2020 of Greater Lafayette, for example, was originally funded by city and county governments and now receives funds from the corporate and nonprofit sectors as well. The chamber of commerce acts as the organization's fiscal agent, and the local community foundation acts as the nonprofit umbrella.

In another example, the Lower Outer Cape Community Coalition received start-up funding from the University of Massachusetts' Office of Community Programs and continues to receive an annual grant from the university. It has also received an annual grant from the Massachusetts Department of Public Health for a number of years. Other funds come from state and federal grants, which usually target specific projects. The coalition's board members recently acted as advisers to help bring a Bureau of Primary Health program to the area, which helps participants to enroll in public health insurance programs. Each of the area's eight towns also provides funds for coalition operations, as do the organization's sponsoring members.

Funding, by all accounts, is a particular challenge in these sparse economic times, requiring the centers to be increasingly creative in resource development. Recently, for example, the Lower Outer Cape Community Coalition has begun to offer professional services, using the processes and products they have developed, including a needs assessment protocol and survey instruments. Jacksonville Community Council Inc. has for many years offered community-based research and consulting services and has developed relationships with communities across the United States and in Canada, Australia, Germany, Korea, Brazil, and other countries around the world. Other initiatives, notably Colorado's Yampa Valley Partners, also rely on partnerships and in-kind contributions. The area's local newspapers, for example, have taken on responsibility for selling advertising, printing, publishing, and distribution for Yampa Valley Partners' annual indicators report as a special newspaper insert.

Measuring Impact

For many of the centers we studied, the community indicators already discussed are the primary means of measuring their impact. Most employ other methods as well; for example, the Lower Outer Cape Community Coalition uses surveys on quality-of-life issues (such as dental health) before and after their initiatives, and Partners for a Healthy Community uses a variety of baseline and benchmark studies.

Although quantitative measures often demonstrate the success of learning democracy centers, perhaps their biggest contribution to the quality of life is the degree to which, as social incubators, they have spawned local solutions to previously intractable problems. For example, the Northern Berkshire Community Coalition of North Adams, Massachusetts, in its role as a community convener, has been instrumental in creating numerous community services, including the area's homeless prevention program and shelter (Family Life Support Center and Louison House) and a unique program that offers access to health care for the uninsured (Ecu-Health Care).[12] The coalition is responsible for bringing an office of Big Brothers and Big Sisters to North Adams. Discussions within monthly coalition-sponsored citizen forums also led to the formation of numerous community task forces, including the Northern Berkshire Collaborative for Non-Violence, the Northern Berkshire Youth Collaborative, the Transportation Association of Northern Berkshire, the Community Wellness Advisory Board, and the Family Economic Self Sufficiency Task Force.

As learning democracy centers have matured and evolved over the years, they have gained the experience, credibility, and capacity to influence public policy. In addition to organizing task forces, the Lower Outer Cape Community Coalition actively advocates for public access to health and human services, and it acts as a watchdog in regard to public policy, practices, and programs in those areas. The coalition has provided the data from their human condition study to each town in the region and discussed the results with each town's human resource committee (which the coalition was instrumental in forming). The next step will be to work with the towns to distribute the data to townspeople who can advance the work of improving conditions. Strongly believing in this approach, executive director Hathaway explained, "We have to do our part in making sure that those involved in decision making, public policy, and resource allocation know about these data and actually use them."

Reflections

The learning democracy centers that we surveyed provide solid evidence that this emerging form of civic engagement, public deliberation, and local capacity building has the potential to revitalize and sustain the practice of participative democracy in America's communities. Each has been in operation for at least ten years, and each has demonstrated its success as an institutionalized, neutral, and trusted convener of the diversity of the community on behalf of the common good. Each has overcome significant barriers—citizen apathy, competing viewpoints, bureaucratic systems and structures, and many others—by taking their time; focusing on what matters most to real people; starting where the energy is; reaching out to business, government, and nonprofit communities; bringing more and more people to the table; drawing on the strengths of the community; giving credit to others; and patiently gaining the trust of a diverse constituency.

Still, these centers are not without significant challenges. Most express a desire to go more deeply into their community to engage those who have been disappointed, disempowered, and disenfranchised; to broaden their reach to embrace regionwide cooperation; and to continually increase the courage, capacity, competence, and commitment of life-affirming, participative, democratic leaders. The

Champlain Initiative, for example, seeks to build the capacity of individual community members to more actively participate in the community, such that the initiative can be a "handle to hang on to" as grassroots citizens become more active in the community. And Pennsylvania's Healthy York County Coalition is cooperating with the community's South George Street Community Partnership's Neighborhood Leadership Corps, working with grassroots leaders to take issues to neighborhoods and educate residents about the issues and their impact.

The experience of the initiatives we examined, and many others like them, demonstrates the potential for local communities all across America to build the capacity and competence required to bring forth innovative, local solutions to complex problems by using a comprehensive set of deliberative processes and practices. We believe that this potential can be realized by calling attention to this emerging phenomenon; by connecting existing initiatives to one another for the purposes of knowledge creation and sharing; by nurturing new and struggling initiatives with support, information, and resources; and by continually telling the stories of what works.

Notes

1. This chapter is based, in part, on extensive interviews and conversations with staff members of learning democracy centers and others in 2003 and 2004. For documentation on quotes and other attributions, contact Carole Schwinn. Contact information is also provided in notes that correspond to each program discussed in this chapter. Communities interested in participating in an on-line community of practice made up of learning democracy centers that is sponsored by The Berkana Institute (www.berkana.org) should contact Carole Schwinn at carole@berkana.org.
2. Kesler, J., and O'Connor, D. (2001, Winter 2001). "The American Communities Movement." *National Civic Review, 90,* 4.
3. Partners for a Healthy Community, Anderson, South Carolina (www.healthy-community.org).
4. Champlain Initiative of Chittenden County, Vermont (www.unitedwaycc.org).
5. Vision 2020 of Greater Lafayette, Indiana (www.ourvision2020.com).
6. Boulder County Civic Forum, Colorado (www.bococivicforum.org).
7. Yampa Valley Partners, Colorado (www.yampavalleypartners.com).
8. Healthy York County Coalition, York, Pennsylvania (www.healthyyork.org).
9. Innovation Partners, Portland, Oregon (www.innovationpartnership.org).
10. Jacksonville Community Council Incorporated, Jacksonville, Florida (www.jcci.org).
11. Community-Building Community, Midvale City, Utah (phone: 801-566-8463).
12. Northern Berkshire Community Coalition of North Adams, Massachusetts (www.nbc coalition.org).

CHAPTER SEVENTEEN

DISAGREEMENT AND CONSENSUS

The Importance of Dynamic Updating in Public Deliberation

Christopher F. Karpowitz, Jane Mansbridge

"There is community consensus." The leaders of Princeton Future, a community group that advocated a deliberative approach to town planning in Princeton, New Jersey, made this claim explicitly at least twice and implied it many more times.[1] One muggy August night in 2002, citizens who had packed into every corner of a borough council meeting room for several hours to vent their frustrations at the outcome and the process heard Princeton Future's advocates at the end sum up the new model of public participation they had offered: "All have been invited to participate. You have been invited to workshops and community meetings. You have been asked questions, and we have listened. Listening has been turned into design." Another speaker hailed both the process and the result as a "remarkable and unusual achievement" that had resulted in communitywide agreement.[2]

But if Princeton Future's participatory model was so successful, why was the public talk at the borough council meeting so contentious? At this and later meetings, the frustration with both the deliberative process and the outcomes that had emerged from it reflects the failure of that process to confront and incorporate potential conflicts. As one citizen put it, "Princeton Future did not allow for real give-and-take."[3]

Whereas the previous chapters in this volume have aimed to describe specific methods of public deliberation, this chapter focuses on the dynamics of deliberation more broadly. Although we look at two specific meeting procedures that are designed to produce deliberation—the consensus-oriented procedure of Princeton Future and the more adversarial procedure of public meetings—our purpose is not so much to document those methods as to raise an issue that pertains to all methods: the importance of an open-minded, ongoing discovery of one another's possibly changing values and interests, which we call *dynamic updating*.

We contend that participants in productive deliberation should continually and consciously update their understandings of common and conflicting interests as the process evolves. In particular, because deliberative norms tend toward consensus, participants must try to alert themselves to possible enduring conflicts in interest and deeply held opinion. It is true that participants should try to forge common interests when this is possible—when they can create new value by expanding the pie or when they can reach a higher goal by transforming their own interests and identities in ways that they will later approve. Yet participants also need to try to discover and probe one another's interests as they appear at any given time. In addition to being an important ingredient in creating more enlightened self-understandings (for example, by allowing parties to see that they really wanted A rather than B), the intensive unpacking involved in the discovery process also aims to minimize obfuscation and manipulation. Too great an emphasis on forging common interests generates unrealistic expectations and obfuscates real conflict. Too great an emphasis on discovering existing interests suggests that interests are fixed, static, waiting to be found. Deliberative groups thus need to engage in a dynamic process of updating in which facilitators probe for possible conflicts as well as possible forms of cooperation and participants feel comfortable in exploring those conflicts as well as in building bonds of solidarity, creating shared value, and finding unexpected points of congruence.

In short, we argue for an interactive process of forging and discovery, with continuing attention to the evolution of conflicting as well as common interests within the deliberative process itself. Failures in such attention, we argue, produced in the Princeton case a backlash against the deliberative process itself. Those failures were illuminated by the presence of an alternative format for deliberation—the relatively adversarial format of public hearings in a series of open borough council meetings. The larger question is the degree to which deeply opposed conflicts in interest, when discovered, can be handled within the deliberative process itself—for example, by building into that process elements of negotiation—or instead remanded to an explicitly adversary process, such as a majority vote or, as in the Princeton case, a mixture of public hearings and decisions by representatives subject to reelection.

Downtown Development in Princeton

Deliberative reform in Princeton was born out of frustration with adversarial politics. The local political system, somewhat unusually, includes two distinct political entities—the geographically larger and more suburban *township* and the more densely populated business district and neighborhoods of the *borough*, which is located wholly inside the township borders. Although borough and township maintain separate local governments, the two entities are similar in population and demographic characteristics,[4] both being much better educated, far wealthier, and with a larger proportion of white residents than the state of New Jersey as a whole.[5]

Although the residents of the borough generally oppose political merger with the township, the two Princetons do cooperate through a regional school board, a regional planning board that includes both borough and township residents, and a single community library. It was the library board's decision to erect a new, larger facility that marked the beginning of community efforts to consider new development downtown, in the borough. After some consideration of alternate sites, the library board secured an agreement between the borough and the township to build a new building in the same location as the old one, near the center of the borough. As part of that agreement, the borough assured the township, which pays the larger share of the tax revenues that support the library, that it would provide "adequate, affordable, and accessible" parking for township residents who wished to drive to the new facility.[6] In addition, the local arts council was planning an expansion that would also require more downtown parking. With library plans in place, borough council members, at the urging of the mayor, began exploring parking alternatives and hired a parking consultant. Because the borough already owned the land surrounding the new library, proposed parking solutions centered on that area. Among the possible parking solutions were plans for a downtown garage.

Princeton Future's Consensus-Oriented Deliberation

With a new library and parking options on the table, some prominent community members—among them a former university president, a former dean of the School of Architecture, and the head of the local Democratic Party—believed that the community ought to think more broadly about its future and its development plans. Envisioning themselves as a new progressive solution to the shortcomings of local government, these citizens insisted that the adversarial traditions of existing political institutions would hamper effective community planning and that citizens had to be more directly involved in the planning process. Absent new opportunities for civic involvement, they predicted, the borough, the township, and the university would not be able to come to agreement about an effective downtown plan. Citing their desire to "help representative democracy" by adding a more "constructive" element of public participation, these leaders founded a new citizens' group called Princeton Future.[7] This extraordinarily well-funded effort was launched with a dramatic three-page newspaper spread that invited all citizens to take part in a collaborative effort to engage in dialogue about their community and its possibilities.[8]

In an open letter that was part of their initial announcement, Princeton Future made it clear that deliberative efforts would be an integral aspect of its approach: "We hope to move forward together with a view toward integrated solutions. We hope to avoid the piecemeal, project-by-project approach which can lead to community frustrations of all sorts, aesthetic dissatisfaction and inequity. *Can we listen carefully to our neighbors? Can we have a respectful dialogue across boundaries that remain fluid long enough for our disagreements to emerge into the sunlight of a covenant of single purpose?*"[9]

Princeton Future had the same deliberative aims that animate many of the programs described in earlier chapters of this book. Deliberation, in this case, was meant to generate consensus that would guide practical decisions about development: "We began to see that the key would be listening to people in small groups. . . . We had to have a process for generating a social vision to inform and direct planning."[10] This process was designed to avoid conflict and to achieve a measure of social harmony: "Our intent is to be cooperative and supportive, not confrontational and preachy. . . . We believe a plan for the future of Princeton's Downtown should seek consensus."[11] The planners hoped that deliberation would yield practical policy suggestions and educate citizens, making them better decision makers.[12]

Beginning in November 2000, Princeton Future held a series of thirty-four small group discussions in local homes and churches. These opportunities for public talk were led by neighborhood coordinators who were trained to lead group sessions, and a careful procedure for recording and categorizing citizens' comments was used at each meeting.[13] The neighborhood meetings focused on developing a "social vision" for Princeton through group discussion. In practice, this meant that moderators instigated discussion with questions about what citizens liked about Princeton and what they would like to improve. In an effort to reach out to African Americans, who had often borne the brunt of past attempts at urban renewal, a special series of four meetings, all moderated by black facilitators, was held in a neighborhood that was historically populated by African Americans. At the conclusion of the series of neighborhood meetings, Princeton Future entered into an agreement with the borough to provide development plans for the block around the new library. Leaders of Princeton Future hired a consulting firm to develop a plan based on citizens' comments.

The plan that Princeton Future drew up on this basis promised a large public square, new walkways connecting the square with other parts of the downtown area, expanded parking in a garage that would include a large underground level and no more than three levels above ground, a downtown food market, and a small number of additional apartments. During the early summer of 2001, Princeton Future sponsored additional public meetings to allow citizens to review and comment on the plans that had been developed. This second round of meetings was also publicized widely, with large newspaper advertisements and thousands of postcards inviting local residents to participate. In July 2001, the borough council voted 4–2 to adopt the Princeton Future plan as a general guideline for development around the new library. Of the two council members in opposition, one said that the plan needed more work, particularly in traffic analysis, and the other, while praising the Princeton Future process, stated that the town should pursue alternative parking solutions.[14]

Throughout the deliberative process and the planning process, Princeton Future's steering committee recognized that diverse interests were present in Princeton.[15] The group's founding insight was, after all, that the interests of the borough, the township, and the university could not be brought together without new, deliberative institutions. In addition, minutes from meetings of the group's leaders show considerable attention to the need to reconcile "social" and "public" interests (defined as social integration and aesthetic improvement) with economic interests, such as the borough's desire to maintain revenue and the developer's need to make a profit. Listening carefully to previously ignored minority groups (especially African Americans and Hispanics from neighborhoods bordering the downtown) would be an important step in articulating this public interest. Princeton Future thus envisioned its deliberative forums as a way to pursue common public goals and resist a planning process that might otherwise be dominated by narrow, private interests. And in fact, many residents did seem to agree that a large public space, affordable markets, additional walkways, and even a small number of additional apartments around the new library would be a valuable improvement over the small parking lot that fronted the old library. In that sense, Princeton Future's claim of consensus was real.

But in its attempts to forge a consensual public interest, Princeton Future failed to engage important conflicts among the various segments of the community. When we analyze the structure of interests, much seems to hang on parking and taxes. The township residents, all of whom had to drive to the new library and all of the other facilities downtown, wanted more parking. Some borough residents, especially those who lived close to the proposed development, resisted the increased traffic that might accompany more downtown parking.[16] Others were deeply suspicious of the university's involvement, believing that its interests were primarily in avoiding payments in lieu of taxes and getting the town to pay for parking for people who came to visit the university. The borough, in turn, wanted to create the parking it had promised in exchange for the new library with as little cost as possible, so as not to increase borough taxes. But the borough council had also promised that in any eventual parking garage, fees would be no higher than those of the parking meters on the street. The downtown merchants were conflicted, wanting more on-street parking (which was not a possibility), not being fully convinced that people would drive to a garage to shop downtown when they could drive to any of the malls surrounding Princeton, and worrying that the little street parking that they had would be made unavailable during the construction of any new development. The developer, finally, simply needed to make a profit.

The facilitators of Princeton Future did not, however, treat the trade-offs among these conflicting goals as hard choices in which some citizens wanted outcomes that others deeply opposed.[17] Nor did they structure the deliberations as negotiating sessions between those who favored more parking and those who opposed raising taxes. This meant that just underneath the surface of Princeton Future's "consensus" lay a host of unresolved, still churning tensions.[18] Instead, the hard trade-offs were made later, often privately, by consultants and the Princeton Future steering committee.

After approving Princeton Future's General Development Plan, the borough council entered into negotiations to hire a developer to work out the specifics of the downtown construction projects. In June 2002, the developer unveiled his proposal, which bore some resemblance to the Princeton Future plan but included a much smaller public plaza, a much larger parking garage, and many more apartments than Princeton Future had recommended.[19]

In response, Princeton Future held a public meeting at which its leaders emphasized the need for "common agreement" about downtown development and highlighted the differences between their proposal and the developer's. Princeton Future's leaders took on the role of advocates for the public interest that they believed they had identified in their deliberative endeavors.

In light of concerns expressed at this meeting and additional negotiations with leaders of Princeton Future, the developer modified his plans, slightly decreasing the size of the garage and increasing the size of the plaza, in addition to making other small changes.[20] From this point on, leaders of Princeton Future publicly supported the developer's proposal, claiming that the community needed to support its elected representatives and that the plan included much of what the citizens who had participated in Princeton Future had hoped to achieve.

The opposition that Princeton Future had not fully recognized emerged when citizens organized petition drives against the plan, wrote letters to the editors of local newspapers, founded community groups, and even picketed outside the borough hall. Content analysis of a local newspaper's letters to the editor reveals consistent opposition to the downtown development plan.[21] A survey conducted by Princeton's Survey Research Center and one of the authors of this chapter found that just over half of the registered voters who had heard of Princeton Future's recommendations either "disagreed" or "strongly disagreed" with the recommendations.[22]

Borough Council Meetings as Public Hearings

Beginning in August 2002, formal public discussion about development in downtown Princeton shifted to a series of borough council meetings, the last of which was held in January 2003.[23] These meetings served as an important supplement to the deliberative process because they gave formal public voice to opposition that had not fully emerged in the earlier consensus-oriented process.

The borough meetings served as public hearings, offering citizens an opportunity to comment publicly about the developer's proposal and the process that led to it. These sessions were generally very well attended, with more than one hundred residents filling the council chambers to overflowing on several occasions. Typically, the mayor allowed several hours for community comment at a time, followed by a few responses from council members. Given that format, talk at the borough council consisted largely of testimony—with citizens standing at the microphone and addressing their elected officials—rather than extended dialogue, although some exchanges between council members and citizens did occur.[24] Speakers frequently expressed great emotion in their speeches. The citizens in opposition became particularly emotional as they tried to break through what they correctly perceived was an existing decision against them. More than once, council members responded with astonishment at the level of interest and passion that the downtown development had evoked.

Speakers at the council meetings addressed both the outcome and the process. Opponents demanded a referendum; for example, one opponent claimed, "Voices of opposition were shouted down at Princeton Future. Opponents have been minimized at every step!" Another, waving her child's fourth-grade civics text, insisted, "We have a right to vote! Princeton Future did not allow for a real give-and-take! Why won't you let the people vote?" Some speakers responded that the Princeton Future deliberative process had been a new, more inclusive, and productive form of referendum and an example to which other towns should look. But the clear majority of citizens present expressed some form of opposition to either the process or the development plan. The Princeton Future process seemed to have produced not consensus but a backlash of anger and frustration.[25]

In contrast to the Princeton Future neighborhood meetings, questions of interests and the difficult trade-offs between them were front and center at the borough council meetings. Hard choices had to be made. Yet at the conclusion of the hearings, despite the many voices in opposition, the borough council voted 5–1 to approve the developer's proposal and move ahead with funding the construction. Indeed, the single council member who had changed his vote from opposition to approval rather provocatively said that he was voting for the plan because he thought it was the right thing to do, despite his belief that the plan would fail overwhelmingly in a referendum. He argued that a referendum would not give the true opinion of an informed public and that the council members were the best informed on these issues because most citizens did not take the time to understand the various aspects of the plan.[26]

Comparing the Two Venues for Public Discussion

Citizens in Princeton thus had an opportunity to discuss downtown development in two distinct contexts—one more unitary in its approach, the other falling closer to the adversary end of the spectrum (see Figure 17.1).[27] Both settings were deliberative in the minimal sense that they represented an opportunity for citizens to give public reasons for their opinions and to hear the opinions of others. Neither setting allowed ordinary citizens final authority, although the public hearings came closer in that the participants were directly trying to influence the ultimate decision makers, whom they could reject at the next election.

Many differences between the two discursive settings reflect their positioning on the unitary-adversary spectrum shown in Figure 17.1. The design of the Princeton Future meetings reflected the planners' beliefs that communitywide agreement could be attained through group discussion focused on common interests.[28] The Princeton Future meetings were often held in the homes of partic-

FIGURE 17.1. TWO DELIBERATIVE SPECTRUMS

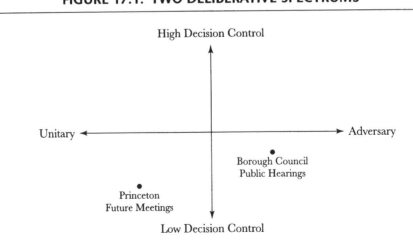

ipants, thereby invoking norms of friendship and neighborliness.[29] The fact that the meetings did not have to come to a binding decision also allowed the groups to avoid facing important conflicts.[30]

Borough council meetings, by contrast, were more adversarial affairs. In these meetings, citizens did not typically engage in dialogue with one another or with their elected representatives. Instead, they stood up and gave testimony, explaining their reasons for supporting or opposing the development, often with reference to their specific interests in the project as business owners, library patrons, property owners, or neighbors directly affected by the development. Council members rarely tried to forge some sort of agreement out of these various perspectives; they simply responded with their own reasons for supporting or opposing the project.

Avoiding Premature Consensus Through Dynamic Updating

Deliberative programs, such as Princeton Future and those described in earlier chapters of this volume, often seek to challenge "politics as usual," which is taken to be an adversarial process in which self-interested individuals compete over who will get what when, and how. There may be less agreement, however, about what the alternative mode of politics should look like. For some, including Princeton Future, the goal is to discover or forge a shared common interest—a full public consensus. For others, common interest is only discovered or created through political struggle, and even then, it remains contested as well as shared.[31]

The more unitary democratic vision can sometimes be achieved through deliberation, and some of the earlier cases described in this book provide clear examples of such outcomes. In some contexts, win-win agreements are discovered when the parties to a negotiation find innovative ways through which both can get what they want at less cost to the others than they had originally expected.[32] In other contexts, misunderstandings can be cleared up and genuinely common interests uncovered.[33] Deliberation can also yield respect and solidarity that enables parties to surmount previously existing differences and create partially new identities for themselves that encompass more compatible interests.

In still other contexts, such as the Princeton case described in this chapter, the costs of attempting to forge a substantive common interest are higher. In contexts that verge on unalterably zero-sum situations, the costs of trying to create consensus include not only time and the likelihood of emotional wear and tear but also the great danger of forced consensus or pseudoconsensus.[34] Participants in deliberative settings aimed at consensus often complain that their objections are overlooked in the group's eagerness to settle the situation. This was certainly the case in Princeton, where opposition groups complained loudly that they had not been heard during the Princeton Future neighborhood meetings. One solution to this problem is to train the group to practice dynamic updating: an ongoing or at least regular process of discovery in which group members try to analyze the state of interests as they see them at each stage of the deliberation.

The failure to gauge accurately the degree of potential common and conflicting interests at the beginning of the deliberative process in Princeton produced an expectation of forging consensus that eventually proved false, and that flawed expectation in turn created a process that eventually fueled considerable anger and opposition to the final plan. The eventual anger and opposition of many participants may not in fact have been greater than would have occurred in the absence of the deliberative process, but many who opposed the eventual outcome certainly blamed the deliberative process. Thus, even if Princeton Future's flawed deliberation did not make the city's problems any worse, it did damage the good name and reputation of deliberation itself, making it harder for future administrations and civic organizations to deploy the deliberative model when the setting *is* right for this mode of public talk.

The failure to facilitate the emergence of conflict in the course of the deliberation compounded the problem.[35] Usually participants will not be able to gauge accurately the degree of potential common and conflicting interests at the beginning of a deliberative process, precisely because identities change, alliances are created and dissolved, and new information emerges in that process. Conflicts may lie submerged through the greater power of some participants to set the agenda,[36] the fear among some participants of the interpersonal costs of raising a conflictual issue,[37] or both. In this case as in many, an elite group set the agenda for the deliberation, expecting a process of "education" that would, over time, naturally tend toward consensus.

In such situations, facilitators and members of any group must try particularly hard to find ways to ensure steady and realistic updating of participants' understandings of one another's values and interests. Too much emphasis on the creation of shared values and solidarity can make it difficult to tease out underlying conflicts in the course of a deliberation. Of course, one cannot know in advance whether a group will move toward consensus or reveal deeper difference, but facilitators can deploy procedures and language that keep the group open to either possibility.

One example might be the discussion process taught by the National Issues Forums (NIF) Institute. As described in Chapter Three of this volume, in the NIF model, it is helpful to seek common ground, but "common ground is neither consensus nor agreement that everyone wants the same thing. . . . As a practical matter, it is necessary to identify enough common ground to move ahead. . . . Through deliberation, . . . participants begin to identify which actions and consequences most people are prepared to live with over the long haul." This sober conception of common ground recognizes the need for joint action but does not overemphasize either the potential for conflict or the potential for commonality. NIF moderators place such emphasis on hard choices that this phrase is the title of one of their most widely circulated pamphlets.[38]

Reflections: The Dream of Unity

The dream of unity dies hard. In 1990, James Morone concluded that "at the heart of American democracy" lies a yearning for a direct, communal politics. The "democratic wish" that Morone found in American history involves a celebration of direct citizen participation that will transform "private into public," "conflict into cooperation," and "bondage into citizenship," culminating in communitywide agreement that will overcome "adversary self-interest." It is a vision of "a single, united people, bound together by a consensus over the public good which is discerned through direct citizen participation in community settings."[39] In *Beyond Adversary Democracy*, Mansbridge agrees: "As a people, we in America are starved for unitary democracy,"[40] meaning a direct, consensus-oriented democracy, aimed at the common good. "Unitary institutions," she argues, "[fill] human needs that adversary institutions cannot."[41]

Moreover, Americans—although perhaps no more than any other group—dislike conflict. In the small town meeting in Vermont that Mansbridge describes, one young farmer told her, "I kinda dread going, because I know when I come home I'm going to have the worst headache I ever had, a splitting headache." Another said he stopped going because he was afraid for his heart. Many townspeople did not go to the meeting, and when you ask them why, said one woman, "they'll say, 'Too damn many arguments!'" The townspeople often described the meeting as "this bickering back and forth," "petty quarrels," a "nasty argument," or a "big fight." As one woman put it, "I just don't like disagreeable situations."[42] John Hibbing and Elizabeth Theiss-Morse have shown more broadly that some citizens, fearing conflict, do not react well when forced to confront the messy disagreements that are an integral part of democratic processes.[43]

Unless conflict is structured into the deliberation, therefore, a deliberative group may well try to avoid difficult trade-offs altogether, preferring to find a consensus on easily available common ground. The Princeton Future deliberation fell into this trap. In deliberation, it is certainly possible to clarify conflict at the same time that one forges common understandings and even common interests. The unsettled question is the degree to which actual negotiations on conflicting interests can be structured into deliberations without undermining pursuit of the common good.[44]

If negotiation cannot be integrated into deliberation, another strategy is to combine relatively unitary with relatively adversary forms of public talk. Lyn Carson and Janette Hartz-Karp suggest experimenting with merging deliberative forms (see Chapter Eight); we suggest also mixing deliberative methods with other modes of public discourse. In the Princeton case, despite the fact that opponents were still not satisfied with the borough council's decision, the more adversarial public hearing at least allowed conflicts to emerge that had been submerged in the deliberative process. It also allowed more instances of testimony.

Those who designed Princeton Future simply did not think through the potential conflicts. If the Princeton Future deliberations had been willing to engage these issues explicitly—both in the planning process and within the deliberation through a dynamic process of updating the participants' understandings of their interests—the deliberative process itself might have been able to encompass and facilitate a mutually attentive exploration of those interests. As it was, however, a relatively static approach, not geared to helping all citizens understand and negotiate their various conflicts, produced what must be considered in hindsight a failed deliberative process. In the end, it was the adversarial public hearings that gave many citizens their real voice.

Notes

1. Sheldon Sturges, Princeton Borough Council meeting, Aug. 13, 2002.
2. Michael Mosteller and Sheldon Sturges, Princeton Borough Council Meeting, Aug. 13, 2002. At that same meeting, another speaker said he was "pleased with the process and the results. I don't know how the process could have gone otherwise." Supporters of Princeton Future regularly expressed such sentiments. As one woman put it during another council meeting, "Princeton Future allowed us to address the problems we share in a new way. . . . Public ideas were incorporated into the process" (Dec. 3, 2003).
3. Dorothy Koehn, Princeton Borough Council meeting, Dec. 10, 2002.
4. According to the 2000 census, the borough includes about 16,000 residents and the township approximately 14,000. Nearly 80 percent of the residents of both the borough and the township are white, with smaller communities of African Americans, Hispanics, and Asians, each of which make up an additional 5 to 10 percent of the population.
5. More than three-quarters of township residents over twenty-five years of age have at least a college education, and almost 50 percent have earned a graduate or professional degree. The median household income in the township is nearly $100,000. Borough residents could also be described as extraordinarily well-educated; nearly 60 percent of borough residents have completed college, and just under 40 percent hold graduate degrees. The median household income in the borough is just over $67,000 per year—only two-thirds that of the township but still more than the $55,000 median figure for the entire state. While the community studied here is clearly unique, those differences allow us to conduct a kind of ideal test of deliberation in action. If there are troubles here, among articulate individuals who understand the issues and have the resources to devote time to talking about them,

then we can expect even more difficulties in communities that do not share the advantages of Princeton. If, on the other hand, the Princeton case reveals successes, then perhaps it can serve as a positive example of successful reform under relatively ideal conditions.

6. The question of what, exactly, "adequate" or "affordable" parking meant became a subject of political debate, although the borough council and library board eventually settled on the idea that it would mean at least eighty-five spaces for library patrons at rates no higher than those paid at parking meters on the street.

7. Robert Geddes, speech at Communiversity event, Princeton, New Jersey, Apr. 27, 2002.

8. In the first few months of its existence, Princeton Future attracted nearly a quarter million dollars in funding. The university contributed significantly, as did area corporations, including Robert Wood Johnson.

9. Geddes, R. Goheen, R. F., Sturges, S. (2000, Sept. 13). "Open Letter to the Community." *Town Topics*, 36 (emphasis in original).

10. Princeton Future. (2002, Feb.). *Princeton Future Annual Report 2002*. Princeton, N.J.: Princeton Future, 3.

11. Geddes, Goheen, and Sturges (2000), "Open Letter to the Community."

12. Capuzzo, J. P. (2002, Dec. 22). "Hot Under the Buttoned-Down Collar." *New York Times*, NJ1. The issue of "education" raises normative questions. If the idea was to bring those who knew less about architecture and urban design around to the same opinions as the experts, then it is unclear to what extent those experts were open to citizen opinions that opposed the experts' fundamental assumptions. Even the Princeton Future's claims for participatory democracy ("All have been invited to participate. You have been invited to workshops and community meetings. You have been asked questions, and we have listened. Listening has been turned [by us] into design.") underscore the top-down character of the process.

13. Leaders of Princeton Future asserted that making accurate records of citizens' comments was a critical part of their efforts. If citizens knew that their comments were being recorded in detailed minutes, they would be more likely to feel that Princeton Future thought the comments were important. Larger group meetings that occurred later in the process were videotaped, and detailed transcripts of the conversations were made available for citizens to review.

14. These mild comments in opposition indicate, as did other features of the process, that although the procedures in the borough council are compatible with adversary democracy, the preferred style of interaction on the council itself is relatively unitary, assuming and searching for a common good, often avoiding overt conflict, and making decisions by consensus whenever possible. As in many towns, there is no sustained party competition in Princeton. All the members of the borough council are Democrats, and no Republican has been elected for quite some time. For these reasons, the borough council could not be counted on to seek out opposition and illuminate conflict. The council's stance as well as the process of Princeton Future led the increasingly frustrated opponents of the plan to claim repeatedly that no one was listening.

15. *Princeton Future Annual Report 2002* stressed the group's goal of achieving "economic, physical, and social" diversity and emphasized the need to create "an affordable balance of shops, services, building types, and green spaces appealing to people across the income spectrum" in Princeton.

16. These residents expressed two related concerns: a garage would bring increased traffic, and it would make it possible for Princeton to grow, becoming less a small town and more like other, larger central business districts in New Jersey, many of which included large parking

garages. The concerns were thus practical (the annoyance of more traffic) and powerfully symbolic (the end of a vision of Princeton as a small academic village).

17. Princeton Future did sponsor sessions in which citizens were asked to respond to various aesthetic trade-offs in the design of buildings and open spaces, but larger trade-offs between various interests were not considered.

18. This was especially problematic, given the deep suspicion that some had toward the university and its interests. Had the question of interests been considered openly, citizens could have voiced their concerns with one another and with representatives of the university in a setting that was less confrontational than the borough council. Instead, these suspicions and resentments remained submerged in the quest to find consensus.

19. During this time, Princeton Future frequently expressed concern that the negotiations between the borough and the developer were occurring in private, behind closed doors. Princeton Future consistently advocated for an open, public process and attributed any public discontent to the borough's unwillingness negotiate openly with the developer.

20. The high water table under the planned public square made it extremely expensive to put more parking underground, as Princeton Future plans called for. This was a critical development, given the controversy that the size of the garage eventually created.

21. Despite the fact that the editors of the newspaper strongly supported the downtown development, approximately 62 percent of letters published between June and December 2002 expressed some form of opposition.

22. Princeton Community Survey, August–November, 2003, conducted by Christopher F. Karpowitz. The survey was sent by mail to a random sample of borough and township registered voters as well as an oversample of those who were more intensely involved in Princeton Future events or who attended borough council meetings. A total of 723 respondents returned the survey, which represents a response rate of 44.88 percent. Among all respondents who attended Princeton Future meetings and responded to the question about the Princeton Future plans, 47.98 percent disagreed or strongly disagreed with the Princeton Future recommendations, while 48.65 percent agreed or strongly agreed and 3.38 percent said they did not know. Among the respondents who did not attend Princeton Future meetings, 57.09 percent disagreed or strongly disagreed with the PF plans, 27.09 percent agreed or strongly agreed, and 15.83 percent said they did not know.

23. The borough council continues to hold meetings at which the downtown development is discussed, but the last meeting before the council's approval of the developer's plans occurred in early 2003. In addition, some discussions occurred in front of the regional planning board, but those were less publicized and less well attended than the borough council meetings.

24. Lynn Sanders urges testimony as an alternative to deliberation, pointing out that the formal reasoning processes that some deliberative theorists advocate may disadvantage individuals who would be more comfortable with simply stating the situation and how they see it affecting them. Sanders, L. M. (1997). "Against Deliberation." *Political Theory, 25,* 347–376.

25. Christopher F. Karpowitz, notes from Princeton Borough Council meeting, Dec. 10, 2002. At earlier meetings, speakers had said that the "mechanism" for public input had been "faulty" (Princeton Borough Council meeting, Nov. 12, 2002), and, commenting on both the Princeton Future and the borough council processes, "We've been trying to participate in this process without being heard. . . . What kind of town center will this be if it brings such divisiveness in its infancy? A true consensus needs to emerge" (Princeton Borough Council meeting, Dec. 3, 2002). Karpowitz attended every borough council meeting on

the downtown development between September 2002 and January 2003, taking extensive notes on the speakers and other aspects of the process. The quotations in this paragraph are from his notes.

26. Indeed, in one of Princeton Future meetings, one citizen participant specifically commented, "I would caution against a referendum. You will have a vote. You will have politicking. Issues get squeezed, passionate and slanted. Someone wins and someone loses. This [Princeton Future] is a wonderful way to decide what the future of this community will be. If people want to come, they know their voices will be heard. This is the best possible way to find out what we want and how we get there" (Princeton Future minutes, Zone One Open Community Meeting, June 19, 2002, in Princeton Future [2003]. *Listening to Each Other: The Downtown Core, The Downtown Neighborhoods.* Princeton, N.J.: Princeton Future).

27. See Mansbridge, J. J. (1983). *Beyond Adversary Democracy* (Chicago: University of Chicago Press) for a full discussion of the distinctions between unitary and adversary democracy. Unitary democracy, which looks back to a distinguished intellectual tradition that includes Rousseau and the political "friendship" of classic Athens, depends on the presence of a common interest that unifies the group and on equal respect among citizens. Identification with the group as a whole allows citizens to make decisions by consensus, as friends. Deliberation is a key element of its politics: "The unitary process of making decisions consists not in the weighing of votes but in the give and take of discussion in a face-to-face setting" (p. 5). The identifying characteristics of unitary democracy thus include equal respect, face-to-face contact, common interests, and consensus.

Adversary democracy, by contrast, takes the conflict of interests as its starting point. Its intellectual heritage includes Hobbes, Locke, Adam Smith, and Madison, all of whom recognized conflict as a central element of political life. For the adversary democrat, egalitarianism is less about equal respect or friendship than about protecting the differing, often clashing interests competing within the political society through the mechanism of the equal vote. Although more recent work on agonistic democracy has stressed the compatibility of enduring and fundamental conflict with deliberation, some theorists consider the democratic exercise of power illegitimate—for example, Arendt, H. (1965). *On Revolution.* New York: Viking Penguin. (Originally published 1963); Cohen, J. (1989). "Deliberation and Democratic Legitimacy." In A. Hamlin and P. Pettit (eds.), *The Good Polity: Normative Analysis of the State.* Cambridge, U.K.: Blackwell; Habermas, J. (1983). "Hannah Arendt: On the Concept of Power." In J. Habermas, *Philosophical-Political Profiles.* (F. G. Lawrence, trans.). Cambridge, Mass.: MIT Press. (Originally published 1976); Wolin, S. (1960). *Politics and Vision.* Boston: Little, Brown. For commentary, see Mansbridge, J. (1995). "Using Power/Fighting Power: The Polity." In S. Benhabib (ed.), *Democracy and Difference.* Princeton, N.J.: Princeton University Press.

28. The Princeton Community Survey confirms that citizens perceived important (and statistically significant) distinctions between the two discursive settings. Respondents were asked, for example, to share their impressions of how important various meeting goals were at the gatherings they attended, ranking each goal on a scale from 0 ("not important at all") to 10 ("very important"). Goals included "teaching people about community development in a neutral, factual way," "allowing people to air differences of opinion and discuss different points of view," "helping people come to agreement about community development," and "persuading people to support a specific approach to community development." Both supporters and opponents of downtown development were far more likely to see education and helping people come to agreement as comparatively more important goals for Princeton

Future than for the borough council. Conversely, borough council meetings were more likely to been seen as places where persuading people to support a specific approach to development was an important goal. That difference makes some intuitive sense, because the purpose of borough council meetings was to debate the merits of a specific community plan that was already on the table, whereas most (though not all) of the Princeton Future meetings were dedicated to finding agreement about principles that would guide the creation of a plan.

29. Some of the larger Princeton Future meetings were held in the borough council chambers, in local churches, or at the university, however.

30. A *contemplative group*, which simply advises, gives an opinion, or discusses, not making a binding decision, will usually, all things equal, produce far less bitter conflicts and, accordingly, far less fear of conflict than an *active group*, which makes a binding decision. Many deliberative forums, such as deliberative polls, America*Speaks,* the National Issues Forum, and the group we analyze here, Princeton Future, are such contemplative groups. In an active group, the stakes are higher and thus the sense of urgency is greater. When a friend takes an opposing position, the conviction that one has been betrayed is far greater when one will have to live with the results of the decision for most of one's life.

31. Pitkin, H. F., and Shumer, S. M. (1982, Fall). "On Participation." *Democracy, 2,* 43–54; Barber, B. R. (1984). *Strong Democracy: Participatory Politics for a New Age.* Berkeley: University of California Press. Pitkin and Shumer as well as Barber maintained what we would now call an "agonistic" side to their understandings of deliberation.

32. Follett, M. P. (1942). "Constructive Conflict." In H. C. Metcalf and L. Urwick (eds.), *Dynamic Administration: The Collected Papers of Mary Parker Follett.* New York: Harper. (Originally published 1925); Fisher, R., and Ury, W. (1983). *Getting to Yes: Negotiating Agreement Without Giving In.* New York: Penguin. (Originally published 1981.)

33. Even in the Princeton Future case, it is clear that the citizens who attended Princeton Future meetings learned something about downtown design and possible plans, even if they vehemently disagreed. Those who attended the meetings were, for example, far more likely to have an opinion about downtown development than those who did not.

34. In the case of the Princeton backlash, failures to check for conflicting interests both initially and throughout the democratic procedure undermined participants' attempts to create a process that, in the words of one of the process entrepreneurs, would "make democracy work better by making it more participatory." Robert Geddes, public speech at Communiversity event, Princeton, New Jersey, Apr. 27, 2002.

35. In fact, Princeton Future's subsequent efforts to promote public participation seem to reflect this recognition. In the case of conflict involving the local arts council, which wanted to expand its building into a historically black neighborhood wary of losing any more ground to development, Princeton Future organized a series of small-group negotiating sessions between members of the arts council, neighbors, and other community residents. This group, moderated by former attorney general Nicholas Katzenbach, attempted precisely the kinds of negotiating between interests that we recommend here. In addition, other recent Princeton Future events have included sessions in which special care was taken to ensure that all interests were represented and guaranteed time to articulate their perspectives.

36. Bachrach, P., and Baratz, M. (1963). "Decisions and Non-Decisions: An Analytical Framework." *American Political Science Review, 57,* 632–642; Lukes, S. *Power: A Radical View.* London: Macmillan, 1974; Crenson, M. A. (1971). *The Un-Politics of Air Pollution: A Study of Non-Decisionmaking in the Cities.* Baltimore, Md.: Johns Hopkins University Press; Gaventa, J. (1980). *Power and Powerlessness.* Urbana: University of Illinois Press.

37. On the fear of conflict, see Rosenberg, M. (1954–1955). "Some Determinants of Political Apathy." *Public Opinion Quarterly, 18,* 349–366; Mansbridge (1983), *Beyond Adversary Democracy;* Eliasoph, N. (1998). *Avoiding Politics: How Americans Produce Apathy in Everyday Life.* Cambridge, U.K.: Cambridge University Press; Hibbing, J. R., and Theiss-Morse, E. (2002). *Stealth Democracy: Americans' Beliefs About How Government Should Work.* Cambridge, U.K.: Cambridge University Press.

38. McAfee, N., McKenzie, R., and Mathews, D. (1990). *Hard Choices.* Dayton, Ohio: Charles F. Kettering Foundation.

39. Morone, J. A. (1990). *The Democratic Wish.* New York: Basic Books, 5–7.

40. Mansbridge (1983), *Beyond Adversary Democracy,* 301.

41. Mansbridge (1983), *Beyond Adversary Democracy,* 4.

42. Mansbridge (1983), *Beyond Adversary Democracy,* 60–65.

43. Hibbing and Theiss-Morse (2002), *Stealth Democracy;* Hibbing, J. R., and Theiss-Morse, E. (1995). *Congress as Public Enemy: Public Attitudes Toward American Political Institutions.* Cambridge, U.K.: Cambridge University Press.

44. Introducing discussion of conflict into contemplative groups might produce precisely the sort of negative reactions and avoidance catalogued by Hibbing and Theiss-Morse (2002) in *Stealth Democracy.* It is also the case that the larger political process should include opportunities for individuals on similar sides of a conflict to create alliances, forge common interests among themselves, and develop common understandings of their adversaries—all processes that inevitably involve some form of deliberation. Investigating the empirical dynamics of "forging conflict" and analyzing the appropriate relation of this process to the full panoply of deliberative norms is a matter for future study.

CHAPTER EIGHTEEN

GROWING GOVERNANCE DELIBERATIVELY

Lessons and Inspiration from Hampton, Virginia

William R. Potapchuk, Cindy Carlson, Joan Kennedy

In the beginning was the group. This is a fundamental truth about human nature and politics, and neither modern nor contemporary political theory has yet to come to terms with it.

CHARLES FREDERICK ALFORD[1]

It's March, two months before elections for city council and mayor. Campaign season is in full swing, and candidates have assembled for the evening's forum. The moderator welcomes the crowd, then draws their attention to the posters on the wall, which list basic rules for public discourse: listen, speak up and be heard, bring an open mind, only one person talks at a time. "These are our group's norms. Candidates, do you think you can follow them for tonight?" Laughter fills the room.

Another poster board is covered with colorful cards. The moderator explains the procedure: a name is drawn; the chosen candidate picks a numbered card from the wall; the moderator reads the question printed on the back of the card; the candidate gives a two-minute answer; then candidates seated to the left and right of the respondent have the option to give their own answers.

The candidates quickly warm to the "Jeopardy"-type game, and debate is lively. Questions cover issues important to the sponsoring group—education, transportation, job training, crime, recreation. Members of the organization weave through the crowd, gathering questions penned by the audience. The moderator announces a new round, same rules. More questions, more discussion.

Candidates deliver closing statements in response to the question, "Why should I vote for you?" Most speak with confidence; they have made a connection with this group of citizens. As they leave for the evening, many express their appreciation for the comfortable atmosphere, the firm guidelines, the skilled facilitation, and the focus on constructive discussion.

A typical evening in the civic life of a city? Perhaps. Now imagine that the sponsoring organization in the above scenario is the Hampton Youth Commission. The moderator, timekeeper, and hosts are all high school students. Most of the audience wears blue jeans and is under the voting age, although those who have recently turned eighteen will have registered by the end of the night. An adult sponsor asks a young person on the way out what she thought of the evening. Her reply: "It made me feel important to my city."

This unlikely scenario typifies how dialogue and deliberation have permeated civic life in Hampton, Virginia, a diverse community of over 140,000 citizens at the mouth of the Chesapeake Bay. Hampton is one of the oldest cities in the United States, but it has changed rapidly over the past fifteen years through creative and painstaking efforts to expand the community's capacity for effective dialogue, deliberation, and collaboration on every kind of public issue.

This chapter explains how this change occurred by discussing the importance of Hampton's governmental structure and general efficiency and its approach to developing a collaborative community; providing three illustrations of how collaborative initiatives in Hampton have taken root; and concluding with some reflections on how to strengthen the connections between the theory and practice of building deliberative, collaborative communities.

The Role of Hampton's Government in Developing Civic Capacity

Although there are many ways to trace the evolution of Hampton's civic culture and its commitment to deliberation, almost all of the threads originate with intentional decisions made by leaders within city government. In Hampton, deliberation is not an "event," as it is in so many other places. Instead, deliberation is integral to deep reforms that have changed government and governance, reweaving and strengthening the community's civic infrastructure.

The impetus for this extraordinary reorientation came from a strategic imperative rather than a grand desire to strengthen democracy or create a collaborative community. Hampton's city leaders found that many neighborhood trends were not healthy. Concerns about youth were accelerating, and the resources that the city could use to address these issues were shrinking. If the leaders wanted to address community problems proactively, they needed community partners, and they needed to become better at working collaboratively with them.

The Council-Manager Model

Hampton's particular form of government facilitated the development and implementation of deliberative and collaborative community processes to address local concerns. Hampton is a council-manager city; a part-time, seven-member city council, with all members elected at large, provides policy leadership for a full-time professional city manager, who directs the staff. A council-manager form of governance (found in a majority of large U.S. cities) differs from a mayor-council form, in which a full-time mayor provides policy leadership and directs the staff. One difference is the length of service of senior staff. Hampton's current city manager has served seven years, and the prior city manager served for thirteen. Directors of departments that interface with citizens and civic organizations average twenty years of service. When citizens are asked annually to evaluate government services, 90 percent provide positive ratings, and their approval often reflects the positive personal relationships.[2]

Thus, senior staff in Hampton have an incentive to build positive working relationships with citizens, for they will be working with the same citizen leaders for decades. Staff speak with pride about the relationships they have nurtured over the years and marvel at how much they have learned from citizens. The strength of these relationships tends to ease the transition to authentic deliberation by moving quickly through the stages of establishing norms and building trust to working on the challenges and opportunities.

Contrast the longevity of Hampton city government's senior staff with peers in Washington, D.C., another city that is striving to build a more deliberative culture[3] (see Chapter Ten). Now in its sixth year, the current mayor's administration has seen four directors for the Department of Housing and Community Development, three for the Department of Parks and Recreation, three for Neighborhood Action, and four directors for the Office of Community Outreach. Thus, it is no wonder that when asked to deliver results within limited time frames, these directors often avoid deliberative processes as potentially slow and time-consuming. Citizens, angry about nondeliberative processes, are unlikely to find the director still around to deal with the issues that have been generated. When a new mayor takes office, often most of the directors are replaced. In this environment, citizens are constantly wary, never knowing whether a community process will be empowering, deliberative, and meaningful, or just a sham.

The form of government also has implications for whether a process is perceived as legitimate—that is, whether sponsors, conveners, participants, and prospective participants are willing to participate in good faith. In an era of cynicism about government and other large institutions, the legitimacy of a process is a critical early test for those who launch deliberative efforts. Long-standing relationships between city directors and citizens lay a strong foundation for processes to be seen as legitimate and authentic.

Efficient City Government

A second favorable aspect of Hampton's political culture is its efficient city government, which (perhaps paradoxically) causes relatively few grassroots groups to form. Many council-manager cities have high-performing local governments that manage ordinary services, such as trash collection, policing, and zoning, and often offer additional services that in other communities might be delivered by a community-based organization or a nonprofit provider. In these cities, one does not often find a proliferation of advocacy groups, since the government incrementally adapts to changing circumstances rather than resisting them. This makes it a less likely target for community organizing. The civic infrastructure often consists of a mixture of homeowner, neighborhood, and citizens' organizations, many of which have very little organizational capacity.

Contrast this with reports from Chicago. In a study area with a population that is approximately four times larger than the city of Hampton's, an impressive array of community-based organizations are critical in fostering civic involvement. Entities such as a community development corporation with over three hundred staff members "arose in direct opposition to a political machine that, in concert with real estate developers, bankers, and other elite institutions, consistently—and often literally—bulldozed over neighborhood interests."[4]

Hampton sought a different path. In the late 1980s, during an update of its comprehensive plan, the city reached a pivotal point in its approach to planning. Joan Kennedy describes the events of that period: "We had gone through a normal, traditional citizen participation thing where you put an ad in the newspaper and tell everybody to come to a meeting. Then you tell them what you're thinking about doing. So we claimed that this plan was going to be the community's vision of where we are going next." Kennedy continued, "I had just done my spiel about how the comprehensive plan is the community's vision. But when I looked around, there was just this sea of angry faces out there. I thought, this must come a lot closer to being these people's nightmare than their vision."[5]

The specific issue that had angered citizens was a proposal to construct a new road through neighborhoods in order to ease growing traffic congestion. The city backed away from the proposal, assembled a stakeholder group, obtained training in collaborative problem solving, and not only addressed the issue of the road but ended up working on all of the contentious issues in the plan. Michael Monteith, the assistant city manager who facilitated the group, reported on the outcomes: "There's no doubt it was the most successful comp plan we've had to date. It is the only one that has dealt with controversial issues in a long term and not a short term way."[6] Rather than bulldozing over neighborhood interests, Hampton city officials painstakingly engaged in a yearlong consensus-building process whose success was rooted in building relationships in order to overcome distrust; utilizing good information; and, ultimately, addressing neighborhood interests.

Although this effort laid the foundation for a new deliberative and collaborative approach to neighborhood planning, it also illuminated a persistent paradox in building a more deliberative civic culture. If dysfunctional and intransigent city administrations foster growth in community organizations and advocacy groups, as in Chicago, how do communities with functional and flexible city administrations foster a strengthening of the civic infrastructure to better support community-driven dialogue, deliberation, and collaborative problem solving?

A Citizen-Focused Approach

Like so many of Hampton's other initiatives, the challenge of improving civic dialogue has been met by a multifaceted approach, including building leadership capacity, creating forums, strengthening citizenship and social capital, reaching out, and continually adapting. We discuss briefly each of these facets.

Building leadership capacity. Hampton was one of the first local governments to create a neighborhood college—a series of evening workshops for current and aspiring neighborhood leaders that combines basic citizen education principles with a focus on neighborhoods. A typical college involves six to twelve sessions, with homework, and focuses on topics like local government organization, public safety and policing, and city budget and finance, as well as skill building in running effective meetings and working with diversity. Many of the three hundred citizen alumni have gone on to lead community projects, run for city council, serve on boards and commissions, and assume leadership roles in neighborhood organizations.

Creating forums. In a significant step toward shared governance, Hampton created the Neighborhood Commission, which comprises representatives from neighborhoods, community-based organizations, nonprofits, schools, business, local government, and youths. The commission provides a mechanism for shared leadership of the city's Neighborhood Initiative, for joint mobilization to implement citywide neighborhood strategies, and for relationship building. In contrast to a typical advisory board comprised solely of citizens who merely offer advice to city staff, the commission includes institutional representatives, makes decisions, allocates funds, and provides leadership. It functions like a collaborative, bringing together citizens and other institutions with a stake in neighborhood efforts. This structure allows differences of opinions among the representatives to be discussed and deliberated and creates a framework that builds consensus among citizens and institutional partners. The previously mentioned Youth Commission as well as the Unity Commission are examples of other forums that have been created by the city.

Strengthening citizenship and social capital. As we mentioned earlier, Hampton's initial impetus for collaborative processes was strategic. Over time, leaders came to recognize that through participatory processes, residents—both youths and adults—became citizens, fully exercising their role in a democratic society. Citizens also formed relationships with each other, helping to build social capital—"the features of social organization, such as networks, norms, and trust, that facilitate coordination and cooperation for mutual benefit."[7]

Reaching out. Hampton leaders recognized that no matter how creative the outreach strategies, many citizens cannot be enticed to begin their civic involvement by sitting in a meeting. Neighborhood Month, which includes house tours, celebrations, parties, and neighborhood clean-ups, draws many residents into an active civic life. Once citizens start connecting with their neighbors through events such as these, they are often more willing to explore participation in various community processes.

Continually adapting. In a balance of art and science, Hampton's leaders have experimented with home-grown community processes through an eclectic mix of strategies and theories in order to create the most successful approach for each situation. Local government has learned what citizens have known all along: there is no cookie-cutter approach to tackling community issues; the results desired should drive the design of the process. Dialogic and deliberative processes are a means of beginning the work, not an end in themselves.

Three Illustrations of the Hampton Approach

Three illustrations demonstrate how Hampton has built a deliberative and collaborative civic culture. The first is a commission addressing race relations; the second returns us to the opening vignette from the Youth Civic Engagement initiative; and the third and most extensive illustration concerns neighborhood planning. In describing these three initiatives, special attention is focused on the role of Hampton's citizens in defining and shaping policy and action, since this subject has been overlooked or underappreciated in recent works on collaborative governance and network governance.[8]

The Citizens' Unity Commission

To follow Hampton's approach to race relations in recent years is to trace the evolution of a model for community deliberation. From adopting a single program to creating an integrated system, city leaders and citizens embarked on a journey that began with solving a problem and arrived at a much larger communitywide agenda.

As an older southern city where people of color make up almost half of the adult population and over 60 percent of those are under age twenty-one, Hampton was ripe for talking about race. Unfortunately, the issue had not emerged in public forums in ways that fostered any type of dialogic process. Then in the early 1990s, city leaders and citizen groups embarked on a new strategic plan for youth and families. This community-based process contacted over five thousand citizens through five stakeholder task forces, to identify the top make-or-break issues that would ensure the healthy development of children and youth.

Over one hundred task force members gathered at the culminating event to present their findings to the city council. One by one, they described an array of important issues ranging from health care to education. Then the youth task force took the podium. In a passionate presentation, they unveiled their top priority: cultural competence and an appreciation of diversity. Their statement: "We are inheriting a world that is not equal. You expect young people to all get along, but your programs and systems haven't even figured that out yet. You adults need to get your act together first before we can hope to succeed."

Study circles were adopted as the first approach to examining issues of diversity (see Chapter Fourteen). With their emphasis on dialogue and focus on bringing together people with differences, the study circles provided an excellent introduction to what would become a growing initiative. In the first year, over 250 people participated in mixed-race groups, drawn to the safety of the circles as a means to explore culture, race, and differences.

When an issue of minority representation in local governance became controversial in 1996, city leaders realized that a more direct deliberative process was needed. Facing a review of its charter, the city convened stakeholders in collaborative decision making. The Charter Review Commission spent two years in sometimes contentious deliberation, exploring the impact of race on citizens and options for equitable representation.

The new council-appointed Citizens' Unity Commission, an outgrowth of the study circles movement and the Charter Review Commission, blended the dialogue approach with a vague and broad mandate to promote "appreciation of diversity" throughout the city. But commissioners and dialogue group participants alike soon tired of the conversation-only model. After a few rounds of groups, leaders convened a forum for feedback on the dialogue process. While they valued the discussions of diversity, participants expressed a desire to go deeper. They wanted to explore not only their own relationships to the issue but also the broad potential of civic activity that could result from their newfound awareness. They asked for education and a forum for action.

Diversity College now invites citizens into a series of sessions that incorporate a variety of deliberative and educational approaches. Dialogue group sessions are an integral part of the college, but so are education, field trips, and planning for action. As a result of this immersion into the complexity of the issue, participants in Diversity College go on to become speakers, facilitate dialogue, serve on boards and commissions, and engage as diversity champions. Their input has been incorporated into Hampton's new community plan under a revised and broader definition of diversity. Their influence has helped to reframe diversity as an asset for Hampton.

Unity commissioners are excited about the incremental change they see in their city and the increased focus on dialogue supported by experiences. Many express appreciation for a community that reaches out to "ordinary citizens" not only to address community problems but to engage in a process that promotes tolerance and civil discourse. They now realize that they are not just solving racial problems in the city but are part of a groundswell of citizens who are contributing to improving the community's quality of life.

The Youth Civic Engagement Initiative

Just as Hampton youth played an important role in the formation of the Unity Commission, their engagement has contributed to the overall creation of collaborative governance in the city. Many communities go to great lengths to include a broad range of citizens in local decision making, but it would be difficult to find a community that has made a more intentional effort to reach out to young people as an underrepresented population than Hampton has. This journey has been a challenging one, a true test of both youth and adult capacity for intergenerational dialogue and change.

The city's Youth Civic Engagement initiative recruits and prepares young people for meaningful roles as volunteers, advisers, and co-creators of public policy. The initiative taps both their innate interest in community life and their passion for improving their neighborhoods, schools, extracurricular activities, and the city itself. Young people in Hampton have become skilled at gathering youth opinion, deliberating about options, and reaching consensus on recommendations. Within local government, they use a deliberative process to create and champion their own component of the Hampton Community Plan. In addition to focus groups and public speak-outs (youth-friendly versions of the public hearing), they have learned to participate in neighborhood planning processes and charrettes. (For more on charrettes, see Chapter Thirteen.)

When opposing groups of adults were locked in debate about the design of land designated for a city park, young people wanted to weigh in with their opinions. Youth commissioners researched options for the site, hosted focus groups to gain youth input, held a dialogue about what they had learned, and then selected two spokespeople to represent them at the upcoming design charrette. The youth representatives' ability to articulate citizen concerns, solve problems, and seek creative solutions ensured that their proposal for a multiuse site emerged with more support than the solutions focused on single uses that were promoted by a few citizens unwilling to participate in dialogue.

Hampton's youth engagement opportunities ensure that young people not only have a powerful voice but have the power and authority to be equal contributors to the decision making within aspects of local government that affect them. This creates a new norm of a responsive, accessible government for the next generation. Not only does the community benefit in the short term, but a new generation of citizens emerges with skills in deliberation and determination to live in a collaborative community.

Neighborhood Planning

Our third illustration of Hampton's deliberative civic culture focuses on the city's efforts at neighborhood planning. When Hampton adopted neighborhoods as a strategic focus in 1993, the scope of neighborhood planning was broadened beyond land use to include social and civic concerns. The strategy called for establishing priorities for implementation that would be sustained by the neighborhood with city support. Staff envisioned neighborhood planning as a tidy process that would identify the most strategic actions needed to improve neighborhood quality of life. Neighborhoods envisioned it as the way to access city resources. Everyone was in for a big surprise.

Neighborhood planning proved to be a slow, messy business, demanding extensive creativity, flexibility, time, and patience. Success was determined by a triple bottom line: inclusiveness, collaboration, and effectiveness.

Inclusiveness. A fully inclusive process must bring together people who can represent the full range of issues, perspectives, and geography in a neighborhood. Issue inclusiveness encompasses physical, social, and civic issues; this is a challenge for neighborhoods because neighborhood issues with the city historically have been physical ones and thus neighborhood leadership typically comes from people concerned about property values and public improvements. Perspective inclusiveness is difficult because public engagement seems to attract people with strongly held but often narrow perspectives; they represent themselves but not others. Geographic representation requires neighborhood organizations with participation and membership from every part of the neighborhood, an atypical occurrence in many communities. Without strong neighborhood organizations, neighborhood leaders do not have a mechanism for learning from and reporting back to a broad base of neighbors.

Collaboration. Earlier collaborative efforts taught Hampton that good decisions depend on good information, relationships, and facilitation. Most neighborhood stakeholders lack accurate information beyond the people and issues of their own street; thus, the city staff's technical expertise with census data, trends, and research plays an important role. Of equal importance in the collaborative process is the ability of city officials to see the neighborhood through the eyes of residents, hearing their history, hopes, and fears. New roles emerge as neighborhood leaders become experts on what matters to the neighborhood and city staff serve as sources of technical resources—a differentiation that sounds good in theory but proves tough in application. Accepting residents' definitions of what is important often feels to staff like compromising their professional expertise. Neighborhood leaders, challenged by the limits of their new role, often come to the table not just as neighborhood experts but with technical solutions as well.

Effectiveness. A neighborhood planning process is effective when there are tangible results. Results usually emerge from careful attention to who is at the table, ownership of the process by those at the table and those who will need to abide by what those at the table have developed, and the implementation of an effective, task-oriented process. In the first neighborhood planning processes, significant time and effort was expended on process design. This allowed time for relationships to develop before more contentious issues were dealt with and created ownership of the process design. However, this relatively purist form of deliberation and collaboration stressed both staff and neighborhood resources to the point of diminished effectiveness. More recent neighborhood planning processes have been more prescriptive, with staff and neighbors seeking a better balance between time spent and impact generated.

Two neighborhood case studies demonstrate the challenges of planning with these criteria in mind. The Aberdeen neighborhood plan was the first developed under Hampton's new neighborhood initiative. Their eighteen-month planning process set strategies and priorities for public improvements, beautification, and services for youth and seniors within a neighborhood bound by a rich and unique history in which leadership is strong and clearly defined.

In Aberdeen, issue inclusiveness occurred naturally because civic leaders were alumni of a long-ago softball team that had grown into an adult group focused on neighborhood social interests. Their inclusiveness challenge was geographic; plan boundaries were far broader than the historic Aberdeen area in which the leaders lived. Involving a church that provided day care for families living outside of the neighborhood's historic area solved the problem; its inclusion gave voice to the issues of those families.

Perspective inclusiveness and collaboration seemed successful as long as the core team of adult leaders worked hard at it. When these leaders assumed that they understood what others in their neighborhood wanted, they were surprised to find their hard work opposed by neighbors who had not been involved in the process.

One factor in Aberdeen's favor is the neighborhood's self-sufficiency and an attitude of "what the neighborhood can do with support from the city" rather than "what the city should do with the neighborhood watching and waiting for it to happen." Their plan was highly successful in the area of effectiveness; the neighborhood organized itself through implementation committees tasked with the top priorities in the plan. Public improvements were a collaborative venture between city staff (who provided materials) and neighborhood volunteers (professional contractors who provided labor). The city even purchased a historic building, which the neighborhood, with grants and volunteer labor, transformed into a museum.

A second planning process, the one for the Greater Wythe Plan, began several years later and covered more neighborhoods, more issues, and more time. It went on for over seven years, burning out both staff and residents. This older area of the city was originally settled along sharply divided racial lines, and this history played out in a poor working relationship between the two sides of the neighborhood. Leaders in the many neighborhoods of greater Wythe were voicing similar concerns to staff's—safety, compliance with codes, declining property values. Staff thought that addressing these issues on a broader scale would bring about more effective solutions and that the process of building relationships, as in previous plans, would work its magic in Wythe.

All the challenges that Aberdeen faced in terms of inclusion and collaboration also occurred in this planning effort. Wythe's challenges were managed through a complex and collaborative design that included a survey to determine what was important across this very large area of over eleven thousand residents.

The concepts and design were laudable in this attempt at multineighborhood planning. It was in the area of effectiveness, however, that this planning process failed. The breadth of issues—both stated, such as safety, and unstated, such as distrust of city government—could simply not be addressed all at once in a planning effort, even one that involved multiple city departments over seven years. To add to the challenge, new and urgent issues, such as the closing of a hospital in this area, kept redirecting the planning team. Oddly, a rather significant list of tangible accomplishments did emerge, but the process so frustrated the city staff and the neighborhoods that a new process design evolved.

In the current generation of neighborhood planning efforts, the staff typically proposes an initial process design, thus saving the many months that neighborhoods often spend on this step. Staff experience with previous plans has built their fluency in matters of process, making this new strategy possible. The initial focus is limited to the top one to three issues, and then implementation starts on a short list of agreed-on strategies before other issues are explored. This shortened planning process of less than a year has been used successfully in the two most recent neighborhood plans. Inherent in these process changes is an understanding that planning is not a one-time event between the city staff and neighborhoods but rather a long-term relationship of planning, doing, learning, and then planning some more.

Reflections on the Theory and Practice of Deliberative Governance

The government of Hampton has consciously evolved into what Archon Fung[9] has dubbed the "supportive center," which skillfully designs, adapts, manages, and participates in a variety of deliberative and collaborative processes to make Hampton "the most livable city in Virginia."[10]

Hampton public officials have recognized "that familiar models of governance do not work because they depend on predictability, approach problems piecemeal, and presume experts can design workable solutions to meet recognized goals."[11] Officials have firmly linked collaborative governance strategies with citizen-oriented deliberative democracy to address challenging problems in neighborhoods and the community, all the while working with severely limited resources.

Those who have led this effort in Hampton have mastered process tools and strategies. They learned from some of the name-brand processes,[12] but often craft their own processes on a meeting-by-meeting basis in over a thousand meetings per year, to meet the unique opportunities and challenges at hand. Skills originally concentrated among a few key leaders and staff have eventually spread to a much broader cross section of the community.

Hampton is still inventing. Current efforts are focused on the development of a community plan, one of the first efforts in the nation to meld a strategic plan with a comprehensive plan, which is typically concerned only with land use. By melding these plans, Hampton is able to create a unified citizen participation process with a focus on future directions for the city rather than separate citizen engagement efforts for the medium-term strategic plan and the long-term comprehensive plan.

As Hampton and other communities continue to refine their practices, deliberative theorists are taking stock of their accomplishments and developing a richer body of work on collaborative community building. In particular, Archon Fung and Eric Olin Wright's *Deepening Democracy* dramatically advances the theory and strategy of deliberative practices.[13] Judith Innes and David Booher's works on network governance and collaborative planning make similar strides.[14] At the time when Hampton started its efforts, works on collaboration in the public arena could be counted on one's fingers. Now, bibliographies citing hundreds of works can be found.[15]

Despite the proliferation of literature, fundamental questions remain unexplored, many centering on the role of citizens. Not only is Hampton concerned about the relationship of youth and adult citizens with local government, but it also attends to the connections between citizens and private, nonprofit, and public organizations. Hampton leaders expect both youth and adult citizens to be coproducers, moving through a process of dialogue, deliberation, collaboration, and action and thus taking responsibility for their community. There are significant bodies of scholarship on volunteerism, neighborhood governance, dialogue, deliberation, and collaboration, but few studies have looked at the intersections among these areas or the developmental stages through which they unfold.

Hampton's approach to collaborative process is substantially informed by the field of conflict resolution, yet the intended audience for most of the works in the field of conflict resolution is third-party mediators. How can this field help community leaders better understand conflict and how to resolve it? In Hampton, the goal of effectiveness—of obtaining real results in the form of better outcomes for children, youth, families, and neighborhoods—remains uppermost. How can some of the lessons from the corporate change and performance management literature, which fully links process and results, be examined and rethought in ways that can inform the use of deliberative and collaborative processes to obtain better outcomes in the public sphere?

These and other important questions become clearer as deliberation theorists and practitioners come together to share insights and experiences. This volume and subsequent work will further narrow the gap between theory and practice, and the development of practical deliberative theory should help current and future community leaders to effectively use inclusive, collaborative, and deliberative processes in their own communities.

Notes

1. Alford, C. F. (1994). *Group Psychology and Political Theory.* New Haven, Conn.: Yale University Press. Thanks to Tali Mendelberg for illuminating this quote.

2. Osbourne, D., and Plastrik, P. (1997). *Banishing Bureaucracy: The Five Strategies for Reinventing Government.* Reading, Mass.: Addison-Wesley, 252.

3. Potapchuk, W. (2002). "Neighborhood Action Initiative: Engaging Citizens in Real Change." In D. D. Chrislip (ed.), *The Collaborative Leadership Fieldbook: A Guide for Citizens and Civic Leaders.* San Francisco: Jossey-Bass.

4. Markus, G. B. (2002). *Civic Participation in American Cities.* Ann Arbor, Mich.: Institute for Social Research, University of Michigan, 17.

5. Osbourne and Plastrik (1997), *Banishing Bureaucracy,* 242.

6. Plotz, D. A. (1991). *Community Problem Solving Case Summaries.* Vol. 3. Washington D.C.: Program for Community Problem Solving, 35.

7. Putnam, R. D. (1993). "The Prosperous Community: Social Capital and Public Life." *American Prospect, 4*(13), 35.

8. None of these otherwise thoughtful works explicitly discusses the role of citizens in governance: Linden, R. M. (2002). *Working Across Boundaries: Making Collaboration Work in Government and Nonprofit Organizations.* San Francisco: Jossey-Bass; Agranoff, R., and McGuire, M. (2003). *Collaborative Public Management: New Strategies for Local Governments.* Washington, D.C.: Georgetown University Press; Healey, P., Magalhaes, C. de, Madanipour, A., and Pendlebury, J. (2003). "Place, Identity, and Local Politics: Analysing Initiatives in Deliberative Governance." In M. A. Hajer and H. Wagenaar (eds.), *Deliberative Policy Analysis: Understanding Governance in the Network Society.* London: Cambridge University Press; Innes, J. E., and Booher, D. E. (2003). *Collaborative Policymaking: Governance Through Dialogue.* In M. A. Hajer and H. Wagenaar (eds.), *Deliberative Policy Analysis: Understanding Governance in the Network Society.* London: Cambridge University Press.

9. Fung, A. (1999, Aug.). "Street Level Democracy: Pragmatic Popular Sovereignty in Chicago Schools and Policing." Paper presented at the annual meeting of the American Political Science Association, Atlanta, Ga., 6. Available at www.archonfung.net.

10. The quotation is from Hampton's formally adopted vision statement.

11. Innes, J. E., and Booher, D. E. (2003). *The Impact of Collaborative Planning on Governance Capacity.* Berkeley, Calif.: Institute of Urban and Regional Development, 6.

12. Name-brand processes are those advocated for and managed by organizations that are usually external to a community. Examples are Future Search, deliberative polling (Chapter Five), the Citizens Jury (Chapter Seven), and the 21st Century Town Meeting (Chapter Ten).

13. Fung, A., and Wright, E. O. (2003). *Deepening Democracy: Institutional Innovations in Empowered Participatory Governance.* London: Verso.

14. See Innes and Booher (2003), *Collaborative Policymaking;* Innes and Booher (2003), *The Impact of Collaborative Planning on Governance Capacity.*

15. Council on Foundations. (2003). *Collaboration: A Selected Bibliography.* Washington D.C.: Council on Foundations.

PART FIVE

CONCLUSION

CHAPTER NINETEEN

FUTURE DIRECTIONS FOR PUBLIC DELIBERATION

Peter Levine, Archon Fung, John Gastil

The earlier chapters of this book demonstrate the large and impressive body of practice in the field of public deliberation. All kinds of people in many countries are gathering, in a wide variety of settings and formats, to discuss and address public issues. There is a growing movement calling for the development of deliberative civic culture and public institutions. Though this momentum is encouraging, as John Gastil and William Keith note in Chapter One, we have been here before. There have been bursts of public deliberation and participation in several periods of the history of the United States—in particular in the Progressive Era before the Second World War. Those earlier movements altered our public discourse and governance, but they ultimately faltered. Therefore, it is crucial that we carefully consider how to assess, improve, sustain, and expand today's experiments. That understanding might then be translated into actions that enhance the deliberative quality of our society and its politics.

In this concluding chapter, we begin by asking what we can expect from deliberative initiatives. This book has demonstrated the full breadth of deliberative approaches, and we note a few of the findings that appear consistent across those different experiences. We then consider the limitations of deliberation as it is currently practiced, as well as the challenges that will arise if and when deliberation becomes a more high-stakes public process. After suggesting ways to advance research on deliberation, we suggest some of the new frontiers for the practice of public deliberation.

What We Can Expect from Deliberation

Although the earlier chapters of this book raise many questions that remain unanswered, they also substantiate several conclusions. First, people are willing to discuss public issues and can sustain serious, in-depth conversations about technical or highly divisive matters. In informal lawn parties, official school councils, and public hearings, and many of the public venues discussed in this book, tens of millions of people in America—and probably hundreds of millions around the globe—deliberate with one another and with government officials about public policies and problems.

To be sure, the desire to deliberate is not universal. Many discussions involve only the most motivated citizens, who volunteer to participate. Many deliberative events also tend to attract individuals who are better-off in terms of income, education, and status. Even when participants are randomly selected, some decline the invitation.[1] Even when an event is mandatory, as in the case of jury service in the United States, deliberators are still somewhat self-selected. Nevertheless, the appetite for deliberation is widespread and cuts across lines of class, occupation, gender, nationality, and culture.

In the United States, 25 percent of adults say they have "attended a formal or informal meeting to discuss a public issue in [the] last year." That quarter of the population is skewed toward more educated people, but African Americans and women are at least as likely as white people and men to say that they have participated in such discussions.[2] Thus, a diverse group of about 50 million adult Americans say that they have been involved in public talk in a given year. Of course, we have no accounting of the deliberative quality of these public discussions, and there are still too few opportunities in the United States for meaningful deliberation. In countries like Brazil and India, very poor people have deliberated in large numbers through programs such those described in Chapter Twelve.

A second conclusion also can be drawn from the previous chapters: when deliberation is well organized, participants *like* it. In fact, they find it deeply satisfying and significant. One Australian member of a consensus conference is quoted in Chapter Six as saying, "It's the most important thing I've ever done in my whole life, I suppose." Often, organizers find that participants are eager to deliberate again.

Although many observers derive intrinsic value from public deliberation, its outcomes can be disappointing. In Chapter Seventeen, for instance, Karpowitz and Mansbridge describe a process that suppressed deep differences, discouraged frank statements and expressions of self-interest, and seriously exaggerated the level of consensus. Participants were infuriated and used the more adversarial format of a public hearing to express their critical views about both the process and the outcome of the deliberation. This is only one way in which a deliberation can go wrong and make people less likely to participate again.

Nevertheless, the fact remains that deliberative democracy often proves deeply fulfilling. This is important because it means that deliberation can reinforce support for itself when it is successful.[3] Research on the American jury has found that a conclusive jury experience, in which jurors deliberate and reach a final verdict, can make the participating jurors more likely to seek out future opportunities for participation in public life, such as voting in elections.[4] In the same way, a rewarding turn at public deliberation sparks future involvement. This has certainly been the experience in some of the longest-running deliberative programs, like the National Issues Forums (Chapter Three) and study circles (Chapter Fourteen), in which today's volunteer participants become tomorrow's forum and study circle organizers. For these participants, deliberation was so rewarding that they felt the impulse to join the nascent deliberation movement and bring that same experience to others.

Third, the products of deliberations are often excellent. Deliberators may be asked to develop budgets, design rural or urban landscapes, make policy recommendations, pose public questions to politicians, or take voluntary actions in their own communities. When the tasks are realistic, the questions are clear and useful, and the discussion is well organized, deliberators often do a good job. They can absorb relevant background materials, seriously consider relevant facts, incorporate and balance a variety of legitimate perspectives and opinions, and make tough choices with full awareness of constraints. Experts are often surprised and impressed by the quality of the public's deliberations, judgments, and actions.[5] Nothing guarantees that a group of citizens will write a wise plan, but neither are judges guaranteed to reach just verdicts or legislators to write good statutes. Although there is no systematic research that compares the outcomes of public deliberation with those of more formal or professional processes (and it is difficult to imagine how such research could be conducted), the preceding chapters show that given the opportunity, ordinary people have frequently proven themselves to be capable of generating impressive outcomes across a wide variety of political contexts and policy issues.[6]

The community of deliberation advocates encompasses many sharp disagreements over techniques and priorities but also an unrecognized overlapping consensus on the criteria for high-quality deliberation. Many of the contributors to this volume discussed criteria explicitly, particularly in Chapters Two, Six, Seven, Eight, Ten, and Eleven.[7] Within this community, there appears to be broad agreement that a successful deliberative initiative has the following features: (1) the realistic expectation of influence (that is, a link to decision makers); (2) an inclusive, representative process that brings key stakeholders and publics together;

(3) informed, substantive, and conscientious discussion, with an eye toward finding common ground if not reaching consensus; and (4) a neutral, professional staff that helps participants work through a fair agenda. Over time, it is also hoped that deliberative processes can (5) earn broad public support for their final recommendations and (6) prove sustainable. Taken together, these objectives are not easily met, but practitioners have found many ways of managing—if not overcoming—the obstacles to deliberation.

Addressing the Limitations of Public Deliberation

Although deliberation has tremendous value and promise for democracy, the chapters in this volume also reveal several important limitations. Here, we discuss four: the elusive nature of public agreement, the challenge of organization, the challenge of scale, and the impact of deliberation on public decisions.

Unity and Disagreement

Deliberation does not often generate a full consensus, especially in larger public bodies. Although people frequently change their views in the process of deliberation and come to understand one another's needs, values, and beliefs better, they rarely reach complete agreement. Because disagreements persist in almost all conversations, a group cannot make a decision without some method, such as voting, that forecloses further deliberation, at least for a period of time. Nevertheless, there is a world of difference between a vote that follows rich deliberation and one in which people simply register their "raw" opinions.

Those convening deliberative events should not create unrealistic expectations about the potential for unity and certainty, but it is probably fruitful to encourage at least the impulse to have an open mind and seek mutual understanding, if not agreement. Public deliberation is valuable when it helps participants to learn the reasons for their disagreements and to distinguish subjects on which they can agree from those on which they are unlikely to reach accord. Deliberation is also valuable when it helps participants to think through, alter, deepen, and stabilize their perspectives through reflection and discussion, even when it does not cause participants' views to converge.

Organization and Facilitation

Good deliberation is not self-generating. The instances of poorly organized public participation that fall below the threshold of proper deliberation—for example, most public hearings and meetings in which participants gather to listen to the content of others' policy choices—far outnumber the properly organized deliberative encounters in which participants hear contesting reasons for diverse options and discuss them. To achieve high-quality deliberation, someone must organize a discursive process, choose a topic, recruit the participants, prepare background materials or invite speakers, provide facilitators, and raise the funds that are necessary to do these things.

In practice, a small group of self-selected leaders must actually organize any process, making choices about methods and agendas. There is no consensus about a best approach that would fit every circumstance.[8] As explained in Chapter Two and demonstrated in the chapters that followed, civic organizers of deliberation are a diverse group with many internal debates. Organizers' decisions can never be perfectly democratic and deliberative, yet they profoundly shape the public discussion that follows. Thus, there is a danger that deliberation will be overly influenced by skilled organizers, but the greater danger is having no competent organization at all.

Scaling Deliberation Up and Out

Two additional challenges for the practice of deliberative democracy concern its scale. To become politically and socially significant, public deliberation initiatives must scale "out" in the sense of directly or indirectly including many more participants. The innovations discussed in this volume typically involve hundreds, or perhaps thousands, of individuals. Those who participate directly in such encounters constitute a far lower percentage of the population than the voters in even the lowest of low-turnout elections. One way to make formal deliberation more salient for more individuals is to increase the frequency with which such events occur. Another way is to link the conversations that occur within these deliberations to the broader public debate that is occurring in the opinion pages of local newspapers, in barbershops, and street corners. This linkage is not easy to accomplish, but it can be done. When dozens of newspapers covered the Listening to the City deliberations on rebuilding lower Manhattan (Chapter Ten), tens of thousands of readers participated, albeit virtually, in a conversation about urban planning. Some newspapers, such as the *Philadelphia Inquirer,* have established a track record of facilitating such deliberation (see Chapters Four, Seven, and Thirteen), and that makes it possible to sustain a deliberative civic conversation even across multiple topics.

In addition to including more participants, public deliberation also faces the challenge of scaling "up" to address problems and policy issues of state, national, and even international concern. The majority of experience and accomplishment for public deliberation concerns local issues such as development and planning, public education, race relations, and the like. But more and more aspects of daily life depend on decisions and actions that occur far beyond the boundaries that separate towns, states, and even nations. A few innovations in public deliberation have focused on issues on a superlocal scale. The Americans Discuss Social Security deliberations in 1997 and 1998 (Chapter Ten), as well as several deliberative polls in the United States, England, and Denmark (Chapter Five), considered national policy issues. National Issues Forums (Chapter Three) generate local deliberations, but they typically address national or global issues. Nevertheless, organized deliberation about such issues remains exceptional, and the policy impact of such initiatives is debatable—a subject we turn to next.

Impact, Authority, and Strategies for Influence

Even high-quality public deliberation does not automatically result in social or political change. Most public deliberations do not directly alter public decisions and actions. Indeed, many practitioners of public deliberation have only recently turned their attention from the question of generating and organizing public discussion to that of linking talk to action. For the results of a deliberative process to count, powerful actors must be encouraged, persuaded, or obliged to heed them. This seldom happens, and rarely does it occur in a fully deliberative way.

Whereas deliberation requires continual openness to new ideas and perspectives, lobbying requires a coherent and consistent position. Rose Marie Nierras, a Filipina activist, offers an example of this tension from her own experience. The Freedom from Debt Coalition in the Philippines has conducted fairly broad deliberations about what should be done about the country's debt to foreign lenders. However, once "there's a common position that the coalition actually can unite [behind], in negotiating with the IMF and the World Bank, with the Philippine Government, that common position is the only position we're willing to deliberate on. Outside the boundaries of that, we're not willing as a coalition to actually entertain any other view than this."[9] If the coalition continued deliberating indefinitely and failed to negotiate with powerful actors, then many participants would lose patience with the endless talk and refuse to participate. In this sense, deliberation is frequently nested in a political context that is not itself fully deliberative.

Deliberation can, however, have a more direct authority, as in the case of the São Paulo Municipal Health Council, described in Chapter Twelve. Another promising example of deliberative authority comes from British Columbia, Canada. In 2003, the British Columbia provincial government established the Citizens' Assembly, which was made up of 160 randomly selected citizens—one man and one woman from each electoral district plus two at-large Aboriginal members. The assembly's task was to evaluate the existing electoral system and, if necessary, propose a new one. On October 24, 2004, after many meetings and public hearings, the assembly voted 146–7 (a 95 percent supermajority, nearly a full consensus) in favor of replacing the existing electoral system with a single transferable vote model, which lets voters rank candidates within districts that have multiple representatives. At press time, this proposal was about to go before the full British Columbia public, and if approved by the voters, it is scheduled to go into effect for the 2009 election.[10]

What the British Columbia model demonstrates is that public deliberation can fit into an institutional arrangement in which it has real authority on issues as fundamental as the electoral process itself. In many countries, legislators might find it advantageous to hand off to a deliberative assembly controversial issues that require sound public policy. In the case of electoral reform, it might be hard for public officials to craft reforms that the public can trust, given officials' inherent conflict of interest on the subject. In the case of tax policy, legislators may prefer that citizens themselves raise taxes and reform the tax structure, lest elected officials draw the ire of those whose taxes go up. There is merit in putting a deliberative assembly's judgment before the voters, as in the British Columbia case, but it is also conceivable that the deliberative body could make a final decision (perhaps subject to the same veto authority that a governor has over a legislature in the United States).

The British Columbia example is exceptional, however, in that the Citizens Assembly originated from within government. Deliberation programs typically are built by citizens (sometimes with the cooperation of public officials) and civic organizations without explicit authority or substantial public influence. To make such deliberative initiatives more consequential, those who organize public deliberations should consider both "inside" and "outside" strategies for influencing public officials.

Inside strategies require creating relationships with policymakers or enacting administrative or legal requirements that compel them to incorporate public deliberations into their decisions. At the minimal end of this empowerment spectrum, notice-and-comment provisions compel officials to respond to concerns raised by participants during their rule-making processes. In more highly empowered processes, public powers and resources are actually delegated to public deliberative bodies. Some neighborhood councils in U.S. cities, for example, exercise substantial zoning authority, and others dispose of substantial public funds for local development and revitalization.

Outside strategies, by contrast, rely on generating political and social pressures that compel officials to respect the results of public deliberation. The Listening to the City event organized by America*Speaks* (Chapter Ten) received extensive coverage from local and national media that in turn created an imperative for the public agencies who sponsored the deliberations to respond to the concerns that participants had raised. In their book *Deliberation Day*, Bruce Ackerman and James Fishkin have developed a compelling argument for how a carefully timed and organized set of public deliberations could alter the character and content of presidential campaigns in the United States.[11]

The most influential and robust institutions of public deliberation will likely incorporate both inside and outside strategies of influence and empowerment. The much lauded and studied participatory budget program of Porto Alegre, discussed briefly in Chapter Twelve, exhibits both elements. From the inside, the participatory budget program is operated by the city's executive and receives elaborate funding and staff support. From the outside, however, no public law institutionalizes the practice of annual popular participation in deliberating about the city's spending priorities. Organizers fear that such institutionalization would dampen the political mobilization that sustains participatory budgeting. Instead, city councillors who receive the budget that grows out of popular participation feel enormous pressure to approve it because of the legitimacy that flows from direct citizen participation and deliberation.

Preserving the Integrity of Consequential Deliberation

To date, most public deliberation has had low stakes, especially in the United States. In some cases, there is no serious effort to change public policy to match the results of the public conversation. The goal of a meeting may be to build networks of citizens, to develop new ideas, to teach people skills and knowledge, to change attitudes, but not to influence government. In other cases, deliberation does have direct consequences for policy. For example, the budget of the District of Columbia is much influenced by the annual Citizens Summit organized by America*Speaks* (see Chapter Ten). In Brazil, municipal health councils formulate and oversee local health policy (see Chapter Twelve). Nevertheless, such cases arise under especially favorable circumstances, when political leaders are either unusually committed to public deliberation or have special incentives to share power with a deliberating group of citizens.

If efforts to promote public deliberation become a more powerful political movement, then citizen deliberation will likely achieve concrete influence, perhaps even when the conditions are unfavorable. At this juncture, deliberation will become a high-stakes process, and with this new status will bring new challenges.

First, who is at the table? In a low-stakes deliberation, it may work well to recruit volunteers, as long as one aims for diversity of background and opinion. However, as soon as the stakes increase, organized interests will dispatch their own foot soldiers. Interest group politics is an acceptable and unavoidable part of democratic politics: "sewn in the nature of man," as James Madison put it.[12] But interest groups are not evenly distributed. For instance, there are effective national groups for developers and landlords but not for renters or the homeless. Second, some groups are not internally democratic or transparent; they don't represent the groups in whose name they speak. And finally, because of problems inherent in collective action, interest groups tend to form around narrow concerns rather than broad ones. Narrow concerns can be legitimate, but interest group politics introduces a bias against general values.

We are used to these problems in conventional representative political institutions to which public deliberation is supposed to be an alternative. But interest groups may be at least as effective in high-stakes citizens' deliberations as in Congress or a town council.

Since meetings of recruited volunteers can be stacked with committed partisans, some organizers randomly select citizens to participate. But random selection has its own problems. It is expensive and practically difficult. Although the cost and logistical challenge may be small relative to the significance of the issues at hand, it is still sometimes a challenge to overcome the resistance to spending more money and committing more time to setting up such a selection process. To date, random selection methods have not been embedded in local networks and associations. Random selection must be organized by some group with a budget and an agenda; thus, the agenda and framing of the discussion can be biased or perceived as biased.

Then there arises the problem of fairness and equality within a discussion. Lynn Sanders notes that "some citizens are better than others at articulating their concerns in rational, reasonable terms." Some are "more learned and practiced at making arguments that would be recognized by others as reasonable ones." Some people are simply more willing to speak; for example, studies of U.S. juries show that men talk far more than women in deliberations. Furthermore, some people "are more likely to be listened to than others." For instance, studies of U.S. juries show that they tend to elect white males as forepersons. Studies of U.S. college students show that white students have much more influence than black students in joint collaborative projects, even controlling for age, socioeconomic status, height, and attitudes toward school.[13]

We have observed how organizers and moderators of low-stakes public deliberation overcome these problems. They deliberately support participants who might be disadvantaged in the conversation. Today's public deliberations are likely to be more equitable than juries or teams of college students because moderators are trained to focus on equality. But what about tomorrow's deliberations? When the stakes go up, individuals with more status or skill will fight back against efforts to support less advantaged participants. They will depict such efforts as politically correct or otherwise biased, and they will use their status, confidence, and rhetorical fluency to win the point.

A skilled facilitator might still manage such difficulties effectively, as was done in the case of the aforementioned British Columbia Citizens Assembly, but the selection of the facilitator itself can be challenged. In Citizens Juries (Chapter Seven), participants have been given the authority to alter discussion rules and even remove the facilitator. That approach—despite its potential for parliamentary-style procedural shenanigans—may be the best way to safeguard the integrity of the process.

Advancing Research

It is difficult to exaggerate academics' interest in deliberative democracy, which has been intense and growing ever since John Rawls and Jürgen Habermas separately advocated it forty years ago. There are too many substantial books to mention, but perhaps one indicator of scholars' interest is the recent publication of at least five anthologies on the topic, most of whose contributors specialize in deliberation.[14]

Unfortunately, most researchers pay little attention to the practices described in this book. There are many other academic fields in which scholars and practitioners do not communicate well or consistently. Why is there such a gap between scholarship and practice in the field of deliberation?

First, most academics are interested in varieties of deliberation that have a clear influence on political outcomes. Therefore, they focus on deliberation in powerful bodies like juries, appellate courts, and legislatures or on long-term discussions that involve millions of people and play out in the mass media and major institutions. For them, a gathering of a few dozen citizens is insignificant. Scholars of deliberation see themselves as too practical and realistic to devote serious attention to experiments like those described in this book. The Brazilian experience with participatory budgeting is a notable exception precisely because it has achieved scale and political impact.

Practical projects could be used as case studies or laboratories to test hypotheses about how people discuss issues. However, only a few of the projects described in this book incorporate designs that are sufficiently controlled to serve as ideal opportunities to address the questions on researchers' agendas. For example, if social scientists want to study whether and when groups converge toward consensus positions, they might feel more confident experimenting with a random sample and a carefully selected series of topics rather than observing a messy and context-dependent process such as a study circle or a National Issues Forum.[15] If they want to assess the effects of deliberation on individuals' attitudes and beliefs, then they might want to select some participants randomly out of a larger pool and leave the rest as a control group, which is impossible in most real-world contexts. Because deliberative polls (Chapter Five) use random selection, they are among the few processes that have been used as formal experiments. The insights derived from deliberative polls are important, but they may not generalize to other practices.

Some of the literature from experimental psychology finds disappointing results when randomly selected groups of people (usually college students) are asked to discuss questions chosen by researchers. For example, such groups often move in the direction of the majority opinion; dissenters drop their opinions in order to go along with the group.[16] Although these are important and challenging results, it is equally important to study what happens when diverse and motivated citizens are recruited to address pressing problems in their communities, provided with balanced materials, guided by skilled moderators, and asked to reach judgments that have real political consequences. Similarly, if we want to observe how interest groups, politicians, and citizens deal with one another in public deliberations, then we need to study practices that are embedded in politics, not experiments with predetermined topics and controlled structures.

One objective of our book is to demonstrate that there is a body of diverse practice that merits serious academic investigation. These projects are valuable experiments precisely because they exist in the real world.

In 2003, the Deliberative Democracy Consortium convened a meeting of thirty leading researchers and practitioners. Despite the very different perspectives of academic scholars and grassroots activists, both groups agreed that the array of practical experiments and projects now under way in deliberative democracy are interesting and promising. In a highly unusual process that itself modeled deliberation, the researchers and practitioners worked together to develop a common research agenda. They decided that the top priorities for research included questions such as the following:

- How does design and structure affect quality of deliberative process and outcomes?
- Under what conditions does deliberation affect public policy?
- In addition to changes in policy, what are other important outcomes of deliberation?
- How should we measure the quality of deliberation?
- What is the relationship between deliberation and advocacy or public involvement?
- What can the deliberative democracy movement learn from other social movements?
- What is the public's interest in deliberation?
- How can the scale of deliberation be increased, and how can it be institutionalized?

New Frontiers for Public Deliberation

There are many new directions in which both researchers and practitioners can take public deliberation. Here, we wish to emphasize three priorities: strengthening the connection between dialogue and deliberation, moving from substantive to cultural conflicts, and considering the potential for cross-national deliberation.[17]

Dialogue and Deliberation

The terms *dialogue* and *deliberation* have become popular in communication and political science, particularly in reference to the role of public discourse in participatory models of democracy.[18] Many uses of these two terms entail considerable conceptual overlap, as is evident in the preceding chapters in this volume. Nonetheless, it is possible to make a clear and useful distinction between them. Public deliberation can be defined as a problem-solving form of discourse that involves problem analysis, establishing evaluative criteria, and identifying and weighing alternative solutions. Through a respectful, egalitarian, and conscientious process, a deliberative body aims for a reasoned consensus but often settles, at least provisionally, for a judicious result based on a more humble decision rule, such as simple or two-thirds majority rule.[19]

When a group seeks to deliberate on a public issue, however, it may be necessary to first engage in dialogue.[20] This form of speech is not as concerned with solving a problem as with bridging linguistic, social, and epistemological chasms between different subgroups of the potentially deliberative body. The members of a group may have incommensurate discourse norms, in which case one participant's preferred method for showing respect (for example, asking a direct, challenging question) might insult another participant. Or subgroups might have contradictory linguistic or semiotic associations—for example, when the display of the Ten Commandments in a public deliberative chamber causes one group to feel honored and another to feel denigrated. Another instance of difference that might require dialogue is when participants have radically different epistemological assumptions. One group may give greater weight to personal testimony, another to statistical evidence, and a third to correspondence with secular or sacred texts (for example, founding documents or holy scriptures). This final difference makes it hard to adjudicate competing claims, because each stands on distinct rhetorical ground, cast in terms of values that are not easily compared.

When differences such as these exist within a group, dialogue can help participants come to recognize and understand one another's point of view. Whereas deliberation focuses on policy choices, dialogue seeks accommodation, reconciliation, mutual understanding, or at the very least, informed tolerance. The particular group procedures for such dialogue are not the central question here, but the general method is to create a group environment that is conducive to honest self-expression, careful self-reflection, and thoughtful probing and perspective taking. Dialogue generally aims to help different subgroups learn about one another through a series of mutual questioning and reflection sessions. It can take many hours or days for a group to move through a series of stages and arrive at the point where participants truly understand one another's standpoints and appreciate the history and conviction of one another's views.[21]

At least in theory, such dialogue can prepare a group for deliberation. Once each subgroup understands how the others think, talk, and reason, it is easier to avoid conceptual confusions, symbolic battles, and epistemological thickets that could otherwise derail a deliberative process. The dialogic phase does not resolve moral disputes or advance policy goals; rather, it prepares group members for the necessary but challenging process of making common decisions together despite deep underlying differences.

Cultural Accommodation

When used as a foundation for subsequent deliberation, the aim of dialogue might be even more modest than in other settings when no deliberation is anticipated. The goal of dialogue might simply be *cultural accommodation*. To accommodate another cultural group means to make room for it within the shared public sphere, so that the groups can coexist peaceably without crowding out or unduly inconveniencing one another. At a minimum, cultural accommodation means giving due consideration to one another's symbols, understandings, and aspirations. Cultural accommodation can also be defined by contrasting it with related but distinct aims: the process involves neither competitive negotiation nor pressing for reasoned consensus. The closest conceptual cousin is strategic compromise, but even that happens later, during the deliberative phase that follows the initial period of dialogue.

The most likely tangible products of accommodation are a modicum of mutual understanding (that is, conscious knowledge of substantive and symbolic differences), a pragmatic commitment to cultural tolerance, and accord on the value of a loosely defined but shared framework for policy discussion (that is, agreement to enter a deliberative phase of public talk).[22] The best possible outcome might be a willingness on the part of all parties to lower the rhetorical stakes of the deliberation that follows. With their greater awareness of one another's distinct standpoints, parties might agree to avoid strategic language that, on reflection, is ineffective at persuading the other side and only prolongs the avoidance of policy talk. Taken together, these accomplishments mean that the participants in a subsequent deliberation enter into it with significantly greater cultural security and appreciation, which will help them defuse the potentially explosive cultural clashes that are inevitable in any sustained policy discussion.[23]

As a hypothetical example, imagine a small group of U.S. citizens engaging in a cultural dialogue about their views on guns and gun control. Each cultural group would have the chance to explain how it views the world, how its deeper values inform its vision of the future, and how it understands the course of history in terms of its cultural traditions. One participant might explain that from his perspective, guns are integral to traditional male roles of father, hunter, and protector. In his view, guns are legitimate signs of military and police authority as well as the authority and status of the household provider. In expressing these values and aspirations, the speaker would also display key words, phrases, and symbols (for example, patriotism, the minuteman), key forms of evidence (for example, accordance with the Second Amendment), and traditional ways of speaking (for example, authoritative declaration). Trained moderators or participants from other cultural backgrounds could, within a restrictive set of discursive guidelines, ask this representative some probing questions in order to further clarify the contours of his particular perspective.[24]

The point here is not to identify policy choices or weigh the pros and cons of conflicting views; rather, it is to illuminate and understand the cultural grounding of a person's perspective. As a result of this dialogue, participants might emerge with a sharper understanding of their points of difference. Within the broad compact of a pluralist society, each group may come to recognize that each other group is entitled to value its distinct set of cultural beliefs, symbols, and practices. This is not to say that participants in dialogue simply become moral relativists and cease debating the merits of private rights versus social responsibilities, community needs versus individual aims, and traditional hierarchies versus egalitarian norms. Rather, the accomplishments are the recognition that each group has a distinct and coherent set of values and styles and the humbling recognition that with few exceptions, those differences are not subject to debate. There might be no points of agreement on substance or style, but it is likely that the groups will arrive at a recognition of the depth of disagreement and the virtue of moving from cultural conflict to policy deliberation. The goal of accommodation and coexistence supplants the dream of consensus on the general will.[25]

Cross-Cultural Dialogue and Deliberation

There are many settings in which it would be appropriate to engage in both dialogue and deliberation in pursuit of cultural accommodation. A popular view of the United States characterizes it as divided between "red" (conservative) and "blue" (liberal) states, a metaphor based on the voting pattern of the 2000 and 2004 presidential elections.[26] At the county level, there are red and blue regions within most states, so the divisions exist not only across but also within the nation's regions. Moreover, there is every reason to believe that the differences between these groups are more than partisan political identity; rather, they reflect deeper cultural divisions. On many issues, such as abortion, gun rights, and nuclear power, the pro and con sides of the debate have distinct cultural characteristics that suggest the need for a dialogue before proceeding directly into deliberation. Other nations across the globe have their own cultural divides, and in each of these contexts, it may also be important to think more in terms of cultural accommodation than the discovery of a common will.

If dialogue and deliberation are appropriate within a political unit as large as a nation, might there be a kind of public deliberation that could occur across national boundaries? The world trade protests we have witnessed across the globe are a testament to the public's sense that it is shut out of international trade negotiations.[27] No international association or trade organization has won the public's trust. The result is a chain of vocal protests, which often devolve into violence as authorities attempt to suppress the most visible public demonstrations and more anarchistic protesters seek to spark public outrage by enticing even more extreme government reaction. Thus, bilateral or international trade is an issue ripe for an open cross-national dialogue, although it is difficult to envision precisely how to integrate such a forum into existing international associations.

An issue that might lend itself to global dialogue is international terrorism. There could be a fruitful conversation among citizens from all parts of the world on the roots of terrorism, the experience of living in terror and being victimized by it, the best methods for addressing it in the long term, and perhaps even the perspectives of those drawn to participate in acts such as suicide bombings. Such a dramatic discussion might even attract a large international audience. If expertly facilitated, it could produce dramatic moments of cross-cultural dialogue and increase mutual understanding. More ambitiously, deliberation on these issues might aim to reach a common set of principles embraced by people who are normally characterized as being unable to speak to one another, let alone live together. Such a body would be unlikely to have legislative authority, but it might help to break through one or more international policy deadlocks by giving renewed hope to political leaders for the ability of the public to overcome its fear, anger, and despair. If effective, such a dialogue could set the stage for a more precise deliberation on what policies best address the threat of global terrorism and the other issues underlying it.

Perhaps this is too much to ask of dialogue and deliberation. After all, this book illustrates a modern history of small victories, not sweeping changes. These successes, though, have often come on issues that were thought to be impossibly contentious and in places where people were unaccustomed to public talk. More-over, many of these processes induced broader changes in the relationships among citizens, the media, and the government. Chapter Eighteen even demonstrates a modest shift toward a more collaborative civic culture.

History asks us to remember that the current deliberative movement could disappear as quickly as it has emerged. Nonetheless, we can go forward with a vigilant optimism. The initiatives described in this book show that deliberation is having a real, positive impact on communities across the globe. With researchers and practitioners working together, we can deeply incorporate deliberation into twenty-first century democracy.

Notes

1. The reason that some programs, like the Citizens Jury, pay participants considerable sums for their participation is that this ensures that very few of those invited decline. Also, demographic and attitudinal balancing, as described in Chapter Seven, can ensure a representative set of participants. Finally, those processes that provide incentives and have rigorous recruitment methods are likely to produce more representative cross sections of the public than more conventional methods of public engagement, such as voting and public hearings. Even jury service, which is ostensibly mandatory in the United States, is not as representative.
2. Delli Carpini, M. X., Cook, F. L., and Jacobs, L. R. (2004, May). "Talking Together: Discursive Capital and Civic Deliberation in America." *Annual Review of Political Science, 7,* 315–344.
3. On the generally self-reinforcing properties of deliberation, see Burkhalter, S., Gastil, J., and Kelshaw, T. (2002). "The Self-Reinforcing Model of Public Deliberation." *Communication Theory, 12,* 398–422.
4. Gastil, J., Deess, E. P., and Weiser, P. (2002). "Civic Awakening in the Jury Room: A Test of the Connection Between Jury Deliberation and Political Participation." *Journal of Politics, 64,* 585–595.
5. This renewed confidence in the public's capabilities is, in itself, an important benefit of deliberation. Over time, it can lead to a greater willingness on the part of governmental leaders to draw the public into public life, as in the case of Hampton, Virginia (Chapter Eighteen).
6. The research that is most relevant to this issue of comparing nonprofessional with professional deliberation concerns the American jury. Studies suggest that over the course of the trial and in their private rooms, juries really do deliberate and reach verdicts quite similar to those that judges reach through their own deliberative process. See Hans, V. P., and Vidmar, N. (2001). *Judging the Jury.* New York: Perseus, 2001; and Hans, V. P. (2000). *Business on Trial: The Civil Jury and Corporate Responsibility.* New Haven, Conn.: Yale University Press.
7. Contributors were not asked to provide such criteria, but many did so spontaneously. This alone is a testament to the fact that this community thinks very carefully about its aims, always looking for ways to improve public discussion methods to better meet these objectives.
8. For a typology of different approaches to convening public meetings, see Gastil, J., and Kelshaw, T. (2000). *Public Meetings: A Sampler of Deliberative Forums That Bring Officeholders and Citizens Together.* Dayton, Ohio: Charles F. Kettering Foundation.

9. Nierras's comments were made at the LogoLink partners' meeting, Institute for Development Studies, University of Sussex, July 2, 2004; transcribed by Peter Levine, and reproduced with the speaker's permission.

10. Details on the Citizens Assembly are available at http://www.citizensassembly.bc.ca.

11. Ackerman, B., and Fishkin, J. (2004). *Deliberation Day.* New Haven, Conn.: Yale University Press.

12. Madison, J. (1982). "The Federalist No. 10." In G. Wills (ed.), *The Federalist Papers.* New York: Bantam, 44.

13. Sanders, L. M. (1997, June). "Against Deliberation." *Political Theory, 25*(3), 347–376.

14. Van Aaken, A., List, C., and Luetge, C. (eds.). (2004). *Deliberation and Decision: Economics, Constitutional Theory and Deliberative Democracy.* Aldershot, U.K.: Ashgate; Bohman, J., and Rehg, W. (eds.). (1997). *Deliberative Democracy: Essays on Reason and Politics.* Cambridge, Mass.: MIT Press; Elster, J., and Przeworski, A. (eds.). (1998). *Deliberative Democracy.* Cambridge, U.K.: Cambridge University Press; Fishkin, J. S., and Laslett, P. (eds.). (2003). *Debating Deliberative Democracy.* Oxford, U.K.: Blackwell; and Macedo, S. (ed.). (1999). *Deliberative Politics: Essays on Democracy and Disagreement.* Oxford, U.K.: Oxford University Press.

15. One of us has tried using National Issues Forums data in a quasi-experimental manner and has experienced these difficulties firsthand. See Gastil, J. (2004). "Adult Civic Education Through the National Issues Forums: A Study of How Adults Develop Civic Skills and Dispositions Through Public Deliberation." *Adult Education Quarterly, 54,* 308–328.

16. Mendelberg, T. (2002). "The Deliberative Citizen: Theory and Evidence." In M. Delli Carpini, L. Huddy, and R. Y. Shapiro (eds.), *Political Decision Making, Deliberation, and Participation: Research in Micropolitics.* Vol. 6. Greenwich, Conn.: JAI Press, 151–193.

17. This section draws on a paper that was developed with Dan Kahan and Don Braman at the Yale Law School. John Gastil is grateful to them for their contribution to the ideas discussed. See Braman, D., Kahan, D., and Gastil, J. (2003, Nov.). "A Cultural Critique of Gun Litigation." Paper presented at a workshop on gun control at Albany Law School, Albany, N.Y.

18. The literature on deliberation has grown to the point where general reviews of its theory and practice are available; for example, Burkhalter, S., Gastil, J., and Kelshaw, T. (2002). "The Self-Reinforcing Model of Public Deliberation." *Communication Theory, 12*(4), 398–422; Ryfe, D. M. (2002). "The Practice of Deliberative Democracy: A Study of 16 Deliberative Organizations." *Political Communication, 19,* 359–377. For critiques, see Pellizzoni, L. (2001). "The Myth of the Best Argument: Power, Deliberation, and Reason." *British Journal of Sociology, 52*(1), 59–86; Sanders, L. M. (1997). "Against Deliberation." *Political Theory, 25*(3), 347–376. Among the most influential works on the subject are Gutmann, A., and Thompson, D. (1996). *Democracy and Disagreement.* Cambridge, Mass.: Harvard University Press; and Fishkin, J. S. (1995). *The Voice of the People.* New Haven, Conn.: Yale University Press.

19. Burkhalter, Gastil, and Kelshaw (2002), "The Self-Reinforcing Model of Public Deliberation," 399–407. This view builds on Gouran, D., and Hirokawa, Y. (1996). "Functional Theory and Communication in Decision-Making and Problem-Solving Groups: An Expanded View." In R. Hirokawa and M. S. Poole (eds.), *Communication and Group Decision-Making.* (2nd ed.) Thousand Oaks, Calif.: Sage, 55–80; and Dewey, J. (1910). *How We Think.* Boston: Heath.

20. Burkhalter, Gastil, and Kelshaw (2002), "The Self-Reinforcing Model of Public Deliberation," 407–411. This conception of dialogue is adapted from Pearce, W. B. and Littlejohn, S. (1997). *Moral Conflict: When Social Worlds Collide.* Thousand Oaks, Calif.: Sage.

21. For examples of different approaches to dialogue, see Pearce and Littlejohn (1997), *Moral Conflict,* 181–210.

22. It is possible that through dialogue, participants will discover some common ground. For instance, an egalitarian might agree with a hierarchist's desired outcome (for example, a world without crime) despite the persisting disagreement about the means through which to achieve that goal. Or an individualist might come to appreciate an egalitarian's way of speaking (for example, passing around a talking stick) as being fair to all individual participants, even while finding it unsuited for his or her own personal discussion style. These points of agreement can help to build mutual trust and respect, but we downplay their likelihood to emphasize the considerable value of the more modest (and more likely) accomplishments of culturally accommodating dialogue.

23. This chapter was completed in the wake of the 2004 U.S. presidential election. Many observers commenting on the result have observed a stark cultural divide in the country, with the bulk of the Kerry and Bush supporters having more cultural differences than similarities. In this context, cultural accommodation may be all the more important as a means of bringing together U.S. citizens to work through controversial public issues.

24. There is no way of knowing in advance precisely how such dialogue would proceed and what it would produce. It might very well uncover points of agreement, but the particular nature of the cultural accommodation is impossible to know prior to the dialogue taking place. Were this not so, dialogue would be an ironic process that appears spontaneous and genuine but is actually scripted and subject to precise prediction.

25. This is consistent with those views of deliberation that downplay consensus, seeing it as an ideal goal rather than an achievable purpose. See, for example, Cohen, J. (1997). *Deliberative Democracy: Essays on Reason and Politics*. Cambridge, Mass.: MIT Press, 407–437.

26. Brooks, D. (2001). "One Nation, Slightly Divisible." *Atlantic Monthly, 288*(5), 53–65.

27. Perhaps surprisingly, the protests themselves offer modest opportunities for a kind of deliberation. See West, M., and Gastil, J. (2004). "Deliberation at the Margins: Participant Accounts of Face-to-Face Public Deliberation at the 1999–2000 World Trade Protests in Seattle and Prague." *Qualitative Research Reports, 5*, 1-7.

RECOMMENDED READING

Ackerman, B., and Fishkin, J. (2004). *Deliberation Day.* New Haven, Conn.: Yale University Press.

Agranoff, R., and McGuire, M. (2003). *Collaborative Public Management: New Strategies for Local Governments.* Washington, D.C.: Georgetown University Press.

Alamprese, J. A. (1995). "National Issues Forums Literacy Program: Linking Literacy and Citizenship." Unpublished report by COSMOS Corporation, Bethesda, Md., for the Charles F. Kettering Foundation.

Alford, C. F. (1994). *Group Psychology and Political Theory.* New Haven, Conn.: Yale University Press.

Andrade, I. (1998). "Descentralização e poder municipal no nordeste: os dois lados da moeda" [Decentralization and municipal power in the North East: Two sides of the coin]. In J. A. Soares (ed.), *O orçamento dos municípios do Nordeste brasileiro* [The municipal budget in the Brazilian Northeast]. Brasília: Paralelo15.

Arendt, H. (1965). *On Revolution.* New York: Viking Penguin. (Originally published 1963.)

Arkansas Blue Ribbon Commission on Public Education. (2002). *Arkansans Speak Up! on Education.* Little Rock: Institute of Government, University of Arkansas at Little Rock.

Bachrach, P., and Baratz, M. (1963). "Decisions and Non-Decisions: An Analytical Framework." *American Political Science Review, 57,* 632–642.

Barber, B. R. (1984). *Strong Democracy.* Berkeley: University of California Press.

Beierle, T. C. (2002). *Democracy On-Line: An Evaluation of the National Dialogue on Public Involvement in EPA Decisions.* Washington D.C.: Resources for the Future. [http://www.rff.org/Documents/RFF-RPT-demonline.pdf]. Retrieved June 8, 2004.

Note: List compiled by Jillien Dube.

Blatner, K. A., Carroll, M. S., Daniels, S. E., and Walker, G. B. (2001). "Evaluating the Application of Collaborative Learning to the Wenatchee Fire Recovery Planning Effort." *Environmental Impact Assessment Review, 21*, 241–270.

Blaug, R. (1999). *Democracy, Real and Ideal: Discourse Ethics and Radical Politics.* Albany, N.Y.: State University of New York Press.

Bobbio, N. (1987). *The Future of Democracy: A Defense of the Rules of the Game.* (R. Griffin, trans.). Cambridge, U.K.: Polity Press.

Brassard, M. (1989). *The Memory Jogger Plus: Featuring the Seven Management and Planning Tools.* Methuen, Mass.: Goal QPC.

Brazilian Association of Collective Health. (1993). *Relatório final da oficina: incentivo à participação popular e controle social em saúde* [Final report: Popular participation and social control in health]. Série Saúde e movimento [Health and movement series]. Vol. 1. Brasília: Brazilian Association of Collective Health.

Briand, M. (1999). *Practical Politics: Five Principles for a Community That Works.* Urbana: University of Illinois Press.

Brown, P., and Levinson, S. (1987). *Politeness: Some Universals in Language.* Cambridge, Mass.: Cambridge University Press.

Burgoon, J. K., and Hale, J. L. (1984). "The Fundamental Topoi of Relational Communication." *Communication Monographs, 51*, 193–214.

Burnheim, J. (1985). *Is Democracy Possible? The Alternative to Electoral Politics.* Cambridge, U.K.: Polity Press.

Button, M., and Mattson, K. (1999). "Deliberative Democracy in Practice: Challenges and Prospects for Civic Deliberation." *Polity, 31*, 609–637.

California Education Master Plan Alliance. (2003, Apr.). "California Education Master Plan Dialogue," [http://www.webdialogues.net/masterplan]. Retrieved June 8, 2004.

California Education Master Plan Alliance. (2003, Apr.). "California Education Master Plan Dialogue, Wrap-Up Evaluation." [http://www.webdialogues.net/cs/emp/download/dlib/183/alliance_eval.doc?x-r=pcfile_d]. Retrieved June 8, 2004.

Campbell, S. vL. (1998). *A Guide for Training Study Circle Facilitators.* Pomfret, Conn.: Topsfield Foundation.

Campbell, S. vL., Malick, A., Landesman, J., Barrett, M. H., Leighninger, M., McCoy, M. L., and Scully, P. L. (2001). *Organizing Community-Wide Dialogue for Action and Change.* Pomfret, Conn.: Topsfield Foundation.

Capuzzo, J. P. (2002, Dec. 22). "Hot Under the Buttoned-Down Collar." *New York Times,* NJ1.

Carneiro, C. (2002, March). "Conselhos: Uma reflexão sobre os condicionantes de sua atuação e os desafios de sua efetivação" [Councils: Challenges for their implementation]. *Informativo CEPAM* [CEPAM Bulletin], *1*(3), 62–70. São Paulo: Fundação Prefeito Faria Lima.

Carson, L., and Martin, B. (1999). *Random Selection in Politics.* Westport, Conn.: Praeger.

Carson, L., White, S., Hendriks, C., and Palmer, J. (2002, July). "Community Consultation in Environmental Policy Making." *The Drawing Board: An Australian Review of Public Affairs, 3*(1), 1–13.

Carvalho, A. (1995). "Conselhos de Saúde No Brasil" [Health Councils in Brazil]. In *Política, Planejamento e Gestao em Saúde. Série Estudos* [Study series: Politics, planning, and health management], no. 3. Rio de Janeiro: Ibam/Fase.

Chambers, S. (1996). *Reasonable Democracy.* Ithaca, N.Y.: Cornell University Press.

Chambers, S. (2003). "Deliberative Democratic Theory." *Annual Review of Political Science, 6*, 307–326.

Cifuentes, M. (2002). "Political Legitimacy of Deliberative Institutions." Unpublished master's thesis, Institute of Development Studies, University of Sussex, Brighton, U.K.

City of Portsmouth. (2004, May). *Portsmouth Master Plan: Vision Statement, Priorities for Action, Goals, Objectives, and Strategies—Draft.* Portsmouth, N.H.: City of Portsmouth.

Clark, S., Wold, M., and Mayeri, H. (1996). "The Key to Community Voter Involvement Project: Fall 1996 Election Study." [http://literacynet.org/slrc/vip/whole.html].

Clary, B. (2000). *Program Evaluation: Maine Youth Study Circles, Project of the Maine Council of Churches, Funded by the Lilly Endowment.* Portland, Maine: University of Southern Maine.

Coelho, V. (2004, Apr.). "Brazil's Health Councils: The Challenge of Building Participatory Political Institutions." *IDS* [Institute of Development Studies] *Bulletin, 35*(2), 33–39.

Coelho, V. (2004). "Conselhos de saúde enquanto instituições políticas: o que está faltando?" [Health councils as political institutions: What is lacking?]. In V.S.P. Coelho and M. Nobre (eds.), *Deliberação e Participação no Brasil* [Deliberation and participation in Brazil]. São Paulo: Editora 34 Letras.

Cohen, J. (1989). "Deliberation and Democratic Legitimacy." In A. Hamlin and P. Pettit (eds.), *The Good Polity: Normative Analysis of the State.* Cambridge, U.K.: Basil Blackwell.

Cohen, J. (1996). "Procedure and Substance in Deliberative Democracy." In S. Benhabib (ed.), *Democracy and Difference.* Princeton, N.J.: Princeton University Press.

Coote, A., and Lenaghan, J. (1997). *Citizens' Juries: Theory into Practice.* London: Institute for Public Policy Research.

Cornwall, A. (2004, Apr.). "New Democratic Spaces? The Politics and Dynamics of Institutionalised Participation." *IDS* [Institute of Development Studies] *Bulletin, 35*(2), 1–10.

Council on Foundations. (2003). *Collaboration: A Selected Bibliography.* Washington D.C.: Council on Foundations.

Crenson, M. A. (1971). *The Un-Politics of Air Pollution: A Study of Non-Decisionmaking in the Cities.* Baltimore, Md.: Johns Hopkins University Press.

Crosby, N. (1995). "The Citizens Jury Process." In O. Renn, T. Webler, and P. Wiedemann (eds.), *Fairness and Competence in Citizen Participation: Evaluating Models for Environmental Discourse.* Dordrecht, Netherlands: Kluwer.

Crosby, N. (1999). "Using the Citizens Jury Process for Environmental Decision Making." In K. Sexton, A. A. Marcus, K. W. Easter, and T. D. Burkhardt (eds.), *Better Environmental Decisions: Strategies for Governments, Business, and Communities.* Washington, D.C.: Island Press.

Crosby, N. (2003). *Healthy Democracy: Empowering a Clear and Informed Voice of the People.* Edina, Minn.: Beaver's Pond Press.

Dahl, R. A. (1989). *Democracy and Its Critics.* New Haven, Conn.: Yale University Press.

Daniels, S. E., and Walker, G. B. (1996). "Collaborative Learning: Improving Public Deliberation in Ecosystem-Based Management." *Environmental Impact Assessment Review, 16,* 71–102.

Daniels, S. E., and Walker, G. B. (1996). "Using Collaborative Learning in Fire Recovery Planning." *Journal of Forestry, 94*(8), 4–9.

Daniels, S. E., and Walker, G. B. (1997). "Collaborative Learning and Land Management Conflict." In B. Solberg and S. Miina (eds.), *Conflict Management and Public Participation in Land Management.* Joensuu, Finland: European Forest Institute.

Daniels, S. E. and Walker, G. B. (2001). *Working Through Environmental Conflict: The Collaborative Learning Approach.* Westport, Conn.: Praeger.

Delli Carpini, M. X., Cook, F. L., and Jacobs, L. R. (2003). "Talking Together: Discursive Capital and Civil Deliberation in America." Paper delivered to meeting of Midwest Political Science Association, Chicago.

Delli Carpini, M. X., Cook, F. L., and Jacobs, L. R. (2004, May). "Talking Together: Discursive Capital and Civic Deliberation in America." *Annual Review of Political Science, 7,* 315–344.

Dienel, P. C. (1978). *Die planungszell: Eine alternative zur establishment-demokratie* [The Planning Cell: An Alternative to Establishment Democracy]. Opladen: Westdeutscher Verlag.

Dienel, P. C. (1997). *Die planungszell: Eine alternative zur establishment-demokratie* [The Planning Cell: An Alternative to Establishment Democracy] (4th ed. with Status Report '97). Opladen: Westdeutscher Verlag.

Dienel, P., and Renn, O. (1995). "Planning Cells: A Gate to 'Fractal' Mediation." In O. Renn, T. Webler, and P. Wiedemann (eds.), *Fairness and Competence in Citizen Participation: Evaluating Models for Environmental Discourse.* Dordrecht, Netherlands: Kluwer.

Dionne, E. J. (2000, Summer). "The State of the Movement." *National Civic Review, 89*(2), 121–138.

Dryzek, J. S. (1990). *Discursive Democracy: Politics, Policy, and Political Science.* Cambridge, U.K.: Cambridge University Press.

Dryzek, J. S. (2000). *Deliberative Democracy and Beyond: Liberals, Critics, and Contestations.* New York: Oxford University Press.

Einsiedel, E. F., Jelsøe, E., and Breck, T. (2001). "Publics and the Technology Table: The Australian, Canadian and Danish Consensus Conferences on Food Biotechnology." *Public Understanding of Science, 10*(1), 83–98.

Eliasoph, N. (1998). *Avoiding Politics: How Americans Produce Apathy in Everyday Life.* Cambridge, U.K.: Cambridge University Press.

Emery, F. E. (1989). *Toward Real Democracy and Toward Real Democracy: Further Problems.* Toronto: Ontario Ministry for Labour.

Fanselow, J. (2002). *What Democracy Feels Like.* Pomfret, Conn.: Topsfield Foundation.

Farkas, S., Friedman, W., and Bers, A. (1996). *The Public's Capacity for Deliberation.* New York: Public Agenda, for the Charles F. Kettering Foundation.

Farrar, C. (in press). "Power to the People." In K. A. Raaflaub, J. Ober, and R. Wallace, with chapters by P. Cartledge and C. Farrar, *The Origins of Democracy in Ancient Greece.* Berkeley: University of California Press.

Farrar, C., Fishkin, J., Green, D., List, C., Luskin, R. C., and Paluck, E. L. (2003, Sept. 18–21). "Experimenting with Deliberative Democracy: Effects on Policy Preferences and Social Choice." Paper presented at the European Consortium for Political Research conference, Marburg, Germany.

Fisher, R., and Ury, W. (1983). *Getting to Yes: Negotiating Agreement Without Giving In.* New York: Penguin. (Originally published 1981.)

Fishkin, J. S. (1991). *Democracy and Deliberation: New Directions for Democratic Reform.* New Haven, Conn.: Yale University Press.

Fishkin, J. S. (1997). *The Voice of the People: Public Opinion and Democracy.* (Rev. paperback ed.) New Haven, Conn.: Yale University Press.

Follett, M. P. (1942). "Constructive Conflict." In H. C. Metcalf and L. Urwick (eds.), *Dynamic Administration: The Collected Papers of Mary Parker Follett.* New York: Harper. (Originally published 1925.)

Font, J. (2004). "Participación ciudadana y decisions públicas: conceptos, experiencias y metodologias" [Citizen participation and public decisions: Concepts, experiences, and methodologies]. In A. Ziccardi (ed.), *Participación ciudadana y políticas socials en el ámbito local* [Citizen participation and social policies in local government]. Mexico: Instituto Nacional de Desarrollo Social [National Institute of Social Development].

Fung, A. (2003). "Recipes for Public Spheres: Eight Institutional Design Choices and Their Consequences." *Journal of Political Philosophy, 11,* 1–30.

Fung, A. (2004). *Empowered Participation: Reinventing Urban Democracy.* Princeton, N.J.: Princeton University Press.

Fung, A., and Wright, E. O. (2003). *Deepening Democracy: Institutional Innovations in Empowered Participatory Governance.* London: Verso.

Gastil, J. (2000). *By Popular Demand: Revitalizing Representative Democracy Through Deliberative Elections.* Berkeley: University of California Press.

Gastil, J. (2004). "Adult Civic Education Through the National Issues Forums: A Study of How Adults Develop Civic Skills and Dispositions Through Public Deliberation." *Adult Education Quarterly, 54,* 308–328.

Gastil, J., and Dillard, J. P. (1999). "Increasing Political Sophistication Through Public Deliberation." *Political Communication, 16,* 3–23.

Gastil, J., and Kelshaw, T. (2000). *Public Meetings: A Sampler of Deliberative Forums That Bring Officeholders and Citizens Together.* Dayton, Ohio: Charles F. Kettering Foundation.

Gaventa, J. (1980). *Power and Powerlessness: Quiescence and Rebellion in an Appalachian Valley.* Urbana: University of Illinois Press.

Gaventa, J. (2004). "Strengthening Participatory Approaches to Local Governance: Learning the Lessons from Abroad," *National Civic Review, 3*(4), 16–27.

Goldman, J. (2004). "Draft Case Study of Portsmouth Study Circles." Cambridge, Mass.: Kennedy School of Government, Harvard University.

Goodin, R. (2004). *Reflective Democracy.* New York: Oxford University Press.

Guild, W., Guild, R., and Thompson, F. (2004, Mar.–Apr.). "21st Century Polling." *Public Power, 62*(2), 28–35.

Gunn, R. W., and Carlitz, R. D. (2003). *Online Dialogue in a Political Context: The California Master Plan for Education.* Pittsburgh, Pa.: Information Renaissance. [http://www.network-democracy.org/camp/report.shtml]. Retrieved June 7, 2004.

Guston, D. H. (1999). "Evaluating the First U.S. Consensus Conference: The Impact of the Citizens' Panel on Telecommunications and the Future of Democracy." *Science, Technology & Human Values, 24*(4), 451–482.

Gutmann, A., and Thompson, D. (1996). *Democracy and Disagreement.* Cambridge, Mass.: Belknap Press.

Habermas, J. (1975). *Legitimation Crisis* (T. McCarthy, trans.). Boston: Beacon Press.

Habermas, J. (1983). "Hannah Arendt: On the Concept of Power." In J. Habermas, *Philosophical-Political Profiles.* (F. G. Lawrence, trans.). Cambridge, Mass.: MIT Press. (Originally published 1976.)

Hansen, K. M. (2003). "Deliberative Democracy and Opinion Formation." Unpublished doctoral dissertation, Department of Political Science and Public Management, University of Southern Denmark.

Hansen, M. H. (1999). *The Athenian Democracy in the Age of Demosthenes: Structures, Principles, and Ideology.* (expanded ed.) Norman: University of Oklahoma Press.

Hartz-Karp, J. (2004, May 14). "Harmonising Divergent Voices: Sharing the Challenge of Decision Making." Keynote address at the New South Wales State Conference of the Institute of Public Administration Australia. [http://www.nsw.ipaa.org.au/07_publications/2004_conf_papers.htm]. Retrieved Jan. 31, 2005.

Harwood, R. (1991). *Citizens and Politics: A View from Main Street America.* Bethesda: Harwood Institute.

Healey, P., Magalhaes, C. de, Madanipour, A., and Pendlebury, J. (2003). "Place, Identity, and Local Politics: Analysing Initiatives in Deliberative Governance." In M. A. Hajer and H. Wagenaar (eds.), *Deliberative Policy Analysis: Understanding Governance in the Network Society.* London: Cambridge University Press.

Heierbacher, S. (2003). "Final Report Submitted to the Kettering Foundation on the Online Survey of Practitioners of Public Deliberation, Conducted by the National Coalition for Dialogue and Deliberation." Unpublished manuscript.

Hendriks, C. M. (2002). "The Ambiguous Role of Civil Society in Deliberative Democracy." Paper presented at the Jubilee Conference of the Australasian Political Studies Association, Australian National University, Canberra. Available at http://arts.anu.edu.au/sss/apsa/default.htm.

Hendriks, C. M. (2002). "Institutions of Deliberative Democratic Processes and Interest Groups: Roles, Tensions and Incentives." *Australian Journal of Public Administration, 61*(1), 64–75.

Hendriks, C. M. (n.d.). "Public Deliberation and Interest Organisations: A Study of Responses to Lay Citizens' Engagement in Public Policy." Unpublished doctoral dissertation. Canberra: The Australian National University.

Hibbing, J. R., and Theiss-Morse, E. (2002). *Stealth Democracy: Americans' Beliefs About How Government Should Work.* Cambridge, U.K.: Cambridge University Press.

Houlé, K., and Roberts, R. (2000). *Toward Competent Communities: Best Practices for Producing Community-wide Study Circles.* Lexington, Ky.: Roberts & Kay, Inc.

"How Have Study Circles Made an Impact? Organizers Report on Their Successes." (2000, Fall). *Focus on Study Circles, 11*(4), 1, 7.

Huckfeldt, R. (1986). *Politics in Context: Assimilation and Conflict In Urban Neighborhoods.* New York: Agathon Press.

Huckfeldt, R., and Sprague, J. (1995). *Citizens, Politics, and Social Communication: Information and Influence in an Election Campaign.* New York: Cambridge University Press.

Information Renaissance. "Dialogue Archives." (n.d.) [http://www.info-ren.org/what/dialogues_projects.shtml]. Retrieved June 10, 2004.

Information Renaissance. (1996, Aug.). "Universal Service/Network Democracy On-Line Seminar." [http://www.info-ren.org/projects/universal-service/]. Retrieved June 8, 2004.

Information Renaissance. (1999, Mar.). "National Dialogue on Social Security." [http://www.network-democracy.org/social-security/]. Retrieved June 8, 2004.

Information Renaissance. (2001, Aug.). "Dialogue on Public Involvement in EPA Decisions: Summary Data Tables." [http://www.network-democracy.org/cgi-bin/epa-pip/show_tables.pl]. Retrieved June 9, 2004.

Information Renaissance. (2002, May). "California Master Plan for Education Dialogue." [http://www.network-democracy.org/camp]. Retrieved June 8, 2004.

Innes, J. E., and Booher, D. E. (2003). *Collaborative Policymaking: Governance Through Dialogue.* In M. A. Hajer and H. Wagenaar (eds.), *Deliberative Policy Analysis: Understanding Governance in the Network Society.* London: Cambridge University Press.

Innes, J. E., and Booher, D. E. (2003). *The Impact of Collaborative Planning on Governance Capacity.* Berkeley, Calif.: Institute of Urban and Regional Development.

Iyengar, S., Luskin, R. C., and Fishkin, J. S. (2004, May). "Considered Opinions on U.S. Foreign Policy: Face to Face Versus Online Deliberative Polling." Paper presented at the annual meetings of the International Communication Association, New Orleans.

John Doble Research Associates. (1996). *The Story of NIF: The Effects of Deliberation.* Dayton, Ohio: Charles F. Kettering Foundation.

Joss, S., and Bellucci, S. (2002). *Participatory Technology Assessment: European Perspectives.* London: Centre for the Study of Democracy.

Joss, S., and Durant, J. (eds.). (1995). *Public Participation in Science: The Role of Consensus Conferences in Europe.* London: Science Museum.

Kirsch, I. S., Jungeblut, A., Jenkins, L., and Kolstad, A. (1993). *Executive Summary of Adult Literacy in America: A First Look at the Results of the National Adult Literacy Survey.* Washington, D.C.: National Center for Education Statistics. [http://nces.ed.gov/naal/resources/execsumm.asp]. Retrieved June 10, 2004. Also available in Kirsch, I. S., Jungeblut, A., Jenkins, L., and Kolstad, A. (1993, Aug. 30). *Adult Literacy in America: A First Look at the Findings of the National Adult Literacy Survey.* NCES 93275. Washington, D.C.: National Center for Education Statistics.

Knight, J., and Johnson, J. (1994). "Aggregation and Deliberation: On the Possibility of Democratic Legitimacy." *Political Theory, 22,* 277–298.

Knoke, D. (1990). *Political Networks: A Structural Perspective.* New York: Cambridge University Press.

Krassa, M. A. (1990). "Political Information, Social Environment, and Deviants." *Political Behavior, 12,* 315–330.

Langlois, G. (2001, Aug. 6). "Online and Involved." *Federal Computer Week, 15*(26), 38. [http://www.fcw.com/fcw/articles/2001/0806/pol-epa-08-06-01.asp]. Retrieved June 10, 2004.

League of Women Voters. (1999). "How to Be Politically Effective: Working Together: Community Involvement in America." [http://www.lwv.org/elibrary/pub/cp_survey/cp_1.html]. Retrieved June 8, 2004.

Lehr, R. L., Guild, W., Thomas, D. L., and Swezey, B. G. (2003, June). "Listening to Customers: How Deliberative Polling Helped Build 1,000 MW of New Renewable Projects in Texas." National Renewable Energy Laboratory, a U.S. Department of Energy Laboratory. Report no. NREL/TP-620-33177. [http://www.nrel.gov/docs/fy03osti/33177.pdf].

Leighley, J. E. (1990). "Social Interaction and Contextual Influences on Political Participation." *American Politics Quarterly, 18,* 459–475.

Leighninger, M. (1998, Fall). "How Have Study Circles Made an Impact?" *Focus on Study Circles, 9*(4), 2, 7.

Leighninger, M. (2002, Summer). "Enlisting Citizens: Building Political Legitimacy." *National Civic Review, 91*(2), 137–148.

Levine, P. (2000). *The New Progressive Era.* Lanham, Md.: Rowman and Littlefield.

Linden, R. M. *Working Across Boundaries: Making Collaboration Work in Government and Nonprofit Organizations.* San Francisco: Jossey-Bass, 2002.

Lobato, L. (1998, Sept. 24–26). "Stress and Contradictions in the Brazilian Healthcare Reform." Paper presented at the annual meeting of the Latin American Studies Association, Chicago.

London, S. (1999). "El Paso Forges Shared Outlook in Forums." In E. Arnone (ed.), *What Citizens Can Do: A Public Way to Act.* Dayton, Ohio: Charles F. Kettering Foundation, 1–3.

London, S. (2004). *Creating Citizens Through Public Deliberation.* Dayton, Ohio: Charles F. Kettering Foundation.

Loyacano, M. (1991). "Attendant Effects of the National Issues Forums." Unpublished manuscript, Charles F. Kettering Foundation, Dayton, Ohio.

Lukes, S. (1974). *Power: A Radical View.* London: Macmillan.

Lumby, C. (1999). *Gotcha: Life in a Tabloid World.* St. Leonards, Australia: Allen & Unwin.

Luskin, R. C., and Fishkin, J. S. (2002, Mar. 22–27). "Deliberation and 'Better Citizens.'" Paper presented at the annual joint sessions of workshops of the European Consortium for Political Research, Turin, Italy.

Luskin, R. C., Fishkin, J. S., and Iyengar, S. (2004, Apr. 23–24). "Deliberative Public Opinion in Presidential Primaries: Evidence from the Online Deliberative Poll." Paper presented at the Voice and Citizenship: Re-thinking Theory and Practice in Political Communication conference, University of Washington.

Luskin, R. C., Fishkin, J. S., and Jowell, R. (2002). "Considered Opinions: Deliberative Polling in Britain." *British Journal of Political Science, 32*, 455–487.

Macpherson, C. B. (1977). *The Life and Times of Liberal Democracy.* Oxford, U.K.: Oxford University Press.

Mallory, B., and Thomas, N. (2003, Sept.–Oct.). "When the Medium Is the Message: Promoting Ethical Action Through Democratic Dialogue." *Change,* 11–17.

Manin, B. (1987). "On Legitimacy and Political Deliberation." *Political Theory, 15,* 338–368.

Mansbridge, J. (1983). *Beyond Adversary Democracy.* Chicago: University of Chicago Press.

Mansbridge, J. (2000). "What Does a Representative Do? Descriptive Representation in Communicative Settings of Distrust, Uncrystallized Interests, and Historically Denigrated Status." In W. Kymlica and W. Norman (eds.), *Citizenship in Diverse Societies.* Oxford: Oxford University Press.

Markus, G. B. (2002). *Civic Participation in American Cities.* Ann Arbor, Mich.: Institute for Social Research, University of Michigan.

Mathews, D. (1994). *Politics for People: Finding a Responsible Public Voice.* Urbana: University of Illinois Press.

Mathews, D. (1998, Dec.). "Dialogue and Deliberation: 'Meaning Making' Is Essential to Decision Making." *Connections, 9*(2), 24–27.

Mattson, K. (2001). *Creating a Democratic Public.* State College: Pennsylvania State University Press.

McAfee, N., McKenzie, R., and Mathews, D. (1990). *Hard Choices.* Dayton, Ohio: Charles F. Kettering Foundation.

McCoy, M. L., and Scully, P. L. (2002, Summer). "Deliberative Dialogue to Expand Civic Engagement: What Kind of Talk Does Democracy Need?" *National Civic Review, 91*(2), 117–135.

McLean, I., List, C., Fishkin, J., and Luskin, R. C. (2000). "Does Deliberation Induce Preference Structuration? Evidence from the Deliberative Polls." Paper presented at the meetings of the American Political Science Association.

Mendelberg, T., and Oleske, J. (2000). "Race and Public Deliberation." *Political Communication, 17,* 169–191.

Mengual, G. (2003, Summer). "Portsmouth, N.H.—Where Public Dialogue is a Hallmark of Community Life." *Focus on Study Circles, 14*(2), 1, 7.

Mengual, G. (2003). *What Works: Study Circles in the Real World.* Adapted from a report by Rona Roberts of Roberts & Kay, Inc. Pomfret, Conn.: Topsfield Foundation.

Metzler, D., McManus, M., Davis, P., Cook, J., and Best H. (2003). *Schools and Communities Working Together: Helping Arkansas Students Succeed.* Little Rock: Institute of Economic Advancement, College of Business, University of Arkansas at Little Rock.

Morone, J. *The Democratic Wish.* New York: Basic Books, 1990.

Moscovici, S. (1976). *Social Influence and Social Change.* New York: Academic Press.

Moscovici, S. (1980). "Toward a Theory of Conversion Behavior." *Advances in Experimental Social Psychology, 13,* 209–239.

Mueller, J. (1999). *Capitalism, Democracy, and Ralph's Pretty Good Grocery*. Princeton, N.J.: Princeton University Press.

Mulkay, M. (1985). "Agreement and Disagreement in Conversations and Letters." *Text, 5,* 201–227.

Nemeth, C. J. (1986). "Differential Contributions of Majority and Minority Influence." *Psychological Review, 93,* 23–32.

Nemeth, C. J., and Kwan, J. (1985). "Originality of Word Associations as a Function of Majority and Minority Influence." *Social Psychology Quarterly, 48,* 277–282.

Office of Environmental Policy Innovation, U.S. Environmental Protection Agency. (Aug. 2003–July 2004). Brochures on public involvement. EPA nos. 233-F-03-005-12, 233-F-03-014. Washington, D.C.: Environmental Protection Agency. Available from the National Service Center for Environmental Publications, P.O. Box 42419, Cincinnati, OH 45242-2419.

Office of Policy, Economics and Innovation, U.S. Environmental Protection Agency. (2003, May). "Framework for Implementing EPA's Public Involvement Policy." EPA 233-F-03-001. Washington, D.C.: U.S. Environmental Protection Agency. [http://www.epa.gov/publicinvolvement/policy2003].

Office of Policy, Economics and Innovation, U.S. Environmental Protection Agency. (2003, May). "Public Involvement Policy of the U.S. Environmental Protection Agency." EPA 233-B-03-002. Washington, D.C.: U.S. Environmental Protection Agency. [http://www.epa.gov/publicinvolvement/policy2003]. Retrieved June 6, 2004.

Oliver, L. P. (1987). *To Understand Is to Act: Study Circles, Coming Together for Personal Growth and Social Change*. Washington, D.C.: Seven Locks Press.

Osbourne, D., and Plastrik, P. (1997). *Banishing Bureaucracy: The Five Strategies for Reinventing Government*. Reading, Mass.: Addison-Wesley.

Paget, G. (1989, Dec.). "Literacy Programs Open Doors for New Readers." *Connections* (Charles F. Kettering Foundation), *3*(1), 10–11.

Pan, D. T., and Mutchler, S. E. (2000). *Calling the Roll: Study Circles for Better Schools: Policy Research Report*. Austin, Texas: Southwest Educational Development Laboratory.

Pitkin, H. F., and Shumer, S. M. (1982, Fall). "On Participation." *Democracy, 2,* 43–54.

Plotz, D. A. (1991). *Community Problem Solving Case Summaries*. Vol. 3. Washington D.C.: Program for Community Problem Solving.

Polletta, F. (2002). *Freedom Is an Endless Meeting: Democracy in American Social Movements*. Chicago: University of Chicago Press.

Pomerantz, A. (1984). "Agreeing and Disagreeing with Assessments: Some Features of Preferred/Dispreferred Turn Shapes." In J. M. Atkinson and J. Heritage (eds.), *Structures of Social Action*. Cambridge, Mass.: Cambridge University Press.

Postman, N. (1985). *Amusing Ourselves to Death: Public Discourse in the Age of Show Business*. New York: Viking Penguin.

Potapchuk, W. (2002). "Neighborhood Action Initiative: Engaging Citizens in Real Change." In D. D. Chrislip (ed.), *The Collaborative Leadership Fieldbook: A Guide for Citizens and Civic Leaders*. San Francisco: Jossey-Bass.

Pozzoni, B. (2002). "Citizen Participation and Deliberation in Brazil." Unpublished master's thesis, Institute of Development Studies, University of Sussex, Brighton, U.K.

Princeton Future. (2002, Feb.). *Princeton Future Annual Report 2002*. Princeton, N.J.: Princeton Future, 3.

Princeton Future. (2003). *Listening to Each Other: The Downtown Core, The Downtown Neighborhoods*. Princeton, N.J.: Princeton Future.

Przeworski, A. (1998). "Deliberation and Ideological Domination." In J. Elster (ed.), *Deliberative Democracy.* Cambridge, U.K.: Cambridge University Press.

Putnam, R. D. (1993). "The Prosperous Community: Social Capital and Public Life." *American Prospect, 4*(13), 35.

Putnam, R. D. (2000). *Bowling Alone: The Collapse and Revival of American Community.* New York: Simon & Schuster.

Pyser, S., and Figallo, C. (2004, Spring). "The 'Listening to the City' Online Dialogues Experience: The Impact of a Full Value Contract." *Conflict Resolution Quarterly, 21*(3), 381–393.

Ralston Saul, J. (1997). *The Unconscious Civilization.* Maryborough, Victoria, Australia: Penguin Books.

Rawls, J. (1996). *Political Liberalism.* New York: Columbia University Press.

Renn, O., Webler, T., and Wiedemann, P. (eds.). (1995). *Fairness and Competence in Citizen Participation.* Dordrecht: Kluwer.

Rosenberg, M. (1954–1955). "Some Determinants of Political Apathy." *Public Opinion Quarterly, 18,* 349–366.

Ryfe, D. (in press). "Does Deliberative Democracy Work?" *Annual Review of Political Science, 8*(1).

Ryfe, D. (Feb. 2003). "An Interim Report on Kinds of Talk in National Issues Forums." Unpublished memo, Charles F. Kettering Foundation, Dayton, Ohio.

Ryfe, D. M. (2003). "The Practice of Public Discourse: A Study of Sixteen Discourse Organizations." In J. Rodin and S. Steinberg (eds.), *Public Discourse in America.* Philadelphia: University of Pennsylvania Press, 184–200.

Ryfe, D. M. (2002). "The Practice of Deliberative Democracy: A Study of 16 Deliberative Organizations." *Political Communication, 19,* 359–377.

Sanders, L. M. (1997, June). "Against Deliberation." *Political Theory, 25*(3), 347–376.

Schiffrin, D. (1990). "The Management of a Cooperative Self During Argument: The Role of Opinions and Stories." In A. D. Grimshaw (ed.), *Conflict Talk: Sociolinguistic Investigations of Arguments in Conversations.* Cambridge, U.K.: Cambridge University Press.

Senge, P. M. (1990). *The Fifth Discipline: The Art and Practice of the Learning Organization.* New York: Doubleday.

Shapiro, I. (1999). "Enough of Deliberation: Politics Is About Interests and Power." In S. Macedo (ed.), *Deliberative Politics.* Oxford, U.K.: Oxford University Press.

Shapiro, I. (2003). *The State of Democratic Theory.* Princeton, N.J.: Princeton University Press.

Sirianni, C., and Friedland, L. (2001). *Civic Innovation in America.* Berkeley: University of California Press.

Smith, G. (2000). "Toward Deliberative Institutions." In M. Saward (ed.), *Democratic Innovation: Deliberation, Representation and Association.* London: Routledge.

Smith, G., and Wales, C. (2000). "Citizens' Juries and Deliberative Democracy." *Political Studies, 48,* 51–65.

Souza Santos, B. (1998). "Participatory Budgeting in Porto Alegre: Toward a Redistributive Democracy." [http://www.ssc.wisc.edu/~wright/santosweb.html].

Stokes, S. (1998). "Pathologies of Deliberation." In J. Elster (ed.), *Deliberative Democracy.* Cambridge, U.K.: Cambridge University Press.

Sunstein, C. (1991). "Preferences and Politics." *Philosophy and Public Affairs, 20,* 3–34.

Sunstein, C. (2002). "The Law of Group Polarization." *Journal of Political Philosophy, 10,* 175–195.

Sunstein, C. (2002). *Republic.com.* Princeton, N.J.: Princeton University Press.

Susskind, L. (1983). *Paternalism, Conflict, and Coproduction: Learning from Citizen Action and Citizen Participation in Western Europe.* New York: Plenum Press.

de Tocqueville, A. (1961). *Democracy in America*. New York: Schocken Books. [originally published in 1835]

Traugott, M. W. (2003). "Can We Trust the Polls? It All Depends." *Brookings Review, 21*(3), 8–11.

Turner, J. C. (1991). *Social influence*. Pacific Grove, Calif.: Brooks/Cole.

U.S. Department of Justice. (2002). "Overview of the Privacy Act of 1974." [http://www.usdoj.gov/04foia/04_7_1.html]. Retrieved June 10, 2004.

U.S. Fish and Wildlife Service. "Overview of the Paperwork Reduction Act of 1995." [http://pdm.fws.gov/opra.html]. Retrieved June 10, 2004.

Verba, S., Schlozman, K., and Brady, H. (1995). *Voice and Equality: Civic Voluntarism in American Politics*. Cambridge, Mass.: Harvard University Press.

Visishtha, P. (2001, July 30). "EPA Takes a People Approach to E-Gov." *Government Computer News, 20*(21), 1, 14. [http://www.gcn.com/vol20_no21/news/4764-1.html]. Retrieved June 8, 2004.

Walsh, K. (2003). *Talking About Politics: Informal Groups and Social Identity in American Life*. Chicago: University of Chicago Press.

Warren, M. (1992). "Democratic Theory and Self-Transformation." *American Political Science Review, 86*, 8–23.

Warren, M. (1996). "Deliberative Democracy and Authority." *American Political Science Review, 90*, 46–60.

Warren, M. (2001). *Democracy and Associations*. Princeton, N.J.: Princeton University Press.

WebDialogues. "Dialogue Archive." [http://www.webdialogues.net]. Retrieved June 8, 2004.

White, S. (2001, Nov.). *Independent Review of Container Deposit Legislation in New South Wales*. Report prepared for Bob Debus, Australian minister for the environment. Vol. 3. Sydney: Institute for Sustainable Futures, 2. [http://www.isf.uts.edu.au/publications/white.html]. Retrieved May 16, 2004.

Wolin, S. (1960). *Politics and Vision*. Boston: Little, Brown.

Wulff, B. (2003, Fall). "Creating a Sandlot for Democracy: The Study Circles Resource Center's Approach to Youth Civic Engagement." *National Civic Review, 92*(3), 12–19.

Wulff, B., Campbell, S. vL., McCoy, M., and Holladay, J. (2003). *Reaching Across Boundaries: Talk to Create Change, A Mix It Up Handbook*. (2nd ed.) Montgomery, Ala.: Mix It Up.

Yankelovich, D. (1991). *Coming to Public Judgment*. Syracuse, N.Y.: Syracuse University Press.

Yankelovich, D. (1999). *The Magic of Dialogue: Transforming Conflict into Cooperation*. New York: Simon & Schuster.

Young, I. M. (1996). "Communication and the Other: Beyond Deliberative Democracy." *Democracy and Difference*. Princeton, N.J.: Princeton University.

Young, I. M. (2000). *Inclusion and Democracy*. New York: Oxford University Press.

INDEX

A

ABA (American Bar Association), 43
Ackerman, B., 278
Adversarial democracy model, 7, 251n.27
After the Revolution (Dahl), 15
Aicher, P., 201, 202
Air America, 17
Alabama Community Leadership Institute, 38
Alford, C. F., 254
American Institute of Architects, 192
American Library Association, 40
The American Prospect (Kuttner), 111
The American Way (Studebaker), 12
Americans Discuss Social Security (1997, 1998), 143, 276
America*Speaks*: as expert-created model, 21; Listening to the City event organized by, 277–278; as public-spirited association, 18; 21st Century Town Meetings convened by, 156, 157, 158, 160, 161, 162
And Justice for All (ABA), 43

Apfel, K., 39
Arendt, H., 30
Atlantic Monthly, 7
Australian Labor Party, 122
The Authoritarian Personality, 14

B

Barber, B., 7, 15
Basic Operational Norms (SUS), 176
Batten Award for Civic Journalism, 193
Bavarian Consumer Protection Project, 84–87
Beck, L., 214
Bell, K., 233
Beyond Adversary Democracy (Mansbridge), 7, 247
Big Choices Symposiums (Medicare), 39
Bill of Rights, adoption of the, 4
Blackburn Institute (University of Alabama), 38
Bloomberg, M., 161
"Blue" (liberal) states metaphor, 284–285
Bonner, P. A., 141

Booher, D., 266
Boulder County (Colorado) Civic Forum, 231–232
Bowling Alone (Putnam), 6, 15, 61
Brazil: legal context of health councils in, 176; Municipal Health Council of São Paulo in, 177–182, 276; participatory mechanisms in, 174–175
Brazilian Constitution (1988), 174
Brazilian Unified Health System (SUS), 176
Brazilian Workers' Party, 178–179, 180
Breast Cancer: We Can Overcome (West Alabama Health Services), 43
Briand, M., 40
Brigham, S., 154
British Columbia Citizens Assembly, 276–277, 280
Burnheim, J., 121
Bush, G. W., 16
Button, M., 20
By the People Citizen Deliberations project, 72, 75, 77

14106212R00193

Made in the USA
Lexington, KY
13 March 2012